Regional Trade and Development Strategies in the Era of Globalization

Akhilesh Chandra Prabhakar
Lovely Professional University, India

Gurpreet Kaur
Lovely Professional University, India

Vasilii Erokhin
Harbin Engineering University, China

IGI Global
DISSEMINATOR OF KNOWLEDGE

A volume in the Advances in Finance, Accounting, and Economics (AFAE) Book Series

Published in the United States of America by
IGI Global
Business Science Reference (an imprint of IGI Global)
701 E. Chocolate Avenue
Hershey PA, USA 17033
Tel: 717-533-8845
Fax: 717-533-8661
E-mail: cust@igi-global.com
Web site: http://www.igi-global.com

Library of Congress Cataloging-in-Publication Data

Names: Prabhakar, Akhilesh Chandra, editor. | Kaur, Gurpreet, 1988- editor. | Erokhin, Vasilii editor.
Title: Regional trade and development strategies in the era of globalization / Akhilesh Chandra Prabhakar, Gurpreet Kaur, and Vasilii Erokhin, editors.
Description: Hershey : Business Science Reference, 2019. | Includes bibliographical references and index. | Summary: “”This book examines the theoretical and practical trends of regional trade and development in the era of globalization”--Provided by publisher”-- Provided by publisher.
Identifiers: LCCN 2019032877 (print) | LCCN 2019032878 (ebook) | ISBN 9781799817307 (hardcover) | ISBN 9781799817314 (paperback) | ISBN 9781799817321 (ebook)
Subjects: LCSH: International trade. | Regionalism--Economic aspects. | Trade blocs | Commercial treaties.
Classification: LCC HF1379 .R43943 2019 (print) | LCC HF1379 (ebook) | DDC 382--dc23
LC record available at https://lccn.loc.gov/2019032877
LC ebook record available at https://lccn.loc.gov/2019032878

This book is published in the IGI Global book series Advances in Finance, Accounting, and Economics (AFAE) (ISSN: 2327-5677; eISSN: 2327-5685)

British Cataloguing in Publication Data
A Cataloguing in Publication record for this book is available from the British Library.

Advances in Finance, Accounting, and Economics (AFAE) Book Series

Ahmed Driouchi
Al Akhawayn University, Morocco

ISSN:2327-5677
EISSN:2327-5685

Mission

In our changing economic and business environment, it is important to consider the financial changes occurring internationally as well as within individual organizations and business environments. Understanding these changes as well as the factors that influence them is crucial in preparing for our financial future and ensuring economic sustainability and growth.

The **Advances in Finance, Accounting, and Economics (AFAE)** book series aims to publish comprehensive and informative titles in all areas of economics and economic theory, finance, and accounting to assist in advancing the available knowledge and providing for further research development in these dynamic fields.

Coverage

- Development Economics
- Economic Policy
- Risk Analysis and Management
- Economics of Risks, Uncertainty, Ambiguity, and Insurance
- Economics of Natural and Environmental Resources
- Microfinance
- Microeconomics
- Economics of Intellectual Property Rights
- Health Economics
- International Economics

IGI Global is currently accepting manuscripts for publication within this series. To submit a proposal for a volume in this series, please contact our Acquisition Editors at Acquisitions@igi-global.com or visit: http://www.igi-global.com/publish/.

The Advances in Finance, Accounting, and Economics (AFAE) Book Series (ISSN 2327-5677) is published by IGI Global, 701 E. Chocolate Avenue, Hershey, PA 17033-1240, USA, www.igi-global.com. This series is composed of titles available for purchase individually; each title is edited to be contextually exclusive from any other title within the series. For pricing and ordering information please visit http://www.igi-global.com/book-series/advances-finance-accounting-economics/73685. Postmaster: Send all address changes to above address.

Titles in this Series

For a list of additional titles in this series, please visit:
https://www.igi-global.com/book-series/advances-finance-accounting-economics/73685

Impact of Mobile Payment Applications and Transfers on Business
Thaisaiyi Zephania Opati (Riara University, Kenya) and Martin Kang'ethe Gachukia (Riara University, Kenya)
Business Science Reference • © 2020 • 311pp • H/C (ISBN: 9781799823988) • US $195.00

Handbook of Research on Social and Economic Development in the European Union
Yilmaz Bayar (Uşak University, Turkey)
Business Science Reference • © 2020 • 614pp • H/C (ISBN: 9781799811886) • US $295.00

Avatar-Based Models, Tools, and Innovation in the Digital Economy
Vardan Mkrttchian (HHH University, Australia) Leyla Gamidullaeva (Penza State University, Russia) and Ekaterina Aleshina (Penza State University, Russia)
Business Science Reference • © 2020 • 288pp • H/C (ISBN: 9781799811046) • US $195.00

Monetary Policies and Independence of the Central Banks in E7 Countries
Hasan Dinçer (İstanbul Medipol University, Turkey) and Serhat Yüksel (İstanbul Medipol University, Turkey)
Business Science Reference • © 2020 • 286pp • H/C (ISBN: 9781799816430) • US $195.00

Handbook of Research on Creating Sustainable Value in the Global Economy
Ulas Akkucuk (Boğaziçi University, Turkey)
Business Science Reference • © 2020 • 562pp • H/C (ISBN: 9781799811961) • US $295.00

Applied Econometric Analysis Emerging Research and Opportunities
Brian W. Sloboda (University of Phoenix, USA) and Yaya Sissoko (Indiana University of Pennsylvania, USA)
Business Science Reference • © 2020 • 270pp • H/C (ISBN: 9781799810933) • US $195.00

Examining the Relationship Between Economics and Philosophy
Ilkben Akansel (University of Bartin, Turkey)
Business Science Reference • © 2020 • 339pp • H/C (ISBN: 9781799810377) • US $205.00

Comparative Approaches to Old and New Institutional Economics
Ilkben Akansel (Bartin University, Turkey)
Business Science Reference • © 2020 • 339pp • H/C (ISBN: 9781799803331) • US $240.00

IGI Global
DISSEMINATOR OF KNOWLEDGE

701 East Chocolate Avenue, Hershey, PA 17033, USA
Tel: 717-533-8845 x100 • Fax: 717-533-8661
E-Mail: cust@igi-global.com • www.igi-global.com

Editorial Advisory Board

Table of Contents

Detailed Table of Contents

China's role in Africa: is it really unilateral domination or is it awakened because of the equation of the situation and interests? Then, how are the character, developments, and forms of cooperation? To answer those questions, this chapter uses a concept of inter-regionalism, in which inter-regional cooperation has several objectives namely balancing, bandwagoning, institution building, rationalizing, agenda-setting, and stabilizing. The emerging collaboration gives China an opportunity to introduce a model of interregional cooperation based on its foreign relations. China introduces a mechanism of cooperation based on "Chinese characteristic" which seems different from the Western perspective. China and Africa's interregional cooperation has been developing not only from economic reasons but has also been influenced by international politics. It is an economic cooperation alternative for Africa and international model alternative from the Chinese perspective. The last is influenced by China's international relations behavior which is based on its character.

This chapter gives a general overview of current integration processes which affect the countries in the regions of Europe and Asia, with a special focus on China and its Belt and Road initiative, from one side, Russia and its integration initiative of the Eurasian Economic Union, from another side, and BRICS as an umbrella format of collaboration between China, Russia, and other countries. In the case of trade in food and agricultural products, the chapter covers the two major rising economic powers with the involvement of China and Russia which are the Eurasian Economic Union and BRICS. The authors interpret their developments in relation to the modification of existing approaches to agricultural trade and establishing food security in the BRICS+ format.

India and Africa have a long partnership history of cooperation for economic development by trade and investment. This framework has become an essential component for development in Africa. Africa is an emerging investment and trade destination due to a large consumer market, high potential of economic growth, improving the business environment and investment regulations, and high rates of return on investment. The depth of relation of India and Africa has been reflected in the patterns of trade and investment, as well as people-to-people interactions, cultural exchanges, and cooperation at the continental and at the regional and bilateral levels. This chapter examines investment and trade patterns

One of the crucial parts of globalization is the upsurge in the volume of Foreign Direct Investment (FDI) inflows across economies. Thus, it becomes inevitable for the mutual benefit of the countries among themselves as it promotes economic cooperation between them. Due to the favorable demography and increasing population size, MINT economies (Mexico, Indonesia, Nigeria, and Turkey) gain particular attention to FDI for GDP growth. Hence, this chapter analyzes the paramount determinants of GDP growth of MINT economies in the period of 2000-2019. To fulfill the purpose of the study, a linear regression model and pooled data analysis statistical technique are employed. GDP is taken as a dependent variable, while some key factors like inflation, unemployment, FDI, and trade openness are taken as independent variables.

The chapter identifies the main determinants of FDI and the factors that constitute the main obstacles to foreign investment attractiveness in a region affected by economic and political instability and even conflict and where investors may face a multitude of political, economic, and security risks. The sample includes 14 Arab countries over the period of 2003-2017. To determine the factors that explain the probability of attracting investment inflows in MENA countries, the study uses a multiple regression model to estimate data in a time series. The authors also use the World Bank's governance indicators to assess the quality of the Arab institutional framework. The results of the panel data estimates through three different regressions reveal that macroeconomic instability combined with political instability constitutes an obstacle to investment. On practical implications, the study suggests that, in general, economic managers should take some economic policy measures to reduce or mitigate risks to encourage foreign investors to invest in MENA countries.

Latin America has been often termed as the lost continent but over the last two decades, both Europe and America have adjusted their policies as per the requirements and opportunities offered by these countries which shows that everything has not been lost. The geopolitical importance of these countries is also immense because of the huge oil reserves that they have apart from other important minerals and materials. These countries have also regrouped since the 1980s and developed the Atlantic Triangle and the Pacific Triangle to take advantage of their strengths. The chapter traces the development of globalization and regionalization in this continent and what it means to the current politico-economic world of today.

Foreword

From economic point of view, globalization occurs when the markets of different countries become more integrated and interconnected through economic transactions that cross national borders. In the book *Regional Trade and Development Strategies in the Era of Globalization* edited by Prof. Prabhakar, Dr. Erokhin, and Dr. Kaur, the positive and negative aspects of globalization and liberalization of trade and capital markets and their influences on the economies of transition are discussed in details using variety of research methods.

Bridging the different experiences of developed, developing, and least developed economies, the uniqueness of their development and spatial discrepancies is the main objective of the book, which is reflected in its content. The research spans over a variety of countries and organizations including BRICS, Southeast Asia, Africa, and the Americas. The authors of the chapters emphasize on the most recent challenges of these economies or provide a post hoc analysis of their experiences from globalization and integration processes and the lessons learned.

The publication covers recessionary trends of capitalism and emergence of global South. The editors and authors look at various policies and practices that have been put in place, and could be put in place, in various developing nations in an attempt to surmount some of the obstacles to economic development such as poverty, unemployment, income inequality, inadequate healthcare and illiteracy, food insecurity, environmental degradation, and other related issues. This book highlights unequal patterns of trade and unequal exchange rate systems and how it has impacted on international trade and what measures some developing nations have taken to adapt to the exigencies of the impact.

I highly recommend this book to those in government and academia who work in the area of international trade and development strategies. New policies have to take into account the negative and positive features of globalization and economic integration. The editors should be complimented in drawing together the large number of authors who made this book possible. The authors of this book are scholars from Asia, Africa, the Middle East, and Latin America, representing respected institutions, universities, and organizations. The variety of talent, expertise, and experience, along the wide scope of topics, make this book a unique collection of information and analysis, and a valuable resource for anyone studying global economy and international market.

Gao Tianming
Harbin Engineering University, China

Preface

Economic development is crucial to any nation that hopes to, not only survive, but also prosper in the face of the ever-changing economic realities of the 21st century. Understanding these economic changes, the principles along which they take place, the effects they create and the concomitant strategies employed to handle these effects, as well as the fast pace at which all these take place, can prove to be daunting to the student of economics.

In view of this, the present book aims to provide the readers with a comprehensive overview of the fundamentals of international economics, from the theoretical assumptions of their underpinning principles through to approaches to overcoming obstacles to economic development, and globalization and its impact on global trade and economic development. The ultimate aims and objectives of the book are to provide the university students, researchers, policymakers, economic actors with a comprehensive overview of globalization and regional initiative trends of trade and development through examining the theoretical and practical experiences of their underpinning principles through approaches to overcome obstacles of globalization and its positive and negative impacts on global trade and economic development.

Since 2008, the series of the systemic crisis occurred in the advanced countries, particularly, in the USA, the EU, and Japan, and then spread to the developing world (India, China, Malaysia, Brazil, and other countries). The most recent trade tensions between the USA and China adversely affect global economy, while the overall trends demonstrate that major economic players adopt protectionist policy. Under free-market-oriented neoliberal economies based on specialization and international division of labor, globalization regime suggests that goods, finance capital, and technology (but not labor mobility) should move freely. It indicates that Thatcher-Reagan's free-market neo-liberal model that dominated economic thinking for thirty years has been discredited. During the past three decades, a combination of large foreign debts, growing fiscal deficits, high inflation, and chronic balance of payments problems forced many developing nations' governments to undertake painful measures to stabilize their economies.

The publication opens with the study of contemporary globalization and emerging regional cooperation initiatives in the context of economic development. In Chapter 1, Dr. Akhilesh Chandra Prabhakar from Lovely Professional University (India) and Dr. Vasilii Erokhin from Harbin Engineering University (China) analyze the trends of the current globalization (new protectionism) and conflicts/contradictions between various forces involved in global economic integration. The authors investigate the trends, status, issues, and impacts of the de-linking project of the South initiatives (which can be seen in the forms of various regional blocks), provide a comprehensive treatment of the subject, and recommend new perspectives on the potential developmental effects of regional cooperation and the implications of regional integration for global economic development.

In Chapter 2, Dr. Akhilesh Chandra Prabhakar and Dr. Rajender Singh (both from Lovely Professional University, India) and Dr. Vasilii Erokhin from Harbin Engineering University (China) continue the study of the contemporary aspects of globalization and focus on the processes of economic integration of African economies with China and India. According to the authors, in the past decades, the global economy has been witnessing the emergence of the Global South, which collectively accounted for about 40% of global trade in 2017, up from 24% in 2001. The traditional pattern of trade, generally skewed towards developed economies, has shifted to a growing South-South trade relationship. The rapidly expanding trade and investment relationship within the China-India-Africa triangle attests to this dynamic change. Chapter 2 reviews China-Africa and India-Africa relations along the lines of trade flows (dynamics, structure, and destinations of exports and imports) and foreign direct investment (stocks accumulated in African countries).

Dr. Tonny Dian Effendi and Dr. Devita Prinanda from Universitas Muhammadiyah Malang (Indonesia) explore China-Africa collaboration. In Chapter 3, they use a concept of inter-regionalism, in which inter-regional cooperation has several objectives namely balancing, bandwagoning, institution building, rationalizing, agenda-setting, and stabilizing. The emerging collaboration gives China an opportunity to introduce a model of interregional cooperation based on its foreign relations. China introduces a mechanism of cooperation based on "Chinese characteristic" which seems different from the Western perspective. China and Africa's interregional cooperation has been developing not only from economic reasons but influenced by international politics. It is an economic cooperation alternative for Africa and international model alternative from the Chinese perspective. The last is influenced by China's international relations behavior which based on its character.

In Chapter 4, Dr. Vasilii Erokhin and Dr. Gao Tianming, both from Harbin Engineering University (China), attempt to give a general overview of current integration processes which affect the countries in the regions of Europe and Asia, with a special focus on China and its Belt and Road initiative, from one side, Russia and its integration initiative of the Eurasian Economic Union, from another side, and BRICS as an umbrella format of collaboration between China, Russia, and other countries. In the case of trade in food and agricultural products, the chapter covers the two major rising economic powers with the involvement of China and Russia which are the Eurasian Economic Union and BRICS. The authors interpret their developments in relation to the modification of existing approaches to agricultural trade and establishing food security in the BRICS+ format.

India and Africa have a long partnership history of cooperation for economic development by trade and investment. This framework has become an essential component for development in Africa. Africa is an emerging investment and trade destination due to a large consumer market, high potential of economic growth, improving the business environment and investment regulations, and high rates of return on investment. In Chapter 5, Dr. Rajender Singh, Dr. Mohamad Aslam, and Dr. Gaibul Preet, from Lovely Professional University (India), and Dr. Sushanta Kumar Mahapatra from IBS Hyderabad, The ICFAI Foundation for Higher Education (India), examine and analyze investment and trade patterns of India-Africa collaboration in the contemporary era of globalization. The study is based on empirical and conceptual aspects by using secondary data. An analysis is carried out by using appropriate econometric tools to make the study more relevant.

In Chapter 6, Dr. Sundip Solanki and Dr. Krishna Murthy Inumula, both from Symbiosis International University (India) study India's trade and development strategies with BRCS, EAC, and SCO in the era of globalization. India's trade with the major economic groups BRCS, EAC, and SCO revealed that there exists a long-run equilibrium relation between BRCS and SCO group of countries trade with

India's economic growth, whereas EAO group of countries does not show any long-run equilibrium relation. It is concluded that 1% change in imports from BRCS countries causes the economic growth to increase by about 0.84% meaning that in the long-run, imports from BRCS countries tend to have a significant impact on economic growth, similarly a 1% change in exports to BRCS countries causes the economic growth to decrease by about 0.53% meaning that in the long-run, exports to BRCS countries tend to have a significant impact on economic growth. Similar to BRCS co-integration model, the SCO group of countries imports are positively affecting, whereas exports are negatively affecting economic growth. The exported items to SCO countries are negatively affecting the economy meaning that exports are not contributing.

One of the solutions to converge the economic interests of India's Look East Policy and foreign economic policies of other countries is the Bay of Bengal Initiative for Multi-Sectoral Technical and Economic Cooperation (BIMSTEC). Its objective is to integrate the regions on both sides of the Bay of Bengal. The development of BIMSTEC countries is indispensable for the forward march of Asia as a whole. In Chapter 7, Dr. Gurpreet Kaur and Dr. Akriti Gupta, both from Lovely Professional University (India), analyze the India-BIMSTEC trade activities after the establishment of BIMSTEC bloc. Gravity model and Auto-Regressive Integrated Moving Average (ARIMA) are used. The model estimates the sets of regression equations to measure the effects of regional trade agreements using ordinary least squares with nation dummies to capture country-specific fixed effects. The study reveals that all coefficients of regional dummy variables are mostly positive and significant, indicating the agreements that tend to enhance more trade than bilateral trade agreements. The authors state that based on India's trade with the BIMSTEC region, there exists a scope for intraregional trade in the future.

In Chapter 8, Dr. Gurpreet Kaur from Lovely Professional University (India) analyze the export competitiveness of India against BIMSTEC countries. To identify the comparative advantage/disadvantage of India's exports with BIMSTEC countries, revealed comparative advantage (RCA) approach is used at HS 6-digit. It provides an understanding of challenges and opportunities that India's export sector faces as it becomes rapidly integrated into global markets. The study identifies those export categories in which India loses, gains, or maintains its comparative advantage with following the stages of comparative advantages. The study concludes that India's export sectors witnessed competitive positioning of some of its product, these trends have not been uniform across all Industries. Rapid export growth of some sector does not imply that the sector is displaying high demand growth in BIMSTEC markets. In an ideal situation, there would be the emergence of an export structure that has a heavy concentration in those industries that exhibit high growth in the BIMSTEC market.

One of the major forums that brings together the representatives of government, business, and academia, from India and other countries is the Indian Ocean Rim Association (IORA). In Chapter 9, Dr. Jasdeep Kaur Dhami and Dr. Manbir Singh, both from CT University (India), analyze India's trade potential with IORA member nations. The main outcome of this chapter is that India should concentrate on ammonium dihydrogen orthophosphate for Australia, gold and semi-manufactured for Singapore, mineral or chemical fertilizers for Thailand, tankers for Malaysia, warp knit fabrics of synthetic fibers for Indonesia, ammonium dihydrogen orthophosphate for South Africa, palm oil and fractions for Sri Lanka, Bangladesh, Mozambique, Tanzania, the United Republic of Yemen, crude palm oil for Kenya, bigeye tunas, frozen for Mauritius, and carded yarn of fine animal hair for Madagascar.

At the turn of the 21st century, globalization of developed and developing countries in the world witnessed institutional inflows from international investors which became the main characteristic of global capital markets. In Chapter 10, Dr. Akriti Gupta, Dr. Gurpreet Kaur, and Dr. Mahesh Sarva, all from

Lovely Professional University (India), assess time-series data from 2000 to 2017 to understand how the different elements that have influenced the foreign institutional investments and helped India become a global market for such investors. The results revealed that political risk, financial market development, trade openness of the country, size of the economy, and rate of return on investment are the important determinants in attracting foreign institutional investments in India. The study also found economic risk and financial market risk played an insignificant role in determining foreign institutional investment in India. The findings of the research help the present government and market regulators to introduce policies aimed at increasing the flow of funds from international institutional investors.

One of the crucial parts of globalization is the upsurge in the volume of Foreign Direct Investment (FDI) inflows across economies. Thus, it becomes inevitable for the mutual benefit of the countries among themselves as it promotes economic cooperation between them. Due to the favorable demography and increasing population size, MINT economies (Mexico, Indonesia, Nigeria, and Turkey) gain particular attention to FDI for GDP growth. Dr. Kunal Dutta from Lovely Professional University (India) analyzes the paramount determinants of GDP growth of MINT economies in the period of 2000-2019. To fulfill the purpose of the study, in Chapter 11, a linear regression model and pooled data analysis statistical technique are employed. GDP is taken as a dependent variable, while some key factors like inflation, unemployment, FDI, and trade openness are taken as independent variables.

In Chapter 12, Dr. Souhaila Kammoun, Dr. Youssra Ben Romdhane, and Dr. Marwa Ben Salem Fakhfakh, all from University of Sfax (Tunisia), identify the main determinants of FDI and the factors that constitute the main obstacles to foreign investment attractiveness in a region affected by economic and political instability and even conflict and where investors may face a multitude of political, economic, and security risks. The sample includes fourteen Arab countries over the period of 2003-2017. In order to determine the factors that explain the probability of attracting investment inflows in MENA countries, the study uses a multiple regression model to estimate data in a time series. The authors also use the World Bank's governance indicators to assess the quality of the Arab institutional framework. The results of the panel data estimates through three different regressions reveal that macroeconomic instability combined with political instability constitutes an obstacle to investment. On practical implications, the study suggests that, in general, economic managers should take some economic policy measures to reduce or mitigate risks in order to encourage foreign investors to invest in MENA countries.

Latin America has been often termed as the lost continent but over the last two decades, both Europe and America have adjusted their policies as per the requirements and opportunities offered by these countries which shows that everything has not been lost. The geopolitical importance of these countries is also immense because of the huge oil reserves that they have apart from other important minerals and materials. These countries have also regrouped since the 1980s and developed the Atlantic Triangle and the Pacific Triangle to take advantage of its strengths. In Chapter 13, Dr. Tanima Dutta from Lovely Professional University (India), Dr. Anupam Rawat from Bhimrao Ambedkar University of Social Sciences (India), and Dr. Arti Mishra from Gauri Shankar Mahavidyalaya (India) trace the development of globalization and regionalization in this continent and what it means to the current politico-economic world of today.

The publication is concluded with the study of regional trade and green innovation development under the NAFTA. In Chapter 14, Prof. Jose Vargas-Hernandez from University of Guadalajara (Mexico) analyzes the elements of an environmentally sustainable regional trade and development under the NAFTA based on the decentralization of the infrastructure. The author assesses how democratization of the territory and innovations in the sphere of institutional design address the complexity of the trade and development challenges. The method employed is the critical analysis supported by a review of the literature and consultation to the experts in the field. It is concluded that the environmentally sustainable capacity planning has a critical role in regional innovation development in specific areas of regional trade and development, economic growth, social inclusion and equality, environmental sustainability, health, education, and business. To achieve these aims, environmentally sustainable regional trade and development require the democratization of the territory and the new institutional design.

The inviting aspect of this book is that, apart from providing clarity, it also provides the context for the discussions on the different facets of economic development. The pedagogical use of case studies provides students with concrete real-life examples that facilitate the grasp of abstract theories and concepts and go a long way towards enlivening classroom discussions. The editors believe that this publication will prove to be a much sought in the institutions of higher learning, not only in developing countries but also in various parts of the world.

Akhilesh Chandra Prabhakar
Lovely Professional University, India

Gurpreet Kaur
Lovely Professional University, India

Vasilii Erokhin
Harbin Engineering University, China

Acknowledgment

This book is a product of research and support of many individuals to whom the editors would like to express their sincere gratitude.

We thank all the chapter contributors from respected universities, research institutes, and organizations. Our acknowledgment is made to the members of the Editorial Advisory Board and international team of reviewers for sharing their precious time, professional experience, valuable recommendations, and insights. We are grateful to Dr. Carlos Correa (Executive Director of South Centre, Geneva), Prof. Sachin Chaturvedi (Director General of Research & Information Systems among Developing Countries, New Delhi), Prof. C. Rangrajan (Former Governor of Reserve Bank of India, and Chancellor of AcFai University IBS), Prof. Prabhat Patnaik (Jawaharlal Nehru University, New Delhi), Prof. Jayati Ghosh (Jawaharlal Nehru University, New Delhi), Prof. K. Kuperan (Universiti Utara Malaysia), Prof. Yusnidah Ibrahim (Associate Vice Chancellor, Universiti Utara Malaysia) who all shaped their ideas and concepts clearly about neo-liberal globalization. Our immense indebted to the colleagues from Lovely Professional University, India, namely, Prof. Shri Ashok Mittal (Chancellor of the LPU), Dr. Sanjay Modi (Executive Dean), and Prof. Rajesh Verma (Dean of Mittal School of Business) for inspiring us to write this book. We are also very thankful to Dr. Mohammad Azam (Pakistan), Dr. Rabiul Islam (Bangladesh), Prof. Ashish Saha (India), Dr. Ahmad Sahidah (Indonesia), Dr. B. Bakhtiyar (Iran), and Dr. Abdullah Sumrahadi (Indonesia). We thank the several thousand students who provided detailed and insightful comments, advices, criticisms, and suggestions for this book. We thank our current and former colleagues and friends who have provided a lot of suggestions and information.

We give our special thanks to Prof. Gao Tianming from Harbin Engineering University (China) who kindly prepared the outstanding foreword for this book.

We sincerely thank the entire IGI Global team for assistance and support throughout the book development process.

The editors appreciate the support of the Fundamental Research Funds for the Central Universities, China (grant no. 3072019CFP0902, HEUCFJ170901).

Suggestions for making improvements in the book from fellow teachers and readers are most welcome.

Acknowledgment

Chapter 1
Globalization:
Reshaping the World Economy in the 21st Century

Akhilesh Chandra Prabhakar
https://orcid.org/0000-0002-1061-6509
Lovely Professional University, India

Vasilii Erokhin
https://orcid.org/0000-0002-3745-5469
Harbin Engineering University, China

ABSTRACT

The chapter focuses on contemporary globalization and emerging regional cooperation initiatives in the context of economic development. The authors analyze the trends of the current globalization (new protectionism) and conflicts/contradictions between various forces involved in global economic integration. The chapter also investigates the trends, status, issues, and impacts of the de-linking project of the South initiatives (which can be seen in the forms of various regional blocks). It also provides a comprehensive treatment of the subject and recommends new perspectives on the potential developmental effects of regional cooperation and the implications of regional integration for global economic development.

INTRODUCTION

It is the dominant global opinion that the balance of power is shifting away from the west to the east. The United Nations Development Program [UNDP] (2013) highlighted that trade among developing countries had been rising up and the trend would continue in the even future. The GDP ratio and trade performance (which has been more than tripled) of the south has surpassed the respective parameters of the developed economies (which have been declining since the 1980s) and finally, the south has acquired capacity to reshape the global economy in the 21st century.

DOI: 10.4018/978-1-7998-1730-7.ch001

The dominant Western multinational corporations open their new branches in China, India, Indonesia, Vietnam, the Republic of Korea, Japan, Malaysia, Hong Kong SAR, Singapore, and Brunei to exploit the abundant natural resources and cheap labor force. According to Bhardwaj (2019), in the 1970-1980s, developed countries shifted production centers to China and South East Asia, where cheap labor was available in abundance. However, China and the countries of South-East Asia, including India and other developing countries, are not fully aware about the effects of western finance capital on society. These countries are preparing themselves for launching Fourth Industrial Revolution (FIR). The FIR lay the power of artificial intelligence, automation, and the Internet of Things (IoT).

After the World War II, Western nations have been enjoyed with rich clubs: G-7, NAFTA (trade block), European Commission (EC), European Union (EU), NATO (military block), World Bank, and IMF (international banking and financial systems – Bretton Woods System), and established (in the decade of the mid 1990s) a forum of World Trade Organization (WTO). A continuation of domination during the last four centuries (first led by the British colonial master before the World War II and then by the USA imperialism until the first decade of 21st century) is now reshaping the world economy towards the eastern bloc: BRICS (Brazil, Russia, India, China, and South Africa) – EAC (East Asian Cooperation) – Shanghai Cooperation Organization (SCO) along-with recently proposed 16-Nations Regional Comprehensive Economic Partnership backed up by China and Russia.

In the 1990s, the balance of forces shifted in the favor of capitalism because of the implosion of the Soviet Union-led Socialist Bloc. The USA posed as single superpower and imposed two types of tactics (direct war and economic sanctions) against developing countries (particularly, Yugoslavia, Iraq, Afghanistan, Libya, Syria, Iran, North Korea, Venezuela, and Russia), and threatened to North Korea and China, as it can be seen particularly in the area of East and South sea with the traditional allies like Japan and South Korea. The USA, however, maintains three pillars of domination: monetary, military, and trade. Developing countries were deviated from the South-South project which was conceived and promoted as a means to reduce the dependence of developing countries on developed markets and enhance the collective bargaining power of developing and least developed nations.

Since 2008, however, the performance of the developed economies has been rather modest and there is no optimism to return to 2007 level in the near future. In this context, the role of G-20 (now G-24) is almost insignificant because G-24 members are not very serious about the solutions. Even developed countries are not prepared to diagnose the crisis properly as they believe that it is a mistake and economic problems can be resolved by correcting measures. A decade long full flagged economic crisis is a systemic crisis of neo-liberal regime which was based on public and private debt interconnected and deregulated free financial flows, free trade mobility under liberalized financial and commodities markets. It may be considered as a great depression which has been created by the imperialist globalization systems itself. The neo-liberal regime creates two major types of problems. First, greater wealth and income inequality among and between nations (e.g. 1% of the richest control 82% of wealth or resources globally). Second, due to the formation of crony corporate financial and commodities bubbles which are themselves embedded within a deeper structural systemic crisis that afflicts contemporary global capitalism, which leads a full flagged economic depression for over a decade long since 2008.

Steinbock (2017) predicts that BRICS combined economic power will surpass that of major six advanced countries: the USA, Japan, the UK, Germany, France, and Italy by the early 2030. By the end of 2020, the size of China's economy will exceed that of the USA. In 2000, China's economy was barely one-tenth of that of the USA, whereas Japan's GDP was still as large as the three largest European economies put together: Germany, the UK, and France. Brazil was struggling for stability, Russian economy had been crushed by US-led reforms, while the change was only beginning in India. By the early 2010s, the world economy looked very different. The US economy was still more than twice as big as that of China but Japan's growth had been sick penalized by stagnation. In Brazil, the Lula era brought about a dramatic catch-up. In India, growth had accelerated. In Russia, President Putin's rule had multiplied the size of the economy by almost six-fold. Despite growth deceleration, which is normal after intensive industrialization, China has strongly internalized capacity to perform well growth potential along-with inclusive development through the participation of the people at massive levels. The value of China's imports and exports of goods totaled $280.9 billion or 3% of global trade. By 2017, its total trade in goods had jumped to $4.1 trillion or 12.4% global trade. While economic growth of the USA is slowing due to structural crisis of the following capitalist mode of production. In the USA, business investment decline (industrial output decreased by 0.2% in July 2019 compared to June 2019). Japan and the core EU economies are also decreasing. The UK economy contracted during the second quarter of 2019, as did Germany. The picture is much the same in Italy, Brazil, Mexico, Argentina, and India. Even China is witnessing a slowing down of its growth rate as a consequence of the world recession (Patnaik, 2019). By 2050, China's economy could be almost 50% bigger than that in the USA, while India may follow in the footprints and surpass the USA a few years later.

Currently India's share of global exports increased from 1.58% in the last quarter of 2017 to 1.71% in the first quarter of 2019. Recent full flagged economic crisis, however, caused a sharp decline in Indian industrial output (from 7.8% to 0.6% in July 2019) due to lack of demand in external and domestic markets. More than 20 million Indian workers have lost their jobs since 2017. Around 94% (450 million) workers are engaged with unorganized (informal) sectors and these unorganized sectors contribute 45% of output to GDP. Among them, 50% earn just less than INR 10,000 ($140) per month, 20% receive less than INR 20,000 ($280) per month, and only 3% of workers receive more than INR 50,000 ($700) per month. These unorganized sectors adversely affected because of demonetization, GST, NPA, and NBFC, and approximately 40 million workers as majority of women workers have lost their jobs in the past three years. In unorganized sectors, investment declined from 37% in 2012-2013 to 30% in 2018-2019. Generally, the authors calculated output growth of organized (formal) sector and on that basis, calculated GDP growth rate and assumed that unorganized sectors also performed the same. But actual figure of unorganized sectors is uncounted.

BACKGROUND

Rising Asia

Asia has been the most important continent in the world economy for many centuries. Until 1820, Asia's GDP accounted for 60% of that of the world. However, after that, Asia experienced a rapid decline where most parts of Asia were colonized by British and other imperial forces. After the World War II, things started to change. Japan invented the export-oriented development model and joined the G-7 club. It was the first to rise in Asia with the U.S. huge capital investment. In the 1960s, the so-called "Four Tigers" (Hong Kong, Taiwan, Singapore, and the Republic of Korea) joined Japan following the same development model. By early 1970s, the development model had been followed by Indonesia, Malaysia, Thailand, and the Philippines. In 1978, China started the policy of reforms and opening up to the world that has led to some stunning achievements. In the past forty years, China has been experimenting Keynesian interventionist policies to maintain the aggregate demand with the aggregate supply under the guiding principles of so-called 'Socialist Market Structures' which is politically controlled and governed by the 'Marxist-Leninist-Maoist' ideologies.

Asia's GDP accounts for about 24% of the global GDP and is forecasted to rise to more than 40% of the world GDP with 60% of the world's population by 2030. The rise of Asia especially that of China differs from those in Europe and the USA. European countries and the USA facilitated their growth by the colonization of Asian and African countries and exploitation of natural resources and cheap labor. China reinforced its credentials as a pro-Third World economic powerhouse by offering $10 billion of concessional loans and exact the same amount announces 'debt-relief' to Africa and pledging to contribute significantly to the continent's skilled human resources base. UNDP (2013) estimates that between 1992 and 2011, China's trade with Sub-Saharan Africa rose from $1 billion to over $140 billion.

India and China succeeded by sharing its growth with others. All countries and continents which have cooperation with India and China benefit at least to some reasonable extent from the growth. India-ASEAN Free Trade Treaty was signed in 2008. India-ASEAN trade have reached $47 billion which is India's 4th ranked with electronics, chemicals, machinery, and textiles almost it's covering 80% of the total (489 items excluding agricultural products). China-ASEAN Free Trade Treaty is effective from 2010. Its 4th trade partner of China will share at least 10% of total China's trade. It is expected to reach over $200 billion between China-ASEAN. It is the world's 3rd largest trade area after NAFTA and the EU. Chinese construction sector will benefit from the imports of raw materials from ASEAN. Even China is trying to sign with the Republic of Korea. Vietnam, Thailand, and Cambodia's textiles, footwear, and steel industries mainly will have to face Chinese competition. However, Thailand will get the biggest Chinese market for their cheapest jewelry and other cosmetics commodities. ASEAN-China's first free trade treaty was signed in 2002, the first round of tax removal started in 2005, the second one in 2007. In 2009, both regions signed an agreement on investment. Indonesia, Brunei, Malaysia, Philippines, Singapore, and Thailand have agreed to reduce 90% of their taxes; if is effective from 2010. Laos, Vietnam, Cambodia, and Burma reduced the taxes on at least 10% of textiles and electronics items in 2015.

Multilateralism and Globalization

Multilateralism is not necessarily the ultimate solution of internal, bilateral, and even multilateral problems, because without changing the existing material, social, economic, and cultural conditions which depend on political and organizational willpower of a nation, multilateralism can only support resolving geopolitical conflicts. Initially, it would be helpful to fulfill the requirements of financial and technological gap by promoting regional cooperation among nations if it is based on complementary mutual interests.

An idea of globalization can be found in the thoughts of the Mont Pelerin Society with antecedents dating back to the great movements of trade and empire across Asia and the Indian Ocean from the 15th century onwards. An early description of globalization was penned by the American entrepreneur-turned-minister Charles Taze Russell who coined the term "corporate giants" in 1897 (Prabhakar, 2003). The foundation of actual concepts and theories of globalization (as popularly known as "neo-liberalism") was developed by Friedrich von Hayek and Milton Friedman of Chicago School. However, it was not used by the economists and social scientists until the 1960s. The term "neo-liberalism" had achieved widespread use in the mainstream press in late 1980s when the actual form of economic policies was implemented by Reagan in the USA and Thatcher in the UK Prabhakar, 2003).

According to Akira (2000), the groundwork for swift international transfer of enormous quantities of funds was laid in the 1970s when trade and capital liberalization also gained momentum in developed capitalist countries, in parallel with the transition of the international monetary system to a floating rate system. By the 1980s, this wave of trade and capital liberalization had extended to semi-developed capitalist countries that had experienced sustained economic growth, and with this came the establishment of a global open-economy system. This, too, spurred the international transfer of funds. This period was also characterized by dramatic growth on a global scale of not only American- but also European- and Japanese-based large corporations, and by an increasing trend toward corporate multinationalization. Multinationalization became another factor accelerating the international movement of funds. The 1980s also saw the rise of "neo-liberalism" represented by "Reaganomics" and "Thatcherism" which may be regarded as the precursors of today's globalization.

Historically, the globalization project was launched during colonial era in Africa and Asia, when Western countries strongly advocated for free flow of goods and commodities because raw materials from colonized countries smoothly supplied to new industrial economies in the UK, France, Italy, the Netherlands, Portugal, and Belgium. There were basic requirements for industrial revolution in the West in the 19th century. But it was slowed down from the beginning of the World War I to the Third Quarter of the 20th century because of the disintegrated balance of forces' emergence of the Socialist USSR after the Bolshevik Revolution (1917), People's Revolution in China (1949), and 'None-alliance Movement led by newly emergence of independent nations of Asia and Africa. The formation of Bretton Woods System (the World Bank and the IMF) after the end of the World War II become matured in the 1950-1960s. This slowdown can be attributed to the inward-looking policies pursued by a number of countries in order to protect their respective industries. The pace of globalization picked up rapidly during the fourth quarter of the 20th century (Prabhakar, 2005).

MAIN FOCUS OF THE CHAPTER

Main Characteristics of the Contemporary Globalization

The contemporary globalization is no different in nature and character from the previous episode of globalization that had been interrupted by the two world wars, the Great Depression, and the post-war adoption of state interventionism within broadly national economic regimes. Indeed, the contemporary globalization is in a continuation of the war resembled in Yugoslavia, Iraq, Afghanistan, Libya, Ukraine, and Syria, and a decade long (2008-2018) Great Depression which has been dominating by the Crony Corporate Finance Capital, military, technology, monetary, and oil lobbies.

In the 1990s, the balance of forces temporarily shifted in the favor of capitalism because of the implosion of the Soviet-led state socialism. De-linking project which was launched by the Soviet Socialist Block and Non-aligned movements of the Third World countries were brushed aside. The USA imposed a new world economic order and posed itself as a unipolar world superpower by using the tactics of military operations and economic sanctions against particular countries and establishing trade mechanism of the World Trade Organization (WTO) (Prabhakar, 2018). This new form of globalism was the process of international finance capital, trade, and technological mobility, but not labor South-North mobility. It promoted four major things at global levels: financial resources, privately-owned corporations, and digitalization and marketization of global economy. In other words, globalization is usually recognized as being driven by a combination of economic, technological, socio-cultural, political, and biological factors. The term can also refer to the transnational circulation of political and academic ideas, languages, popular cultures, regional economies, and societies which closely interact with each other through a global network of communication, transportation, finance, and trade. National economies have been integrated to global economy by trade, FDI, capital flows, migration, spread of technology, and military presence.

The current wave of capital flows and trade to semi-capitalist developing countries (particularly, in East and South-East Asia) can be seen with the opening market along with financial and trade liberalization which has been practiced by the US, the EU, and Japanese based transnational and multinational corporations in the beginning of the 1970s. The same corporate multinational groups are now internalizing their financial movements in the semi-feudal-semi-capitalist developing countries. This contemporary phase of globalization forces argues that the role of the state should be minimized by following "laissez-fair" and "international division of labor". By following these two principles, both producers and consumers will benefit. Although, on the name of greater individual freedom for capital and trade mobility, labor and technological North-South mobility is restricted. Trade in agricultural and primary commodities from the South to the North has not increased, but multinational corporations have lead the economic sectors in developing countries of the South. The free trade and free-market regime is similar to that in colonialism, and fail to change material conditions of the south. It was basically revival of Adam Smith's philosophy. They further argue that by implementing neo-liberal policies and export-oriented growth and development strategies, efficiency, productivity, and competitiveness of the workers, in short, the productive forces' capacity will be greater. With large scale of integrated economies, people will be enjoying more than previously. This assumption was also a myth prediction.

Thus, under free-market competition, classical form of industrial capitalism has been transformed into 'crony capitalism' dominated by international capital controlled by multinational corporation of the USA, the EU, Japan, and Canada. With currency domination through the activities of stock markets and share markets, a win-win situation for big corporate houses is only based on the personal relationship between business leaders, top-level influential policymakers, bureaucrats, and ruling groups of politicians by receiving huge amounts of tax incentive and other types of rebate and concession. These ruling elite groups focus on the exchange of favors for bribes between state and business; politics drove policy choices that bureaucrats were not autonomous from political interference in setting policy and that business and political elites struggled with each other over who would reap the rents to be had.

Current Global Economic Scenario

International trade has always been dominated by big multinational and transnational corporations. Fifteen top multinational and transnational corporations control 72% of international trade. The centralization of capital during digitalization, capitalization, and privatization leads an engine of jobless output growth model which turns into the great depression because of lack of demand. Privately owned business is based on either public or private debt. By early 2018, global debt stocks had risen to nearly $250 trillion (three times global income) from $142 trillion a decade earlier. The ratio of global debt to GDP is now nearly one-third higher than in 2008. Private debt has exploded, especially in emerging markets and developing countries, whose share of global debt stock increased from 7% in 2007 to 26% in 2017. The ratio of credit to non-financial corporations to GDP in emerging market economies increased from 56% in 2008 to 105% in 2017. Vulnerability is reflected in cross-border capital flows which have not just become more volatile but turned negative for emerging and developing countries as a group since late 2014, with outflows especially large in the second quarter of 2018. The banks have grown even bigger on the back of public money; opaque financial instruments are again de rigueur; shadow banking has grown into a $160 trillion business, twice the size of the global economy; over-the-counter derivatives have surpassed the volume of $500 trillion (United Nations Conference on Trade and Development [UNCTAD], 2018).

According to the World Bank (2019), global economic growth is to be declined to 2.6% by the end of 2019. It may be reflected in terms of poor performance in trade and investment. However, World Bank (2019) projected to gradually rise to 2.8% by 2021, and predicated on continued benign global financing conditions and a modest recovery in emerging market and developing economies (EMDEs). Global Business Risks are also declining because of trade war between China and the USA. Other problems are rising global debt (both public and private), growing income and wealth inequality, and unemployment which lead to adverse developments and faced more significant challenges today than they did in the early 2000s (World Bank, 2019).

The widening gaps across firms have been particularly marked in the digital world. Of the top 25 big tech firms (in terms of market capitalization), 14 are based in the USA, three in the EU, three in China, four in other Asian countries (Republic of Korea, Japan, Singapore, and Malaysia), and one in Africa. The top three big tech firms in the USA have an average market capitalization of more than $400 billion, compared with an average of $200 billion in the top big tech firms in China, $123 billion in Asia, $69 billion in Europe, and $66 billion in Africa. What has been significant is the pace at which the benefits of market dominance have accrued in this sector: Amazon's profits-to-sales ratio increased from 10% in 2005 to 23% in 2015, while that for Alibaba increased from 10% in 2011 to 32% in 2015. Rising inequality, together with the higher propensity to save of the rich, creates a bias towards under consumption or, alternatively, has encouraged debt-led consumption enabled by financial deregulation.

Tax and many other types of incentives provided by the government to the largest private corporate houses and the removal of the pension and bonus schemes of the contractual workers are major reason for inequality between corporate employers and employees and among the skilled and unskilled labor. According to Jipson and Jitheesh (2018), growing inequality in China has been accompanied by the reduction in poverty, but this has not been the case in India, Brazil, and almost all other countries of the South.

Current explosion of debt levels around the world suggests the urgency of a better, more just and effective system of sovereign debt management, in which the burden of adjustment is not disproportionately borne by citizens and workers in a country, but shared more equitably among those responsible for creating the problem, including creditors.

Corporate firms or industries seek to boost profitability through rent-seeking strategies, such as intensifying international competition between workers and government to reduce labor and tax costs, crushing or buying up competitors to build up market dominance and increase markups, etc. The unfortunate truth is that the attempts of big firms to enhance their own market position through such strategies only make the broader economic system more fragile and vulnerable since together they lead to more inequality, under-consumption, debt, and consequently, macroeconomic vulnerability.

Overall economic performance of developing countries is slowdown and faces the risks of instability (Prabhakar, 2016, 2017). Since the colonial regime and even after independence of Asian and African countries, the western multinational and transnational corporations have been controlling resources in developing countries. According to UNCTAD (2018), multinational corporations offshore tax hubs result in an estimated $100 billion in annual tax revenue losses for developing countries. According to

Correa (2019), around thirty least developed and other vulnerable countries are either in or at high risk of debt distress. Western Rich Nations have reduced the commitment for financial assistance or foreign aid around 0.7% of their GNIs (as their official commitment) to developing countries.

China-USA Trade War

China and the USA have recently launched a tariff war. In 2017, the U.S. trade deficit in goods and services was $566 billion (trade deficit in goods alone was $810 billion). The largest trade deficit of $375 billion was with China. The initial tariff imposed by the USA on Chinese goods is now generalized for other countries including India. The U.S. Government has recently announced for the break-up of the Special Trade Preferences Agreement with India. Since the beginning of 2018, technological domination to capture the world market (i.e. competition between Apple vs Hawaii) has been adversely influencing the global economy to reverse the gear of globalization project by isolating each other and following protectionist policy. Due to trade war protectionist policy, approximately $0.5 trillion worth of commodities have been restricted almost seven times in the last year 2018, which has been creating uncertainties in the global business environment.

In view of a decline in economic performance at domestic level and an increase in external indebtedness, the USA have embarked on protectionist policy by persuading emerging countries like China and India to accept new rules (Patnaik, 2019). Chandrasekhar (2019) stated that the initial tariff spat was clothed by the USA in the rhetoric of generalized protectionism, which included a rewrite of the North American Free Trade Agreement (NAFTA) and exit from the Trans-Pacific Partnership. Trade war with China is aimed at forcing China to step back in its drive to become global economic superpower. The rhetoric against China is not just that it runs large trade and current account surpluses with the USA or that it steals technological secrets to bolster its competitiveness, but that the activities of its firms pose a national security threat to the USA.

USA-India Adverse Trade Relations

The US government has dismissed the trade preference system (many countries including India and African countries have been enjoyed it for a long time) and banned 2,000 items of Indian goods and services in the US market from June 5, 2019. India-USA merchandise trade balance was favorable as much as $27.3 billion in 2017. In 2018, it is supposed to decline by $4 billion owing to increased Indian demand for a range of US goods, in particular, civilian aircraft and energy. About a decade ago, US share in India's imports was 8.5%. Today, it has declined down to 5.7%. Over the same period, China's share has increased from less than 11% to over 16%. India, in short, has been moving from US sources to Asian sources for its imports (Patnaik, 2019).

UNCTAD (2018) highlights that the immediate pressures are building around escalating tariffs and volatile financial flows but behind these threats to global stability is a wider failure, since 2008, to address the inequities and imbalances of our hyper-globalized world. New pressures are weighing down on multilateralism. In the interdependent world, inward-looking solutions do not offer a way forward; the challenge is to find ways to make multilateralism work for all and for the health of the planet.

Growth of Emerging Economies

In the coming decade, secular stagnation in the USA, the EU, and Japan will sustain relatively low growth, whereas large emerging economies despite relative deceleration will continue their historical catch-up. By the mid-21st century, BRICS could be some 50% bigger than their advanced counterparts. Currently, BRICS contributes to more than 50% of the world's economic growth. This emerging group along with the EAC and the SCO strive to replace the Western-dominated international financial system and reshape the world economy by following the principles of South-South cooperation which is based on mutually beneficial relationships, and claim not to attach to their cooperation any policy conditions on what type of development model partner countries should adopt. This, accordingly, would undermine the principles of mutual respect for national sovereignty, non-interference in each other's internal affairs, and solidarity at the basis of the Non-Aligned Movement and the struggle for independence from colonialism that characterized the common past of many countries in Asia, Africa, and Latin America.

BRICS committed to transparent, non-discriminatory, open, free, and inclusive international trade. Protectionism and unilateralism run counter to the spirit and rules of the WTO. However, traditional donors, including multilateral development banks, have always approached their interactions with developing countries as donor-aid recipient relationships, largely based on altruism and policy conditions attached to their cooperation efforts. The overall development model informing such conditionality followed most often the Western-type of approach to economic development, with policies and investment underlined by E-governance principles and the institutional and regulatory frameworks to ensure an enabling environment for market-led growth. The recent focus by traditional donors on the centrality of trade liberalization and private crony corporate sectors led development implies that the industrialization path of a country should be primarily left to market forces and international competitiveness.

The establishment of BRICS and its affiliated institutions such as the New Development Bank (NDB) and the Contingent Reserve Arrangement initiatives make an effort to fulfill the financial requirements of developing countries. China's connectivity initiative appears to offer such a model for cooperation, which is seen as less exploitative and more relevant to mutual development. In fact, BRICS is influential platform which is promoting financial flow to the South. The NDB provides more loans than any other bank in the world. This cooperation has resulted in an increase in foreign direct investment, trade, technology transfer, energy resources, and infrastructure projects. The NDB provided $2.5 billion loans to member countries. Despite the fact that Brazil is a huge commodity market, South Africa and Russia are rich in natural resources, India has an enormous agricultural economy, and China is the largest exporter of manufactured commodities with the biggest production capacity, intra-trade between BRICS countries remains abysmal. For example, in 2015, intra-trade stood at about $250 billion; it is expected almost doubling to $500 billion by 2020. In the long run, it would be more constructive to promote better regional connectivity and intra-regional connectivity, to pave the way for regional and trans-regional economic integration.

Among BRICS nations, there are trilateral groupings as it can be seen in the formats of Russia-China-South Africa, Brazil-India-South Africa, and Russia-China-India lobbies. However, Brazil and India play sometimes dwell tactics like cooperation and competition with China, because the right-wing social and political forces fight, compromise, and bargain with China and at the same time with the USA, it is a speed-breaker of BRICS' sprite.

International trade of some emerging countries including other developing countries has also accelerated (e.g. the share of BRICS GDP has increased from 5.4% in 1990 to 22.2% in 2016). In 2015, the five BRICS countries represent over 3.1 billion people or about 41% of the world population; four out of five members (excluding South Africa) are in the top ten of the world by population. As of 2018, these five nations have a combined nominal GDP of $18.6 trillion, about 23.2% of the gross world product, combined GDP (PPP) of around $40.55 trillion (32% of world's GDP PPP), and an estimated $4.46 trillion in combined foreign reserves. Overall, BRICS is forecasted to expand by 4.6% in 2016 from a growth of 3.9% in 2015.

China's Miracle

Thirty years ago, China had a tiny footprint in the global economy and little influence outside its borders, save for a few countries with which it had close political and military relationships. The situation has completely changed and China becomes the second-largest economic and military superpower (what it called: the world's manufacturing workshop), a leading investor across the globe from Africa to Latin America, the largest creditor of the USA, and increasingly, a major source of research and development.

There is not a single business anywhere in the world that has not felt China's impact either as a low-cost supplier or a formidable competitor. The British scholar and journalist According to Jacques (2005), not only is China the next economic superpower, but the world order that it will construct will look very different from what we have had under American leadership. Americans and Europeans blithely assume that China will become more like them as its economy develops and its population gets richer. The Chinese and their government are wedded to a different conception of society and polity-community based rather than individualist based, state-centric rather than liberal. As Steinbock (2017) forecasts, by 2050, Chinese economy could be almost 50% bigger than that of the USA, while the Indian economy may follow in the footprints and surpass the USA a few years later. Japan and the core EU economies follow far behind (Figure 1).

Figure 1. Projected GDPs in PPP of major economies by 2050, $ trillion
Source: Authors' development based on PricewaterhouseCoopers (2017)

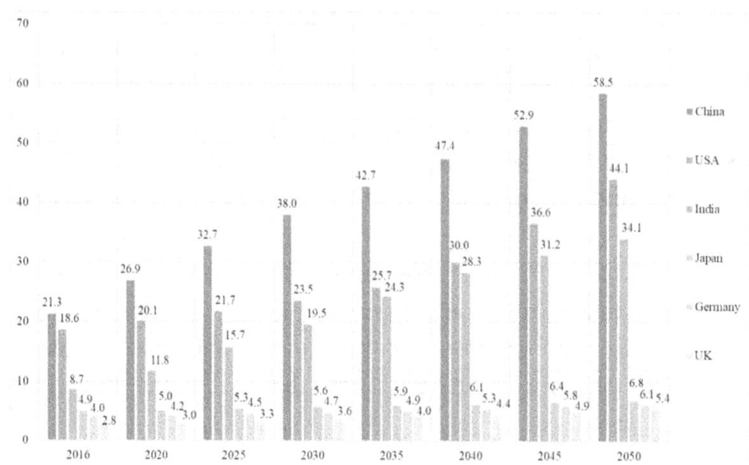

What will the catch-up by the BRICS economies mean in terms of global economic power? In 2000, the major advanced nations, as reflected by the G6, were almost ten times bigger than the BRICS. In the aftermath of the global crisis, their dominance had shrunk dramatically. In 2010, they were only three times as large as the BRICS. In 2016, BRICS' collective economic power surpassed that of the G6, while by the 2050s, BRICS could be some 50% bigger than their advanced counterparts (Figure 2).

Indonesia could become the fourth-largest economy in the world, while Mexico and Turkey could grow bigger than Germany and France, respectively. Meanwhile, the economies of new rising powers (Saudi Arabia, Nigeria, Egypt, Pakistan, Iran, the Philippines, and Vietnam) could each prove bigger than that of Italy. Thus, outside the BRICS-EAC-SCO, East and the South-East Asia, other developing countries' export shares remained either constant or and in some cases even declined, other than during the rising phase of the commodity price super-cycle, when major commodity exporters registered a temporary increase of their market shares (UNCTAD, 2018).

Regional Trade: Challenges and Opportunities

The economic aspect of regionalization may be described as efforts to form free-trade zones and – through the creation of common markets, the coordination of economic policies, and the implementation of joint economic policies – to form even larger economic zones. This trend is represented by the European Community (EC) and the EU in Europe, NAFTA in North America, MERCOSUR in South America, Organization of African Unity (OAU) in Africa, and other regional organizations. In Asia, ASEAN, BRICS-SCO-EAC, Bay of Bengal Initiative for Multi-Sectoral Technical and Economic Cooperation (BIMSTEK), Indian Ocean Rim, Asia-Pacific Economic Cooperation, and RCEF (proposed) trade and economic blocs have been initiated towards the intensifying regional economic integration through investment, technology, set-up joint-ventures to promote trade cooperation, and finally to achieve the goals of self-reliance based on mutual interests by respecting sovereignty of each-other. It will certainly create a necessary material condition for "Pan-Asianism" (Akira, 2000).

Figure 2. Projected GDPs in PPP of BRICS and G6 economies by 2050, $ trillion
Source: Authors' development based on PricewaterhouseCoopers (2017)

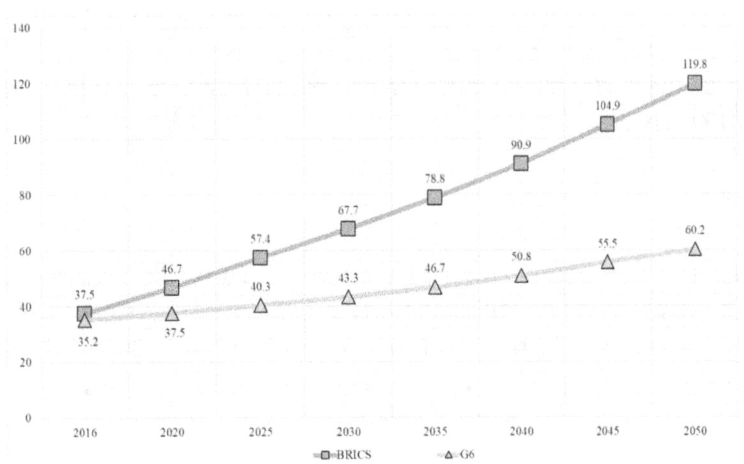

RCEP: 16-Nations Regional Comprehensive Economic Partnership

RCEP is the world's largest economic bloc. It is covering nearly half of the global economy. It comprises ten ASEAN members (Brunei, Cambodia, Indonesia, Malaysia, Myanmar, Singapore, Thailand, the Philippines, Laos, and Vietnam) and their six FTA partners – India, China, Japan, the Republic of Korea, Australia, and New Zealand. RCEP negotiations were formally launched in November 2012 at the ASEAN Summit in Cambodia. In 2017, prospective RCEP member states accounted for a population of 3.4 billion people with a total GDP (PPP) of $49.5 trillion, approximately 39% of the world's GDP with the combined GDPs of China and India making up more than half that amount. The GDP (PPP) of RCEP member states is likely to amount to nearly $250 trillion by 2050 with the combined GDPs of China and India making up more than 75% of the amount. RCEP's share of the global economy could account for half of the estimated $0.5 quadrillion global GDP (PPP) by 2050.

Strategy for Cooperation and Competition Between India and China

The integration of the domestic economy through the twin channels of trade and capital flows has accelerated in the past two decades which, in turn, led to the India's GDP reaching $2.47 trillion in 2017-2018 and $2.76 trillion in 2018-2019. Total exports from India (merchandise and services) have increased by 8.73% by $483.92 billion in 2018-2019, while total imports have increased by 9.42% to $577.31 billion. In 2019, end exports are expected to reach $540 billion (Government of India, n.d.).

India-China bilateral trade reached $84.44 billion with 40% increase Indian exports to China in 2017. India's exports to China include antibiotics, diesel engines and granite amid, textile manufacturers, aluminum, copper, etc. India urges to cut the bilateral trade deficit with China by $10 billion down to $53 billion. The surge in exports was mainly due to greater demand for marine products, grapes, raw cotton, and plastic raw materials. India's imports may increase by $29 billion annually during the post-RCEP period implying a revenue loss by as much as 1.3% of GDP.

India has registered trade deficit in 2018-2019 with as many as eleven RCEP member countries, including China, the Republic of Korea, and Australia – out of the grouping of sixteen nations that are negotiating the mega trade pact since November 2012.

India's imports from China decreased down to $5.9 billion in February 2018 from $6.1 billion in January 2018. In 2014-2018, India's imports from China reached an all-time high of $6.5 billion in December 2017 and a record low of $2.3 billion in February 2014.

The South Asian nation's exports to China jumped by 31% up to $17 billion in the financial year ended March 31, 2019 (Srivastava, 2019).

South-South Trade

One of the clearest trends of contemporary globalization is that the developing South is catching up with the developed North in terms of GDP and trade (International Trade Centre [ITC], 2019). The total GDP of the South increased from $7.6 trillion in 2000 to $30.9 trillion in 2016, implying that the South's share in world income rose from 28.0% to 40.6% in real terms. Gross savings in the South increased to $9.7 trillion in 2016 compared to $9.1 trillion in the North (Mohanty, Franssen, & Saha, 2019). While trade between developed countries declined from over 50% of global goods exports in the mid-1990s to 36% in 2017, South-South trade or trade between developing countries increased from 13% to 28% (Rajanayagam, 2019).

In 1995-2018, total trade of developing economies increased by 8 times. There was a decline in 1998 due to decrease in the intra-trade group from 42% to 39%. Another slight decline in 2001 was observed in time series data due to the drop in trade with the rest of world. In 2009, global recession affected trade volume in a negative way for both intra trade and trade with the rest of the world. There was major decline in 2013-2015 due to the stagnation of intra group trade as well as trade with the rest of the world. In crux, since 2015 onwards, an improvement has been evidencing (Figure3).

In 2018, the share of developing economies of Asia, America, Africa, and Oceania in total world's merchandise exports reached 42.08% (including the share of developing countries of Asia – 32.78%) (Figure 4).

Figure 3. Total trade of developing countries in 1995-2018, $ trillion
Source: Authors' development based on UNCTAD (2019)

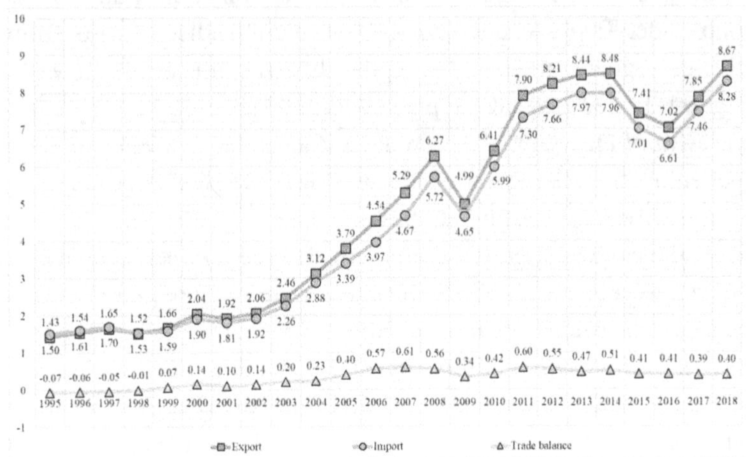

Figure 4. Total merchandise exports from developing countries in 1950-2018, percentage of total world
Source: Authors' development based on UNCTAD (2019)

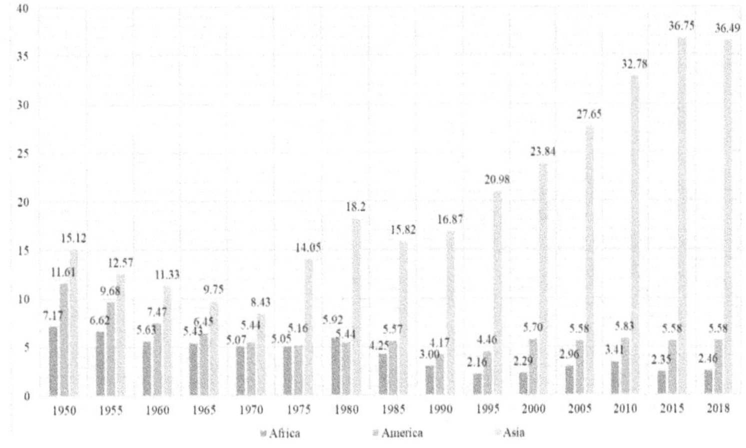

Similar to the role of developing countries in world exports, the share of developing economies in total world's merchandise imports has been increasing since the 1980s, specifically, by means of emerging economies of Asia (Figure 5).

South-South trade exhibits a pattern in which one region (Asia) acts as the center of gravity for the majority of trade flows from other regions. The rising importance of South-South trade is mostly related to the trade performances of East Asian economies (Priyadarshi, 2015). Asia is incontestably the world's most important hub, as it is both the largest exporter and the largest importer in South-South trade (Mohanty et al., 2019). Particularly, China has emerged to the world's biggest merchandise exporter and the dominating player in South-South trade. In 2018, China alone accounted for over 25% of exports and over 30% of imports of all South-South trade (Priyadarshi, 2015).

Intra-group trade is a minor component of South-South trade, particularly, in Oceania and Africa. The bulk of South-South trade occurs among countries within the same region, especially, among developing countries in Asia. Asia's dominance in South-South exports can be explained to a certain extent by its sheer economic size as well as by its greater participation in international trade than Africa and Latin America (Table 1). Rajanayagam (2019) reports that international trade patterns have shifted eastwards due to China's economic growth and fragmentation of production along value chains. Both factors have intensified intra-group trade. Two decades ago, 41% of merchandise exports from developing Asian countries went to other emerging markets in the region. In 2018, it is over 53% with eighteen of the top twenty South-South goods trade flows taking place within Asia.

The remarkable growth of emerging, developing, and even least developed countries of the Global South has been propelled by, first, rising trade in technology-intensive goods and, second, the proliferation of regional trade agreements (Mohanty et al., 2019).

South-South trade is the world's largest in communications equipment, chemicals, electric and other machinery, and basic metals. For instance, South-South trade accounts for about 50% of world's trade in communication equipment. Another feature of South-South trade which is particularly observed in exports is the reliance on primary commodities, in particular oil, gas and coal, and petroleum products. This is particularly the case for developing countries in Latin America, Africa and the Middle East. Primary products account for about a third of exports in both South-South and South-North trade (Table 2).

Figure 5. Total merchandise imports to developing countries in 1950-2018, percentage of total world
Source: Authors' development based on UNCTAD (2019)

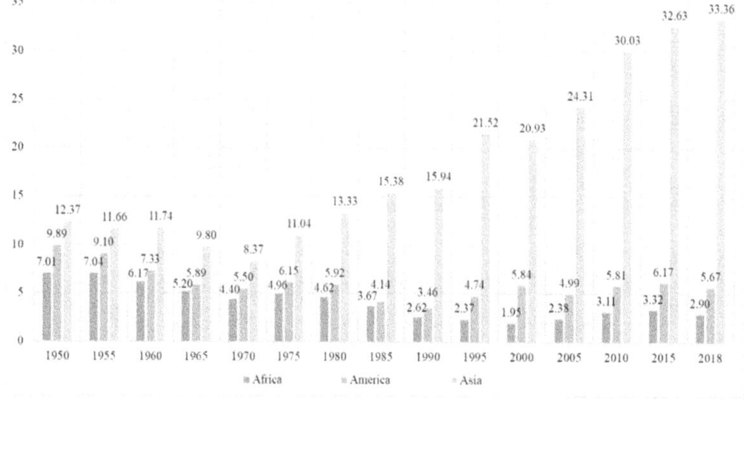

Table 1. Intra-trade and extra-trade of Global South countries in 1995-2018, percentage by destination

Countries	1995		2000		2005		2010		2015		2018	
	IG	W	IG	W	IG	W	IG	W	IG	W	IG	W
Africa	12.01	87.99	9.38	90.62	9.53	90.47	13.81	86.19	17.94	82.06	15.26	84.74
America	20.50	79.50	17.84	82.16	18.66	81.34	19.97	80.03	17.26	82.74	16.14	83.86
Asia	42.22	57.78	41.65	58.35	46.58	53.42	51.46	48.54	53.60	46.40	53.85	46.15
Oceania	0.35	99.65	2.41	97.59	3.99	96.01	2.90	97.10	2.81	97.19	2.62	97.38

Note: IG – intra-group; W – rest of the world
Source: Authors' development based on UNCTAD (2019)

Table 2. Intra-trade and extra-trade of Global South countries by products in 1995-2018, percentage by destination

Countries	1995		2000		2005		2010		2015		2018	
	IG	W	IG	W	IG	W	IG	W	IG	W	IG	W
Africa												
Food items	15.05	84.95	17.47	82.53	18.46	81.54	26.66	73.34	26.04	73.96	23.77	76.23
Ores and metals	5.02	94.98	7.90	92.10	8.13	91.87	6.55	93.45	6.26	93.74	11.97	88.03
Fuels	6.03	93.97	5.01	94.99	5.29	94.71	6.62	93.38	10.26	89.74	9.08	90.92
Manufactured goods	24.44	75.56	18.66	81.34	19.78	80.22	33.70	66.30	33.62	66.38	25.52	74.48
Chemical products	30.33	69.67	27.62	72.38	26.64	73.36	32.88	67.12	39.16	60.84	29.13	70.87
Machinery	28.87	71.13	20.13	79.87	16.83	83.17	36.81	63.19	29.35	70.65	19.96	80.04
Electronic goods	55.61	44.39	64.53	35.47	47.43	52.57	49.21	50.79	44.31	55.69	37.47	62.53
Iron and steel	20.59	79.41	12.37	87.63	15.98	84.02	23.29	76.71	28.49	71.51	28.28	71.72
Textile and clothing	9.54	90.46	7.09	92.91	7.13	92.87	11.88	88.12	15.20	84.80	12.53	87.47
America												
Food items	17.56	82.44	18.51	81.49	14.43	85.57	16.80	83.20	15.12	84.88	14.21	85.79
Ores and metals	12.00	88.00	12.64	87.36	12.30	87.70	9.26	90.74	7.45	92.55	5.96	94.04
Fuels	26.56	73.44	28.28	71.72	21.66	78.34	19.46	80.54	24.80	75.20	24.32	75.68
Manufactured goods	22.50	77.50	15.49	84.51	20.79	79.21	26.88	73.12	19.63	80.37	17.80	82.20
Chemical products	48.44	51.56	49.32	50.68	47.35	52.65	50.08	49.92	49.09	50.91	44.59	55.41
Machinery	15.81	84.19	9.53	90.47	15.90	84.10	20.21	79.79	12.76	87.24	11.85	88.15
Electronic goods	9.57	90.43	6.16	93.84	10.93	89.07	10.27	89.73	7.30	92.70	6.16	93.84
Iron and steel	21.36	78.64	23.88	76.12	25.00	75.00	33.03	66.97	24.80	75.20	23.72	76.28
Textile and clothing	21.48	78.52	11.72	88.28	15.29	84.71	28.90	71.10	23.22	76.78	23.55	76.45

continues on following page

Table 2. Continued

Countries	1995		2000		2005		2010		2015		2018	
	IG	W	IG	W	IG	W	IG	W	IG	W	IG	W
Asia												
Food items	45.27	54.73	44.99	55.01	45.61	54.39	54.16	45.84	56.91	43.09	58.05	41.95
Ores and metals	61.64	38.36	62.35	37.65	70.08	29.92	70.03	29.97	67.90	32.10	66.83	33.17
Fuels	40.73	59.27	45.42	54.58	49.88	50.12	59.32	40.68	66.02	33.98	64.71	35.29
Manufactured goods	41.42	58.58	39.91	60.09	44.44	55.56	47.95	52.05	50.10	49.90	50.57	49.43
Chemical products	69.25	30.75	65.41	34.59	62.82	37.18	62.24	37.76	60.04	39.96	62.88	37.12
Machinery	40.88	59.12	41.56	58.44	47.10	52.90	51.16	48.84	54.93	45.07	55.47	44.53
Electronic goods	22.33	77.67	20.84	79.16	27.88	72.12	31.84	68.16	34.89	65.11	33.84	66.16
Iron and steel	64.97	35.03	58.42	41.58	64.09	35.91	62.14	37.86	59.05	40.95	59.16	40.84
Textile and clothing	39.29	60.71	34.31	65.69	30.79	69.21	30.29	69.71	33.68	66.32	32.39	67.61
Oceania												
Food items	0.22	99.78	4.34	95.66	9.42	90.58	6.18	93.82	5.03	94.97	6.08	93.92
Ores and metals	0.01	99.99	2.62	97.38	0.17	99.83	0.11	99.89	0.47	99.53	0.24	99.76
Fuels	0.39	99.61	0.91	99.09	4.46	95.54	5.05	94.95	2.65	97.35	2.28	97.72
Manufactured goods	1.21	98.79	2.58	97.42	3.99	96.01	6.34	93.66	7.49	92.51	5.79	94.21
Chemical products	3.09	96.91	7.62	92.38	22.87	77.13	15.93	84.07	7.95	92.05	8.12	91.88
Machinery	1.86	98.14	9.09	90.91	5.68	94.32	9.09	90.91	8.25	91.75	6.90	93.10
Electronic goods	0.85	99.15	1.78	98.22	4.88	95.12	26.44	73.56	17.79	82.21	9.97	90.03
Iron and steel	0.03	99.97	0.29	99.71	0.36	99.64	0.34	99.66	0.57	99.43	0.33	99.67
Textile and clothing	0.15	99.85	0.45	99.55	1.41	98.59	5.78	94.22	11.05	88.95	14.97	85.03

Note: IG – intra-group; W – rest of the world
Source: Authors' development based on UNCTAD (2019)

The proliferation of regional trade agreements fuels up the growth of intra- and inter-regional trade. However, in Global South countries, tariffs and trade barriers are still higher compared to those in developed economies. According to Rajanayagam (2019), the average tariff in low- and middle-income nations is 4.3% compared with 2.0% in high-income countries. Tackling remaining trade barriers via regional trade deals and collaboration in the formats of BRICS, SCO, EAC, and other initiatives would provide greater opportunities for developing countries to expand trade flows.

BRICS-SCO-EAC Initiatives

There are many factors that underline improved economic and trade outlook of the Global South countries, development of international collaboration in trade being one of the major of them. The three major alliances of developing countries (BRICS, SCO, and EAC) have a potential to expand and improve economic, financial, investment, and trade collaboration between themselves.

Collaboration in BRICS-SCO format looks promising. It has been developing in the past years, including in the shape of various international forums. For instance, the one in Russia in September 2019 aims at the elaboration of conditions for the development and support of small business in the regions of SCO and BRICS countries, a barrier-free cooperation, financial, legal, and infrastructure support of small business, and strengthening of positions of the export-oriented entities (logistics, certification, customs procedures) (Chamber of Commerce and Industry of the Republic of Bashkortostan, 2019). As the SCO has recently started dealing with economic and financial issues, collaboration between China, India, Russia, and other developing countries and emerging economies in an extended SCO-BRICS format will definitely play a decisive role in the geopolitical future of Eurasia. In the light of the expansion of China's Belt and Road Initiative, Russia's turn to the East, and accession of India and Pakistan to the SCO, the BRICS-SCO format is becoming a prospective platform for collaboration in the macro-region of Eurasia (Stuenkel, 2015).

In Africa, boosting economic and trade cooperation between developing and least developed countries should envisage an establishment of a partnership between BRICS and African sub-regional integration organizations, such as the EAC and others (Southern African Development Community (SADC) and Common Market for Eastern and Southern Africa (COMESA)) that enhances the overall development capacity of Africa (Bawa, Bohler-Muller, Fikeni, Zondi, & Naidu, 2013). BRICS countries should strengthen relations by establishing sub-regional and continental economic and trade cooperation mechanisms that inform engagements with Africa's regional integration groupings. Under these mechanisms, support for trade facilitation can be explored. Since until recently, African integration organizations have achieved little success in terms of promoting and strengthening modes of trade and production cooperation, BRICS countries may contribute by identifying investment destinations and contributing financial resources (as China has been doing in various parts of Africa for a number of years).

Emerging Northern Dimension: Integration and Collaboration Initiatives in the Arctic

In recent decades, international northern cooperation between Arctic and non-Arctic states has become more institutionalized and dynamic (Erokhin, Gao, & Zhang, 2019; Erokhin, 2019). One of the major themes of international collaboration in the Arctic is the establishment of economic and trade linkages between the countries of the region and collaborating states. In particular, the activities of the Arctic Economic Council include establishing strong market connections between Arctic states, encouraging public-private partnerships for infrastructure developments, and promoting stable and predictable regulatory frameworks, among others. Various formats are used – from the multilateral international cooperation within the Arctic Council to the cooperation with and between international organizations and forums, in addition to bilateral inter-state relations (Heininen, 2012). Non-Arctic states are keen to strengthen their role in the Arctic. They assert that their participation in international cooperation in that region is as useful as it is warranted and legitimate (Bartenstein, 2015). However, non-Arctic countries, with widely varying levels of commercial and political participation are diverse in their approaches and levels of engagement (Coates & Holroyd, 2017). So far, among non-Arctic countries, the use of polar transport routes has received the most attention in Japan, especially regarding the Northern Sea Route (NSR) (Tonami, 2014). Critically depending on maritime deliveries of energy resources and goods and export of its products to the European and US markets, Republic of Korea is interested in diversification of its supply routes and modes for natural resources.

One of the most active players in the Arctic region is China. The role of the country in the Arctic grows as China explores the possibilities of opening the Arctic passages as alternative routes for its Belt and Road Initiative (BRI) and investigates the social, economic, and political implications of this engagement in the Arctic (Gao, 2019). Specific implementations of the BRI and China-Nordic diplomatic model for achieving sustainable development in the region have to be concerned. Another area to study is the investment collaboration between Arctic and non-Arctic countries. Perspectives on the development and commercial use of transport and trade routes in the Arctic, polar logistics, and development of infrastructure in the High North are also among the hot topics for all Arctic actors to investigate. The effects of climate change in the region have to be discussed in view of biodiversity, sustainable fisheries management, and food security. In terms of commercial potential, one of the promising industries is Arctic tourism, however, careful studies have to be carried out to ensure the sustainable development of Arctic territories in the light of the growing tourist mobility.

SOLUTIONS AND RECOMMENDATIONS

In order to increase competitiveness in the global market, Global South economies should transform economic growth drivers, seize existing opportunities, reduce dependence on factors of production (investment and labor), and increase reliance on innovation and quality. The major challenge would be development of a favorable external environment through establishment of effective ties with other countries and alliances. The countries should emphasize comprehensive multilateral agreements on matters including goods, services, competition, intellectual property and short-term labor flows, to promote open markets between them and further amplify the impact of trade liberalization on investment, production, and employment. This study has demonstrated positive dynamics and potentials of such formats, as BRICS, SCO, EAC, and others. Participating countries need to make full use of those emerging markets and resources to expedite their economic transformations and improve their positions in increasingly globalized value chains.

FUTURE RESEARCH DIRECTIONS

The major trend of future research activities in relation to developing economies and their role in the global market should be aimed at facing new challenges of globalization and multilateralism. Until recently, Global South has been focused on domestic development, but in order to keep growing, the economies of the South will have to face new global challenges. Particularly, investigations have to be directed on exploration of economic and trade cooperation of developing economies with international community. For instance, China has proposed the "five connections" development plan (policy exchange, road network, trade talks, currency circulation, and people-to-people friendship), which encourages cooperation at practical and cultural levels (Erokhin, 2016). There are similar initiatives in India and other developing countries aimed at the determination of the optimal allocation of resources between sectors in order to maximize long-run economic growth. Existing practices and challenges of such initiatives require investigation.

In the northern dimension, future research has to be based on the study of the contemporary issues of international cooperation on the sustainable development of the Arctic in the formats of the Arctic Council, the Nordic Council, and various trans-Arctic interactions between Arctic and non-Arctic countries. China, Republic of Korea, and Japan are the most active non-Arctic actors in the region; however, future studies should also consider Arctic aspirations of Singapore, India, and countries of Central Europe.

CONCLUSION

Free financial and trade mobility of neo-liberal version of globalization is going to over in near future. The series of global economic and financial crises in the USA and other developed nations clearly indicates that the collapse of neo-liberalism led by the Thatcher-Reagan free-market model that dominated thinking for three decades has been discredited. World economy should be integrated through financial flow, trade, and technological mobility under the guidance of the World Bank and the IMF to fulfill the requirements of investment and technology transfer of the desired countries to promote economic growth and development by increasing efficiency of the workers (on the basis of international division of labor or specialization), productivity and competitiveness through trade and FDI promotions in free and openness conditions of the market (e.g. laissez-fair environment). In this process, various countries follow the same monetary and fiscal policies, and trade and commercial policies provided guidelines, principles, and regulations set by the WTO, World Bank, and the IMF at global level. The world has witnessed that in the last four decades of globalized economic order, there has been created not only wealth but also income and wealth inequalities among and between the nations. Few emerging countries like China, India, Brazil, Russia, Vietnam, the Republic of Korea, and South Africa, however, have maintained high rates of GDP growth but (except China and Vietnam) other emerging economies have adopted a jobless growth models where new job opportunity has been narrowing and the existing employment has been found at risks.

The problem of the current neo-liberalism has no longer commanded the consent of the mass of the population. However, the fact that neo-liberalism could not survive without entering into an alliance with the sectarian right-wing feudal-capitalist has led state authoritarianism. That is why it has moved towards an alliance with international finance capital led and growing inequality. The idea of a total delinking would be disastrous. It could be better a selective delinking and the search for autonomous regionalities though bioregionalism for self-reliance based on sustainable and inclusive development with freedom and equality. The idea is to build alternative geographies of interrelations, but the global perspective (e.g. on global warming) is critical.

ACKNOWLEDGMENT

This study is supported by the National Social Sciences Fund of China (grant no. 18BGJ004).

REFERENCES

Akira, K. (2000). *A Note on Globalization and Regional Integration*. Retrieved August 22, 2019, from https://project.iss.u-tokyo.ac.jp/kikkawa/iss-1.pdf

Bartenstein, K. (2015). The "Common Arctic": Legal Analysis of Arctic and non-Arctic Political Discourses. In L. Heininen, H. Exner-Pirot, & J. Plouffe (Eds.), *Arctic Yearbook 2015* (pp. 264–280). Akureyri: Northern Research Forum.

Bawa, A., Bohler-Muller, N., Fikeni, S., Zondi, S., & Naidu, S. (Eds.). (2013). *BRICS and Africa: Partnership for Development, Integration and Industrialisation*. Pretoria, South Africa: The Department of International Relations and Cooperation.

Bhardwaj, A. (2019). Fourth Industrial Revolution: Decay of Liberalism and Withering Away of the Left. *Economic and Political Weekly*, *54*(30), 12–14.

Chamber of Commerce and Industry of the Republic of Bashkortostan. (2019). *The Fifth Small Business Forum of the SCO and BRICS Regions Takes Place on September 26-27, 2019*. Retrieved August 24, 2019, from https://sco-brics.ru/en/registration-reliz/

Chandrasekhar, C. P. (2019). *Looming Economic War*. Retrieved August 22, 2019, from https://frontline.thehindu.com/columns/C_P_Chandrasekhar/article27546724.ece

Coates, K. S., & Holroyd, C. (2017). Non-Arctic States and Their Stake in Arctic Sustainability. In K. Keil & S. Knecht (Eds.), *Governing Arctic Change* (pp. 207–228). Cham, Switzerland: Springer. doi:10.1057/978-1-137-50884-3_11

Correa, C. (2019). *Financing for Development*. Washington, DC: United Nations.

Erokhin, V. (2016). Rising Economic Powers among Economies in Transition: Is There Enough Space on the Global Market? In V. Erokhin (Ed.), *Global Perspectives on Trade Integration and Economies in Transition* (pp. 1–25). Hershey, PA: IGI Global. doi:10.4018/978-1-5225-0451-1.ch001

Erokhin, V. (2019). Arctic Connectivity for Sustainable Development: Major Actors, Policies, and Approaches. In V. Erokhin, T. Gao, & X. Zhang (Eds.), *Handbook of Research on International Collaboration, Economic Development, and Sustainability in the Arctic* (pp. 24–54). Hershey, PA: IGI Global. doi:10.4018/978-1-5225-6954-1.ch002

Erokhin, V., Gao, T., & Zhang, X. (Eds.). (2019). *Handbook of Research on International Collaboration, Economic Development, and Sustainability in the Arctic*. Hershey, PA: IGI Global. doi:10.4018/978-1-5225-6954-1

Gao, T. (2019). Going North: China's Role in the Arctic Blue Economic Corridor. In V. Erokhin, T. Gao, & X. Zhang (Eds.), *Handbook of Research on International Collaboration, Economic Development, and Sustainability in the Arctic* (pp. 133–161). Hershey, PA: IGI Global.

Government of India. (n.d.). *Latest Trade Figures*. Retrieved August 22, 2019, from https://commerce.gov.in

Heininen, L. (2012). Arctic Strategies and Policies. Inventory and Comparative Study. Akureyri: The Northern Research Forum; The University of Lapland.

International Trade Centre. (2019). South-South Trade Helps Firms Build Competitiveness, Met Growth Goals. Retrieved August 23, 2019, from http://www.intracen.org/news/South-South-trade-helps-firms-build-competitiveness-meet-growth-goals/

Jacques, M. (2005). *China Is Well on Its Way to Being the Other Superpower*. Retrieved August 23, 2019, from https://www.theguardian.com/world/2005/dec/08/china.comment.

Jipson, J., & Jitheesh, P. M. (2018). *There Is a Structural Crisis of Capitalism*. Retrieved August 22, 2019, from https://frontline.thehindu.com/other/there-is-a-structural-crisis-of-capitalism/article10107168.ece

Mohanty, S. K., Franssen, L., & Saha, S. (2019). *The Power of International Value Chains in the Global South*. Geneva, Switzerland: International Trade Centre.

Patnaik, P. (2019). *The Global Shift to the Right*. Retrieved August 22, 2019, from https://peoplesdemocracy.in/2019/0602_pd/global-shift-right

Prabhakar, A. (2003). A Critical Reflection on Globalisation and Inequality: A New Approach to the Development of the South. *African and Asian Studies*, *2*(3), 307–345. doi:10.1163/156920903322661735

Prabhakar, A. (2005). Globalisation, Poverty & Inequality: A Study of India, China, the USA and OECD, *VIKLP*.

Prabhakar, A. (2016). Trade and Economic Integration in BRICS: Towards Multi-Polarity. In V. Erokhin (Ed.), *Global Perspectives on Trade Integration and Economies in Transition* (pp. 45–57). Hershey, PA: IGI Global. doi:10.4018/978-1-5225-0451-1.ch003

Prabhakar, A. (2017). *The Current Global Recession: A Theoretical and Empirical Investigation into Developed and BRICS Economies*. London, UK: Emerald Group.

Prabhakar, A. (2018). *Comparative Economic Systems and Welfare Economics*. New Delhi, India: ISARA.

PricewaterhouseCoopers. (2017). *The Long View. How Will the Global Economic Order Change by 2050?* London, UK: PricewaterhouseCoopers.

Priyadarshi, S. (2015). *South-South Trade and Its Implications for the World Economy*. Retrieved August 23, 2019, from https://internationalbanker.com/finance/south-south-trade-and-its-implications-for-the-world-economy/

Rajanayagam, S. (2019). *South-South Trade. Trade between Developing Countries Is Evolving*. Retrieved August 23, 2019, from https://www.gbm.hsbc.com/insights/global-research/south-south-trade

Srivastava, S. (2019). *India Is Said to Have Cut Trade Deficit with China by $10 Billion*. Retrieved August 22, 2019, from https://economictimes.indiatimes.com/small-biz/trade/exports/insights/india-is-said-to-cut-trade-deficit-with-china-by-10-billion/articleshow/68902529.cms?from=mdr

Steinbock, D. (2017). *The Global Economic Balance of Power Is Shifting*. Retrieved August 22, 2019, from https://www.weforum.org/agenda/2017/09/the-global-economic-balance-of-power-is-shifting

Stuenkel, O. (2015). *BRICS and SCO: Russia's Big Summit.* Retrieved August 24, 2019, from https://www.postwesternworld.com/2015/07/01/brics-russias-summit/

Tonami, A. (2014). Future-Proofing Japan's Interests in the Arctic: Scientific Collaboration and a Search for Balance. *Asia Policy*, *18*(1), 52–58. doi:10.1353/asp.2014.0027

United Nations Conference on Trade and Development. (2018). *Trade and Development Report 2018.* Geneva, Switzerland: United Nations Conference on Trade and Development.

United Nations Conference on Trade and Development. (2019). *Statistics Database* [Data file]. Retrieved August 24, 2019, from http://unctad.org/en/Pages/Statistics.aspx

United Nations Development Programme. (2013). *Human Development Report 2013. The Rise of the South – Human Progress in a Diverse World.* New York, NY: United Nations Development Programme.

World Bank. (2019). *Global Economic Prospects, June 2019: Heightened Tensions, Subdued Investment.* Washington, DC: World Bank.

ADDITIONAL READING

Awokuse, T. O. (2007). Causality between Exports, Imports, and Economic Growth: Evidence from Transition Economies. *Economics Letters*, *94*(3), 389–395. doi:10.1016/j.econlet.2006.08.025

Awokuse, T. O. (2008). Trade Openness and Economic Growth: Is Growth Export-Led or Import-Led? *Applied Economics*, *40*(2), 161–173. doi:10.1080/00036840600749490

Begum, S., & Shamsuddin, A. F. M. (1998). Exports and Economic Growth in Bangladesh. *The Journal of Development Studies*, *35*(1), 89–114. doi:10.1080/00220389808422556

Dodaro, S. (1993). Exports and Growth: A Reconsideration of Causality. *Journal of Developing Areas*, *27*(2), 227–244.

Dollar, D., & Kraay, A. (2004). Trade, Growth, and Poverty. *Economic Journal (London)*, *493*(114), F22–F49. doi:10.1111/j.0013-0133.2004.00186.x

Dritsaki, M., Dritsaki, C., & Adamopoulos, A. (2004). A Causal Relationship between Trade, Foreign Direct Investment and Economic Growth for Greece. *American Journal of Applied Sciences*, *1*(3), 230–235. doi:10.3844/ajassp.2004.230.235

Ekanayake, E. M. (1999). Exports and Economic Growth in Asian Developing Countries: Cointegration and Error-Correction Models. *Journal of Economic Development*, *24*(2), 43–56.

Emery, R. F. (1967). The Relation of Exports and Economic Growth. *Kyklos*, *20*(4), 470–486. doi:10.1111/j.1467-6435.1967.tb00859.x

Fajana, O. (1979). Trade and Growth: The Nigerian Experience. *World Development*, *7*(1), 73–78. doi:10.1016/0305-750X(79)90009-3

Fan, C. C. (1992). Foreign Trade and Regional Development in China. *Geographical Analysis*, *24*(3), 240–256. doi:10.1111/j.1538-4632.1992.tb00264.x

Fan, C. C. (1992). Regional Impacts of Foreign Trade in China, 1984-1989. *Growth and Change*, *23*(2), 129–159. doi:10.1111/j.1468-2257.1992.tb00576.x

Feder, G. (1983). On Exports and Economic Growth. *Journal of Development Economics*, *12*(1-2), 59–73. doi:10.1016/0304-3878(83)90031-7

Harrison, A. (1996). Openness and Growth: A Time-Series, Cross-Country Analysis for Developing Countries. *Journal of Development Economics*, *48*(2), 419–447. doi:10.1016/0304-3878(95)00042-9

Hatemi-J, A. (2002). Export Performance and Economic Growth Nexus in Japan: A Bootstrap Approach. *Japan and the World Economy*, *14*(1), 25–33. doi:10.1016/S0922-1425(01)00071-8

Henriques, I., & Sadorsky, P. (1996). Export-Led Growth or Growth-Driven Exports? The Canadian Case. *The Canadian Journal of Economics. Revue Canadienne d'Economique*, *29*(3), 540–555. doi:10.2307/136249

Jung, W. S., & Marshall, P. J. (1985). Exports, Growth and Causality in Developing Countries. *Journal of Development Economics*, *18*(1), 1–12. doi:10.1016/0304-3878(85)90002-1

Kavoussi, R. M. (1984). Export Expansion and Economic Growth. *Journal of Development Economics*, *14*(1), 241–250. doi:10.1016/0304-3878(84)90052-X

Lewer, J. J., & van den Berg, H. (2003). How Large Is International Trade's Effect on Economic Growth? *Journal of Economic Surveys*, *17*(3), 363–396. doi:10.1111/1467-6419.00198

Liu, X., Burridge, P., & Sinclair, P. J. N. (2002). Relationships between Economic Growth, Foreign Direct Investment and Trade: Evidence from China. *Applied Economics*, *34*(11), 1433–1440. doi:10.1080/00036840110100835

Lunenborg, P. (2019). *"Phase 1B" of the African Continental Free Trade Area (AfCFTA) Negotiations*. Geneva: The South Centre.

Musila, J. W., & Yiheyis, Z. (2015). The Impact of Trade Openness on Growth: The Case of Kenya. *Journal of Policy Modeling*, *37*(2), 342–354. doi:10.1016/j.jpolmod.2014.12.001

Tah, K. A., Czerniak, C., Levine, A., Wiggin, K., & Osondu, I. N. (2019). Foreign Trade and Economic Growth in South Africa. *Asia-Pacific Journal of Accounting & Economics*, *17*(1), 1–10. doi:10.1080/16081625.2019.1567352

Were, M. (2015). Differential Effects of Trade on Economic Growth and Investment: A Cross-Country Empirical Investigation. *Journal of African Trade*, *2*(1-2), 71–85. doi:10.1016/j.joat.2015.08.002

KEY TERMS AND DEFINITIONS

BRICS: An economic initialization for the developing countries of Brazil, Russia, India, China, and South Africa referred to the idea that by 2050, China and India will become the world's dominant suppliers of manufactured goods and services, while Brazil, Russia, and South Africa would be similarly dominant as suppliers of raw materials.

East Asian Cooperation (Community): A proposed trade bloc for the East Asian and Southeast Asian countries that may arise out of either ASEAN Plus Three or the East Asia Summit.

Emerging Economies: Rapidly growing and volatile economies that are progressing toward becoming advanced, promise huge potential for growth, but also pose significant political, monetary, and social risks.

Globalization: The spread of products, technology, information, and jobs across national borders and cultures; economic interdependence of nations around the globe fostered through free trade.

Multilateralism: A process of organizing relations between groups of three or more states which is generally considered to comprise the principles of indivisibility of interests among participants, a commitment to diffuse reciprocity, and a system of dispute settlement intended to enforce a particular mode of behavior.

Regional Comprehensive Economic Partnership: A proposed international free trade agreement among ten member countries of the ASEAN (Brunei, Cambodia, Indonesia, Laos, Malaysia, Myanmar, the Philippines, Singapore, Thailand, and Vietnam) and six Asia-Pacific countries with whom ASEAN has existing free trade agreements (Australia, China, India, Japan, New Zealand, and the Republic of Korea).

Shanghai Cooperation Organization: A permanent intergovernmental international organization, which comprises eight member states (China, India, Kazakhstan, Kyrgyzstan, Pakistan, Russia, Tajikistan, and Uzbekistan), which main goals strengthening mutual trust and neighborliness among the member states; promoting their effective cooperation in politics, trade, the economy, research, technology and culture.

Chapter 2

Economic Integration of African Economies With China and India

Akhilesh Chandra Prabhakar
https://orcid.org/0000-0002-1061-6509
Lovely Professional University, India

Vasilii Erokhin
https://orcid.org/0000-0002-3745-5469
Harbin Engineering University, China

Rajender Singh Godara
https://orcid.org/0000-0002-7568-0819
Lovely Professional University, India

ABSTRACT

In recent decades, the global economy has been witnessing the emergence of the Global South, which accounted for about 40% of global trade in 2017, up from 24% in 2001. The traditional pattern of trade, generally skewed towards developed economies, has shifted to a growing South-South trade relationship. The rapidly expanding trade and investment relationship within the China-India-Africa triangle attests to this dynamic change. This study reviews China-Africa and India-Africa relations along the lines of trade flows (dynamics, structure, and destinations of exports and imports) and foreign direct investment (stocks accumulated in African countries). The authors emphasize existing problems and challenges in China-Africa and India-Africa trade and investment integration and reveal opportunities for the three sides to collaborate with an aim to spur economic growth.

INTRODUCTION

Africa is surrounded by the Mediterranean Sea, Suez Canal, the Red Sea, Indian Ocean, Atlantic Ocean, and Sinai Peninsula. The African continent is the world's second-largest. It covers an area of 30.2 million km^2 which is equivalent to almost 20.4% of the total world's land area. In terms of population, Africa

DOI: 10.4018/978-1-7998-1730-7.ch002

has more than 900 million people which is 14% of the world's total population. In Africa, there are 55 countries, out of which 48 countries are considered as Sub-Saharan Africa and seven countries relate to North Africa. Africa is rich in natural resources; however, the majority of African economies are dominated by agricultural production with around 80-90% population living in rural areas.

In economic terms, the continent is divided into four parts. The southern parts of Africa are the most prosperous (based on agricultural, industrial, and trade performances) and people enjoy freedom and democracy along-with socio-political stability, whereas the other parts striving for democracy, freedom, and social and political stability. South Africa, Nigeria, Mauritius, Kenya, and Egypt are the richest nations in Africa, while the poorest economies are Somalia, Burundi, Eritrea, and Ethiopia.

The collective GDP of the African countries is estimated to reach $2.6 trillion by 2020. Consumer spending is on the rise with Sub-Saharan Africa's consumers projected to generate up to $1.4 trillion by 2020. Urban food markets are set to increase fourfold to exceed $400 billion by 2030, requiring major agribusiness investments in processing, logistics, market infrastructure, and retail networks (Chakrabarti & Ghosh, 2014). Africa is estimated to be home to 30% of the world's mineral reserves, and an even higher proportion of deposits of gold, platinum, diamonds, and manganese. However, despite rich natural resources and hard-working workforce, Africa is the most backward continent in the world. Despite rich natural resources, Africans are still poor and backward community, because of its poor economy, lack of education, lack of access to health care, uneducated people, few businesses, poverty, and civil wars which erupt every now and then. Coupled with corruption by whoever is running the government. Be aware though that it is beautiful and rich in natural resources, (gold and diamonds) but this is the irony for other countries enjoy their wealth but still they remain poor and undeveloped despite all that.

In the most of Sub-Saharan African countries, people's source of income the lowest as around less than $765 of GNI per-capita annually. Ethiopia, Eritrea, Somalia, and Burundi are the worst-off whereas only $90 per capita of GNI. Gabon and Botswana have considered middle-income countries but the two-thirds of population live below the poverty line. North Africa has found generally rich because of oil resource. Western Africa has also oil and diamonds but diamonds bought and sold in the USA. Africa is the world's largest producer of cocoa beans and peanuts (as 75% of cacao and over 30% of peanuts), but rural people are very poor, while agricultural productivity is at the lowest standard.

Other natural resources like precious minerals and diamonds are abundant in the south and east of a line from the Gulf of Guinea to the Sinai Peninsula; extensive oil, gas, and phosphate deposits occur in sedimentary rocks to the north and west of this general line.

Major fishing grounds are found over the wider sections in the continent's North West, South West, South Africa, and North West Madagascar. Despite Africa's enormous potential for hydroelectric power production, only a small percentage of it has been developed due to the lack of internal capability including skilled manpower and capital and technology.

BACKGROUND

Exploitative Nature of the Western Countries in Africa

Africa's huge reserves of mineral wealth are divided up between the giant multinationals based in Europe and the USA – local people are unlikely to receive a share of the huge profits being made. Petroleum oil, gold and diamond, and other natural resources of Africa are directly controlled by 4,000 US and

EU based multinational companies (MNCs) (e.g. 98.3% of Ghana's gold remains in the hands of multinational corporations). These new colonial policies which are directly responsible for many of Africa's contemporary problems. The true effects of new colonialism are psychological and that domination by a foreign power creates a lasting sense of inferiority and subjugation that creates a barrier to growth and innovation. With the entry of MNCs into export-oriented agriculture, a serious threat of dispossession of small and marginal farmers is becoming a reality with grave social consequences. The IMF's recommendations saw the continent's currencies drop by an average of 50%, the selling off of government-owned industries, and the slashing of government spending.

Africa has been marginalizing by the colonial legacies and practices. Africa's industrialization process is an unfinished task. Africa's trade share has been declining even in primary sector. Traditional donors, including the multilateral development banks, have always approached their interactions with African countries as donor-aid recipient relationships, largely based on altruism and policy conditions attached to their cooperation efforts. The overall development model informing such conditionality followed most often the western-type of approach to economic development, with policies and investment underlined by key governance principles and the institutional and regulatory frameworks to ensure an enabling environment for market-led growth. The recent focus by traditional donors on the centrality of trade liberalization and private-sector-led development implies that the industrialization path of a country should be primarily left to market forces and international competitiveness (Rampa & Bilal, 2011).

Since the decade of 1990s, 40 out of 48 Sub-Saharan African countries followed the IMF's restructuring plans. The World Bank's Structural Adjustments Programme (SAP) has dismantled existing rural and urban systems but has not built new ones, and the SAP has not been successful in Africa. In many African transitional economies, rural situation was marked by continuing economic stagnation, poor performance of industrial production, low incomes, and the rising vulnerability of poor people. In the past three decades of liberalization, privatization and globalization (LPG) practice has failed due to above-mentioned reasons including lack of access to the western markets for small and medium scale enterprises (SMEs).

The Potential of African Economic Integration With the Emerging Economies

The African continent is preparing itself to build and intensify the relationship with the emerging nations such as China, India, Brazil, Russia, Indonesia, Turkey, and South Korea since the developed nations, particularly, the USA and the EU, have denied to extend foreign-aid package to Africa in the 21st century. China and India are the two major investors and trade partners of African countries. The western nations have withdrawal financial support such as foreign-aid, donation and special types of trade preferences from Africa since 2008. International financial organizations like the World Bank and the IMF are unable to provide even conditionality-based loan as per financial requirements of Africa (especially, for infrastructural development).

China and India's engagement with Africa has come at a time when the business climate has improved across Africa and interest in Africa as a market has grown (Cheru & Obi, 2010). This emerging engagement has been increasingly studied by many scholars worldwide. The studies have been focusing on the nature of the shift in China's and India's strategic vision of Africa in terms of politics, ideology and economic development (Roy, 2014), merchandise trade between China and Africa and between India and Africa (Nowak, 2016), and China's and India's presence in Africa from the perspectives on South-South relations (Moyo, 2016). India and China reinforced their credentials as a pro-Third World economic powerhouses by offering billions of dollars (e.g. China provides $10 billion of concessional loans, more than the World Bank, the IMF, and the EU, and India provided $5 billion of concessional loan) and exact the same amounts both countries announce 'debt-relief' to Africa and pledging to contribute significantly to the continent's skilled human resources base. In this direction, China-Africa Forums and India-Africa Forums are the main bridges which actively play a vital role by the states to avoid competition among stakeholders and promote regional economic cooperation by following South-South principles.

In the era of globalization, China and India have emerged to global economic powers. Africa has rich natural resources but unable to exploit it. Africa has an opportunity to participate enthusiastically and must integrate with the Chinese and Indian economies. Therefore, Africa can enjoy with the most favorable conditions of emerging markets of China and India.

Thus, China and India have been sharing developmental and technical knowledge with Africa, on complimentary basis and providing all kinds of institutional supports for capacity building. These countries established joint-ventures in operational areas such as banking and finance, paper mills, petroleum oil, chemicals and engineering, food processing, leather, wooden, medicines, and build infrastructures such as: health and educational building constructions, electrification, water supply, road, railway, bridges, flyover, and facilitate educational and technical training by providing direct fellowship for African students and sending experts team to Africa to train them. China and India facilitate preferential free trade areas (PTAs/FTAs) to Africa, which are based on the principles of Bandung Consensus' in 1955 for mutual interests and benefits, and mutual respect for sovereignty, non-interference in each other's internal affairs, and solidarity at the basis of the Non-Aligned Movement and the freedom Struggles against western colonialism that characterized the common past of many Asian, African, and Latin American countries, and to avoid to claim to attach to their cooperation on what types of development model adopted by Africa.

Bandung Consensus (1955)

Bandung in Indonesia is where newly emerged independent countries of Africa and Asia had gathered, and created a new platform for an alternative path of development by promoting trade, investment, and technology transfer between developing countries, to achieve the ultimate goal of self-reliance economy (Prabhakar, 2014), by creating their institutional structures and mechanisms such as to establish a Global System of Trade Preferences among developing countries and set-up state-run trade organizations.

The African Continental Free Trade Area (AfCFTA)

The African Continental Free Trade Area (AfCFTA), which entered into force on 30 May 2019, represents a unique collaborative effort by African countries to bolster regional and continental economic integration, in a world marked by increasing protectionism and use of unilateral trade measures.

In order to make the agreement operational for trade in goods, negotiations on tariff concessions need to be concluded and negotiating outcomes need to be inserted into the agreement. This policy brief focuses on the expected economic impacts of tariff liberalization under the AfCFTA, the tariff negotiation modalities and discusses some legal and practical issues related to the implementation of these modalities (Lunenborg, 2019).

Trade Performance in the Era of Globalization

Globalization and trade liberalization have developed a new measure of the scale of export dumping by the EU and the USA in Africa. Sub-Saharan Africa seems to have been left behind and marginalized by globalization. Around 60% of Europe's trade is being among the European countries. While Africa only accounts for 15% of intra-Africa trade. For example, the continent only accounts for a dismal 2% of the global cocoa revenue despite producing about 75% of the world's cocoa (Ofori-Atta, 2016).

Agricultural superpowers are exporting their agricultural products at high price in Africa than the one-third lower of African products. While subsidized exports from rich countries are driving down prices for exports from Africa to the western countries' market, and devastating the prospects for small-holder agriculture.

Around 80-90% of African workers are employed by the agricultural sector, with about three-fifths of African farmers are still subsistence farmers, and these small farmers do not access outside markets. Larger farms tend to grow cash crops such as coffee, cotton, cocoa, and rubber. These farms, normally operated by large corporations, cover tens of square kilometers and employ large numbers of laborers.

- The EU and the USA protect their own agricultural sectors with high import tariffs and offer subsidies to their farmers, which many contend leads the overproduction of such commodities as grain, cotton, and milk.
- The global price of such products is continually reduced until Africans are unable to compete.

MAIN FOCUS OF THE CHAPTER

China-Africa

Trade

China is second-highest trading partner of African countries, behind the USA and ahead of France and the UK. Since the early 2000s, there has been a rapid growth in China-Africa trade due to increasing demand for natural resources in booming Chinese economy. 85% of China's import from Africa come from five oil-rich countries such as Angola, Equatorial Guinea, Nigeria, the Republic of Congo, and Sudan. Chinese companies also import a significant amount of non-oil commodities such as timber, copper, and diamonds. United Nations Development Programme (2013) estimated that China's trade with Sub-Saharan Africa rose from \$1 billion to more than \$140 billion from 1992 to 2011. In 2010-2014, however, on the background of rising prices for hydrocarbons, foreign trade balance was negative for China. As the price decreased and global financial crisis emerged in 2014-2016, the volume of China's imports from Africa decreased substantially (Figure 1).

The top three items in China's export to Africa are machinery and transport equipment (33.67% in total exports in 2018), manufactured goods (30.52%), and miscellaneous manufactured articles (24.69%) (Table 1). While African countries aim to produce their own machinery in the future, many zones still rely on machinery imports to kickstart the process. A sudden decline in Chinese machinery exports to Africa may impact industrial zones development under the China-Africa Industrial Capacity Cooperation Fund.

Figure 1. China-Africa trade in 1995-2018, $ billion
Source: Authors' development based on United Nations Conference on Trade and Development [UNCTAD] (2019)

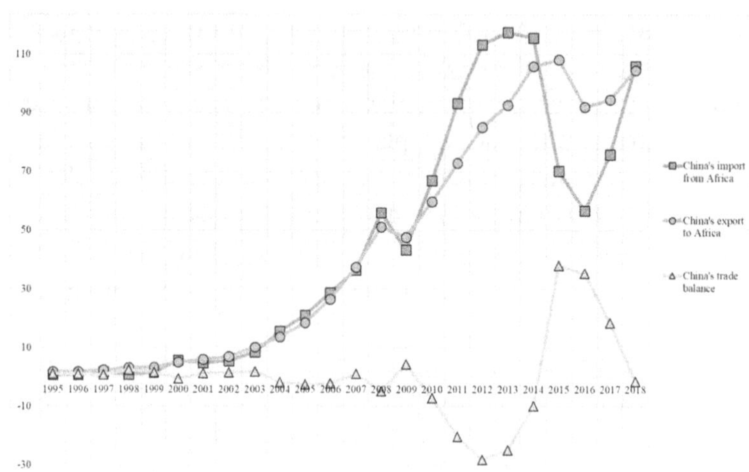

Table 1. China's exports to Africa in 1995-2018, product groups

Product	1995		2000		2005		2010		2015		2018	
	$ billion	share in total, %	$ billion	share in total, %	$ billion	share in total, %	$ billion	share in total, %	$ billion	share in total, %	$ billion	share in total, %
Food and live animals	0.150	8.23	0.417	8.33	0.530	2.85	1.560	2.61	2.408	2.22	2.750	2.63
Beverages and tobacco	0.006	0.33	0.020	0.40	0.042	0.23	0.060	0.10	0.074	0.07	0.099	0.09
Crude metals	0.022	1.21	0.040	0.80	0.112	0.60	0.253	0.42	0.533	0.49	0.571	0.55
Mineral fuels	0.008	0.44	0.065	1.30	0.121	0.65	0.517	0.86	0.613	0.57	1.024	0.98
Animal and vegetable oils	0.000	0.00	0.001	0.02	0.005	0.03	0.006	0.01	0.008	0.01	0.010	0.01
Chemicals	0.138	7.57	0.310	6.19	1.092	5.87	3.398	5.68	6.450	5.95	7.176	6.86
Manufactured goods	0.699	38.36	1.532	30.60	5.758	30.95	17.326	28.97	32.724	30.21	31.908	30.52
Machinery and transport equipment	0.435	23.87	1.316	26.28	6.500	34.94	25.215	42.16	36.306	33.52	35.202	33.67
Miscellaneous manufactured articles	0.342	18.77	1.285	25.66	4.108	22.08	11.458	19.16	29.125	26.89	25.812	24.69
Commodities and transactions	0.019	1.04	0.021	0.42	0.336	1.81	0.017	0.03	0.074	0.07	0.003	0.00
Total all products	1.822	100.00	5.007	100.00	18.604	100.00	59.810	100.00	108.317	100.00	104.552	100.00

Source: Authors' development based on UNCTAD (2019)

China-Africa trade has been dominated by resource-rich African countries. According to the value of bilateral trade, the most important China's trading partners in Africa in 2018 are South Africa, Nigeria, and Egypt (Figure 2).

The top three items in China's import from Africa are mineral fuels (49.45% in total imports in 2018), crude metals (19.57%), and manufactured goods (17.08%) (Table 2). Since the mid-1995s, the share of mineral fuels in total imports has been increasing, while that of crude metals has been decreasing. Compared to 1995, China almost stopped importing chemicals from Africa (14.32% and 0.80% in total imports in 1994 and 2018, respectively).

African trade is largely concentrated on a few countries. South Africa and Angola taken together make up over 50% of China's import from Africa. Other major exporters to China in the region are Congo, Democratic Republic of Congo, Libya, Zambia, Gabon, Ghana, Guinea, and Equatorial Guinea (Figure 3).

China has implemented eight major initiatives with African countries, covering fields such as industrial promotion, infrastructure connectivity, trade facilitation, green development, capacity building, healthcare, people-to-people exchanges, and peace and security under an umbrella of South-South cooperation within the frameworks of the United Nations 2030 Agenda for Sustainable Development, and the African Union's Agenda 2063.

China provides inputs in production activities through establishing joint-ventures and set-up direct industries, and One Belt One Road Initiative (BRI) transforming infrastructures such as railway, roads, bridges, electrification, water supply networks, hospital, schools, etc. (Erokhin, 2017). These initiatives

Figure 2. China's top ten export destinations in Africa in 2018, % of total exports to African countries
Source: Authors' development based on UNCTAD (2019)

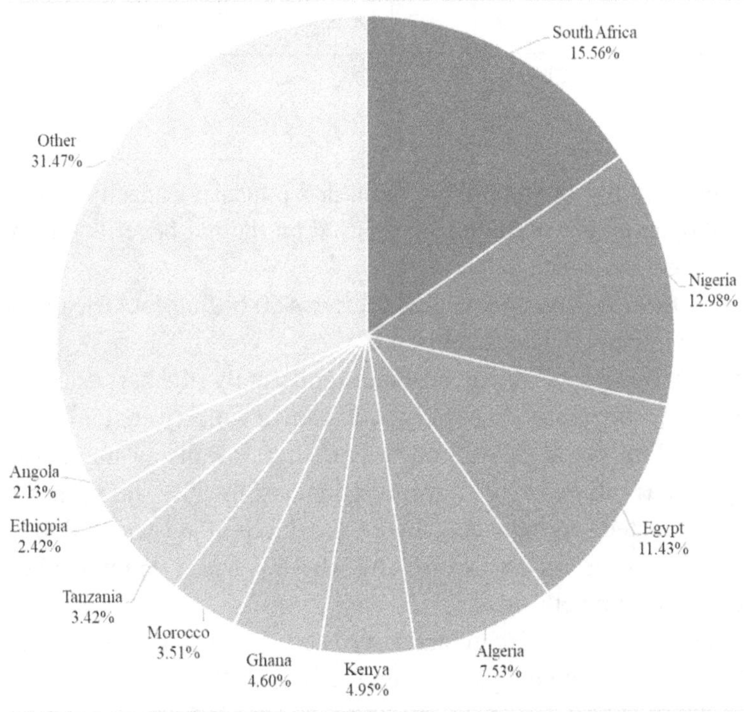

Table 2. China's imports from Africa in 1995-2018, product groups

Product	1995		2000		2005		2010		2015		2018	
	$ billion	share in total, %	$ billion	share in total, %	$ billion	share in total, %	$ billion	share in total, %	$ billion	share in total, %	$ billion	share in total, %
Food and live animals	0.007	0.95	0.061	1.10	0.117	0.56	0.208	0.31	0.512	0.73	0.824	0.78
Beverages and tobacco	0.021	2.86	0.099	1.78	0.131	0.62	0.173	0.26	0.756	1.08	0.870	0.82
Crude metals	0.319	43.52	0.867	15.61	3.125	14.84	11.966	17.84	12.656	18.01	20.756	19.57
Mineral fuels	0.262	35.74	3.670	66.07	14.622	69.42	41.519	61.91	27.525	39.18	52.435	49.45
Animal and vegetable oils	0.000	0.00	0.000	0.00	0.003	0.01	0.039	0.06	0.043	0.06	0.060	0.06
Chemicals	0.105	14.32	0.086	1.55	0.290	1.38	0.789	1.18	0.533	0.76	0.850	0.80
Manufactured goods	0.016	2.18	0.376	6.77	2.002	9.51	8.494	12.67	12.605	17.94	18.115	17.08
Machinery and transport equipment	0.002	0.27	0.074	1.33	0.291	1.38	0.344	0.51	0.353	0.50	0.481	0.45
Miscellaneous manufactured articles	0.001	0.14	0.006	0.11	0.017	0.08	0.134	0.20	0.294	0.42	0.366	0.35
Commodities and transactions	0.000	0.00	0.315	5.67	0.464	2.20	3.401	5.07	14.980	21.32	11.289	10.65
Total all products	0.733	100.00	5.555	100.00	21.062	100.00	67.066	100.00	70.258	100.00	106.045	100.00

Source: Authors' development based on UNCTAD (2019)

not only promote South-South cooperation, but build and intensify capacity development, create new job opportunities, and open up new trading routes based on mutual benefits for both sides, which has averaged growth of around 30% since 2008.

Chinese financial institutions and companies invested $60 billion to Africa to achieve the goals of greater prosperity which ultimately lead a better life.

Since 1980s, China-Africa partnership contribute significantly (the best examples are the Tanzania-Zambia Railway, and the Mombasa-Nairobi railway in Kenya which were built by China and still constructing over 6,200 km of railway in other countries of Africa). Railway attained an occupancy rate of over 95%. Road projects has lowered cargo transportation cost by 80% and pushed up Kenya's GDP by around 1.5% which was created approximately 50,000 local jobs along-with 1,000 transport professionals. It shows that the relationship between China and Africa is based on mutual benefits, equality, and well-being of the societies from both sides.

South African Financial Services Group Standards Bank works with the Industrial and Commercial Bank of China (ICBC) to provide funding to the value of $835 million for the Morupule B Power Project in Botswana, and a $400 million debt refinance with Equinox, a $470 million export finance facility to the Ethiopian Hydro Power plant, and a $5.5 billion financial advisory mandate to the Ghanaian Rail-

Figure 3. China's top ten import sources in Africa in 2018, % of total imports from African countries
Source: Authors' development based on UNCTAD (2019)

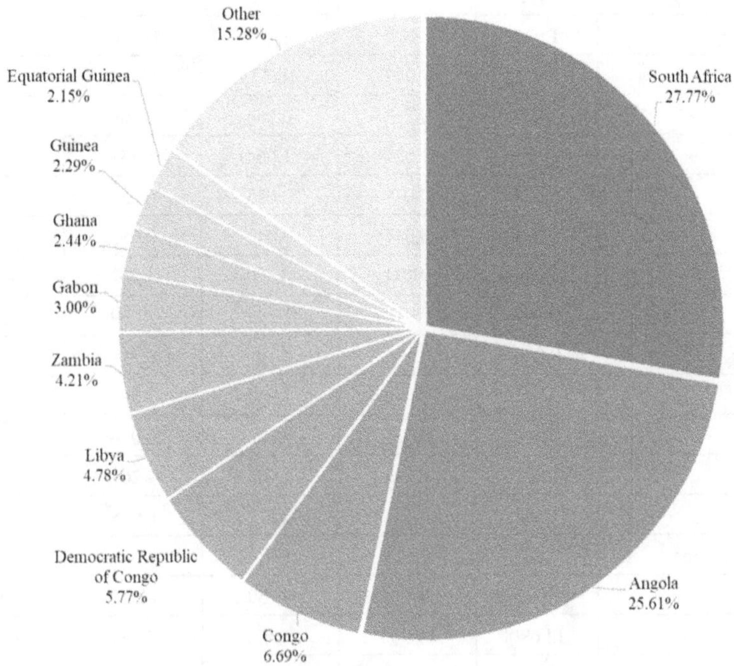

way, and the $1.3 billion sale of mining company Metorex to Jinchuan, and the sale of a 25% stake in black economic empowerment investment holding company Shanduka to CIC for R2 billion (Prabhakar, 2016, 2017).

Investment

Since 1995, African countries have accumulated almost $900 billion of inward FDI as stocks. Among the countries of Africa, the major recipients of foreign investment are South Africa, Egypt, and Nigeria (Table 3).

The three top recipients have substantially increased FDI stocks since 1995. South Africa made a skyrocket start in the late 1990s, but after 2010, its share in the total inflow of foreign investment to Africa decreased. Egypt, Nigeria, and Morocco have emerged as new destinations of foreign investment after 2005. Since 2010, on the wave of growing oil prices and the rise of China, Algeria, Sudan, Congo, and Ghana have joined the club of major FDI recipients (Figure 4).

China is the largest investor in Africa with over 700 Chinese corporations operating in different parts of the continent. China has become an important partner of African countries to fulfill their requirements (particularly, in infrastructural gap) (Prabhakar, 2016).

In 2018, China's FDI stock in African countries totaled $43.3 billion, out of which 17.26% accumulated in South Africa, 8.97% in Democratic Republic of Congo, and 6.61% in Nigeria. China's investments projects in Africa are located in many countries of the continent, the geography of locations is very diverse, top ten destinations amount to about 60% of China's aggregated FDI stock in Africa (Figure 5).

Table 3. Inward foreign direct investment in Africa in 1995-2018, stock, $ billion

Economy	1995	2000	2005	2010	2015	2018
Algeria	1.671	3.379	8.222	19.540	26.227	30.602
Angola	2.921	7.977	16.336	32.458	32.312	23.704
Benin	0.049	0.213	0.284	0.604	1.632	2.257
Botswana	1.126	1.827	1.664	3.351	5.018	4.826
Burkina Faso	0.074	0.028	0.075	0.354	1.745	2.707
Burundi	0.034	0.047	0.047	0.013	0.252	0.243
Cabo Verde	0.038	0.192	0.360	1.252	1.572	1.989
Cameroon	0.379	0.917	2.248	3.099	5.138	7.224
Central African Republic	0.080	0.104	0.198	0.511	0.626	0.658
Chad	0.331	0.576	3.040	3.594	4.860	6.101
Comoros	0.019	0.021	0.024	0.060	0.107	0.122
Congo	1.022	1.893	3.006	9.261	15.237	25.566
Cote d'Ivoire	1.567	2.483	4.512	6.978	7.381	10.234
Democratic Republic of Congo	0.541	0.617	1.974	9.368	19.982	24.021
Djibouti	0.023	0.040	0.159	0.878	1.629	2.219
Egypt	14.690	19.955	28.882	73.095	94.307	116.385
Equatorial Guinea	0.175	1.060	4.124	9.413	13.357	14.111
Eritrea	-	0.337	0.423	0.666	0.886	1.055
Eswatini	0.535	0.536	0.786	0.927	0.521	0.802
Ethiopia	0.165	0.941	2.821	4.206	10.937	22.253
Gabon	0.751	-	0.363	3.287	6.750	10.335
Gambia	0.185	0.216	0.372	0.323	0.399	0.407
Ghana	0.826	1.554	2.145	10.080	26.397	36.126
Guinea	0.131	0.263	0.581	0.486	2.140	4.797
Guinea-Bissau	0.020	0.038	0.006	0.063	0.134	0.199
Kenya	0.732	0.932	1.114	5.449	10.839	14.421
Lesotho	0.179	0.330	0.193	0.929	0.572	0.614
Liberia	2.698	3.247	3.788	10.206	7.880	8.703
Libya	0.766	0.471	2.021	16.334	18.462	18.462
Madagascar	0.172	0.141	0.250	4.383	5.619	6.360
Malawi	0.230	0.358	0.553	0.963	0.714	1.399
Mali	0.342	0.132	0.872	1.964	3.014	4.464
Mauritania	0.095	0.146	1.608	2.372	6.478	7.408
Mauritius	0.253	0.683	0.805	4.658	4.364	5.313
Morocco	5.126	8.842	20.752	45.082	49.671	64.227
Mozambique	0.356	1.249	2.578	4.331	29.274	40.664
Namibia	1.708	1.276	2.453	3.595	5.095	6.727
Niger	0.327	0.045	0.100	2.251	5.165	6.534

continues on following page

Ta ble 3. Continued

Economy	1995	2000	2005	2010	2015	2018
Nigeria	16.256	23.786	26.345	60.327	89.735	99.685
Rwanda	0.051	0.055	0.077	0.422	1.402	2.265
Senegal	0.374	0.295	0.358	1.699	3.431	5.304
Seychelles	0.346	0.515	0.809	1.701	2.762	3.023
Sierra Leone	0.242	0.284	0.300	0.482	1.042	2.002
Somalia	0.002	0.004	0.022	0.566	1.598	2.725
South Africa	15.014	43.451	96.693	179.565	126.755	128.809
Sudan	0.166	1.398	6.901	15.690	24.404	27.669
Togo	0.301	0.087	0.235	0.565	1.568	1.790
Tunisia	10.967	11.545	16.840	31.364	31.772	26.792
Uganda	0.277	0.807	2.024	5.575	10.567	13.333
United Republic of Tanzania	0.620	2.781	4.439	9.712	17.805	20.712
Zambia	3.186	3.966	5.409	7.433	16.488	20.435
Zimbabwe	0.496	1.238	1.383	1.814	3.967	5.433

Source: Authors' development based on UNCTAD (2019)

Figure 4. Africa's top ten recipients of FDI in 1995-2018, stock, $ billion
Source: Authors' development based on UNCTAD (2019)

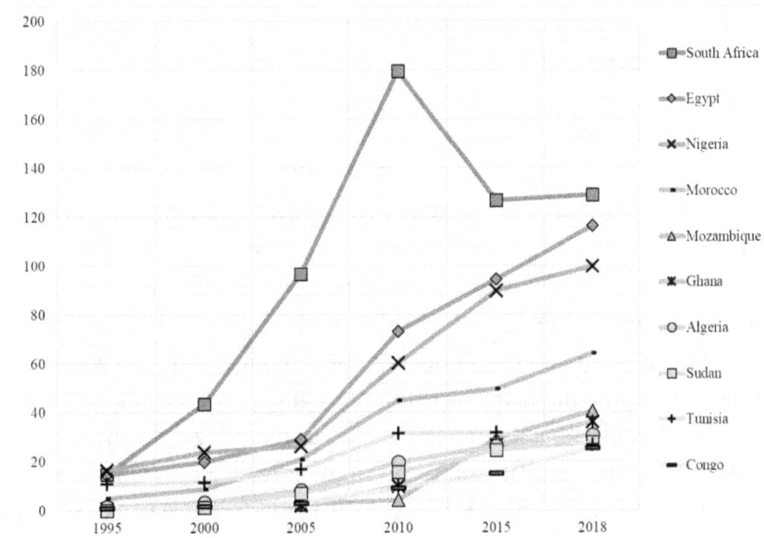

Figure 5. China's top ten destinations of FDI in Africa in 2018, stock
Source: Authors' development based on UNCTAD (2019)

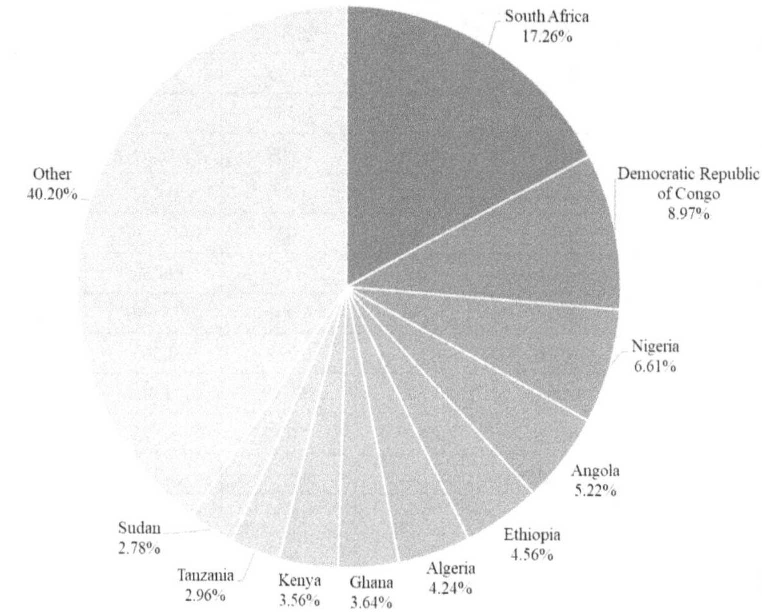

China's FDI in Africa are concentrated in construction, mining, and manufacture of goods, as well as in the sectors of financial services and intermediation and information transmission, computer services, and software (Figure 6).

Despite the growing importance of China as a source of investment resources for Africa, Chinese business operations and other economic activities have been criticized by the scholars who argue that China is not directly involved in local business or even failed to promote local business. According to Wethal (2018), Chinese-led construction projects (especially, in case of Mozambique) are the weak or backward linkages with the local operating systems to any extent for further build local industrial capabilities, and social infrastructures to create new business environment for local business community.

Annually, China-Africa Forum (FOCAC) is participated by the majority of African countries. During the past FOCAS summit, China has declared $10 billion (previous) debt relief, which made a great accomplishment and tariff exemption and the same amount provided with concessionary loans to Africa. It was more worth relaxations than the IMF/World Bank or any other developed countries including the USA and the EU provided. Besides that, China launched various programs such as allowed 100 African postdoctoral fellows to carry out scientific and technological research in China. Since 2012, China has increased the number of scholarships up to 5,500, and around 20,000 African professionals have been already trained. China constructed 50 schools and trained 1,500 school principals and teachers for Africa. In the sphere of agricultural production and improving food security in Africa, China increased the number of its agricultural technology demonstration centers and sent 50 agricultural technology teams to train 2,000 agricultural technology personnel. In the field of health-care, China provided medical equipment and anti-malaria materials worth $73.2 million to 30 hospitals and 30 malaria prevention and treatment centers. Around 3,000 doctors and nurses would also be trained under this initiative. China opened its market for African products, with provisions of duty-free access to 95% of the products produced by the

Figure 6. China's FDI stock in Africa in 2018, sectors
Source: Authors' development based on UNCTAD (2019)

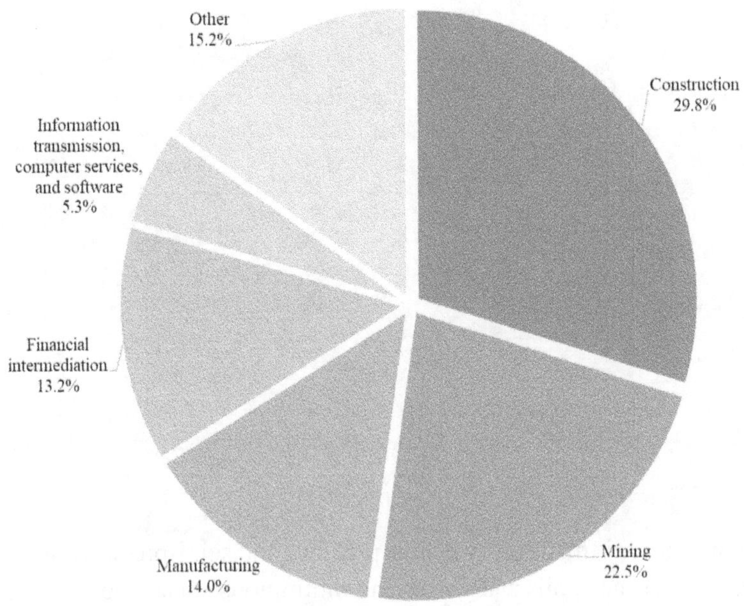

least developed African countries. Twelve Chinese companies signed with worth $ 1.9 billion and assured that it would not monopolize Africa's resources. Chinese SME's (which are around 42 million) are well organized with wide international networks, and currently, SME sectors play a major role in Africa.

India-Africa

Trade

Introduction of GST and Demonetization in India caused a debacle setback for the growing trade relationship between India and African countries over years. Despite some decline, trade relations are still very important and efficient to the two parties and the growth of the economy and the local markets. India and Africa have adopted new trade policy which is anticipated to have a positive impact on bilateral trade. In 2002, India launched the Focus Africa initiative with an aim to strengthen trade tie-ups with African countries. In 2009, Pan African e-network project was launched. The main objectives were to facilitate digital infrastructures like Tele-education and satellite system for E-Governances and Resource mapping.

India's exports to India jumped by 19.2% up to $27.84 billion in August of 2018 boosted by the sales of chemicals (39.9%), petroleum products (31.8%), gems and jewelry (24%), engineering goods (21.2%), and drugs and pharmaceuticals (18.2%). Indian exports of agricultural commodities to African countries remained significantly high from 2010 to 2014 but declined in 2016-2018. Since the mid-1990s, India-Africa trade balance has been negative for India with particular drops in 2008 and 2011 and a continuing decline starting from 2016 on (Figure 7).

Figure 7. India-Africa trade in 1995-2018, $ billion
Source: Authors' development based on UNCTAD (2019)

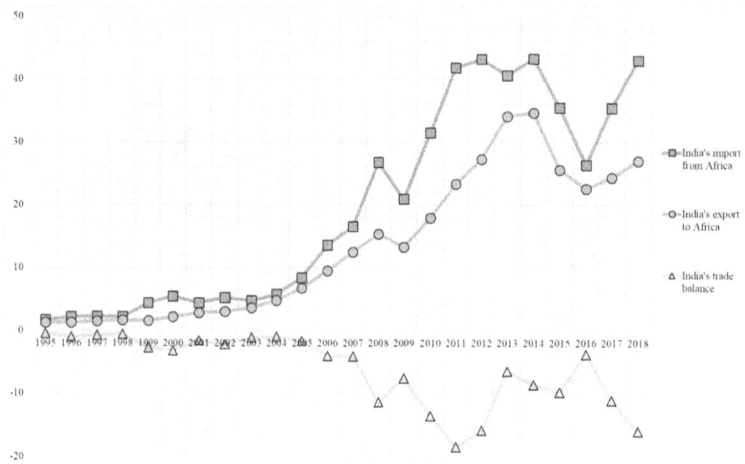

India's export to the worlds is made up by pearls, precious and semi-precious stones, and jewelry (16% of total shipments), mineral fuels, oils and waxes and bituminous substances (12%), vehicles, parts and accessories (5%), nuclear reactors, boilers, machinery and mechanical appliances (5%), pharmaceutical products (5%), and organic chemicals (4%). India's export to Africa is rather diverse, it is made up by machinery and transport equipment (23.51% of total exports to Africa in 2018), chemicals (21.36%), manufactured goods (17.32%), and mineral fuels (16.68%) (Table 4).

Globally, India's main export partners are the USA (15% of total exports), United Arab Emirates (11%), Hong Kong (5%), China (4%), Singapore (4%), and the UK (3%). In Africa, India's top export destinations in 2018 are South Africa, Egypt, Nigeria, Kenya, Tanzania, Mauritius, Algeria, Djibouti, Mozambique, and Sudan (Figure 8).

India's import from Africa is not as diversified as its export to the continent. It is dominated by mineral fuels which share in total imports have been growing since 1995 and has reached 63.13% in 2018. Other import items are commodities and transactions (12.43% of total India's import from Africa in 2018), manufactured goods (7.62%), crude metals (6.61%), chemicals (4.72%), and food and live animals (4.56%) (Table 5).

Major portion of imports originate from Nigeria (particularly, oil and other mineral fuels) – 31.02% in the structure of imports by countries in 2018. Other large suppliers to India are South Africa, Angola, Ghana, Algeria, Egypt, Mozambique, Morocco, Botswana, and Tanzania (Figure 9).

Investment

Investment relations between India and Africa can be traced back to the 1960 when some large Indian companies invested in Eastern African countries on the wave of independence movement in the continent. In recent years, bilateral investment flows have surged. According to Africa Export-Import Bank and Export-Import Bank of India (2018), between 2010 and 2014, the stock of Indian FDI in Africa rose from $11.9 billion to $15.2 billion making India the eighth-largest investor in Africa. India has a vast area for investment in Africa where on one hand state-owned companies are investing in sectors

Table 4. India's exports to Africa in 1995-2018, product groups

Product	1995		2000		2005		2010		2015		2018	
	$ billion	share in total, %	$ billion	share in total, %	$ billion	share in total, %	$ billion	share in total, %	$ billion	share in total, %	$ billion	share in total, %
Food and live animals	0.318	24.11	0.175	7.99	0.882	13.12	1.047	5.85	3.287	12.82	3.215	11.90
Beverages and tobacco	0.005	0.38	0.006	0.27	0.027	0.40	0.160	0.89	0.145	0.57	0.121	0.45
Crude metals	0.014	1.06	0.046	2.10	0.063	0.94	0.172	0.96	0.235	0.92	0.385	1.43
Mineral fuels	0.001	0.08	0.001	0.05	0.770	11.46	4.109	22.97	5.293	20.64	4.506	16.68
Animal and vegetable oils	0.001	0.08	0.004	0.18	0.011	0.16	0.010	0.06	0.014	0.05	0.022	0.08
Chemicals	0.160	12.13	0.382	17.45	1.036	15.41	2.820	15.77	5.017	19.57	5.768	21.36
Manufactured goods	0.448	33.97	0.983	44.91	2.057	30.61	3.691	20.64	4.315	16.83	4.678	17.32
Machinery and transport equipment	0.276	20.92	0.362	16.54	1.417	21.08	5.004	27.98	5.462	21.30	6.350	23.51
Miscellaneous manufactured articles	0.086	6.52	0.212	9.68	0.377	5.61	0.827	4.62	1.859	7.25	1.953	7.23
Commodities and transactions	0.010	0.76	0.017	0.78	0.081	1.21	0.046	0.26	0.013	0.05	0.011	0.04
Total all products	1.319	100.00	2.189	100.00	6.721	100.00	17.887	100.00	25.640	100.00	27.008	100.00

Source: Authors' development based on UNCTAD (2019)

like energy, power, and infrastructure and on the other hand India is investing in sectors like agriculture, pharmaceuticals, telecommunications and mining (Khan & Arora, 2017). India's African investments are often in natural resource industries, textiles, information and communications technology, banking, and automotive industries (Table 6).

India has supported the establishment of pan-African institutions with many projects, including the Pan African E-Network Project with three universities in Ghana, Cameroon, and Uganda and a telemedicine center in Tanzania, the India-Africa Institute of Foreign Trade, the India-Africa Institute of Agriculture and Rural Development, the India-Africa Civil Aviation Academy, the India-Africa Institute of Education, Planning and Administration, and the India-Africa Institute of Information Technology (Wagner, 2019).

The flow of FDI has not been unidirectional. Between 2010 and 2014, the stock of African FDI in India increased from $57.0 billion to $73.3 billion, with FDI from Africa in India accounting for almost 23% of the country's FDI stock in 2014. Mauritius has established itself as a major source of FDI for India, even overtaking Singapore to become the top source of FDI in India in 2016-2017. Mauritius is a widely used conduit for Indian inward and outward FDI, owing to the island nation's advantageous tax conditions. South Africa, Seychelles, Swaziland, and Morocco are among the other largest African investors in India.

Figure 8. India's top ten export destinations in Africa in 2018, % of total exports to African countries
Source: Authors' development based on UNCTAD (2019)

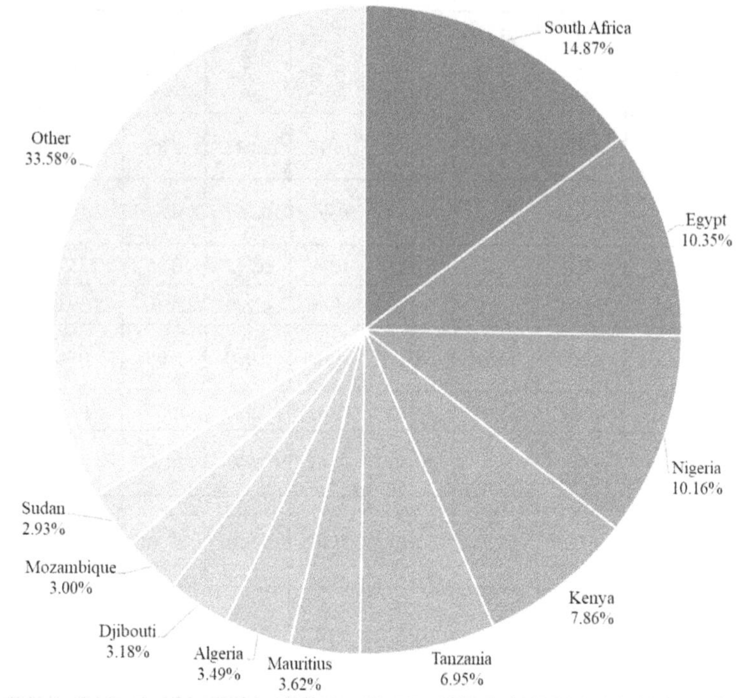

Figure 9. India's top ten import sources in Africa in 2018, % of total imports from African countries
Source: Authors' development based on UNCTAD (2019)

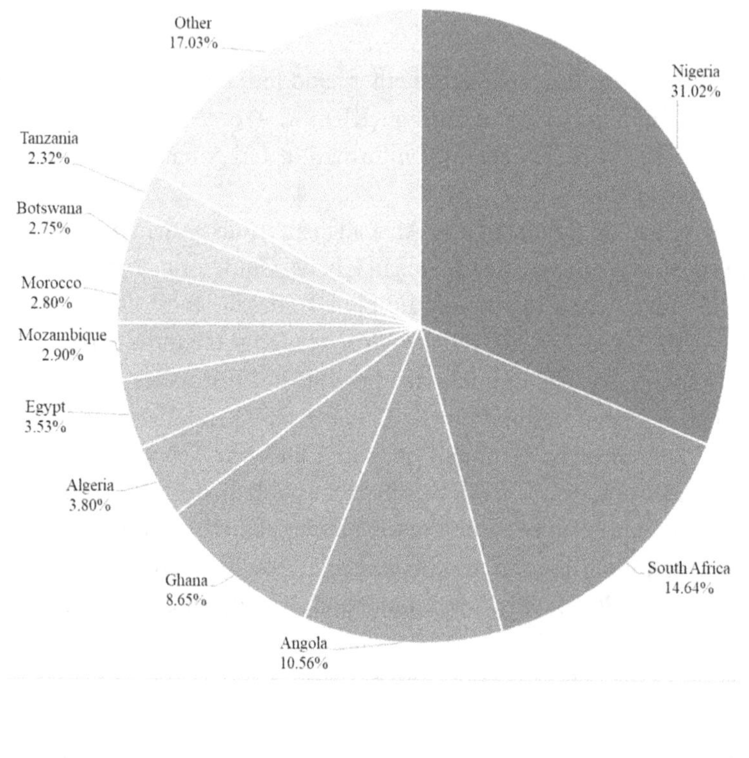

Table 5. India's imports from Africa in 1995-2018, product groups

Product	1995		2000		2005		2010		2015		2018	
	$ billion	share in total, %	$ billion	share in total, %	$ billion	share in total, %	$ billion	share in total, %	$ billion	share in total, %	$ billion	share in total, %
Food and live animals	0.186	10.66	0.287	5.28	1.115	13.29	0.815	2.59	1.973	5.56	1.962	4.56
Beverages and tobacco	0.000	0.00	0.001	0.02	0.002	0.02	0.004	0.01	0.005	0.01	0.007	0.02
Crude metals	0.187	10.72	0.443	8.15	2.560	30.52	1.404	4.46	2.656	7.49	2.841	6.61
Mineral fuels	0.708	40.57	3.239	59.57	0.685	8.17	23.400	74.32	21.564	60.79	27.133	63.13
Animal and vegetable oils	0.000	0.00	0.006	0.11	0.001	0.01	0.005	0.02	0.003	0.01	0.006	0.01
Chemicals	0.530	30.37	0.707	13.00	1.359	16.20	1.741	5.53	1.288	3.63	2.030	4.72
Manufactured goods	0.121	6.93	0.114	2.10	1.000	11.92	0.800	2.54	1.701	4.80	3.275	7.62
Machinery and transport equipment	0.004	0.23	0.152	2.80	0.336	4.01	0.158	0.50	0.305	0.86	0.323	0.75
Miscellaneous manufactured articles	0.000	0.00	0.006	0.11	0.013	0.16	0.027	0.09	0.034	0.10	0.062	0.14
Commodities and transactions	0.009	0.52	0.481	8.85	1.278	15.24	3.131	9.94	5.943	16.75	5.343	12.43
Total all products	1.745	100.00	5.437	100.00	8.387	100.00	31.485	100.00	35.471	100.00	42.981	100.00

Source: Authors' development based on UNCTAD (2019)

Table 6. India's major investment projects in Africa

Sectors	Countries
Mining, oil and gas, and other extraction of natural resources	
oil and gas	Cote d'Ivoire, Libya, Mozambique, Libya, South Sudan, Sudan
coal	Mozambique, Zambia
copper	Zambia
Agriculture	
tea production	Uganda, Rwanda
floriculture	Ethiopia, Kenya
Services	
telecommunications	Kenya
health care	
information technology	Ethiopia, South Africa
banking	Botswana, Ghana, Kenya, Mauritius, South Africa, Uganda, Zambia
Manufacturing	Ghana, Nigeria
Pharmaceuticals	Nigeria

Source: Authors' development based on Africa Export-Import Bank and Export-Import Bank of India (2018)

According to Africa Export-Import Bank and Export-Import Bank of India (2018), the growth of investment flows can be attributed to several developments in India and Africa.

First, India was traditionally highly restrictive in releasing the foreign exchange necessary for Indian firms to invest abroad given capital scarcity and limited foreign exchange resources. However, economic reforms since the 1990s have relaxed these restrictions and, with the overall investment ceiling on outward Indian investment abolished in 2003, Indian companies are now largely free to invest abroad, thus facilitating greater outward investments. In addition, India has signed bilateral investment agreements with thirteen African countries.

Second, with faster economic growth, India's energy requirements have also increased dramatically such that energy security concerns have come to occupy a prominent position in India's foreign policy discourse. The diversification of energy suppliers and investment in oil and gas ventures abroad became important objectives of India's foreign policy and an important avenue for India's investment in Africa.

SOLUTIONS AND RECOMMENDATIONS

In recent years, the governments of China, India, and African countries have implemented initiatives to nurture and expand multilateral trade and investment relationship. These efforts have been welcomed by most of the African countries as they increasingly seek to diversify export markets and strengthen partnerships. However, there are many questions which arise in terms of future policies in the area of trade and investment integration. Particularly, according to Johnston and Yuan (2014), the question is what does it mean that some neighboring economies in Africa have deeper trade and investment ties with China and India, and others not, yet are otherwise simultaneously seeking to regionally integrate? Answering this question will help to devise onward policies for maximized mutual benefit of China and India from one side and African countries from the other. Economic policy suggestions can only be envisaged by taking into consideration the specific nature of individual countries.

The recommendations on possible improvement of economic, trade, and investment ties within China-India-Africa triangle include the study of the effectiveness of China's and India's bilateral trade and investment treaties between different African countries and how this impacts trade and investment relations and success and broader economic growth in the continent. Research exploring the institutional relations between and requirements of foreign investors, including expectations of local ownership, transfer for technology, and training of local staff, might also be re-visited toward relevant application to the African case. The latter could serve to directly and explicitly embed lessons from China's and India's experience of FDI absorption into Africa's own investment ties with China and India, where and as relevant. Detailed country or sub-regional case studies would also be insightful.

The effectiveness of large infrastructure projects requires closer and more detailed analysis. Particularly, Chinese large infrastructure projects, suffering from high political risk in recipient countries, have been becoming more expensive and less efficient. China and India should thus pay more attention to domestic politics of recipient countries. In turn, African countries should strengthen their governance institutions. African countries may be able to reap significant benefits from furthering regional integration in respect to the rules governing Chinese investment (Renard, 2011).

FUTURE RESEARCH DIRECTIONS

In this chapter, the analysis of China-Africa and India-Africa relations has been conducted along the lines of trade flows (dynamics, structure, and destinations of exports and imports) and foreign direct investment (stocks accumulated in African countries). While the data analyzed in this study are not exhaustive, they shed light on opportunities for future research that can address the complexity of China-India-Africa relationships and identify the potential for the three sides to collaborate with an aim to spur economic growth within this triangle.

McMillan (2019) emphasized that the increasing focus on productive sectors in high-growth countries suggested that there could be opportunities for Chinese and Indian investment in African countries to create jobs, supply local markets, and create linkages and knowledge spillovers to local firms. These effects require further investigation with due account to contemporary development in the global market, trade tensions between China and the USA, and increasing economic influence of China and to some extent, India in Africa in particular and in the developing part of the world in general (Prabhakar, 2003, 2005, 2018; Erokhin, 2016).

While in this study, the authors overviewed the big picture of trade and investment collaboration between China and India from one side and the entire continent of Africa from the other, a regional focus on the countries of Northern, Western, Eastern, Southern, and Central Africa may show the differences in specific features of trade and investment links. A new strand of research (Brautigam, Diao, McMillan, & Silver, 2017) demonstrates some positive synergies between Chinese and local manufacturing firms in Ethiopia, and the potential for them to develop in Ghana, Nigeria, and Tanzania. All four of these countries belong to the group of Africa's fastest-growing economies.

CONCLUSION

In the past decades, Africa has been emerging as an attractive investment destination for its high rate of growth, a rising middle class, and its resource abundance, particularly in energy. Chinese and Indian companies have made huge investments in many African countries. In addition, the emergence of African multinationals and growing South-South cooperation saw several African companies invest in India and China to take advantage of the two biggest consumer markets in the planet.

However, there are many problems, drawbacks, and challenges on the way to effective trade and investment collaboration in China-India-Africa triangle. The economies of the majority of African countries are developing rather slowly due to colonial legacies or practices, public debt, and lack of infrastructures in various fields. Still, there are vast scopes and opportunities for Africa to intensify economic integration with India and China. Most of the countries in Africa have abundant natural resources. This advantage should be utilized and developed further by adopting advanced and innovative technologies and proper use of resources for the purpose of the development of African economies.

Nevertheless, both continents have millions of citizens and still population is growing fast hence the demand also increases daily. Therefore, in order to meet the increasing demand, further development of these relationships is necessary since it benefits all participating sides. Trade and investment integration can not only promote trade but also support for local development and contribute to the wellbeing and wealth of large population in Africa, China, and India.

ACKNOWLEDGMENT

This study is supported by the Fundamental Research Funds for the Central Universities, China, grant no. 3072019CFP0902, HEUCFJ170901.

REFERENCES

Africa Export-Import Bank, & Export-Import Bank of India. (2018). *Deepening South-South Collaboration: An Analysis of Africa and India's Trade and Investment*. Heliopolis: Africa Export-Import Bank.

Brautigam, D., Diao, X., McMillan, M., & Silver, J. (2017). *Chinese Investment in Africa: How Much Do We Know?* Washington, DC: International Food Policy Research Institute.

Chakrabarti, S., & Ghosh, I. (2014). FDI in Africa: A Comparison of the Indian and Chinese Experience. *Procedia: Social and Behavioral Sciences*, *157*, 340–352. doi:10.1016/j.sbspro.2014.11.038

Cheru, F., & Obi, C. (2010). *The Rise of China and India in Africa: Challenges, Opportunities, and Critical Interventions*. London, UK: Zed Books.

Erokhin, V. (Ed.). (2016). *Global Perspectives on Trade Integration and Economies in Transition*. Hershey, PA: IGI Global. doi:10.4018/978-1-5225-0451-1

Erokhin, V. (2017). How to Shape the Market: China's One Belt One Road Initiative. In M. Malovic, & K. Roy (Eds.), *The State and the Market in Economic Development: In Pursuit of Millennium Development Goals* (pp. 144–156). Brisbane, Australia: The IIDS Australia Inc.

Johnston, L. A., & Yuan, C. (2014). China's Africa Trade and Investment Policies: Review of a "Noodle Bowl". *African East-Asian Affairs*, *4*, 6–41.

Khan, S. M., & Arora, K. (2017). Scope of India's and China's Investment in African Continent. *Procedia Computer Science*, *122*, 691–697. doi:10.1016/j.procs.2017.11.425

Lunenborg, P. (2019). *"Phase 1B" of the African Continental Free Trade Area (AfCFTA) Negotiations*. Geneva, Switzerland: The South Centre.

McMillan, M. (2019). *Chinese Investment in Africa*. Retrieved September 2, 2019, from https://www.theigc.org/blog/chinese-investment-africa/

Moyo, S. (2016). Perspectives on South-South Relations: China's Presence in Africa. *Inter-Asia Cultural Studies*, *17*(1), 58–67. doi:10.1080/14649373.2016.1138615

Nowak, W. (2016). China-Africa and India-Africa Trade in the Years 2000-2014. *Procedia Economics and Finance*, *39*, 140–146. doi:10.1016/S2212-5671(16)30261-1

Ofori-Atta, P. (2016). *Backward Integration Key to Africa's Growth Prospects*. Retrieved September 2, 2019, from https://www.theafricareport.com/1743/backward-integration-key-to-africas-growth-prospects/

Prabhakar, A. (2003). A Critical Reflection on Globalisation and Inequality: A New Approach to the Development of the South. *African and Asian Studies*, *2*(3), 307–345. doi:10.1163/156920903322661735

Prabhakar, A. (2005). Globalisation, Poverty, & Inequality: A Study of India, China, the USA and OECD, *VIKLP*.

Prabhakar, A. (2014). *South-South Trade and Technological Cooperation: A Case Study of India and East Africa*. New Delhi, India: Shodh Ganga.

Prabhakar, A. (2016). Trade and Economic Integration in BRICS: Towards Multi-Polarity. In V. Erokhin (Ed.), *Global Perspectives on Trade Integration and Economies in Transition* (pp. 45–57). Hershey, PA: IGI Global. doi:10.4018/978-1-5225-0451-1.ch003

Prabhakar, A. (2017). *The Current Global Recession: A Theoretical and Empirical Investigation into Developed and BRICS Economies*. London, UK: Emerald Group.

Prabhakar, A. (2018). *Comparative Economic Systems and Welfare Economics*. New Delhi, India: ISARA.

Rampa, F., & Bilal, S. (2011). *Emerging Economies in Africa and the Development Effectiveness Debate*. Maastricht, The Netherlands: European Centre for Development Policy Management.

Renard, M.-F. (2011). *China's Trade and FDI in Africa. Belvedere*. African Development Bank.

Roy, S. (2014). *China and India, "Rising Powers" and African Development: Challenges and Opportunities*. Uppsala, Sweden: The Nordic Africa Institute.

United Nations Conference on Trade and Development. (2019). *Statistics Database*. Retrieved September 1, 2019, from http://unctad.org/en/Pages/Statistics.aspx

United Nations Development Programme. (2013). *Human Development Report 2013. The Rise of the South – Human Progress in a Diverse World*. New York, NY: United Nations Development Programme.

Wagner, C. (2019). *India's Africa Policy*. Berlin, Germany: German Institute for International and Security Affairs.

Wethal, U. (2018). Beyond the China Factor: Challenges to Backward Linkages in the Mozambican Construction Sector. *The Journal of Modern African Studies*, *56*(2), 325–351. doi:10.1017/S0022278X18000150

ADDITIONAL READING

Ademola, O. T., Bankole, A.-S., & Adewuyi, A. O. (2016). China-Africa Trade Relations: Insights from AERC Scoping Studies. In S. Henson & O. F. Yap (Eds.), *The Power of the Chinese Dragon* (pp. 69–97). London: Palgrave Macmillan. doi:10.1007/978-1-137-57449-7_4

African Forum and Network on Debt and Development. (2008). *Mapping Chinese Development Assistance in Africa*. Harare: AFRODAD.

Aguilar, C. G. (2010). South-South Relations in the New International Geopolitics. *Global Studies Review*, *80*(22), 2–7.

Alden, C. (2007). *China in Africa*. London: Zed Books.

Alfaro, L., Rodríguez-Clare, A., Hanson, G. H., & Bravo-Ortega, C. (2004). Multinationals and Linkages: An Empirical Investigation [with Comments]. *Economía*, *4*(2), 113–169.

Amendolagine, V., Boly, A., Coniglio, N. D., Prota, F., & Seric, A. (2013). FDI and Local Linkages in Developing Countries: Evidence from Sub-Saharan Africa. *World Development*, *50*, 41–56. doi:10.1016/j.worlddev.2013.05.001

Anshan, L. (2007). China and Africa: Policy and Challenges. *China Security*, *3*(3), 69–93.

Auffray, C., & Fu, X. (2015). Chinese MNEs and Managerial Knowledge Transfer in Africa: The Case of the Construction Sector in Ghana. *Journal of Chinese Economic and Business Studies*, *13*(4), 285–310. doi:10.1080/14765284.2015.1092415

Biggeri, M., & Sanfilippo, M. (2007). Understanding China's Move into Africa: An Empirical Analysis. *Journal of Chinese Economic and Business Studies*, *7*(1), 31–54. doi:10.1080/14765280802604714

Bräutigam, D. (2011). Aid with Chinese Characteristics: Chinese Foreign Aid and Development Finance Meet the OECD-DAC Aid Regime. *Journal of International Development*, *23*(5), 752–764. doi:10.1002/jid.1798

Bräutigam, D., & Tang, X. (2011). African Shenzhen: China's Special Economic Zones in Africa. *The Journal of Modern African Studies*, *49*(1), 27–54. doi:10.1017/S0022278X10000649

Broadman, H. G. (2008). China and India Go to Africa: New Deals in the Developing World. *Foreign Affairs*, *87*(2), 95–109.

Chen, C., Goldstein, A., & Orr, R. J. (2009). Local Operations of Chinese Construction Firms in Africa: An Empirical Survey. *International Journal of Construction Management*, *9*(2), 75–89. doi:10.1080/15623599.2009.10773131

Cheru, F., & Obi, C. (2011). Chinese and Indian Engagement in Africa: Competitive or Mutually Reinforcing Strategies? *Sino-Indian Relations*, *64*(2), 91–110.

Cissé, D. (2013). South-South Migration and Sino-African Small Traders: A Comparative Study of Chinese in Senegal and Africans in China. *African Review of Economics and Finance*, *5*(1), 17–28.

Corkin, L. (2012). Chinese Construction Companies in Angola: A Local Linkages Perspective. *Resources Policy*, *37*(4), 475–483. doi:10.1016/j.resourpol.2012.06.002

Dicken, P. (2011). *Global Shift: Reshaping the Global Economic Map in the 21st Century*. London: Sage.

Foster, V., Butterfield, W., & Chen, C. (2009). *Building Bridges: China's Growing Role as Infrastructure Financier for Sub-Saharan Africa*. Washington, DC: World Bank Publications. doi:10.1596/978-0-8213-7554-9

Gu, J. (2009). China's Private Enterprises in Africa and the Implications for African Development. *European Journal of Development Research*, *21*(4), 570–587. doi:10.1057/ejdr.2009.21

Harman, S., & Brown, W. (2013). In from the Margins? The Changing Place of Africa in International Relations. *International Affairs*, *89*(1), 69–87. doi:10.1111/1468-2346.12005

Herbertson, K. (2011). Leading while Catching Up? Emerging Standards for China's Overseas Investments. *Sustainable Development Law and Policy*, *11*, 22–43.

Kragelund, P. (2009). Knocking on a Wide-Open Door: Chinese Investments in Africa. *Review of African Political Economy*, *36*(122), 479–497. doi:10.1080/03056240903346111

Mawdsley, E. (2012). *From Recipients to Donors – Emerging Powers and the Changing Development Landscape*. London: Zed Books.

Mold, A. (2012). Will It All End in Tears? Infrastructure Spending and African Development in Historical Perspective. *Journal of International Development*, *24*(2), 237–254. doi:10.1002/jid.2818

Morris, M., Kaplinsky, R., & Kaplan, D. (2012). *One Thing Leads to Another: Promoting Industrialisation by Making the Most of the Commodity Boom in Sub-Saharan Africa*. Raleigh, NC: LULU Press.

Morrissey, O. (2012). FDI in Sub-Saharan Africa: Few Linkages, Fewer Spillovers. *European Journal of Development Research*, *24*(1), 26–31. doi:10.1057/ejdr.2011.49

Moumouni, G. (2010). China's Relations with African Sub-regions: The Case of West Africa. [African Union Commission]. *The Bulletin of Fridays at the Commission*, *3*(1), 25–43.

Njoh, A. J. (2000). Transportation Infrastructure and Economic Development in Sub-Saharan Africa. *Public Works Management & Policy*, *4*(4), 286–296. doi:10.1177/1087724X0044003

Pannell, C. W. (2008). China's Economic and Political Penetration in Africa. *Eurasian Geography and Economics*, *49*(6), 706–730. doi:10.2747/1539-7216.49.6.706

Vines, A. (2007). China in Africa: A Mixed Blessing? *Current History (New York, N.Y.)*, *106*(700), 213–219.

Weng, X., Buckley, L., Blackmore, E., Vorley, B., Schoneveld, G., & Cerutti, P. O. … Jønsson, J. (2018). Chinese Investments and Africa's Smallscale Producers: Disruptions and Opportunities: Empirical Analysis of Primary Sectors in Tanzania, Zambia and Zimbabwe. London: International Institute for Environment and Development.

Yi-Chong, X. (2014). Chinese State-Owned Enterprises in Africa: Ambassadors or Freebooters? *Journal of Contemporary China*, *23*(89), 822–840. doi:10.1080/10670564.2014.882542

KEY TERMS AND DEFINITIONS

African Continental Free Trade Area (AfCFTA): A unique collaborative effort by African countries to bolster regional and continental economic integration in a world marked by increasing protectionism and use of unilateral trade measures.

Economic Integration: An arrangement among nations that typically includes the reduction or elimination of trade barriers and the coordination of monetary and fiscal policies. Economic integration aims to reduce costs for both consumers and producers and to increase trade between the countries involved in the agreement.

Foreign Direct Investment: An investment made by a firm or individual in one country into business interests located in another country. Generally, FDI takes place when an investor establishes foreign business operations or acquires foreign business assets, including establishing ownership or controlling interest in a foreign company.

Globalization: The spread of products, technology, information, and jobs across national borders and cultures; economic interdependence of nations around the globe fostered through free trade.

North Africa: The northern part of Africa, especially the region north of the tropical rain forest and comprised of Morocco, Algeria, Tunisia, Libya, and that part of Egypt west of the Gulf of Suez.

Sub-Saharan Africa: The area of the continent of Africa that consists of all African countries that are fully or partially located south of the Sahara.

Chapter 3
China in Africa:
A Cooperation With Chinese Characteristics

Tonny Dian Effendi
https://orcid.org/0000-0002-7494-5715
Universitas Muhammadiyah Malang, Indonesia

Devita Prinanda
University of Muhammadiyah Malang, Indonesia

ABSTRACT

China's role in Africa: is it really unilateral domination or is it awakened because of the equation of the situation and interests? Then, how are the character, developments, and forms of cooperation? To answer those questions, this chapter uses a concept of inter-regionalism, in which inter-regional co-operation has several objectives namely balancing, bandwagoning, institution building, rationalizing, agenda-setting, and stabilizing. The emerging collaboration gives China an opportunity to introduce a model of interregional cooperation based on its foreign relations. China introduces a mechanism of cooperation based on "Chinese characteristic" which seems different from the Western perspective. China and Africa's interregional cooperation has been developing not only from economic reasons but has also been influenced by international politics. It is an economic cooperation alternative for Africa and international model alternative from the Chinese perspective. The last is influenced by China's international relations behavior which is based on its character.

INTRODUCTION

China and Africa have been establishing long-standing relationships. The Asian-African Conference in Indonesia also strengthened the relationship on the basis of two similarities. Firstly, they were both located in the Asian and African regions that were then against colonialism. Secondly, they also have the same perspective against colonialism. During the Cold War, their relationship continued where China

DOI: 10.4018/978-1-7998-1730-7.ch003

and Africa were, again united by similar situations and problems. African countries are experiencing economic problems and lack of the world's attention, whereas China needs the support from many countries in international politics and faced the "isolation" of Western countries and other Asian countries due to the Communism issue. In the post-Cold War, following China's economic development, the relationship between China and Africa continued and increased. Even some opinions say that China has to dominate Africa through foreign aid, investment, and trade.

This chapter discusses the history and cooperation building built by China and Africa. Chinese domination in Africa, such as some opinions say, is it really unilateral domination or is it awakened because of the equation of the situation and interests? Then, how are the character, developments, and forms of cooperation? To answer those questions, this chapter uses a concept in the international relations study called interregionalism. In this concept, interregional cooperation has several objectives namely balancing, bandwagoning, institution building, rationalizing, agenda setting, and stabilizing. The initial function of regional cooperation is balancing were the countries in the region are trying to make balancing through their inter-cooperation. The second goal is to put cooperation as an effective way to look strong by conducting alliances. When two objectives are reached, the next goal is to establish a strong cooperation institution to facilitate the dialogue and the continued or enhance the cooperation. This was then strengthened by the agreement that became a mechanism in regional and international cooperation. Agenda setting aims to compile some important issues for example about good governance, liberal democracy, and human right. And lastly is the development of cooperation that leads to economic growth.

When the authors discuss China's cooperation in Africa from the inter-regionalism concept, the existence of compatibility and incompatibility is observed. In the context of balancing and bandwagoning, history should be referred to. Initially, the cooperation between China and Africa is precisely because they both experience similar situation and problems in international politics. Therefore, at first, the cooperation was not built on the domination of either party. China and Africa at the time, both faced a weak economic situation, which seen negatively from other the international world. Africa was considered as a poor continent with many internal problems, whereas China was seen as poor country (during the Cold War) with the Communism ideology (which is contrary to the most of the world's countries). Those conditions caused them to cooperate to offset their outside forces (Western and more advanced economies).

In subsequent developments, that cooperation formed institutional building in several mechanisms such as the Forum on China-Africa Cooperation (FOCAC). Starting at this stage appears to be a difference or perhaps more called deviations with the explanation of the concept of inter-regionalism. Cooperation forums built by China and Africa contain the values or establish certain norms in the cooperation influenced by China and Africa. As Deng Xiaoping, China's economic reform leader, said that China did not look into the background of its partners because the most important was that they could do mutually beneficial cooperation. The highest value is a commitment to the cooperation. This then affects the agenda setting, where the main focus is to increase the cooperation with no involvement in the domestic affairs of the country involved. While in the concept of inter-regionalism, the issues could be good governance, liberal democracy, and human right issues, which is most likely that China will avoid it in the context of interference with the country's domestic affairs other. These things are possible to be discussed but as an effort to improve cooperation rather than as an order to be implemented in practice. The development mechanism, however, looks consistent in China-Africa cooperation that focuses on economic development from the very beginning. It is further strengthened by China's economic and development cooperation mechanisms, called the Belt and Road Initiative (BRI), which also involves many African countries. While on the other hand, African countries themselves have carried out many internal consolidation with the emergence of several intraregion organizations such as the African Union (AU), the South African Development Community (SADC), the Economic Community of West African States (ECOWAS), and East African Community (EAC).

Ultimately, the question that arises is how to identify the form of cooperation built by China in Africa through the concept of interregionalism? Again, as many of the examples that China has often brought about some of its policies that appear to be "anomaly" of thought Western perspective or theory is the concept of "with Chinese characteristics". When China has seen an anomaly in the implementation of its Socialisms (not entirely the same as Western Socialism thought) they called it the Socialism with Chinese characteristic. When China offers a free trade concept which is precisely set up on a bilateral agreement in a multilateral forum (this is turning from the World Trade Organization (WTO) where the agreements are multilateral and can be applied bilaterally) then they create unimpeded trade or free trade with Chinese characteristic. Some of the mechanisms in the BRI cooperation appear to be different and weird compared with Western-style economic cooperation that has been known. And returning to Chinese and African cooperation, this chapter saw that that cooperation looks like interregionalism with Chinese characteristic by doing some things such as explanations in Western concepts, but doing modifications or adjustments with characters and values built by China with non-interference and peaceful coexistence.

BACKGROUND

This chapter describes the content analysis of China and regional groups in Africa. The authors review the phenomenon by using institutional approach. China manages regional forum to establish long term relation with African states. Accordingly, dialog activities, memorandums of understanding (MoUs), and agreements are the predominant endeavours in maintaining relation. Through inter-regionalism, this research detailed the dynamics of both regions in undertaking cooperation.

Interregionalism is a formal process of integration between a region to other regions. Interregionalism can not only be seen in economic cooperation but also can be selected from the post-hegemonic international system genesis. Hybrid inter-regionalism is the relationship between regional organizations with single nations in other regions. In other terms, it is also said to be quasi-inter-regionalism. Usually, hybrid inter-regionalism refers to a relation with single power state from another region.

Through a number of forums in approaching regional organizations in Africa, China benefited in the form of direct agreements with the groups of countries in Africa. Engagement among African states and China makes an easier way for China to get trust in many countries at the same time. To avoid losing bargaining value in the region, China chooses an approach to supranational levels toward regional and sub-regional organizations in Africa.

MAIN FOCUS OF THE CHAPTER

China's Engagement With the African Union

As an external actor, China has a capability to influence regional cooperation in Africa. African countries feature China as an alternative relation compared to western development models. Although bilateral relations are the most efficient to achieve goals, institutional approach with the AU acquires China to have a strong position as an external actor in the African continent.

The institutional approach had major beneficial for China. However, this does not mean that this approach eliminates bilateral cooperation between China and the AU member countries. China advances substantial interests through multilateral forum. FOCAC was establish in 2000 as the dialog mechanism between 53 African states and China.

FOCAC has a multidimensional scope by mapping cooperation in political, economic, trade, and social sectors. Political cooperation undertakes the high level visit and dialog around regional issues. Communication and partnership in this sector initiate action plan. As in ongoing effort, political discourse within the FOCAC consults to multilateral institution such as the United Nations (UN) and the WTO. Political consultation is managed to achieve the ideal result. In addition, the FOCAC facilitates ministerial, parliament, judiciaries, and local government levels in regional dialog. Thus, the establishment of sister-city or sister-province is inevitable.

In economic sector, the FOCAC presents economic framework for both parties. The FOCAC emphasizes in reinforcing agricultural sector to comply food security. China contributes to the reinforcement of African agriculture by dispatching professional agricultural technology, investing in food processing industry, and exporting machine and technology. This collaboration framework is also coped by the Food and Agriculture Organization of the United Nations (FAO). Aside of agriculture, the FOCAC facilitates investment environment and trade for both parties. There are several economic dialogues participated by associating political leaders and businesses. One of the high-level dialogs is Conference of Chinese and African Entrepreneurs (Forum on China-Africa Cooperation [FOCAC], 2006). In financial sector, Africa and China established China-Africa Development Fund in 2007. It was recognized in Beijing to cultivate robust investment through funding program for African states (China-Africa Development Fund, 2013). In infrastructure sector, China engages in building African infrastructure. China delegates expertise, technician, and management team to construct telecommunication, transportation, power plant, and so forth.

Social development partnership between China and Africa comprises the principle of sustainable development. China commits the assistance to increase development standard in Africa. Besides, the FOCAC emerged China-Africa Inter-Governmental Human Resource Development Plan. This plan culminated sustainable training for African professional worker. The FOCAC also conducts ministerial-level dialog on education. China-Africa Forum of Ministers of Education arises scholarship for students, training for teacher, and establishing Confucius institutes. There are also dialog and action plan in tourism, media, terrorism, culture, and environment dialog in enhancing sustainable development (FOCAC, 2006).

The authors argue that through multidimensional dialog in the FOCAC's framework, China could constitute comprehensive access in Africa. Through the FOCAC and the involvement of the AU in the FOCAC, China's access to consensus approval is easier. So that China can probe cooperation without tough negotiations. The AU has an external strategy in several areas. With China's huge involvement in the development of the African region, the AU prioritized its strategy to China.

Within the FOCAC, both parties can establish deeper relations to strengthen the strategic partnership between Africa and China. China is Africa's biggest cooperation partner, especially in trade and investment sectors. This has positive implications for Africa's regional economic growth. Value of trade between China and Africa has continued to increase since 2000. China has implemented a special plan on trade with Africa through several approaches.

At first, the AU commission was involved as an observer in the FOCAC. In 2011, however, the AU commission became a member of the FOCAC. The FOCAC 2013-2015 action plan was dedicated to the development of the AU and Chinese relations. One of them was the establishment of the AU delegation in Beijing as a diplomatic mission. Since 2012, the AU associated into the conference and arranged action plan within the FOCAC. The AU and other regional organization in Africa committed to develop regional integration through strategic dialogue mechanism and cooperation. Several MoUs are generated by the dialog within the FOCAC. The MoU consists of consensus on building infrastructure such as railway, highway, and other infrastructure (FOCAC, 2015).

One of the AU development projects is the New Partnership for Africa's Development (NEPAD). The NEPAD was established in 2010 with the main goal to eradicate poverty, promote sustainable growth and development, integrate Africa in the world economy, and accelerate the empowerment of women. Through relations between China and the AU, China supports the implementation of the NEPAD by synergizing assistance and projects provided with development programs in Africa (Information Office of the State Council, 2013).

The FOCAC and the NEPAD have similar objectives. Both have prioritized sectors which are infrastructure, human resource development, and agriculture. Infrastructure development in Africa supported by China, go along with the strategy described in the FOCAC and the NEPAD (Wenping, 2006). China helps Africa's infrastructure programs through project assistance and funding. Road, railway, port, and energy development by building power plants and renewable development technologies are constructed by Chinese companies. Financing sector is carried out by the China Export-Import Bank. In 2000, the total cost expended by China for Africa's infrastructure development was $1 billion, and it increased to $8 billion in 2006 (Foster, Butterfield, Chen, & Pushak, 2008).

This institutional relationship is characterized by several forums and projects. One of them is the Sino-African Media Forum on Cooperation. In this forum, the importance of media to the change the socio-political landscape in Africa is discussed. The first meeting with the theme of exchange, cooperation, and development was officiated in 2012. This forum was expected to support cooperation and closeness between Africa and China through strengthening media and the press. China also provided training for African journalists (African Union, 2012). Then, the forum is held regularly. In 2016, the third meeting was convened in Beijing. The meeting agreed on the importance of media in publicizing investment opportunities both in China and Africa. Media is important to provide public awareness about the potential of partnerships within the FOCAC. Special topics discussed in the third round are media policies and regulation in China and Africa. The challenge of media platforms is to broadcast relevant issues related to Africa-China cooperation by targeting a broad audience (African Union, 2016).

In 2014, a conference involving representatives of the AU commissions, AU members, the media, businesspeople, and others were called in Addis Ababa. In that meeting, a strategic partnership between Africa and China was declared. In the AU Commission's statement, the relations between the AU and China were a win-win partnership. Ethiopian Prime Minister Hailemariam Desalegn confirmed that the strategic partnership is potential to encourage technology transfer by the establishment of Chinese industries in Africa (African Union, 2014a).

In another forum, HE Fatima Haram Acyl, the Commissioner for the Department of Trade and Industry of the African Union Commission, said that the essential key to have good growth was the implementation of pro-industry policies. The background of China's successful industrialization could deliver a constructive impact on the industrialization in Africa. With the industrialization, it will reinforce economic growth as a major supporter of poverty alleviation (African Union, 2014b).

China and Africa have significant differences in GDP. It provides special attractions for Africa to connect with China. In 2015, China's GDP exceeded $10 trillion, while the aggregated GDP of the entire African continent was only $2.6 trillion (Figure 1).

Foreign aid, investment, and loan drive an increase in African GDP. That is why Chinese assistance has implications for economic growth in Africa. Since the FOCAC was established, economic growth in Africa has increased (Figure 2).

In 2015, China committed to provide about $60 billion as funding assistance packages in the form of financial and technical assistance. The focuses of China's aid were first for infrastructure development. Second, increasing industrialization and modernization of the agricultural sector. China offered an agricultural development project by bringing 30 agricultural experts to Africa to get them achieving rural living standards. Apart from that, there were collaborative research programs between Chinese and African agricultural research institutes. Third, educational assistance such as scholarships with 30,000 government scholarships, visiting programs, and training for 1,000 professional media. Next, through the Happy Life program, China has been contributing to the reduction of poverty in Africa with a focus on

Figure 1. Comparison of GDP of China and the African region, $ billion
Source: International Monetary Fund [IMF] (2019)

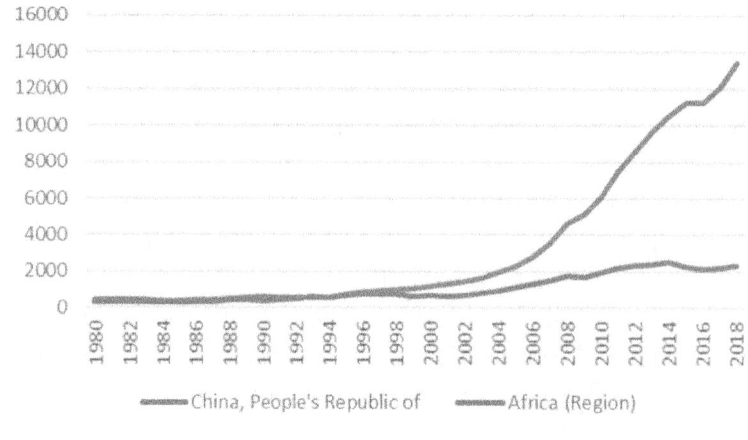

Figure 2. Comparison of economic growth in China and the African region, annual percentage change
Source: IMF (2019)

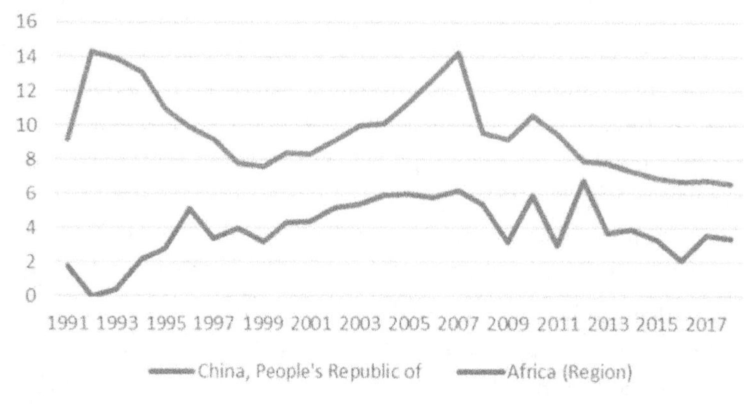

women and children. Fifth, in the security sector, China provided $60 million assistance to the AU for African standby force and African capacity for the immediate response to the crisis (African Union, 2016).

Within the form of cooperation carried out, trade between China and African region has been increasing annually. In 2010, China's total trade with Africa (exports and imports) amounted to $127 billion. The value had increased until 2017, the total trade between the two regions reached $170 billion (National Bureau of Statistics of China, 2018).

China and SADC: An Extension Partnership

The SADC is a sub-regional organization in South Africa consisting of 16 countries, namely, Angola, Botswana, Comoros, Democratic Republic of Congo, Eswatini, Lesotho, Madagascar, Malawi, Mauritius, Mozambique, Namibia, Seychelles, South Africa, Tanzania, Zambia, and Zimbabwe. SADC's main agenda includes economic and non-economic development goals. Countries in the southern part of Africa are those that struggle for economic growth. This is inseparable from the conditions and political stability in several countries in the region.

In the economic sector, the SADC approved the 2008 free trade practice. With the reduction of tariffs for intra-trade in the SADC region, it could support industrialization, expansion of employment opportunities, the opening of foreign direct investment (FDI), and increasing the quantity and quality of domestic production. The SADC has a trade and compliance monitoring mechanism to monitor free trade area activities, especially to identify and reduce non-tariff barriers.

To support economic and non-economic goals, the SADC also has inter-regional cooperation with other regions both inside Africa and outside Africa. The SADC collaborates with the AU, the NEPAD, the EAC, and the COMESA. Cooperations between these institutions aim to combine existing projects, especially in the regional security sector and economic integration. The European Union (EU) is one of SADC's partners in establishing relationships with external actors. The Economic Partnership Agreement (EPA) between the EU and the SADC can increase SADC's economic growth. In addition, the SADC has close relations with the USA and China as external powers (Southern African Development Community [SADC], 2012).

China has a special intimacy with the SADC marked by China's ambassador to Botswana assigned as China's representation in SADC. The SADC and China generally conceive special forums or create forums within the FOCAC. As of May 2018, the SADC executive secretary accepted China as a strategic partner at the meetings in Botswana. This meeting was also arranged to complete the Framework Agreement on Economy, Trade, Investment, and Technical Assistance.

In August 2018, the SADC organized the summit of Heads of States and Government on the theme "Promoting Infrastructure Development and Youth Empowerment for Sustainable Development". For completing the goals regarding that theme, the SADC invited China to contribute to the achievement of regional goals (SADC, 2016). The intense partnership between the SADC and China is in investment. The states of South Africa experience high production costs in manufacturing. Therefore, China considerably invested in mineral sector (East African Community [EAC], 2017). China not only constructed infrastructure in mining sector, but also contributed to the investment in manufactured industry.

China and the SADC do not have a set of agreements like the EU did. But the commitment to win-win cooperation between the two parties tightened by the method of cooperation that was built. China was committed to build infrastructure in South African region. China dispatched its state and private companies to carry out projects and invest in SADC member states. China contributed as much as TZS

40 billion to the development of Tanzania Zambia Railway Authority. China was also active in contributing to developing ICT in the SADC by placing its flagship multinational company such as TCL Corporation, Lenovo, and Huawei. In addition, the elimination of debt was the main key for the country to focus on economic growth. China abolished Zambia's debt amounted to $211 billion in 2006 which made Zambia's debt plummeted. In the education sector, China has built many schools in that region (Rowland, 2009). China also invests in the South African region in the leather, iron, and steel sectors, cement, malaria medicine, and so on.

The SADC and China also had the arrangement in security issues. In September 2018, both parties discussed peace and security. This meeting supported the FOCAC declaration on peace and security where China was committed to supporting the SADC as well as China supporting Africa as a whole. China is committed to providing grants as an effort to support peace and security at the SADC.

The authors argued that the cooperation between China and the SADC was the extension of China-Africa relations. There is no specific mechanism in maintaining collaboration, but the projects taken under the action plan of the FOCAC.

The EAC and China: A Progress of Economic Relation

The EAC is one of the sub-regional organizations consisting of member states in Eastern African region such as the Republics of Burundi, Kenya, Rwanda, South Sudan, the United Republic of Tanzania, and the Republic of Uganda. Since 2005, the countries have agreed to have a customs union. The custom union applied includes the agricultural and food security sectors, health, immigration and labor, industry and SME development, tourism, and trade. Since 2010, the EAC has implemented a common market to open up the wide transfer of goods, services, workers, and capital. The EAC continued to develop strengthening regional economic integration by implementing monetary union in 2013. The establishment of the East Africa Monetary Union (EAMU) agreed on the establishment of a single currency and harmonization of monetary and financial policies.

The EAC has an agreement with the EU within the EAC-EU Economic Partnership Agreement. This a kind of agreement which aims to eliminate tariff and non-tariff barriers between East Africa and Europe. But not all member states had ratified the agreement even though the negotiations have reached finalization (European Commission, 2019). Aside from the EU, the EAC has close relations with China through the agreements and forums. In establishing diplomatic relations, China's ambassador in Tanzania was assigned as China's representatives at the EAC. In November 2017, China appointed an ambassador in Tanzania (Wang Ke) as China's representative at the EAC. The function of the delegation is to facilitate China's efforts in establishing a relationship with the regional bloc (EAC, 2017). Although, the EAC also has the relation with single power such as Turkey and Germany.

The EAC and China signed a framework agreement on the economy, trade, investment, and technical cooperation in November 2011. The signing aimed to increase the volume of trade and investment of both parties. In 2011, the number of Chinese investments in the East African region exceeded $750 million (EAC, 2011). It was convinced that such agreement could reinforce the commitment of the East African region and China. Therefore, the trade value continued to increase from 2011 worth to $3.8 billion and in 2015, reached the value to $5.2 billion (Figure 3).

One of imperative forums between the EAC and China was the EAC-China High-Level Forum on Air Traffic Management (ATM). In November 2018, this forum discussed the form of cooperation and support of China to the EAC in the transfer of technology and the purchase of airplanes from China.

Figure 3. Trade value between China and EAC countries
Source: National Bureau of Statistics of China (2018)

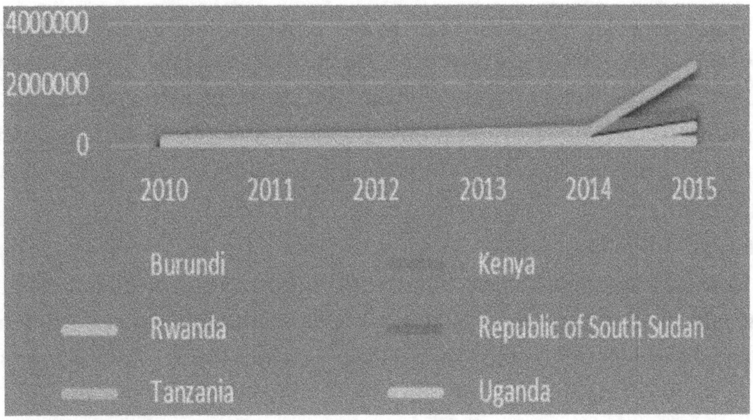

This meeting culminated the agreement of technology transfer from China to East African states. One of the projects established was the EAC Upper Flight Information Region (EAC-UFIR). In the course of meeting, several actors were involved, including Civil Aviation Administration of China (CAAC), China Electronic Group Cooperation (CETC), EAC Director for Infrastructure, Kenya Civil Aviation Authority, and so on (EAC, 2019).

In November 2018, the Chinese ambassador in Tanzania provided a grant of $200,000 to support the integration of the East African region. The signing of this assistance agreement was carried out at the EAC headquarters in Tanzania. The intended support was for infrastructure development so that the region's economy could continue to mature (EAC, 2018).

In 2018, the EAC claimed that it did not approve of a FTA with China. This FTA is intended to provide a booster to trade between the two sides. However, as a principal reason for rejecting FTA, the EAC explained the importance of protecting domestic industries. Intra-regional trade in East Africa is adequately low. Several projects of infrastructure are still constructed with the involvement from external states. The governments of the region criticize that infrastructure should utilize local products for raw material. Nonetheless, China dominated the supply chain of materials. Consequently, the EAC should evaluate common external tariff to bolster intra-regional trade.

Comprehensive Relation Between ECOWAS and China

The ECOWAS is a regional economic integration consisted of the countries in the West African region. The ECOWAS member countries have different backgrounds and histories in colonialism. English, French, and Portuguese are the three official languages used in the ECOWAS. Before colonialism, the West African region was hosted to many empires of major empires such as Ghana, Mali Songhai, Wolof, Oyo, Benin, and Kanem Bornu.

As an economic community, the ECOWAS aims to promote economic cooperation and regional integration as a tool for accelerating economic development in West Africa. Regional integration is the most feasible and appropriate tool in achieving and accelerating sustainable development of the states in the West African region. The ECOWAS was established with the aim of encouraging economic and political cooperation between the countries in the West African region. This is in line with the efforts of countries in the West African region in pushing the diverse dimensions of socio-cultural development in West Africa. Therefore, the ECOWAS must be able to become a building block needed as an effort to build peace and security in the West African region. Besides the ECOWAS designed to improve people's living conditions in the West African region, to ensure the rate of growth, and to create an economic and conducive environment to economic development and integration. In 1976, Cape Verde, one of the two Lusophone countries, joined the ECOWAS, while Mauritania withdrew from the ECOWAS in December in 2000 (Economic Community of West African States [ECOWAS], 2019).

China maintains good relations and cooperation with twelve ECOWAS member states except for Senegal, Gambia, Burkina Faso, and Liberia. The relationship was established through bilateral cooperation between China and twelve countries. In the early 1990s, the Chinese government has expressed its support in international forums such as the UN regarding various kinds of efforts made by the ECOWAS in restoring peace in the West African region. In July 1998, China's deputy foreign minister, Ji Peiding attended the UN summit on Sierra Leone. In a meeting of the 2nd UN Security Council foreign minister in Africa, Tang Jiaxuan, the Chinese foreign minister called on the international community to respect and better support the efforts made by the ECOWAS regional organization in preventing and resolving conflicts. In his speech, Tang Jiaxuan also called on the international community to provide assistance to West Africa, both in the form of money and logistics needed for victims in West Africa.

China appreciated the efforts made by the ECOWAS to resolve conflicts in Sierra Leone. In August 2000, China chose to resolve the special court assistance in Sierra Leone on the UN security council at the request of the Sierra Leone government. China attached great importance carried out by the ECOWAS. China ready to join international community in positive efforts that the ECOWAS tried to push especially in terms of promoting economic integration and maintaining peace in the West African region.

In 2011, China invested $15 billion in West Africa. The grant is for supporting the economic projects in 50 countries with more than 2,000 investors. The partnership began in 2008 at ECOWAS-Beijing economic and commercial forum. At the forum, China and the ECOWAS together discussed the interests of both sides in various sectors such as the food sector in terms of agriculture. Some ECOWAS member states that directly benefited from the cooperative relations were Ghana, Nigeria, and Sierra Leone.

In 2012, the second China-ECOWAS forum was held. The two sides agreed to strengthen relations in the context of foreign direct investment. The Chinese government together with the ECOWAS member countries are engaged in strengthening the relations by signing a framework in several fields of cooperation as a form of increasing economic cooperation between China and the ECOWAS. The focus of the cooperation is the increase in trade, investment, and technical cooperation between China and the ECOWAS. By signing the agreement, China and the ECOWAS have made a major agreement in strengthening the relationship. China also has a strong commitment to supporting integration in the African region. The ECOWAS is one of the strongest regional blocs that applies market policy and its member country has a strong commitment to development in the West African region. It is important for China to be fully committed to the ECOWAS countries in creating economic activities and driving the pace of regional economic growth with the aim to improve the welfare of the people in each member country. Therefore, both China and the ECOWAS have a shared determination especially in improving and building infrastructure in the West African region, both transnational and trans-regional infrastructure (Economic and Commercial Section of the Consulate General of the People's Republic of China in Lagos, 2012).

Certain large Chinese companies are placed in West Africa both in the food and energy fields such as the Standard Plastics Industry in Nigeria, Hongkong Huachang Group, Chongqing Overseas Labor Company Ltd. China's presence at the ECOWAS helps in encouraging and creating strategic and competitive markets.

On April 22nd, 2016, China's ambassador for Niger and the representatives for the ECOWAS met in Abuja. During the meeting, the two sides exchanged their views on future China-ECOWAS relations. China supports and respects the important role of the ECOWAS in maintaining peace and security and promoting economic development and regional integration in West Africa. Chinese relations and the ECOWAS are proceeded well by forming partnerships that are profitable for both countries (Embassy of the People's Republic of China in the Federal Republic of Nigeria, 2016).

There was a new agreement between Chinese construction entrepreneurs and the ECOWAS. The ECOWAS member states needed infrastructure development to support economic development in the West African region. In the form of collaboration, the Trans-West African Coastal Highway and the Trans-West African Railway were involved. On January 20, 2016, the ECOWAS commission signed five memoranda of understanding with the CGC Overseas Construction Group (CGCOC) in Abuja. In this agreement, China and the ECOWAS agreed to build a road network in the West African region that connects twelve countries from Mauritania to Nigeria. In addition to highways, China and the ECOWAS also agreed to build a railroad network that links several countries such as Benin, Burkina Faso, Ivory Coast, Ghana, Niger, Nigeria, and Togo. Other facilities discussed in the collaboration were the construction of telecommunications infrastructure facilities in West Africa, as well as cooperation in the field of regional aviation in the West African region and the construction of a building for the new ECOWAS office. Economic cooperation and investments that have been established between China and the ECOWAS have an impact on the increasing investment climate in West African countries. Until 2017, the partnership between China and Ghana has gone into an economic cooperation agreement related to Chinese exports in Ghana. Whereas, Nigeria has an important agreement with China regarding oil refineries (Pirolli, 2014).

Trade between China and West Africa have special characteristics where West African countries export a lot of raw materials while China exports manufactured goods. But the technology transfer obtained through Chinese investment provides a structural transformation in West Africa's export-import activities. In 2010, although raw material export figures were still high, the West African countries were able to export their manufactured goods to China (Aidehou, Yang, & Ehikioya, 2014).

China imports raw materials from West African countries (Figure 4). Generally, China needs to import crude oil. However, the West African region has diverse natural resources which are also needed by China to meet its national needs, especially for industrial needs. China gets oil from Guinea. In addition, China imports wood from Guinea and Liberia. China also needs cotton from several countries such as Benin, Burkina Faso, Mali, and Ivory Coast. Iron and metals are also commodities needed by China from Nigeria (Broadman, Isik, Plaza, Ye, & Yoshino, 2006).

China also exports technology, machinery, and equipment for transportation in all countries in West Africa (Figure 5).

The purpose of building facilities and technology is to ensure that the area can become a place for China to open factories and companies. Thus, improving technology in West Africa, it will be in line with the increasing development of business empires in China.

Figure 4. Export data by commodities from West African region to China, $ thousand
Source: World Trade Integrated Solution [WITS] (2019)

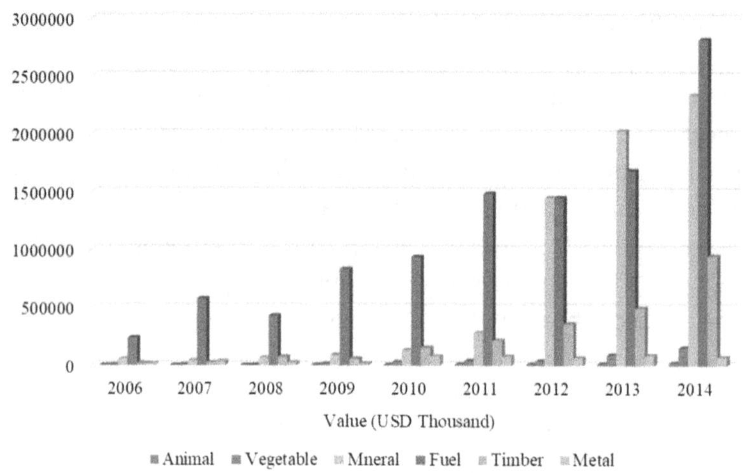

Figure 5. Export value of transportation, machine, and transportation equipment from China to West Africa
Source: WITS (2019)

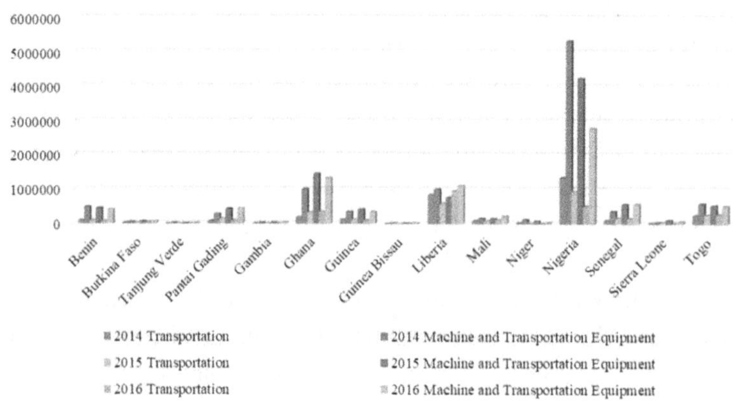

Interregionalism Approach

Regionalism is the study which does not only discuss how to build regional integration and improve institutions in the region, but also discuss how the relationship between the region with external factors. Regionalism also discusses how the region relates to external parties or other regions. Interregionalism is a situation or process in which two regions or more interact with each other. In other sense, inter-regionalism can be said to be region-region interactions.

After the Cold War, regional organizations increased their regional relations to balance their institutions at the global level. Therefore, the system formed is a multilayered system of global governance. This system proved the existence of international governance that is regulated by many actors ranging from countries, regions, globally, to the provisions agreed between regions (Valle, 2008). This phenomenon then strengthens the amount of inter-regional cooperations.

According to Hänggi (2000), interregionalism is divided into three forms. First is the relationship between regional groups. The first form leads to a dialogue between one regional group and the others. One example of the first form of interregionalism is a dialogue carried out by the European Community and the ASEAN. The second form is bi-regional and trans-regional relations. What distinguishes it from the first form, this second form does not only carry out inter-regional dialogue but has formed the membership even though the new institutions are a combination of the two. An example of regional relations is the Asia-Europe Meeting (ASEM) while the example of trans-regional relations is the East Asia – Latin America Forum (EALAF). The EALAF consists of thirteen Asian countries, twelve Latin American countries, Australia, and New Zealand. So that the EALAF is said to be a trans-regional relationship because it's country's participation exceeds two regions. The third form is the relationship between regional groups with single power. This relation explains the hybrid form where there is a dominant state such as the EU and China, the EU and the USA, and so on in cooperation with a region (Hänggi, 2000).

There are four forms of inter-regionalism, namely inter-regionalism, trans-regionalism, quasi-inter-regionalism, and mega-regions. Inter-regionalism is a general form of relations carried out by two regions, either regional groups or regional integration, that has become an institution. Trans-regionalism is an inter-regional dialogue that also involves non-state actors such as corporations and non-governmental organizations (NGOs). Quasi-inter-regionalism is the relationship of regional organizations or regional groups with other countries outside the region. In general, the countries invited to cooperate are the dominant countries in other regions. While mega-regions are large regions that are connected to each other like Asia-Pacific Cooperation (APEC) (Baert, Scaramangli, & Soderbaum, 2014).

The functions of inter-regionalism include balancing, band wagoning, institution building, rationalizing, agenda setting, identity building, stabilizing, and development. Inter-regionalism's functions can be grouped into three main perspectives: neorealism, institutional liberalism, and social constructivism. The first function is balancing. Balancing is an effort to balance the institutions. This function is in the realist and institutionalist argument where the formation of cooperation between the regions to compete with other forces or other institutions. When looking at external roles in the African region, China is not a single player. Colonialism formed a close relationship between African countries with former colonizers such as France and the UK. The contribution of former colonial countries is still significant for Africa, such as the example of how France played a role in peace conflict in Mali. The EU, through the EPA framework with the ACP countries (Africa, Caribbean, and Pacific) which has been ratified by a number of countries in Africa is a match for China in controlling the market in Africa. Otherwise, the SADC has close relations with the USA toward agreements. China's involvement in the SADC gave a new alternative for the SADC to develop.

Band wagoning is a way to fuse a state or region with other external actors with the aim of strengthening their power. China merged to form a new institution in Africa called the FOCAC. This has an impact on both parties in terms of strengthening each power. For China, involvement in African regionalism could change the perception of African states. African countries put great sympathy to China. Most of the African states broke diplomatic relation with Taiwan and re-established diplomatic relation with China. Lately, in 2016 and 2018, Gambia and Burkina Faso did that (Solomon, 2018).

Institution building explains the function of cooperation between regions to build strong institutions. This function explains how to establish structures and establish norms in the collaboration process. Institutions must be able to facilitate inter-regional dialogue activities. As a consequence of inter-regional negotiations is to make intra-regional institutions stronger. This function is in line with social constructivism wherein strengthening institutions along with strengthening norms and values within the institution. The FOCAC is a forum built by the African region and China. The FOCAC is an initiative of African countries themselves to establish a forum that facilitates dialogue between China and Africa. The FOCAC holds regular meetings every three years to discuss diplomacy, trade, security, and investment activities. In addition, the dialogue between China and several sub-regional organizations in Africa also has implications for strengthening these institutions. As in the ECOWAS, China provides assistance for the development of the ECOWAS building in March 2018 (ECOWAS, 2018).

Rationalizing explains the importance of the agreements agreed between regional groups as a solution to the ineffectiveness of the agreements at the multilateral or global level. Mechanisms for coordination, cooperation, and negotiation in inter-regional dialogue can create new regulations that are mutually agreed upon. The activity can also facilitate multilateral issues. As explained earlier, relation with China is an alternative for Africa despite engaging the West. Moreover, the characteristics of China in providing loans and assistance are very different from other multilateral systems. China did not pay attention to the country's domestic political system which was invited to cooperate.

Agenda setting is a derivative function of multilateral cooperation. This function explains how objectives at the international level are adopted within the framework of inter-regionalism. The agenda which is generally discussed in inter-regional dialogue forums includes good governance, liberal democracy, and human rights. Seeing from the forums held, this relationship still places universal value as agenda-setting in dialogue and discussion. Such as the placement of peace and security on the media forum between China and the AU.

Identity building means the existence of solidarity or shared identity as a result of cooperation among different regions. China and Africa have different identities. However, through long term cooperation built, China has a moral duty for Africa. Moral duty was imposed on China as solidarity to the African community. This moral duty made China labeled a friendly state (Delgado, 2015).

Stabilizing and development explains the functions of creating prosperity and security for both parties. In addition, this function shows how collaboration implicate to economic growth (Baert et al., 2014). Both China and Africa had an increase in economic growth. This was also caused by the trade volume that is increased every year.

SOLUTIONS AND RECOMMENDATIONS

Looking at some of the above facts, the authors see some important points from the inter-regional cooperation between China and Africa. First, cooperation starts from the same interests that is the desire to build an economy through mutually beneficial cooperation. The built-in economic cooperation is interesting because, first, it came from the same problem in economic development. It looks like a coalition of economies to build a common economic power, in the name of cooperation among developing or less developed countries. On the one hand, Africa requires China in the context of economic assistance or cooperation that does not require a change of domestic political or democratization, which is, of course, difficult to obtain from Western countries where the majority of them are democratic ones. On the other hand, China requires the support of African countries in international politics which is to provide support to Chinese representatives in the UN including in the context of Taiwan issues. Relationships on the basis of the equation of these conditions and situations become a major capital of China-Africa economic cooperation. Second, both sides meet some elements of the concept of inter-regionalism but with modifications or adjustments. They also have a commitment to build a joint institution in strengthening cooperation in the form of institutional building or institutionalization of the cooperation. They also follow the agenda-setting stage, but in this context, again due to the equation of the situation and conditions, the agenda that is given is the agenda which strongly characterizes the situation of their condition. Therefore, issues about democracy, the environment, and human rights, for example, are tailored to their situation and condition, or in other words according to their perspective rather than following the Western model. Most likely, in the Western view, the cooperation organizations built by China and Africa are considered to be only concerned with economic interests and are less concerned with other aspects (politics and democracy), but for China and Africa, the agenda was constructed from their own interests and adapted to the situation and conditions so that it did not conform to the Western perspective.

Thirdly, interregional cooperation conducted by China and Africa seems to be loose or not rigid. This precisely illustrates the characteristic of Chinese behavior in its international relations. China's foreign relations principle is peaceful coexistence. It is translated with the cooperation and prioritizing without mutually interference with each country's domestic affairs. From the Chinese perspective, the interregional cooperation with Africa is seen as mutually beneficial cooperation, without pressure and for mutual benefit in a peaceful way. The most important of these is the economic cooperation that provides advantages for China and Africa, and the African countries that work together are not forced to do this cooperation. Although between China and Africa has a problem in domestic politics, for example, but it is considered not a problem in this cooperation, it is possible that the domestic problem should not mutually interfere with each other. These adjustments are the characteristics of Chinese international behavior which may be appropriate or resemble a Western look, but fundamentally different principles, or better known as "with Chinese characteristic". The use of this term as a differentiator from the Western perspective. This addition of Chinese characteristics demonstrates the existence of something different, unique, and distinctive from China in the application of a fundamental policy to the same concept of Western view.

FUTURE RESEARCH DIRECTIONS

Future research directions in the area of China and Africa should be focused on translating academic work into policy briefs, op-eds, and long-form articles. China's natural resource-backed loans raise questions about the continent's future and its capacity for sustainable development which require thorough study. Studies of China's Africa strategy (or lack thereof) have been overwhelmingly focused on China's economic interests in Africa, the role played by Chinese government and companies, and the economic and social impacts of such activities on the ground. The study of the role of African countries in the economic development of China is also needed.

CONCLUSION

Interregional cooperation between China and Africa could not be divided from the history of their relations and international politic. International politics has carried them in one group on the basis of the same situation and conditions. It is becoming an important capital in establishing economic cooperation between them. China and Africa's interregional cooperation was originally an alternative for Africa when it was difficult to establish cooperation and trust from the West in relation to their domestic political situation. On the other hand, it also an alternative for China to get support for its international relations. However, this alternative is next not only an alternative to difficulty but also an alternative in an outlook for cooperation between countries. That is, if initially, cooperation with China is as an alternative because of the situation, in its development, this cooperation is as an alternative model of cooperation that has a difference with the Western model that has been used in inter-state economic cooperation. The term "with Chinese characteristic" not only shows a model built by China but also as an identity, a typical thing that distinguishes with the model of economic cooperation that has been presented and it is sourced to the principle of China's peaceful coexistence. Finally, the interregional cooperation between China and Africa demonstrates a higher level of confidence from China to introduce alternative concepts built precisely from their own experiences.

REFERENCES

African Union. (2012). *The First Sino-African Media Forum on Cooperation – Beijing, China*. Retrieved October 5, 2019, from https://au.int/en/newsevents/20120822-0

African Union. (2014a). *Countries in Africa and China Renew Their Commitment to Jointly Eliminating Poverty – Africa-China Poverty Reduction and Development Conference*. Retrieved October 5, 2019, from https://au.int/en/newsevents/14665/countries-africa-and-china-renew-their-commitment-jointly-eliminating-poverty

African Union. (2014b). *Statement by the Chairperson of the African Union Commission*. Addis Ababa: African Union.

African Union. (2016). *The 3rd Forum on China-Africa Media Cooperation, Beijing, People's Republic of China, 21 June 2016*. Retrieved October 5, 2019, from https://au.int/en/newsevents/30802/3rd-forum-china-africa-media-cooperation-beijing-people-s-republic-china

Aidehou, K. C. L., Yang, S. Y., & Ehikioya, B. (2014). Ecowas Member Countries Trade with China: Analysis of Structural Transformation. *International Journal of Innovation and Applied Studies*, *8*(2), 756–769.

Baert, F., Scaramangli, T., & Soderbaum, F. (Eds.). (2014). *Intersecting Regionalism. Regions, Global Governance and The EU*. London, UK: Springer. doi:10.1007/978-94-007-7566-4

Broadman, H. G., Isik, G., Plaza, S., Ye, X., & Yoshino, Y. (2006). *Africa's Silk Road: China and India's New Economic Frontier*. Washington, DC: World Bank. doi:10.1596/978-0-8213-6835-0

China-Africa Development Fund. (2013). General Introduction. Beijing: China-Africa Development Fund.

Delgado, D. L. (2015). Discourse, Identity, and International Development Cooperation: China, Africa and FOCAC. *Asia-Pacific Social Science Review*, *15*(2), 1–18.

East African Community. (2011). *Press Release: EAC and China Sign Framework Agreement to Boost Trade, Investment*. Retrieved October 5, 2019, from https://assets.aspeninstitute.org/content/uploads/files/content/images/ghd/China_EAC_Press_Release_11.17.2011.pdf

East African Community. (2017). *China Accredits Envoy to EAC Bloc.* Retrieved October 5, 2019, from https://www.eac.int/press-releases/151-international-relations/899-china-accredits-envoy-to-eac-bloc

East African Community. (2018). *EAC, China Sign Financing Agreement.* Retrieved October 5, 2019, from https://www.eac.int/press-releases/155-resource-mobilization/1293-eac,-china-sign-financing-agreement

East African Community. (2019). *EAC-China Forum on Air Traffic Management Concludes in Arusha.* Retrieved October 5, 2019, from https://www.eac.int/press-releases/629-1106-662-eac-china-forum-on-air-traffic-management-concludes-in-arusha

Economic and Commercial Section of the Consulate General of the People's Republic of China in Lagos. (2012). *China, ECOWAS Move to Strengthen Ties.* Retrieved October 5, 2019, from http://ng2.mofcom.gov.cn/article/bilateralvisits/201212/20121208488755.shtml

Economic Community of West African States. (2018). *ECOWAS Signs MOU with China for the Construction of the New ECOWAS Commission Headquarters.* Retrieved October 5, 2019, from https://www.ecowas.int/ecowas-signs-mou-with-china-for-the-construction-of-the-new-ecowas-commission-headquarters/

Economic Community of West African States. (2019). *History.* Retrieved October 5, 2019, from https://www.ecowas.int/about-ecowas/history/

Embassy of the People's Republic of China in the Federal Republic of Nigeria. (2016). *Gu Xiaojie Met with New President of ECOWAS Commission.* Retrieved October 5, 2019, from http://ng.china-embassy.org/eng/zt/ecowas/t1358045.htm

European Commission. (2019). *East African Community (EAC).* Retrieved October 5, 2019, from https://ec.europa.eu/trade/policy/countries-and-regions/regions/eac/

Forum on China-Africa Cooperation. (2006). *Forum on China-Africa Cooperation. Beijing Action Plan (2007-2009).* Retrieved October 5, 2019, from https://www.focac.org/eng/zywx_1/zywj/t280369.htm

Forum on China-Africa Cooperation. (2015). *The Forum on China-Africa Cooperation. Johannesburg Action Plan (2016-2018).* Retrieved October 5, 2019, from https://www.focac.org/eng/zywx_1/zywj/t1327961.htm

Foster, V., Butterfield, W., Chen, C., & Pushak, N. (2008). *Building Bridges: China's Growing Role as Infrastructure Financier for Sub-Saharan Africa*. Washington, DC: International Bank for Reconstruction and Development.

Hänggi, H. (2000). Interregionalism: Empirical and Theoretical Perspectives. Paper presented at the *Workshop "Dollars, Democracy and Trade: External Influence on Economic Integration in the Americas"*. Los Angeles.

Information Office of the State Council. (2013). *China-Africa Economic and Trade Cooperation (2013).* Beijing, China: Information Office of the State Council.

International Monetary Fund. (2019). *GDP, Current Prices.* Retrieved October 5, 2019, from https://www.imf.org/external/datamapper/NGDPD@WEO/CHN/AFQ

National Bureau of Statistics of China. (2018). *China Statistical Yearbook*. Beijing, China: National Bureau of Statistics of China.

Pirolli, M. (2014). *ECOWAS: From Economic Cooperation and Development to Security. A Revision of the Mandate of Progress towards Future Rules?* Retrieved October 5, 2019, from http://mediterraneanaffairs.com/ecowas-from-economic-cooperation-and-development-to-security-a-revision-of-the-mandate-or-progress-towards-future-rules-part-2/

Rowland, D. B. (2009). *U.S.-Chinese Relation with the Southern African Development Community (SADC) Countries: How It Can Make A Difference*. Washington, DC: Georgetown University.

Solomon, S. (2018). *Once Influential in Africa, Taiwan Loses All but One Ally*. Retrieved October 5, 2019, from https://www.globalsecurity.org/wmd/library/news/taiwan/2018/taiwan-180526-voa01.htm

Southern African Development Community. (2012). *About SADC*. Retrieved October 5, 2019, from https://www.sadc.int/about-sadc

Southern African Development Community. (2016). *China and the SADC Secretariat Commit to Enhance Cooperation*. Retrieved October 5, 2019, from https://www.sadc.int/news-events/news/china-and-sadc-secretariat-commit-enhance-cooperation/

Valle, V. M. (2008). *A Case Study of the European Union and Mercosur*. Mexico: University of Mexico.

Wenping, H. (2006). Engaging with NEPAD: A View from China. Johannesburg, South Africa: Royal African Society; South African Institute of International Affairs.

World Trade Integrated Solution. (2019). *China Product Exports by Country*. Retrieved October 5, 2019, from https://wits.worldbank.org/CountryProfile/en/Country/CHN/Year/LTST/TradeFlow/Export/Partner/by-country/Product/Total

ADDITIONAL READING

Ajakaiye, O., & Kaplinsky, R. (2009). China in Africa: A Relationship in Transition. *European Journal of Development Research, 21*(4), 479–484. doi:10.1057/ejdr.2009.30

Asche, H., & Schüller, M. (2008). *China's Engagement in Africa: Opportunities and Risks for Development*. Eschborn: GTZ.

Burke, C., Corkin, L., & Tay, N. (2007). *China's Engagement of Africa: Preliminary Scoping of African Case Studies, Angola, Ethiopia, Gabon, Uganda, South Africa, and Zambia*. Stellenbosch: University of Stellenbosch.

Cornelissen, S., & Taylor, I. (2000). The Political Economy of China and Japan's Relationship with Africa: A Comparative Perspective. *The Pacific Review, 13*(4), 615–633. doi:10.1080/095127400455350

Goldstein, A., Pinaud, N., Reisen, H., & Chen, X. (2006). The Rise of China and India: What's. In *It for Africa?* Paris: Organization for Economic Co-operation and Development.

Kurlantzick, J. (2006). *Beijing's Safari: China's Move into Africa and Its Implications for Aid, Development, and Governance*. Washington, DC: Carnegie Endowment for International Peace.

McCormick, D. (2008). China and India as Africa's New Donors: The Impact of Aid on Development. *Review of African Political Economy*, *35*(1), 73–92. doi:10.1080/03056240802011501

Mohan, G., & Tan-Mullins, M. (2009). Chinese Migrants in Africa as New Agents of Development? An Analytical Framework. *European Journal of Development Research*, *21*(4), 588–605. doi:10.1057/ejdr.2009.22

Van Dijk, M. P. (2011). *The New Presence of China in Africa*. Amsterdam: Amsterdam University Press.

Winters, L. A., & Yusuf, S. (Eds.). (2007). *Dancing with Giants, China, India and the Global Economy*. Washington, DC: World Bank. doi:10.1596/978-0-8213-6749-0

KEY TERMS AND DEFINITIONS

African Union (AU): An organization of African states established with an aim to encourage economic development and political stability through increased cooperation between its members.

Belt and Road Initiative (BRI): A global development strategy adopted by the Chinese government involving infrastructure development and investments in over 150 countries and international organizations in Asia, Europe, Africa, the Middle East, and the Americas.

East African Community: An intergovernmental group formed in 1967, which includes Kenya, Uganda, Burundi, Rwanda and Tanzania, that promotes social and economic cooperation.

Economic Community of West African States (ECOWAS): A regional political and economic union of fifteen countries located in West Africa, which mission is to promote economic integration in industry, international transport, telecommunications, energy, agriculture, natural resources, international trade, monetary and financial, social, and cultural themes.

Forum on China-Africa Cooperation (FOCAC): An official forum between the People's Republic of China and all states in Africa (with the exception of Eswatini).

Interregionalism: A situation or process in which two regions or more interact with each other. In another sense, inter-regionalism can be said to be region-region interactions.

Southern African Development Community (SADC): An inter-governmental organization which goal is to strengthen socio-economic cooperation and integration as well as political and security cooperation among the countries of southern Africa.

Chapter 4
China and the Eurasian Economic Union:
A Future of Agricultural Trade in BRICS+ Format

Vasilii Erokhin
https://orcid.org/0000-0002-3745-5469
Harbin Engineering University, China

Gao Tianming
Harbin Engineering University, China

ABSTRACT

This chapter gives a general overview of current integration processes which affect the countries in the regions of Europe and Asia, with a special focus on China and its Belt and Road initiative, from one side, Russia and its integration initiative of the Eurasian Economic Union, from another side, and BRICS as an umbrella format of collaboration between China, Russia, and other countries. In the case of trade in food and agricultural products, the chapter covers the two major rising economic powers with the involvement of China and Russia which are the Eurasian Economic Union and BRICS. The authors interpret their developments in relation to the modification of existing approaches to agricultural trade and establishing food security in the BRICS+ format.

INTRODUCTION

Until the present time, the countries of BRICS and the Eurasian Economic Union (EAEU) have been focusing on their domestic developments, but in order to be competitive on the global market, they will have to face new global challenges. Integration gains momentum. Neither single country, even such giants as the USA or China, is able to compete. Investigations have to be directed on the exploration of economic and trade cooperation of BRICS and EAEU countries between themselves and with the international community (Hartwell, 2016).

DOI: 10.4018/978-1-7998-1730-7.ch004

Until recently, there have been many studies related to the integration of BRICS or EAEU economies. Radulescu, Panait, and Voica (2014) analyzed the importance of the BRICS group as representatives of emerging countries in the global economy; Rasoulinezhad and Jabalameli (2018) explored the similarities of trade integrations in the BRICS member countries in the previous decades; Shaygani, Abolhasani Hastiani, Ghaffari, Sadeghi Shahdani, and Fadaee (2015) studied the effects of imposed exchange rate arrangements on the trade volume of BRICS countries using the generalized gravity model; Nashier (2015) examined the integration among the stock markets of BRICS and found evidence for both the short-term static and long-term dynamic integration between the stock markets. Mostafa and Mahmood (2018) analysed the history and evolution of the EEU as well as its success, challenges, and prospects; Dragneva and Wolczuk (2017) explained the political origins of the EAEU, its architecture and its progress; Vinokurov (2017) reviewed the state of Eurasian institutions, the single market for goods and services, the state of mutual trade and investment flows among member states, ongoing work to eliminate non-tariff barriers, and problems pertaining to the efficient coordination of macroeconomic policies. Few studies, however, addressed the potential convergence between BRICS and EAEU formats, particularly, in various BRICS+ formats with deeper involvement of Russia, China, and other countries into parallel integration processes. Russia is the country which somehow links BRICS and EAEU being a member of both alliances. China is an ultimate engine, a driving force of economic development and integration in the region. China has recently proposed the "five connections" development plan (policy exchange, road network, trade talks, currency circulation, and people-to-people friendship), which encourages cooperation at practical and cultural levels. China's recent Belt and Road Initiative is meant to integrate the economies of Eurasia through physical and cyber-connectivity, energy pipelines, industrial parks, and smart cities. The plan involves more than 60 countries, representing a third of the world's total economy and more than half the global population (Mariani, 2013).

BRICS and the Eurasian Economic Union should become the core pillars of a new international order, defined by a multipolar world with a greater role of China (Fedorenko, 2015). The EAEU is primarily a Russian initiative, but in 2015, China and Russia commenced talks to harmonize the two initiatives (Kukushkina & Ostrovskaya, 2013; Linn & Tiomkin, 2006). The initiative is not without its challenges. In the case of trade in agricultural product and food, the chapter summarizes the overview of the major competitive advantages and existing weaknesses of the EAEU economies, particularly, Russia, and BRICS economies, particularly, China in their integration into the global market (Golam & Monowar, 2018). While China is not a member of the EAEU, it is an interested observer. Should the EAEU sign Free Trade deals with China, it will have created an effective Free Trade Zone in the China-Mongolia-Russia Economic Corridor stretching from North-West China to Moscow covering all points in between (Makarov & Sokolova, 2016; Kembayev, 2016). There are signs this could occur. The EAEU has already signed off an FTA with Vietnam while India has also just agreed on an FTA, mainly concentrating on the textiles area.

This may link the rapidly growing markets in Asia and Europe's economies, mature, rich in industrial and technological achievements. At the same time, this will allow BRICS countries and EAEU to become more commercially viable in the competition for investors, for creating new jobs, for advanced enterprises. Although this scenario may take some time to develop, the future for the EAEU-BRICS relations in a BRICS+ format is feasible.

BACKGROUND

Eurasian Economic Union

The Eurasian Economic Union originated from the Commonwealth of Independent States in 2000 and was transformed into the EAEU in 2014. EAEU was established for effective promotion of free movement of goods, services, capital, and labor between participating countries (Armenia, Belarus, Kazakhstan, Kyrgyzstan, and Russia), and as a Central Asian version of the European Union. While the EAEU may appear small in terms of its members, it still represents about 183 million people spread amongst the vast territory from the Baltic Sea on the West to the Pacific Ocean on the East.

Participating countries are Armenia, Belarus, Kazakhstan, Kyrgyzstan, and Russia. Russia currently provides about 1.0% of the world food export and 2.7% of the world food import. Over the recent decades, Russia has been a net importer of agricultural commodities and food. Moreover, the share of the country in the total world food import has been growing since the very fall of the Soviet Union. Food Foreign-Trade-to-GDP ratio has been growing over two decades onwards. The outrun growth of the Food Import-to-GDP ratio in comparison with the Food Export-to-GDP ratio should be noted. Even in 2014, when Russia's domestic food market experienced two tendencies, unfavorable for import (depreciation of food import because of the devaluation of the national currency and import ban, introduced in August 2014), Import/Production ratio remained above 43% (Table 1).

Russia, Belarus, and Kazakhstan are leaders in the EAEU on agricultural production (Figure 1). Belarus increases its agricultural production quite rapidly, while Kazakhstan slows down. Agricultural production in Kazakhstan is rather seasonal, and very much dependent on climatic conditions and yield of wheat (Kudaibergenova, 2016), while Belarus is rather more diversified. Agricultural production in Armenia is growing, but the country is not self-sufficient. Trade balance in food and agricultural commodities is negative. Import/Production ratio is 0.43 in 2017 which means that import comprises about 43% of total agricultural production of the country.

Belarus is the country which focuses on agricultural production the most among other countries of the EAEU. Volume of agricultural production have been growing rapidly starting from 1995 and increased up to $4.2 billion in 2017. Being the leading food producer, Belarus is also a leading food exporter among the four countries under consideration. The country substantially increased its export in 2014, when Russia imposed a ban on import of agricultural products from certain countries of the world, and deliveries started to go through Belarus. Agricultural export from Belarus has been growing steadily, while Kazakhstan's export has been fluctuating in parallel with production of wheat (Figure 2).

Russia, Kazakhstan, and Belarus (in 1995-2005 and 2015) are all net importers of food and agricultural products. Belarus increases its import from the EU, process raw agricultural commodities, or just repacks food products, labels them and then export them to Russia – this is the way how food products of the EU origin come to Russia in circumvention of the food ban, being formally produced in Belarus. Belarus is the best performer among other EAEU countries in relation to food independence. Being heavily dependent on import deliveries of food products and agricultural commodities in the mid-1990s, the country was able to decrease its dependency.

Kazakhstan, on the contrary, turned to become a consumer-oriented country – import deliveries of food are growing, trade balance is negative, and Import/Production ratio is rather high – 0.43 in 2017, which means that above 40% of food on the domestic market is of foreign origin. Kyrgyzstan is more or less in the same position as Kazakhstan – growing deficit in trade in agricultural commodities and food

Table 1. Agricultural production and trade in EAEU economies in 1995-2017, $ million

Economy / parameter	1995	2000	2005	2010	2015	2016	2017
Armenia							
Production	523	444	935	1,575	1,818	1,729	1,723
Export	34	31	111	165	377	475	562
Import	220	198	280	722	661	613	736
Trade turnover	254	229	391	887	1,038	1,088	1,298
Trade balance	-186	-167	-169	-557	-284	-138	-174
Import/GDP	0.42	0.45	0.30	0.46	0.36	0.35	0.43
Export/GDP	0.07	0.07	0.12	0.10	0.21	0.27	0.33
Belarus							
Production	2,193	1,282	2,584	5,089	3,547	3,291	4,231
Export	89	495	1,319	3,191	4,169	4,016	5,035
Import	664	1,027	1,562	2,748	4,278	3,830	4,627
Trade turnover	753	1,522	2,881	5,939	8,447	7,846	9,662
Trade balance	-575	-532	-243	443	-109	186	408
Import/GDP	0.30	0.80	0.60	0.54	1.21	1.16	1.09
Export/GDP	0.04	0.39	0.51	0.63	1.18	1.22	1.19
Kazakhstan							
Production	2,535	1,484	3,639	6,678	8,686	6,254	7,064
Export	518	87	669	1,934	2,117	2,105	2,359
Import	375	217	1,131	2,207	3,125	2,703	3,015
Trade turnover	893	304	1,800	4,141	5,242	4,808	5,374
Trade balance	143	-130	-462	-273	-1,008	-598	-656
Import/GDP	0.15	0.15	0.31	0.33	0.36	0.43	0.43
Export/GDP	0.20	0.06	0.18	0.29	0.24	0.34	0.33
Kyrgyzstan							
Production	607	468	701	837	939	874	933
Export	88	67	93	312	144	149	193
Import	96	80	166	544	567	458	638
Trade turnover	184	147	259	856	711	607	831
Trade balance	-8	-13	-73	-232	-423	-309	-445
Import/GDP	0.16	0.17	0.24	0.65	0.60	0.52	0.68
Export/GDP	0.14	0.14	0.13	0.37	0.15	0.17	0.21
Russia							
Production	26,368	14,502	32,524	51,004	56,482	53,745	63,327
Export	1,382	1,286	3,860	7,506	15,996	16,845	20,507
Import	12,535	8,379	19,346	34,658	24,285	23,282	27,756
Trade turnover	13,917	9,665	23,206	42,164	40,281	40,127	48,263
Trade balance	-11,153	-7,093	-15,486	-27,152	-8,289	-6,437	-7,249

continues on following page

Table 1. Continued

Economy / parameter	1995	2000	2005	2010	2015	2016	2017
Import/GDP	0.48	0.58	0.59	0.68	0.43	0.43	0.44
Export/GDP	0.05	0.09	0.12	0.15	0.28	0.31	0.32

Source: Authors' development based on United Nations Conference on Trade and Development [UNCTAD] (2019)

Figure 1. Agricultural production in EAEU countries in 1995-2017, $ million
Source: Authors' development based on UNCTAD (2019)

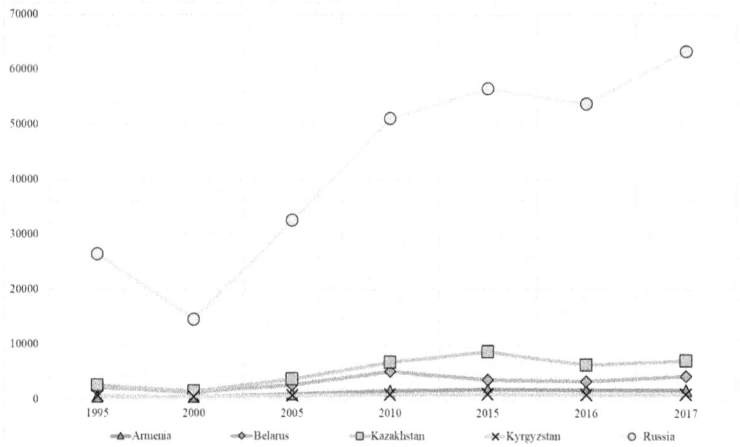

Figure 2. Export of food and agricultural products from EAEU countries in 1995-2017, $ million
Source: Authors' development based on UNCTAD (2019)

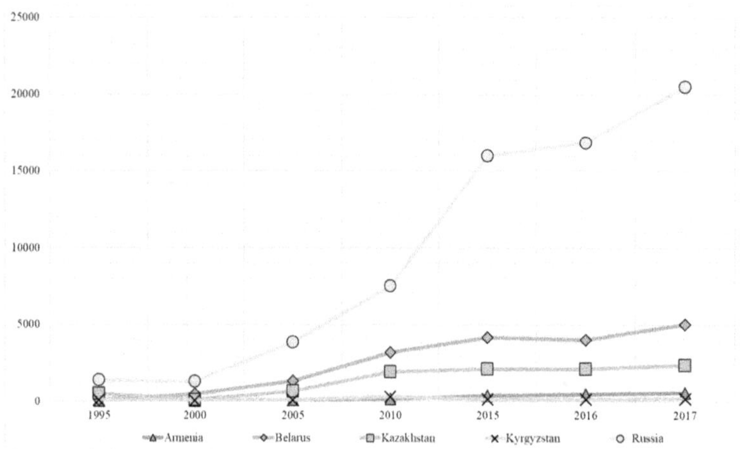

Figure 3. Import of food and agricultural products to EAEU countries in 1995-2017, $ million
Source: Authors' development based on UNCTAD (2019)

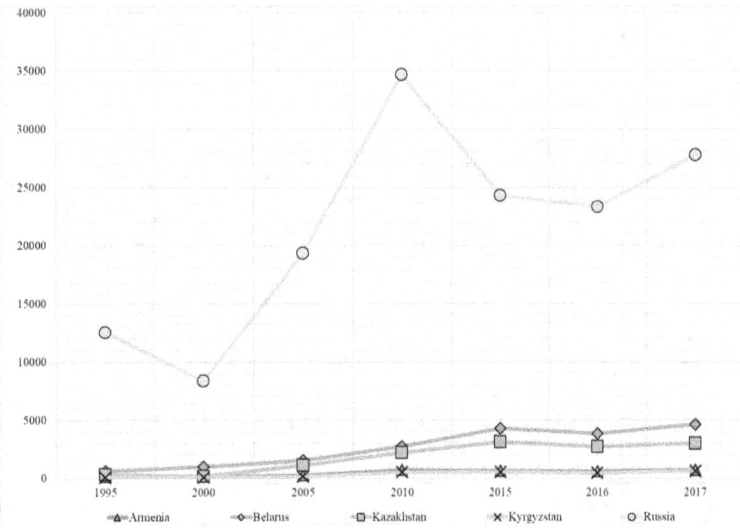

(Kudaibergenova, 2016). The country accessed the World Trade Organization (WTO) in 1999 which resulted in the immediate response on the domestic market in 2000 and onwards – negative trade balance (Kudaibergenova, 2016) (Figure 3).

Russia, regardless of the world's biggest territory and high volumes of domestic agricultural production, remains a net importer of agricultural commodities. Currently, over 44% of Russia's agricultural GDP is produced by imports. Russia received up to 55% of its agricultural imports from the countries it has so far sanctioned, including the EU. Until recently, Russia was not among the WTO members. Russia's accession to this global trading system in 2012 and membership of its major EAEU and BRICS trade partners in the WTO are considered as precondition of essential structural changes in interregional and even international trade. However, latest trade sanctions imposed on both sides between Russia and Western countries, demonstrated, that WTO had not much to do with those changes. The real threats for Russian agricultural market and trade are unilateral actions, which completely distort trade patterns and destroy trade links between countries and regions. Trade restrictions threat sustainable development not only because of their direct effects (market volatilities, destruction of trade linkages, etc.) but largely because of the hidden ones (distortion of natural economic order, establishment of artificial market environment and overprotection) (Molchanov, 2016).

BRICS

BRICS is an association of five major emerging national economies: Brazil, Russia, India, China, and South Africa. The BRICS members are countries, distinguished by their large, fast-growing economies and growing influence on regional and global affairs (Prabhakar, 2016). As of 2017, five BRICS countries represent almost 3 billion people, which are 40% of the world population, with a combined nominal GDP of $18.8 trillion, which is about 20% of the world GDP. Agricultural production and trade in food and agricultural products are important contributors to GDP in all of the five BRICS countries (Table 2).

Table 2. Agricultural production and trade in BRICS economies in 1995-2017, $ million

Economy / parameter	1995	2000	2005	2010	2015	2016	2017
Brazil							
Production	37,791	30,519	41,471	90,910	77,840	85,450	91,888
Export	13,259	12,808	30,432	60,836	70,982	67,998	77,612
Import	5,756	3,665	3,210	8,373	8,817	10,184	9,929
Trade turnover	19,015	16,473	33,642	69,209	79,799	78,182	87,541
Trade balance	7,503	9,143	27,222	52,463	62,165	57,814	67,683
Import/GDP	0.15	0.12	0.08	0.09	0.11	0.12	0.11
Export/GDP	0.35	0.42	0.73	0.67	0.91	0.80	0.84
China							
Production	145,306	180,511	273,558	598,647	1,010,227	992,940	1,006,231
Export	12,299	13,559	24,635	44,153	63,173	66,205	68,998
Import	9,236	9,043	21,541	59,556	102,671	99,652	113,459
Trade turnover	21,535	22,602	46,176	103,709	165,844	165,857	182,457
Trade balance	3,063	4,516	3,094	-15,403	-39,498	-33,447	-44,461
Import/GDP	0.06	0.05	0.08	0.10	0.10	0.10	0.11
Export/GDP	0.08	0.08	0.09	0.07	0.06	0.07	0.07
India							
Production	90,911	100,394	145,122	284,278	346,890	369,670	398,444
Export	5,912	5,418	9,001	18,199	29,954	29,062	34,352
Import	1,660	3,101	6,653	13,652	20,751	21,575	24,229
Trade turnover	7,572	8,519	15,654	31,851	50,705	50,637	58,581
Trade balance	4,252	2,317	2,348	4,547	9,203	7,487	10,123
Import/GDP	0.02	0.03	0.05	0.05	0.06	0.06	0.06
Export/GDP	0.07	0.05	0.06	0.06	0.09	0.08	0.09
Russia							
Production	26,368	14,502	32,524	51,004	56,482	53,745	63,327
Export	1,382	1,286	3,860	7,506	15,996	16,845	20,507
Import	12,535	8,379	19,346	34,658	24,285	23,282	27,756
Trade turnover	13,917	9,665	23,206	42,164	40,281	40,127	48,263
Trade balance	-11,153	-7,093	-15,486	-27,152	-8,289	-6,437	-7,249
Import/GDP	0.48	0.58	0.59	0.68	0.43	0.43	0.44
Export/GDP	0.05	0.09	0.12	0.15	0.28	0.31	0.32
South Africa							
Production	5,436	4,038	6,160	8,961	6,607	6,442	7,981
Export	2,779	2,232	3,990	8,231	8,547	8,426	9,612
Import	1,409	1,254	2,451	5,493	5,961	6,234	6,525
Trade turnover	4,188	3,486	6,441	13,724	14,508	14,660	16,137

continues on following page

Table 2. Continued

Economy / parameter	1995	2000	2005	2010	2015	2016	2017
Trade balance	1,370	978	1,539	2,738	2,586	2,192	3,087
Import/GDP	0.26	0.31	0.40	0.61	0.90	0.97	0.82
Export/GDP	0.51	0.55	0.65	0.92	1.29	1.31	1.20

Source: Authors' development based on UNCTAD (2019)

China is the largest producer of food and agricultural products among BRICS economies (Huang & Yang, 2017). In 2002, China entered the WTO. In fifteen years after the accession, the country has become the leading producer and consumer of food and agricultural products among BRICS countries, with $1 trillion worth of agricultural production, and $113.4 billion of agricultural import. Trade balance in agricultural commodities has been remaining negative since 2008 (Figure 4).

Due to a huge domestic market, China is not able to export much of its agricultural products (Fan, 1997; Gale, Hansen, & Jewison, 2015). Brazil is the leader on the volume of agricultural export. India is also increasing its export. India, the second biggest country in the world in terms of its population, on the contrary to China, has been able to ensure a positive trade balance in food and agricultural commodities (Ghosh & Ghoshal, 2017) (Figure 5).

Smaller economies of BRICS and the EAEU (South Africa and Belarus, respectively) tend to be more export-oriented compared to such big agricultural producers as China and India (Figure 6).

China is the most distinct importer among the BRICS economies with over $113 billion of import in 2017. Other countries are well below China (Figure 7). South Africa, being the smallest economy and food producer among the BRICS countries, is very dependent on import of food, and the dependency is rising. China, India, and Brazil are quite stable in terms of Import/GDP ratio

Figure 4. Agricultural production in BRICS countries in 1995-2017, $ million
Source: Authors' development based on UNCTAD (2019)

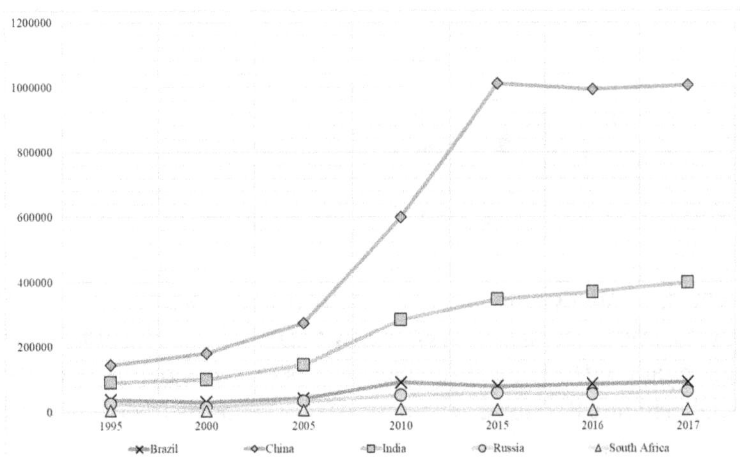

Figure 5. Export of food and agricultural products from BRICS countries in 1995-2017, $ million
Source: Authors' development based on UNCTAD (2019)

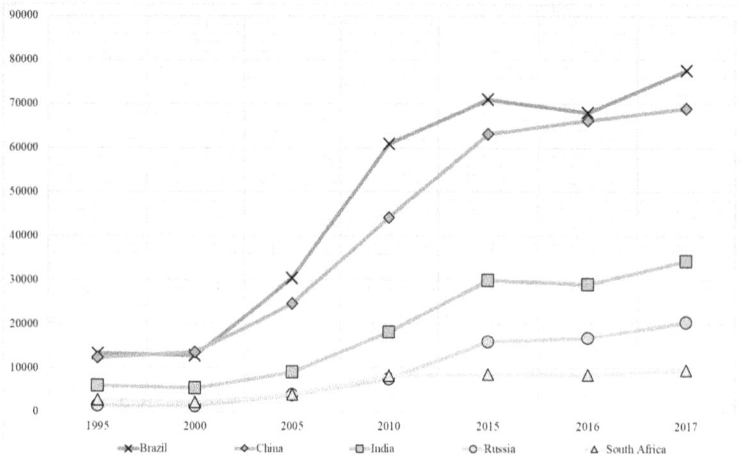

Figure 6. Export/Production ratio in agricultural sector in BRICS and EAEU countries in 1995-2017
Source: Authors' development based on UNCTAD (2019)

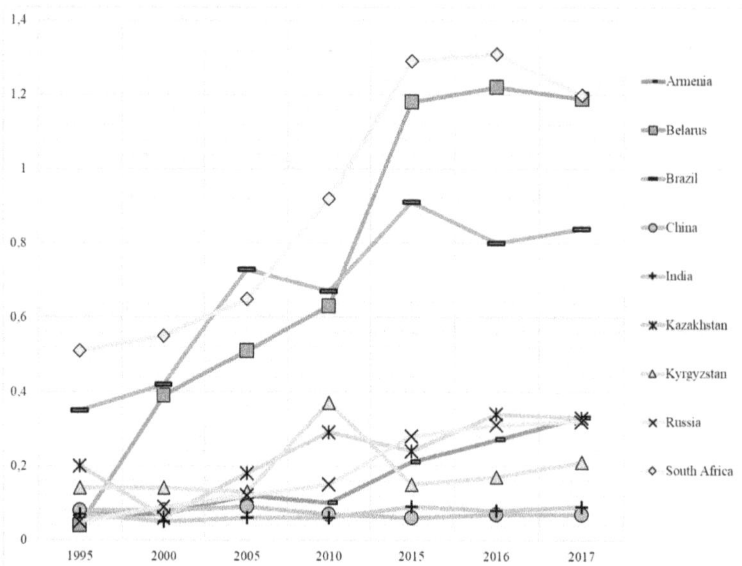

Being export-oriented, smaller economies are also the most dependent on import of food and agricultural products. South Africa is the smallest economy in BRICS and the most dependent on import of food. Import/Production ratio is 0.82 in 2017, which means that the country imports almost as much as it produces domestically (Figure 8). However, South Africa keeps its trade balance positive.

Figure 7. Import of food and agricultural products to BRICS countries in 1995-2017, \$ million
Source: Authors' development based on UNCTAD (2019)

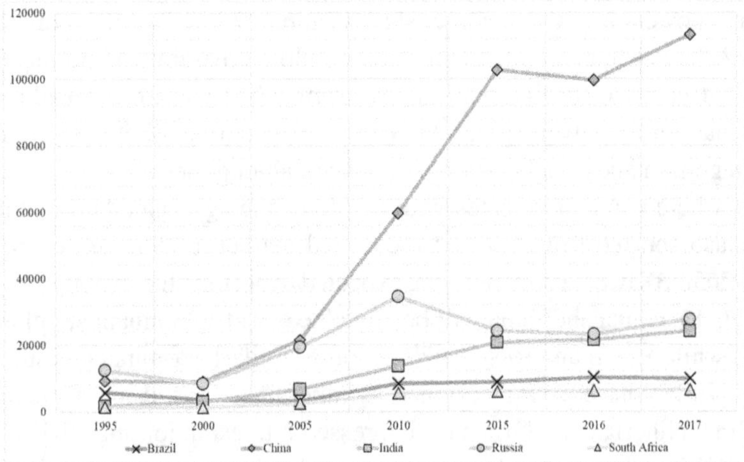

Figure 8. Import/Production ratio in agricultural sector in BRICS and EAEU countries in 1995-2017
Source: Authors' development based on UNCTAD (2019)

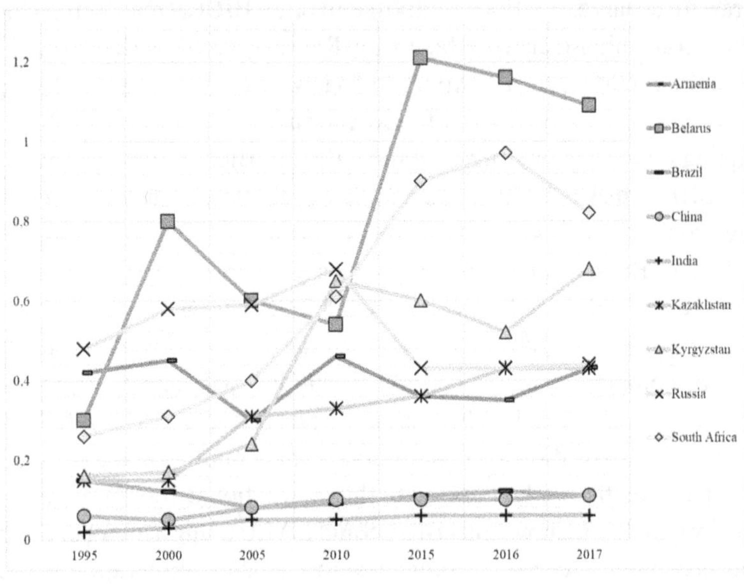

MAIN FOCUS OF THE CHAPTER

BRICS and EAEU: A Possible Convergence of Interests in BRICS+ Format

Shares of the BRICS countries on the global market are rather small, except China. In spite of the BRICS common core as an alliance of emerging economies, politically, economically and geographically BRICS countries have little in common. Member countries have unequal economic resources. As can be seen from GDP, FTT, and market share breakdowns, China is the dominating economic force within BRICS. Its economy is bigger than those of all the other BRICS combined are. China is now the world's second-largest economy, after the USA. There is a distinct tendency on the global market: recognized economic powers lose their market shares (minus 9.1 percentage points for the EU during 1995-2014; minus 2.4 percentage points for the USA) while emerging economies and their alliances rise. For the past two decades, China has made a pass from only 2.8% of the global market share in 1995 up to 10.8%. China has certain advantages, which are expected to facilitate its economic growth in the future, and wise integration and collaboration policies are among them.

BRICS alliance, where China dominates with 61.0% of the aggregated GDP and 64.7% of the aggregated FTT, has also spurred from 6.3% of the global market in 1995 up to 16.6% in 2017. As of Goldman Sachs, by 2050 BRICS's economies are expected to become the major global economic powers (The World Bank, 2018). China and India will become the world's dominant suppliers of manufactured goods and services, while Brazil and Russia will become similarly dominant as suppliers of raw materials. Indonesia and Turkey have been mentioned as candidates for full membership in BRICS, while Argentina, Egypt, Iran, Nigeria, and Syria have expressed interest in joining BRICS. With inclusion of these economies, BRICS is expected to become the world largest economic alliance in the near future.

Since the emergence of geopolitical tensions with the USA and the EU in 2014, Russia has been becoming particularly interested in establishing alternative integration networks with BRICS countries, specifically, by potential convergence of BRICS and EAEU formats (Diener, 2015). Russia has an economy based on raw materials extraction as opposed to other BRICS members, which try to focus their economies on innovation and high-tech manufacturing. Russia needs those technologies for development, as well as BRICS common market for its exports. In view of escalating sanctions, growing trade, and financial isolation from Western countries, BRICS is becoming an alternative for Russia (Bugajski, 2008).

Indeed, participating countries, not only Russia, value its BRICS membership. There is a range of opportunities, which BRICS may bring to participating economies. BRICS has a common core; it unites a group of emerging economies that grow fast, but until now had no chance to influence on global economic regulations. Recent Russia's and China's policies are aimed at the development of a multipolar world, as the Belt and Road Initiative (Bondaz, Cohen, Godement, Kratz, & Pantucci, 2015).

Until the present time, BRICS and EAEU countries have been focused on their domestic developments, but in order to be competitive on the global market, they will have to face new global challenges. Integration gains momentum. Neither single country, even such giants as the USA or China, is able to compete. Investigations have to be directed on exploration of economic and trade cooperation of BRICS and EAEU countries between themselves and with the international community.

Russia is the country which somehow links BRICS and EAEU being a member of both alliances. China is an ultimate engine, a driving force of economic development and integration in the region. China has recently proposed the "five connections" development plan (policy exchange, road network, trade talks, currency circulation, and people-to-people friendship), which encourages cooperation at practical and cultural levels. China's Belt and Road Initiative is meant to integrate the economies of Eurasia through physical and cyber-connectivity, energy pipelines, industrial parks, and smart cities. The plan involves more than 60 countries, representing a third of the world's total economy and more than half the global population. In Eurasia, BRICS and the EAEU are expected to become the core pillars of a new format of international collaboration.

Measuring Food Security and Export Potentials

Although free trade in BRICS, EAEU, and any other formats of international collaboration is a key factor in promoting economic growth, there are specific markets, which require specific approaches (Yu, Elleby, & Zobbe, 2015; Nath et al., 2015). Food market is one of them due to its vital importance for securing nutritional requirements of the population (Lawrence & McMichael, 2012). Providing the population with food in sufficient quantity and variety is a challenge, which includes a range of issues of food production, import dependence and export orientation of the food market, solvency and dietary patterns of the population (Warr, 2011; Mahendra Dev & Zhong, 2015). Many governments are re-examining their strategies for dealing with domestic agricultural production and food security concerns (Tian, Hu, Wang, & Huang, 2016; Zhang, 2016). BRICS and EAEU countries support domestic farmers, protect domestic agricultural and food markets, and in such a way achieve food self-sufficiency. However, the problem is that self-sufficiency is considered as just a share of the domestic market occupied by food products of domestic origin. However, the idea of food security or food sovereignty is wider. It reflects the quality of consumed products and sufficient level of consumption in terms of nutrient intakes (Zhu, 2016). Such approach requires determination of volume of domestic food market expressed in physical terms, which is required for ensurance of rational food security based on the annual average population and recommended reference nutrient intakes, released by the World Health Organization (WHO). To measure food security and evaluate the export potential of a country, the actual volume of food products produced domestically and, what is important, consumed domestically should be measured (Benesova, Maitah, Smutka, Tomsik, & Ishchukova, 2017; Ishchukova & Smutka, 2013a, 2013b). This value is calculated as a difference between the overall volume of food consumption in the country during a period of time, and volume of import during the same period.

$$I_i = \frac{\frac{Im_i}{x_i} - Im_i}{P_i \times R_{WHO}} \tag{1}$$

Im – import volume of selected agricultural product, kg;
x – share of imports on domestic market;
P – population of a country, people;
R_{WHO} – recommended annual reference nutrient intake, kg per capita
i – reference period (year).

Food market is diverse which embarrasses any kinds of generalizations (Yu, Feng, Hubacek, & Sun, 2016). That is why the methodology has to be implemented to such staple foods recommended by the WHO as grain, meat and meat products, milk and milk products, vegetables, and eggs.

In the case of Russia's domestic market of meat and meat products and milk and dairy products, Federal State Statistics Service of the Russian Federation (2019) reports that approximately 76-79% of domestic consumption is met by domestic production (Import-Consumption ratio or current independence). However, it is burgeoning poverty, not competitiveness of domestic producers, quality of their products, or food embargo, which is behind such high food independency levels (Erokhin, 2017). People tend to consume less. Apart from food independence, food security issues have to be considered.

Figure 9. Reported food independence and calculated security on selected food products in Russia
Source: Authors' development based on Federal State Statistics Service of the Russian Federation (2019)

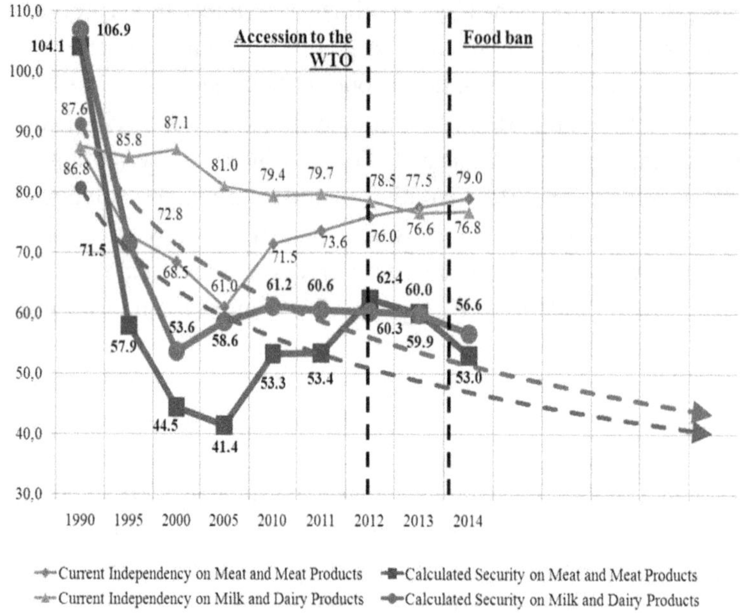

Calculation of Russia's real food security levels on meat and dairy products conducted on the basis of the WHO medical standards of safe food consumption shows the tremendous gap between the reported level of food independence and real level of food security (Figure 9).

In case of Russia, it is demonstrated that domestic food markets in BRICS and EAEU countries are influenced by internal factors (low competitiveness of food producers, their financial instability, outdated facilities, infrastructure, lowering effective demand, etc.), not only external ones. This is a common situation for the EAEU and BRICS countries, that is why influences of certain factors on food security have to be assesses. This could be done by regression analysis. The authors' methodology employs seventeen parameters:

GDP: Volume of agricultural production.
DS: Aggregated state support of domestic farmers.
E: Volume of agricultural export.
I: Volume of agricultural import.
TQ: Foreign trade (import plus export) / volume of agricultural production ratio.
FI: Food independence (governmental statistics).
FS: Calculated food security.
PRF: Profitability of domestic farmers.
PSE: Share of personal subsidiary plots in aggregated agricultural production.
ER: National currency / USD exchange rate.
WFPI: World food price index.
DEPI: Domestic export food price index.
DPPI: Domestic food producers index.

Winf: Average annual inflation, world.
Dinf: Average annual inflation, domestic.
P: Population of a country.
S: Average monthly real wages.

The idea is to find out the most impacting factors for such parameters, as volume of agricultural and food production (national GDP in agriculture), food independence, and export of agricultural commodities and food. In case of Russia, profitability of domestic agricultural producers causes a positive influence on volume of agricultural production, while share of personal subsidiary plots in aggregated agricultural production has a negative impact on volume of agricultural production. This is because of the specifics of agricultural production in Russia, where big farms dominate over less productive small producers. Aggregated state support of domestic agricultural and food producers has a positive influence on food independence. In order to ensure food independence, the government has to provide support to domestic producers according to the WTO boxes – amber and green. Volume of export is influenced in a positive manner by external factors, such as world food price index and average annual inflation. Both these factors encourage producers to export in seeking higher profits. Food security is positively influenced by import and domestic production, which both saturate domestic market with food products and make them available for local consumers (Table 3).

To balance foreign trade in food and agricultural commodities and to ensure sustainable and diversified distribution system on the domestic food market, promotion of export potentials is required (Erokhin, 2018). Development of export potential in the conditions of trade integration and liberalization is considered as a factor of increasing competitiveness of a country on the global market (He, Huang, & Zhang, 2016; Kravchenko & Sergeeva, 2014). However, in case of food security problems, there is always an issue what exactly to export, and whether food producers should continue exporting in case of deficit of food products on the domestic market (Huang, Wei, Cui, & Xie, 2017).

Table 3. Regression analysis of food security factors in Russia in 2017

<table>
<tr><th colspan="2">M_1</th><th colspan="2">M_2</th><th colspan="2">M_3</th></tr>
<tr><th>Regressand (dependent) Y</th><th>Regressors (independent) X</th><th>Regressand (dependent) Y</th><th>Regressors (independent) X</th><th>Regressand (dependent) Y</th><th>Regressors (independent) X</th></tr>
<tr><td rowspan="9">GDP (Y_1)</td><td>DS</td><td rowspan="9">FI (Y_2)</td><td>GDP</td><td rowspan="9">E (Y_3)</td><td>GDP</td></tr>
<tr><td>TQ</td><td>DS*</td><td>DS</td></tr>
<tr><td>PRF*</td><td>E</td><td>ER</td></tr>
<tr><td>PSE**</td><td>I**</td><td>WFPI*</td></tr>
<tr><td>WFPI</td><td>ER</td><td>DEPI</td></tr>
<tr><td rowspan="2">DEPI</td><td>Winf</td><td>DPPI</td></tr>
<tr><td>Dinf</td><td>Winf*</td></tr>
<tr><td rowspan="2">DPPI</td><td>DEPI</td><td rowspan="2">Dinf*</td></tr>
<tr><td>DPPI</td></tr>
</table>

Note: * most positive effect on FS; ** most negative effect on FS
Source: Authors' development

In order to be able to discover the priority export directions, the five-step methodology is suggested. It includes consequential calculation of three foreign trade indices (Balassa, or Revealed Comparative Advantage; Vollrath, or Relative Trade Advantage; and Lafay), with further breakdown of agricultural commodities by competitiveness for export, and differentiation of supportive, or promotional, or protection measures in view of competitiveness.

The approach is applicable not only to agricultural commodities but to any other industry since it allows to discover relative competitive advantages of various countries in export and correspondingly differentiate adaptation measures in the conditions of growing degree of trade integration.

First step is Balassa Index which is used to measure revealed comparative advantage of a country. On the basis of this index, a country is defined as being specialized in exports of a certain product if it's market share in that product is higher than the average or, equivalently, if the weight of the product of the country's exports is higher than its weight of the exports of the reference area.

$$RCA = \frac{\frac{X_{ij}}{X_{it}}}{\frac{X_{nj}}{X_{nt}}} = \frac{\frac{X_{ij}}{X_{nj}}}{\frac{X_{it}}{X_{nt}}} \tag{2}$$

X: Export.
i: Country.
j: Commodity group (domestic food market).
t: Commodity group (global food market).
n: Group of countries.

A country reveals comparative advantages in products for which this indicator is higher than 1, showing that its exports of those products are more than expected on the basis of its importance in total exports of the reference area (Balassa, 1965). The idea behind this approach is to gain some understanding of how that export performance accounts for the total exports of certain products in the world market and how they compare to others who also engage in the same type of exports. Conducting a revealed comparative advantage analysis can provide information that can aid in reversing an unfavorable trend, improve the flow of trade, and also help to stabilize the economy of a nation or industry.

Vollrath Index allows considering not only export, but also import, and demonstrating net trade advantages and disadvantages (Vollrath, 1985).

$$RTA = \frac{\frac{X_{ij}}{X_{it}}}{\frac{X_{nj}}{X_{nt}}} - \frac{\frac{M_{ij}}{M_{it}}}{\frac{M_{nj}}{M_{nt}}} \tag{3}$$

X: Export.
i: Country.

j: Commodity group (domestic food market).
t: Commodity group (global food market).
n: Group of countries.

The Lafay index, by taking into account imports, allows to control for intra-industry trade and re-export flows; in this sense, it is superior to the traditional Revealed Comparative Advantages index. Moreover, unlike other two indexes as the Balassa index and the Vollrath index, it also controls for distortions induced by macroeconomic fluctuations.

$$LI_{ij} = \frac{1000}{Y_i} \times \frac{2 \times \left(X_{ij} \times M_i - X_i \times M_{ij} \right)}{X_i + M_i} \tag{3}$$

X: Export.
M: Import.
i: Country.
j: Commodity group (domestic food market).

Since comparative advantages are structural, by definition, it is crucial to eliminate the influence of cyclical factors, which can affect the magnitude of trade flows in the short run. The Lafay index takes into account these effects by considering the difference between each item's normalized trade balance and the overall normalized trade balance. Finally, the Lafay index weights each product's contribution according to the respective importance in trade.

Approaches to the Promotion of Agricultural Trade between BRICS+ Countries

The methodology is universal, since it allows to group agricultural and food commodity products, or any other products, on their competitiveness degree in purpose of differentiation of adaptation measures in the conditions of trade liberalization. When there is a threefold concurrence of three indexes, it is assumed that a product is positively competitive on the international market, and trade competitive advantages have to be implemented. When Balassa Index is more than 1, and Vollrath and Lafay are above 0, it is assumed that a product is conditionally competitive, and support and development of comparative competitive advantage are required. For the remaining product groups, not included to positively competitive or conditionally competitive ones, an arithmetical average is calculated. When the product's indexes are above this arithmetical average, they are considered conditionally non-competitive, and it is assumed that a comparable competitive advantage has to be established. When the product's indexes are below this arithmetical average, it is considered non-competitive, and it is assumed that such product has to be supported on a domestic market, without any attempts to exporting (Table 4).

The resulting effect of the methodology is differentiation of measures to promote export potentials of BRICS and EAEU countries on the global food market. Measures should be differentiated for various products and various countries, so there may be dozens of various measures (Table 5).

In general, products which are positively competitive would require diminishing of administrative barriers to export, transition from export embargo practices to customs and tariff regulations, and development of production and logistics infrastructure, including easier access to foreign markets (Gao, Ivolga,

Table 4. Grouping of agricultural and food commodity groups on their competitiveness degree in purpose of differentiation of adaptation measures in the conditions of trade liberalization

Groups	Competitiveness criteria	Target effect of adaptation measures
Positively Competitive (PC)	Threefold concurrence: $RCA_{av} > 1$ $RTA_{av} > 0$ $LI_{av} > 0$	Implementation of trade competitive advantage
Conditionally Competitive (CC)	$RCA_i > 1$ $RTA_i > 0$ $LI_i > 0$	Support and development of comparative competitive advantage
Conditionally Non-Competitive (CNC)	$RCA_{av} > RCA_{CNC+NC}$ $RTA_{av} > RTA_{CNC+NC}$ $LI_{av} > LI_{CNC+NC}$	Establishment of comparative competitive advantage
Non-Competitive (NC)	Threefold concurrence: $RCA_{av} < RCA_{CNC+NC}$ $RTA_{av} < RTA_{CNC+NC}$ $LI_{av} < LI_{CNC+NC}$	Support of competitiveness on the domestic food market

Source: Authors' development

Table 5. Differentiation of measures to promote export potentials of BRICS and EAEU countries on the global food market

Commodity group	Measures to be implemented
Positively Competitive (PC)	General economic measures: 1. Diminishing of administrative barriers to export 2. Transition from export embargo practices to customs and tariff regulations. WTO Green Box: 1. Development of production and logistics infrastructure, including access to foreign markets
Conditionally Competitive (CC)	General economic measures: 1. PR and information promotion of domestic products to foreign markets (exhibition and fairs, publishing, research). 2. Support of "niche" productions going to export WTO Amber Box: 1. Subsidized loans for development of export production 2. Subsidized insurance of export-oriented productions WTO Green Box: 1. Development of production and logistics infrastructure, including access to foreign markets
Conditionally Non-Competitive (CNC)	WTO Amber Box: 1. Income support of agricultural and food producers 2. Reduction of production costs
Non-Competitive (NC)	WTO Amber Box: 1. Income support of agricultural and food producers 2. Reduction of production costs WTO Green Box: 1. Promotion of domestic demand through subsidies to consumers 2. Programs for ensurance of sustainable development and diversification of rural economy

Source: Authors' development

& Erokhin, 2018). Conditionally competitive products would benefit from a combination of promotion measures and support in the forms of subsidized loans, insurances, or any other support measures out of the WTO Amber Box. Indirect economic measures focused in increase of competitiveness are needed for those products which are conditionally non-competitive, for example, income support or reduction of production costs. Non-competitive products have to be targeted on a domestic market, and buyers have to be somehow rewarded for buying locally-produced products – through subsidies to consumers, or development of local production in rural areas (Erokhin & Gao, 2018; Gao, 2017).

SOLUTIONS AND RECOMMENDATIONS

The countries of the EAEU and BRICS have particular competitive advantages as well as weaknesses in the view of the development of agricultural production and trade in BRICS+ format. EAEU countries have abundant natural and labor resources and high agricultural potential. EAEU countries have traditional close economic, trade, and social ties between themselves. The major obstacles to effective integration are low diversification of output and export, dependence on fossil-fuel exports, weak infrastructures, low effective demand on domestic markets, and corruption. These obstacles are common for all five EAEU countries, including Russia.

Although Goldman Sachs forecasts Russia to grow into the world's sixth economy by 2050, currently it is smaller than most of the developed countries (The World Bank, 2018). Being under Western sanctions, Russia has been the worst performer among the EAEU economies since 2014. During the 2000s, lack of comprehensive structural reforms was masked by a growth fueled by sizeable oil revenues. Recent events around Russian-Ukrainian crisis clearly exposed economic weakness of such a growth model. In conditions of growing isolation from Western countries, cooperation with China and involvement to the Belt and Road Initiative may become an alternative for Russia, since it gives access to new export markets for Russia's oil and gas, and new sources for agricultural and merchandise imports.

In order to breakthrough on the global market, EAEU and BRICS countries have to transform economic growth drivers, seize existing opportunities, reduce dependence on factors of production (investment and labor), and increase reliance on innovation and quality. The major challenge would be development of a favorable external environment through establishment of effective ties with neighbor countries and alliances. The countries need to make full use of emerging markets and resources to expedite their economic transformations and improve their positions in increasingly globalized value chains.

The biggest BRICS economy, China supports Russia in promoting regional integration within the EAEU framework and agrees to launch talks with the EAEU on an economic and trade cooperation deal. The two sides vowed to discuss the docking of the Belt and Road Initiative and the EAEU construction, saying that they agreed to set up a dialogue mechanism for the integration. They pledged to maintain a continuous and stable economic growth in the region, strengthen regional economic integration, and safeguard peace and stability in the region. There are several perspectives of China-Russia economic and trade relation in view of integration of the EAEU and Belt and Road Initiative and in such a way extending the BRICS format:

- Expansion of investment and trade cooperation, optimization of trade structure and cultivation of new growth points for economy and employment.

- Facilitation of mutual investment, launch of major investment cooperation projects and jointly building of industrial parks and cross-border economic cooperation zones.
- Improvement of interconnection in logistics and transportation, and collaboration on infrastructure construction projects.
- Development of trade-facilitating mechanisms in ripe areas, formulation of common policies in fields of common interests, establishment of a free trade zone between China and the EAEU.
- Creation of a better environment for medium- and small-sized enterprises that can play an important role in boosting regional economic cooperation.
- Promotion of local-currency settlement in bilateral trade and cooperation in export credit, insurance and trade financing among many other fields.
- Enhancement of financial cooperation through the Silk Road Fund and the Asian Infrastructure Investment Bank.
- Promotion of regional and global multilateral cooperation and expansion of international trade.

FUTURE RESEARCH DIRECTIONS

Future studies related to the potential convergence between BRICS and the EAEU formats in relation to trade in agricultural and food products should ensure that the new format establishes a clearly defined mechanism for collaboration between all involved countries taking into account the differences in various fields of national regulations. Implementation of particular measures of state support of domestic agricultural production and protection of domestic farmers has to be ensured on a long-term basis by all participating countries and has to be integrated into all policies of participating states. Financial and economic sustainability is also important, especially in the view of the economic slowdown of China, recession in Russia, and emerging trade and economic tensions in the global economy. Interregional financial institutions have to be investigated, established, and supported by both BRICS and EAEU countries in order to ensure financial stability in the region and support smaller economies in both of the blocks. One of the most important directions of future research is how to reduce poverty and ensure social development. Concentrating on large-scale investment projects, BRICS and EAEU countries should pay attention to the study of social development effects, creation of job opportunities, and development of rural areas.

CONCLUSION

Transforming paradigm of international economic relations causes rising influence of integration and trade liberalization on domestic food markets of developing and emerging countries. Experiences of the EAEU and BRICS countries demonstrate direct links between trade integration (accession to the WTO) and growth of dependency of domestic food markets on import. In the mid-term and long-term perspective, the effects of trade integration show up. Internal bottlenecks may become accelerators of food security and economic sovereignty problems when trade liberalization goes on.

What has to be done in such a situation? Adaptation of domestic food markets of the EAEU and BRICS countries in the conditions of trade integration and liberalization should have two major directions: promotion of external opportunities and overcoming of internal bottlenecks. Most of the EAEU countries are heavily dependent on import deliveries of agricultural products and food (food dependency), in addition to the discovered nonconformance of food consumption volumes to international standards (food insecurity), that is why the attention has to paid to the quality of domestic consumption, not only its quantity. Promotion of external opportunities should include development of food export potential in the conditions of trade integration and liberalization and should be founded on discovery of comparative advantages and their promotion on the global and domestic food markets.

ACKNOWLEDGMENT

This study is supported by the Fundamental Research Funds for the Central Universities, China, grant no. 3072019CFP0902, HEUCFJ170901.

REFERENCES

Balassa, B. (1965). Trade Liberalization and Revealed Comparative Advantage. Manchester School of Economics and Social Science, 33, 99-123.

Benesova, I., Maitah, M., Smutka, L., Tomsik, K., & Ishchukova, N. (2017). Perspectives of the Russian Agricultural Exports in Terms of Comparative Advantage. *Agricultural Economics – Czech, 63*, 1-13.

Bondaz, A., Cohen, D., Godement, F., Kratz, A., & Pantucci, R. (2015). *One Belt, One Road: China's Great Leap Outward*. London, UK: European Council on Foreign Relations.

Bugajski, J. (2008). *Expanding Eurasia: Russia's European Ambitions*. Washington, DC: Center for Strategic and International Studies.

Diener, A. C. (2015). Parsing Mobilities in Central Eurasia: Border Management and New Silk Roads. *Eurasian Geography and Economics*, *56*(4), 376–404. doi:10.1080/15387216.2015.1078736

Dragneva, R., & Wolczuk, K. (2017). *The Eurasian Economic Union: Deals, Rules and the Exercise of Power.* London, UK: Chatham House, the Royal Institute of International Affairs.

Erokhin, V. (2017). Factors Influencing Food Markets in Developing Countries: An Approach to Assess Sustainability of the Food Supply in Russia. *Sustainability*, *9*(8), 1313. doi:10.3390u9081313

Erokhin, V. (2018). Contemporary Foreign Trade Policy of China in the Region of Central and Northeast Asia. In A. C. Ozer (Ed.), *Globalization and Trade Integration in Developing Countries* (pp. 27–54). Hershey, PA: IGI Global. doi:10.4018/978-1-5225-4032-8.ch002

Erokhin, V., & Gao, T. (2018). Competitive Advantages of China's Agricultural Exports in the Outward-Looking Belt and Road Initiative. In W. Zhang, I. Alon, & C. Lattemann (Eds.), *China's Belt and Road Initiative: Changing the Rules of Globalization* (pp. 265–285). London, UK: Palgrave Macmillan. doi:10.1007/978-3-319-75435-2_14

Fan, S. (1997). Production and Productivity Growth in Chinese Agriculture: New Measurement and Evidence. *Food Policy*, *22*(3), 213–228. doi:10.1016/S0306-9192(97)00010-9

Federal State Statistics Service of the Russian Federation. (2019). *Russia in Figures*. Retrieved June 13, 2019, from http://www.gks.ru/wps/wcm/connect/rosstat_main/rosstat/en/main/

Fedorenko, V. (2015). *Eurasian Integration: Effects on Central Asia*. Washington, DC: Rethink Institute.

Gale, F., Hansen, J., & Jewison, M. (2015). *China's Growing Demand for Agricultural Imports*. Washington, DC: U.S. Department of Agriculture, Economic Research Service.

Gao, T. (2017). Food Security and Rural Development on Emerging Markets of Northeast Asia: Cases of Chinese North and Russian Far East. In V. Erokhin (Ed.), *Establishing Food Security and Alternatives to International Trade in Emerging Economies* (pp. 155–176). Hershey, PA: IGI Global.

Gao, T., Ivolga, A., & Erokhin, V. (2018). Sustainable Rural Development in Northern China: Caught in a Vice between Poverty, Urban Attractions, and Migration. *Sustainability*, *10*(5), 1467. doi:10.3390u10051467

Ghosh, I., & Ghoshal, I. (2017). Implications of Trade Liberalization for Food Security under the ASEAN-India Strategic Partnership: A Gravity Model Approach. In V. Erokhin (Ed.), *Establishing Food Security and Alternatives to International Trade in Emerging Economies* (pp. 98–118). Hershey, PA: IGI Global.

Golam, M., & Monowar, M. (2018). Eurasian Economic Union: Evolution, Challenges and Possible Future Directions. *Journal of Eurasian Studies*, *9*(2), 163–172. doi:10.1016/j.euras.2018.05.001

Hartwell, C. A. (2016). Improving Competitiveness in the Member States of the Eurasian Economic Union: A Blueprint for the Next Decade. *Post-Communist Economies*, *28*(1), 49–71. doi:10.1080/14631377.2015.1124554

He, M., Huang, Z., & Zhang, N. (2016). An Empirical Research on Agricultural Trade between China and "The Belt and Road" Countries: Competitiveness and Complementarity. *Modern Economy*, *7*(14), 1671–1686. doi:10.4236/me.2016.714147

Huang, J., Wei, W., Cui, Q., & Xie, W. (2017). The Prospects for China's Food Security and Imports: Will China Starve the World via Imports? *Journal of Integrative Agriculture*, *16*(12), 2933–2944. doi:10.1016/S2095-3119(17)61756-8

Huang, J., & Yang, G. (2017). Understanding Recent Challenges and New Food Policy in China. *Global Food Security*, *12*, 119–126. doi:10.1016/j.gfs.2016.10.002

Ishchukova, N., & Smutka, L. (2013a). Comparative Advantage: Products Mapping of the Russian Agricultural Exports. *AGRIS On-Line Papers in Economics and Informatics*, *5*(3), 13–24.

Ishchukova, N., & Smutka, L. (2013b). Revealed Comparative Advantage of Russian Agricultural Exports. *Acta Universitatis Agriculturae et Silviculturae Mendelianae Brunensis*, *61*(4), 941–952. doi:10.11118/actaun201361040941

Kembayev, Z. (2016). Towards a Silk Road Union? *Chinese Journal of International Law*, *15*(3), 691–699.

Kravchenko, A., & Sergeeva, O. (2014). China Policy in the Area of Food Security: Modernization of Agriculture. *Pacific Rim: Economics, Politics, Law*, *32*(4), 57–65.

Kudaibergenova, D. (2016). Eurasian Economic Union Integration in Kazakhstan and Kyrgyzstan. *European Political Science*, *17*(1), 97–112.

Kukushkina, J., & Ostrovskaya, E. (2013). Current Issues and Prospects of Eurasian and European Economic Integration. *International Organizations Research Journal, 8*(4), 214–228.

Lawrence, G., & McMichael, P. (2012). The Question of Food Security. *International Journal of Sociology of Agriculture and Food, 19*(2), 135–142.

Linn, J. F., & Tiomkin, D. (2006). The New Impetus towards Economic Integration between Europe and Asia. *Asia Europe Journal, 4*(1), 31–41. doi:10.100710308-006-0046-6

Mahendra Dev, S., & Zhong, F. (2015). Trade and Stock Management to Achieve National Food Security in India and China? *China Agricultural Economic Review, 7*(4), 641–654. doi:10.1108/CAER-01-2015-0009

Makarov, I., & Sokolova, A. (2016). The Eurasian Economic Union and the Silk Road Economic Belt: Opportunities for Russia. *International Organisations Research Journal, 11*(2), 40–57. doi:10.17323/1996-7845-2016-02-40

Mariani, B. (2013). *China's Role and Interests in Central Asia*. London, UK: Saferworld.

Molchanov, M. (2016). Russia's Leadership of Regional Integration in Eurasia. In S. Kingah, & C. Quiliconi (Eds.), *Global and Regional Leadership of BRICS Countries* (pp. 113–133). Cham, Switzerland: Springer International Publishing. doi:10.1007/978-3-319-22972-0_7

Mostafa, G., & Mahmood, M. (2018). Eurasian Economic Union: Evolution, Challenges and Possible Future Directions. *Journal of Eurasian Studies, 9*(2), 163–172. doi:10.1016/j.euras.2018.05.001

Nashier, T. (2015). Financial Integration between BRICS and Developed Stock Markets. *International Journal of Business and Management Invention, 4*(1), 65–71.

Nath, R., Luan, Y., Yang, W., Yang, C., Chen, W., Li, Q., & Cui, X. (2015). Changes in Arable Land Demand for Food in India and China: A Potential Threat to Food Security. *Sustainability, 7*(5), 5371–5397. doi:10.3390u7055371

Prabhakar, A. C. (2016). Trade and Economic Integration in BRICS: Towards Multi-Polarity. In V. Erokhin (Ed.), *Global Perspectives on Trade Integration and Economies in Transition* (pp. 45–57). Hershey, PA: IGI Global. doi:10.4018/978-1-5225-0451-1.ch003

Radulescu, I. G., Panait, M., & Voica, C. (2014). BRICS Countries Challenge to the World Economy New Trends. *Procedia Economics and Finance, 8*, 605–613. doi:10.1016/S2212-5671(14)00135-X

Rasoulizhad, E., & Jabalameli, F. (2018). Do BRICS Countries Have Similar Trade Integration Patterns? *Journal of Economic Integration, 33*(1), 1011–1045. doi:10.11130/jei.2018.33.1.1011

Shaygani, B., Abolhasani Hastiani, F., Ghaffari, A., Sadeghi Shahdani, M., & Fadaee, M. (2015). Effects of Exchange Rate Arrangements on Trade Cooperation in BRICS Countries. *Asian Economic and Financial Review, 5*(3), 563–578. doi:10.18488/journal.aefr/2015.5.3/102.3.563.578

The World Bank. (2018). *Central Asia. China (and Russia) 2030 – Implications for Agriculture in Central Asia*. Washington, DC: The World Bank.

Tian, D., Hu, N., Wang, X., & Huang, L. (2016). Trade Margins, Quality Upgrading, and China's Agri-Food Export Growth. *China Agricultural Economic Review, 8*(2), 277–298. doi:10.1108/CAER-12-2013-0156

United Nations Conference on Trade and Development. (2019). *Statistics Database* [Data file]. Retrieved June 14, 2019, from http://unctad.org/en/Pages/Statistics.aspx

Vinokurov, E. (2017). Eurasian Economic Union: Current State and Preliminary Results. *Russian Journal of Economics*, *3*(1), 54–70. doi:10.1016/j.ruje.2017.02.004

Vollrath, T. (1985). *Dynamics of Comparative Advantage and the Resistance to Free Trade*. Washington, DC: United States Department of Agriculture.

Warr, P. (2011). *Food Security vs. Food Self-Sufficiency: The Indonesian Case*. Canberra, Australia: The Australian National University.

Yu, W., Elleby, C., & Zobbe, H. (2015). Food Security Policies in India and China: Implications for National and Global Food Security. *Food Security*, *7*(2), 405–414. doi:10.100712571-015-0432-2

Yu, Y., Feng, K., Hubacek, K., & Sun, L. (2016). Global Implications of China's Future Food Consumption. *Journal of Industrial Ecology*, *20*(3), 593–602. doi:10.1111/jiec.12392

Zhang, H. (2016). Food in Sino-U.S. Relations. From Blessing to Curse? In F. Wu & H. Zhang (Eds.), *China's Global Quest for Resources. Energy, Food and Water* (pp. 100–118). London, UK: Routledge.

Zhu, Y. (2016). International Trade and Food Security: Conceptual Discussion, WTO and the Case of China. *China Agricultural Economic Review*, *8*(3), 399–411. doi:10.1108/CAER-09-2015-0127

ADDITIONAL READING

Anderson, K., Jha, S., Nelgen, S., & Strutt, A. (2013). Re-Examining Policies for Food Security in Asia. *Food Security*, *5*(2), 195–215. doi:10.100712571-012-0237-5

Andronova, I. (2016). Eurasian Economic Union: Opportunities and Barriers to Regional and Global Leadership. *International Organisations Research Journal*, *11*(2), 7–23. doi:10.17323/1996-7845-2016-02-07

Blanchard, J.-M. F., & Flint, C. (2017). The Geopolitics of China's Maritime Silk Road Initiative. *Geopolitics*, *22*(2), 223–245. doi:10.1080/14650045.2017.1291503

Bratersky, M. (2016). Isolationism versus Geopolitics: The Dual Role of the Eurasian Economic Union in Global Governance. *International Organisations Research Journal*, *11*(2), 58–70. doi:10.17323/1996-7845-2016-02-58

Estevadeordal, A., Freund, C., & Ornelas, E. (2008). Does Regionalism Affect Trade Liberalization Toward Nonmembers? *The Quarterly Journal of Economics*, *124*(4), 1531–1575. doi:10.1162/qjec.2008.123.4.1531

Ghose, B. (2014). Food Security and Food Self-Sufficiency in China: From Past to 2050. *Food and Energy Security*, *3*(2), 86–95. doi:10.1002/fes3.48

Ghosh, I., & Chakrabarti, S. (2016). Inward and Outward Foreign Investments of the Asian Economies in Transition and India: Determinants of FDI and India's Prospects in CLMV. In V. Erokhin (Ed.), *Global Perspectives on Trade Integration and Economies in Transition* (pp. 212–237). Hershey, PA: IGI Global. doi:10.4018/978-1-5225-0451-1.ch011

Henneberry, S. R., & Diaz, C. C. (2015). Food Security Issues: Concepts and the Role of Emerging Markets. In A. Schmitz, P. L. Kennedy, & T. G. Schmitz (Eds.), *Food Security in an Uncertain World* (pp. 63–79). Bingley, UK: Emerald Group. doi:10.1108/S1574-871520150000015005

Horska, E., Moroz, S., & Galova, J. (2016). The EU – Ukraine – Russia Crisis Triangle: Evidence of Local and Global Consequences for International Trade. In V. Erokhin (Ed.), *Global Perspectives on Trade Integration and Economies in Transition* (pp. 105–125). Hershey, PA: IGI Global. doi:10.4018/978-1-5225-0451-1.ch006

Huang, J., & Rozelle, S. (2006). The Emergence of Agricultural Commodity Markets in China. *China Economic Review*, *17*(3), 266–280. doi:10.1016/j.chieco.2006.04.008

Khanna, T., & Palepu, K. G. (2010). *Winning in Emerging Markets: A Road Map for Strategy and Execution*. Boston, MA: Harvard Business Press.

Lardy, N. R. (2002). *Integrating China into the World Economy*. Washington, DC: Brookings Institution Press.

Obydenkova, A. (2011). Comparative Regionalism: Eurasian Cooperation and European Integration. The Case for Neofunctionalism? *Journal of Eurasian Studies*, *2*(2), 87–102. doi:10.1016/j.euras.2011.03.001

Roberts, S. P., & Moshes, A. (2016). The Eurasian Economic Union: A Case of Reproductive Integration? *Post-Soviet Affairs*, *32*(6), 542–565. doi:10.1080/1060586X.2015.1115198

Sakwa, R. (2016). How the Eurasian Elites Envisage the Role of the EEU in Global Perspective. *European Political Science*, *17*(1), 4–22.

Samokhvalov, V. (2016). The New Eurasia: Post-Soviet Space between Russia, Europe and China. *European Political Science*, *17*(1), 82–96.

Svetlicinii, A. (2018). China's Belt and Road Initiative and the Eurasian Economic Union: "Integrating the Integrations". *Public Administration Issues, Special Issue*, 7-20.

Tarr, D. G. (2016). The Eurasian Economic Union of Russia, Belarus, Kazakhstan, Armenia, and the Kyrgyz Republic: Can It Succeed Where Its Predecessor Failed? *Eastern European Economics*, *54*(1), 1–22. doi:10.1080/00128775.2015.1105672

Ustyuzhanina, E. (2016). The Eurasian Union and Global Value Chains. *European Political Science*, *17*(1), 35–45.

Vasilieva, N., & Lagutina, M. (2013). Eurasian Economic Unit Project in Experts' Evaluations. *International Organisations Research Journal*, *8*(4), 229–242.

Wilson, J. L. (2016). The Eurasian Economic Union and China's Silk Road: Implications for the Russian-Chinese Relationship. *European Political Science*, *17*(1), 113–132.

Windfuhr, M., & Jonsen, J. (2005). *Food Sovereignty: Towards Democracy in Localized Food Systems*. Heidelberg, Germany: FIAN ITDG Publishing. doi:10.3362/9781780441160

Wittman, H., Desmarais, A., & Wiebe, N. (2010). *Food Sovereignty: Reconnecting Food, Nature and Community*. Oakland, CA: Food First Books.

Yanikkaya, H. (2003). Trade Openness and Economic Growth: A Cross-Country Empirical Investigation. *Journal of Development Economics*, *72*(1), 57–89. doi:10.1016/S0304-3878(03)00068-3

Zhang, H., & Chen, G. (2016). China's Food Security Strategy Reform: An Emerging Global Agricultural Policy. In F. Wu, & H. Zhang (Eds.), *China's Global Quest for Resources. Energy, Food and Water* (pp. 23–41). London, UK: Routledge.

Zhou, Z. (2010). Achieving Food Security in China: Past Three Decades and Beyond. *China Agricultural Economic Review*, *2*(3), 251–275. doi:10.1108/17561371011078417

KEY TERMS AND DEFINITIONS

Belt and Road Initiative: A development strategy proposed by the Chinese government in 2013 and focused on the improvement of connectivity and collaboration among the countries of Eurasia through the increase of China's role in global affairs.

BRICS: The association of five major emerging national economies: Brazil, Russia, India, China, and South Africa.

Eurasian Economic Union: The union between Armenia, Belarus, Kazakhstan, Kyrgyzstan, and Russia established with an aim of effective promotion of free movement of goods, services, capital, and labor between participating countries.

Food Security: A condition when people have access to sufficient amounts of safe and nutritious food and are therefore consuming the food required for normal growth and development, and for an active and healthy life.

Food Self-Sufficiency: An extent to which a country can satisfy its food needs from its own domestic production.

Foreign Trade: A system of international commodity-money relations composed of foreign trade activities of all countries worldwide.

Trade Liberalization: A process of reduction or elimination of constraints in the sphere of international trade, including reduction or removal of customs tariffs, import quotas, abolishment of multiple exchange rates, and simplification of administrative requirements to import and export operations.

Trade Protectionism: A set of measures to limit imports or promote exports by putting up barriers to trade that countries use to limit unfair competition from foreign industries.

Chapter 5
India-Africa Trade and Investment Cooperation for Economic Development

Rajender Singh Godara
https://orcid.org/0000-0002-7568-0819
Lovely Professional University, India

Mohamad Aslam
Lovely Professional University, India

Gaibul Preet
https://orcid.org/0000-0001-7001-3462
Lovely Professional University, India

Sushanta Kumar Mahapatra
IBS Hyderabad, The ICFAI Foundation for Higher Education, India

ABSTRACT

India and Africa have a long partnership history of cooperation for economic development by trade and investment. This framework has become an essential component for development in Africa. Africa is an emerging investment and trade destination due to a large consumer market, high potential of economic growth, improving the business environment and investment regulations, and high rates of return on investment. The depth of relation of India and Africa has been reflected in the patterns of trade and investment, as well as people-to-people interactions, cultural exchanges, and cooperation at the continental and at the regional and bilateral levels. This chapter examines investment and trade patterns of India-Africa collaboration in the contemporary era of globalization. The study is based on empirical and conceptual aspects by using secondary data. An analysis uses appropriate econometric tools to make the study more relevant.

DOI: 10.4018/978-1-7998-1730-7.ch005

INTRODUCTION

Trade and investment have emerged as a powerful aspect for modern international relations (Erokhin, 2015, 2016). African continent appeared a new epicenter for global business activities. Trade and investment relationship between India and Africa is motivated by positive economic environment in changing international scenario that creates sound economic relations. After liberalization and globalization of Indian economy the trade and investment between India and Africa has been increasing. The increasing trends are due to liberalized policy of India and African countries and India's duty-free tariff scheme, announced in April 2008, for 49 least developed countries out of 33 African countries were got benefitted (Nayyar & Aggarwal, 2014).

India has undertaken significant investment initiatives to make its strategic partnership with Africa stronger. In 1996-2016, investments from India to Africa reached $54 billion. The progress made by both sides sustained and attributable to the reciprocal trade relationship established. The Indo-African partnership is based on good equity – economic- principle. Nigeria is major exporter to India with the value of export $7.7 billion in 2017, making it the top import source for India (about 26% of India's total imports). The second-largest supplier is South Africa with $5.8 billion, the third-largest is Angola with $2.6 billion in 2016-2017.The share of other African countries in India's import from the region is about 40%.Major import items of India from African countries are crude oil, edible fruits, and nuts. India's main export items to Africa are petroleum products, pharmaceutical products, and vehicles.

Trade and investment relationships between India and African countries are regulated by India-Africa Trade Agreements to increase the trade, economic activity by joint ventures. These relationships are beneficial for trade between India and Africa. The major export items of India are manufactured goods, machinery, transportation equipment, food, pharmaceutical products, automobiles, telecoms. India's major import items in trade with African countries are crude oil, petroleum, gold, and inorganic chemical products. This situation reflects India's high demand for energy resources because India is comparatively high developed and industrialized than most African countries. India mainly exporting finished products to African countries and importing raw materials from African countries (crude oil from Algeria, Angola, Cameroon, Congo, Egypt, Equatorial Guinea, Kenya, Gabon, Ivory Coast, Libya, Nigeria, and Sudan, edible fruits and nuts, particularly, cashew nuts). India is importing raw cotton, gold, and precious stones from other African countries. India imports gold, coal, iron, steel, inorganic chemicals, and mineral ores from South African countries, inorganic chemicals, fertilizers, and mineral fuel from North Africa, iron, steel, vegetables, edible nuts, coffee, inorganic chemicals, coffee, and crude oil from East and Central Africa (Roy, 2013).

BACKGROUND

India and Africa have a long partnership history of cooperation between each other in the spheres of economic development, trade, and investment. This cooperation has become an essential component for the development of Africa. However, a fresh search of cooperation opportunities in this region is now needed. In this chapter, an attempt has been made to examine and analyze India-Africa trade patterns and evaluate the potential for cooperation among both regions in the present era of globalization. The depth of the relations has been reflected in the patterns of trade and investment, as well as people-to-people interactions, cultural exchanges, and cooperation at the continental, regional, and bilateral levels. In recent years, there is a strong trade and investment relations between India and Africa. These relations are promoting socio-political and commercial issues, capacity building, development cooperation, and economic and technological initiatives for India and Africa (Prabhakar, 2005).

Both Africa and India have performing very well with full dedication to build up the relationship for trade and development. Through this partnership the trade between India and Africa has increased ten-times, it was $7.2 billion in 2001 to rise up to $78.0 billion in 2014, but it was declines to $59.9 billion in 2017 due to declines in the commodity and oil price decline overall the developing economy in the world (African Export-Import Bank & Export-Import Bank of India, 2018).

MAIN FOCUS OF THE CHAPTER

India-Africa Trade

Total trade between India and Africa increased almost thirteen-fold between 2001 and 2018 and stood at $68.46 billion in 1018. India's exports to Africa increased from $2.81 billion in 2001 up to $26.95 billion in 2018 registering an impressive growth rate. India's exports to Africa were at the peak in 2014 at $34.63 billion. India's imports from Africa, on the other hand, increased from $2.44 billion in 2001 to $41.51 billion in 2018 (Table 1; Figure 1).

Annual growth rate for India's export to the world and Africa was 12.41% and 6.88%, respectively (Table 2; Figure 2).

During 2001-2007, compound growth rate for exports was 22.17%for the world and 28.14%for Africa. During 2007-2013, compound growth rate of India's export was 14.95%for the world and 18.28% for Africa. In 20013-2018, compound growth rate for India's export was (-0.82%)for the world and (-4.58%) for Africa(Table 3; Figure 3).

India's import from Africa is rather unstable with the peaks in 2006, 2010, and 2017, and breakdowns in 2009, 2013, and 2015-2016 (Table 4; Figure 4).

Table 1. India-Africa trade in 2001-2018, $ billion

Years	India's imports from Africa	India's exports to Africa	Years	India's imports from Africa	India's exports to Africa
2001	2.44	2.81	2010	31.44	17.89
2002	3.30	3.02	2011	39.78	23.35
2003	3.26	3.62	2012	43.02	27.31
2004	3.38	4.80	2013	39.42	34.08
2005	4.93	6.73	2014	40.37	34.63
2006	12.76	9.47	2015	33.78	25.64
2007	18.31	12.44	2016	26.14	22.61
2008	26.65	15.38	2017	35.80	24.38
2009	21.12	13.31	2018	41.51	26.95

Source: Authors' development based on Government of India (n.d.)

Figure 1. India-Africa export, import, and trade balance in 2001-2018, $ billion
Source: Authors' development based on Government of India (n.d.)

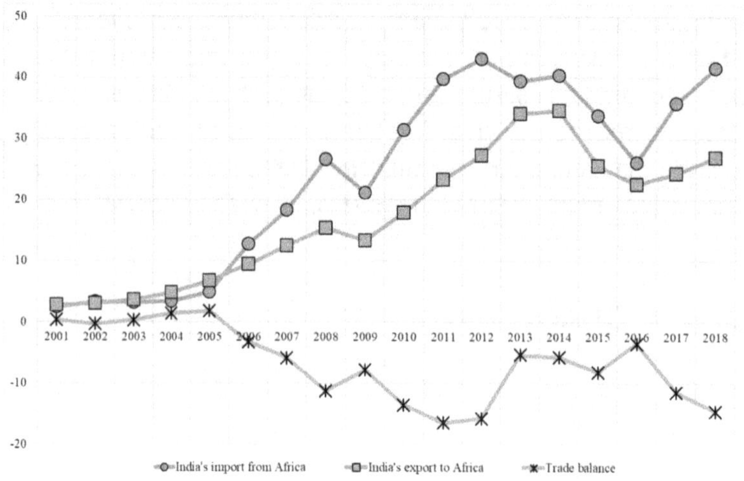

Table 2. India's export to the world and Africa in 2002-2018, annual growth rate in percentage

Years	World	Africa	Share of Africa in total export	Years	World	Africa	Share of Africa in total export
2002	12.41	6.88	6.41	2011	26.89	23.38	8.12
2003	15.60	16.67	6.02	2012	-4.12	14.53	7.74
2004	21.80	24.62	6.10	2013	13.98	19.84	9.43
2005	24.36	28.65	6.33	2014	-6.00	1.60	10.12
2006	17.20	28.89	6.71	2015	-20.11	-35.06	10.91
2007	16.93	23.88	7.81	2016	-1.56	-13.38	9.70
2008	19.77	19.12	8.53	2017	12.01	7.23	8.69
2009	-2.88	-15.57	8.46	2018	8.42	9.56	8.24
2010	19.80	25.58	7.53				

Source: Authors' development based on Government of India (n.d.)

Table 3. India's export to Africa, compound growth rate in 2001-2018, %

Region	2001-2007	2007-2013	2013-2018
World	22.17	14.95	-0.82
Africa	28.14	18.28	-4.58

Source: Authors' development based on Government of India (n.d.)

In terms of the compound growth rate of India's import from Africa, it has been slowing down since the early 2000s to only 1.04% in 2013-2018 (Table 5; Figure 5).

India's export to Africa is rather diverse. The major export item is mineral fuels followed by vehicles, pharmaceutical products, machinery, and cereals (Figure 6).

Figure 2. India's export to the world and Africa in 2002-2018, annual growth rate in percentage
Source: Authors' development based on Government of India (n.d.)

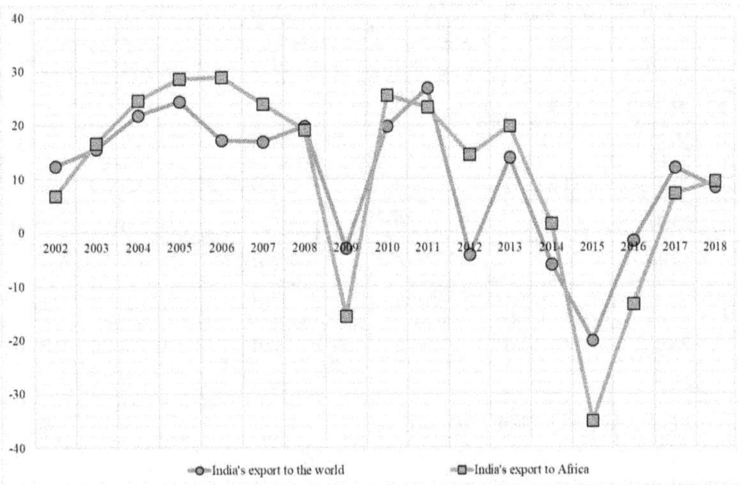

Figure 3. India's export to Africa, compound growth rate in 2001-2018, %
Source: Authors' development based on Government of India (n.d.)

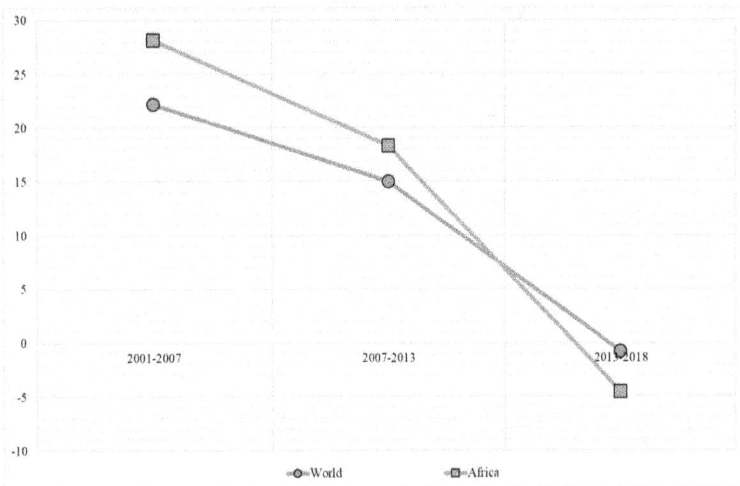

India's import from Africa is more homogeneous compared to its export – the share of mineral fuels in total import is about 63% (Figure 7).

India's main export destination in Africa is South Africa (17% in total exports). Among other export destinations are Kenya, Egypt, Nigeria, Tanzania, Mauritius, Mozambique, Algeria, Ghana, and Ethiopia (Figure 8).

Among African countries, major suppliers to India are Nigeria, South Africa, Angola, Egypt, Morocco, Ghana, Algeria, Tanzania, Libya, and Botswana (Figure 9).

Table 4. India's import from Africa, annual growth rate in percentage in 2002-2018

Years	World	Africa	Share of Africa in total import	Years	World	Africa	Share of Africa in total import
2002	11.80	26.26	4.81	2011	24.30	20.96	8.98
2003	20.68	-1.49	5.75	2012	5.43	7.52	8.60
2004	26.82	3.67	4.50	2013	-4.92	-9.13	8.80
2005	29.73	31.37	3.42	2014	-1.45	2.35	8.46
2006	20.96	61.41	3.50	2015	-17.56	-19.50	8.79
2007	18.49	30.30	7.16	2016	-9.54	-29.21	8.65
2008	30.75	31.30	8.37	2017	19.67	26.97	7.33
2009	-18.51	-26.22	8.44	2018	12.52	13.76	8.06
2010	23.89	32.84	7.93				

Source: Authors' development based on Government of India (n.d.)

Figure 4. India's import from Africa, annual growth rate in percentage in 2002-2018
Source: Authors' development based on Government of India (n.d.)

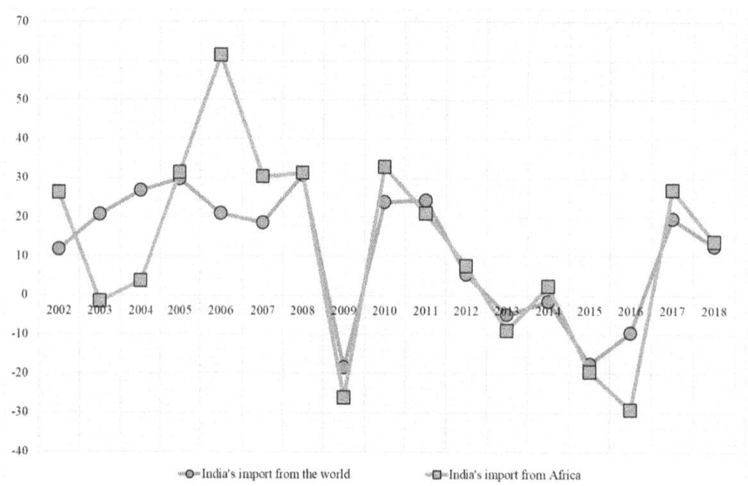

Table 5. India's import from Africa, compound growth rate in 2001-2018, %

Region	2001-2007	2007-2013	2013-2018
World	27.59	13.44	1.72
Africa	39.95	13.63	1.04

Source: Authors' development based on Government of India (n.d.)

Figure 5. India's import from Africa, compound growth rate in 2001-2018, %
Source: Authors' development based on Government of India (n.d.)

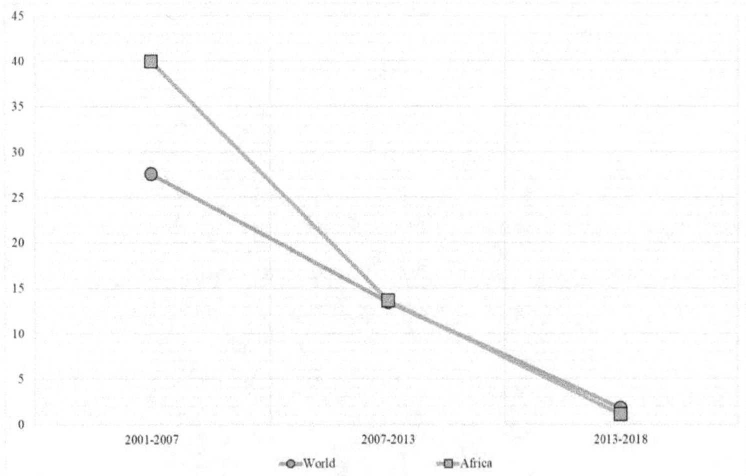

Figure 6. India's export to Africa in 2001-2018, commodity shares, %
Source: Authors' development based on Government of India (n.d.)

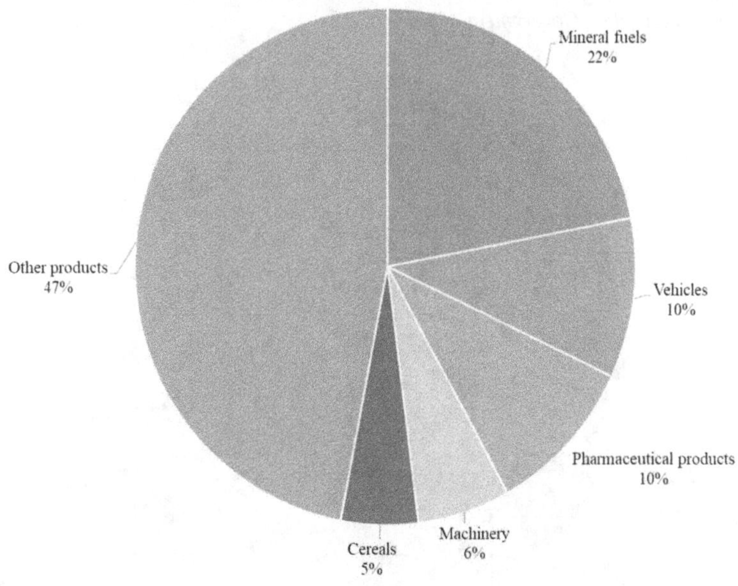

Foreign Direct Investment

Investment flows between India and Africa has been increased in last two decades due to good economic growth rate, favorable business environment, and relaxations in rule for investment, increasing profits on investment and expanding consumerism. India's outside investment flows has been increased from $44 million during 1980-1989 to $700 million during 1990-1999 and went up to $79.3 billion during 2000-2009. India's OFDI stock took a major leap from $78 million in 1980 to $1.7 billion in 2000 and increased up to $96.9 billion in 2010.

Figure 7. India's import from Africa in 2001-2018, commodity shares, %
Source: Authors' development based on Government of India (n.d.)

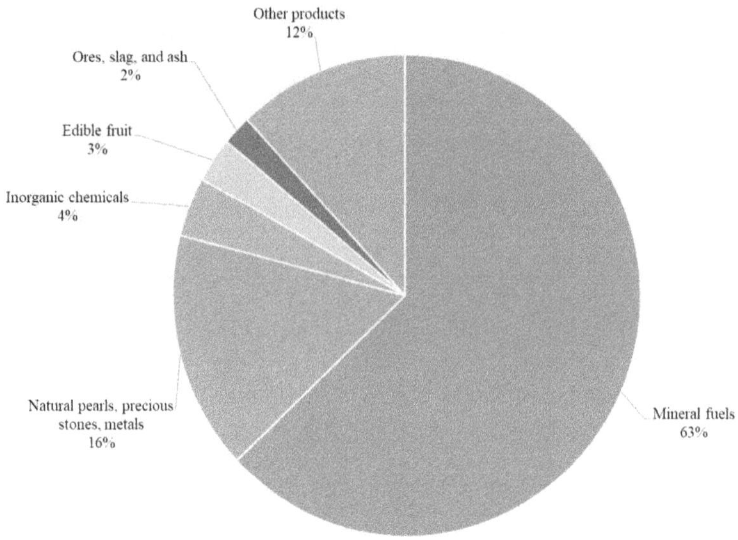

Figure 8. India's export to Africa in 2001-2018, countries shares, %
Source: Authors' development based on Government of India (n.d.)

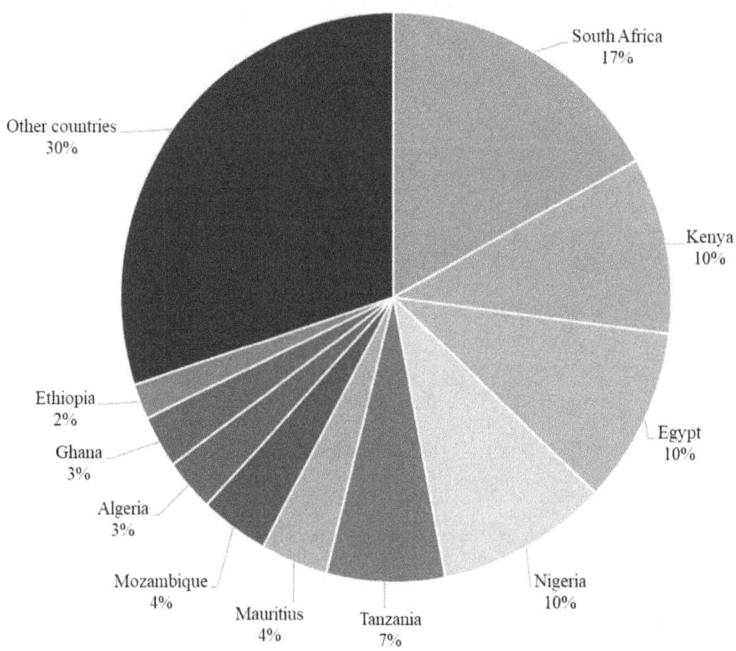

Indian investors entered to African region to reap the benefit from the market and resource by making investment to explore the potentiality of forward and backward linkage. Indian investment mainly concentrated in oil, gas, and mining in the primary commodities market of African countries. In Africa, manufacturing sector is dominated by automobile and pharmaceutical sectors. Indian companies create

Figure 9. India's import from Africa in 2001-2018, countries shares, %
Source: Authors' development based on Government of India (n.d.)

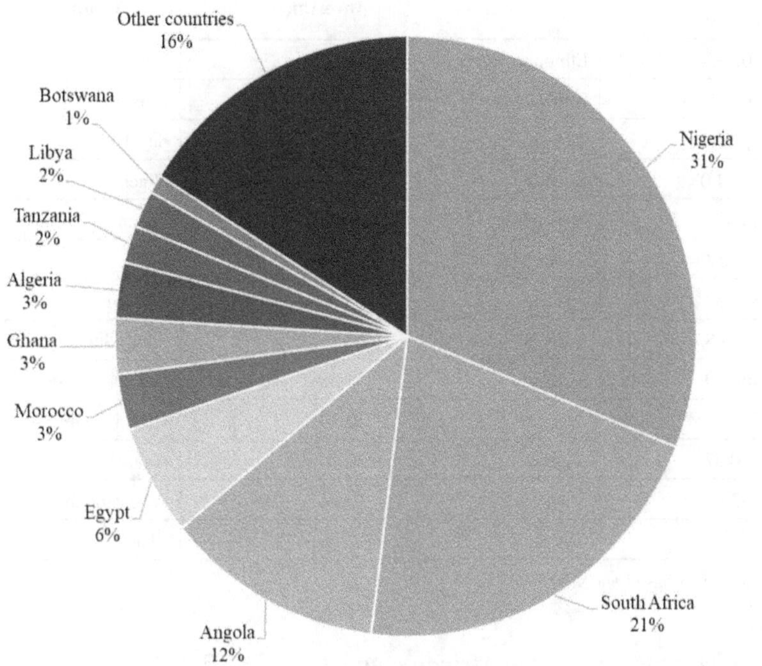

new production capacity, generate employment, and transfer of technology through Greenfield investments and joint ventures according to the requirement of African countries. The factors like socio-cultural, host country policies, regional integration agreements, bilateral investment treaties, and gross domestic product growth motivates Indian investors to invest in Africa.

In 2010, India's investment was $11.89 billion and increased up to $13.31 billion in 2017. Despite this increase, the share of the world investment made by India in African countries was 16.67% and slightly decreased to 16.31% (Table 6).

India's top investment destination in Africa is Mauritius with over $102 billion investment in 2010-2017 (Table 7).

The share of Mauritius in overall India's investment in Africa is 83%. Other countries have rather modest shares in India's investment in the region (Figure 10).

Table 6. India's investment in African countries in 2010-2017, $ billion

Years	2010	2011	2012	2013	2014	2015	2016	2017
India's investment to Africa	11.89	16.38	23.64	13.82	15.10	18.18	11.58	13.31
India's investment to the world	71.32	78.54	93.41	90.16	89.01	90.78	72.51	81.35
Share of investment to Africa in total India's investment to the world	16.67	20.86	25.31	15.33	16.97	20.02	15.97	16.36

Source: Authors'development based onInternational Monetary Fund [IMF] (n.d.)

Table 7. India's investment in top-ten African countries in 2010-2017, $ million

Country	Investment volume	Country	Investment volume	Country	Investment volume
Mauritius	102,834.94	Ethiopia	142.61	Namibia	10.78
Zambia	10,428.37	Zimbabwe	124.83	Botswana	10.67
South Africa	2,665.43	Tanzania	106.16	Seychelles	9.34
Libya	1,651.03	Uganda	83.70	Niger	7.04
Nigeria	1,649.46	Madagascar	71.48	Sudan	5.44
Gabon	901.52	Cameroon	52.06	Mali	3.96
Mozambique	830.53	Senegal	46.26	Malawi	2.14
Morocco	812.48	Gambia	36.73	South Sudan	1.91
Ghana	460.60	Liberia	35.38	Guinea-Bissau	1.04
Egypt	272.52	Algeria	20.79	Côte d'Ivoire	0.33
Eswatini	230.97	Rwanda	20.76	Angola	0.30
Tunisia	192.63	Mauritania	15.24	Western Sahara	0.27
Kenya	145.07	Congo	12.86	Chad	0.19

Source: Authors' development based on IMF (n.d.)

Figure 10. India's investment in top-ten African countries in 2010-2017, %
Source: Authors' development based on IMF (n.d.)

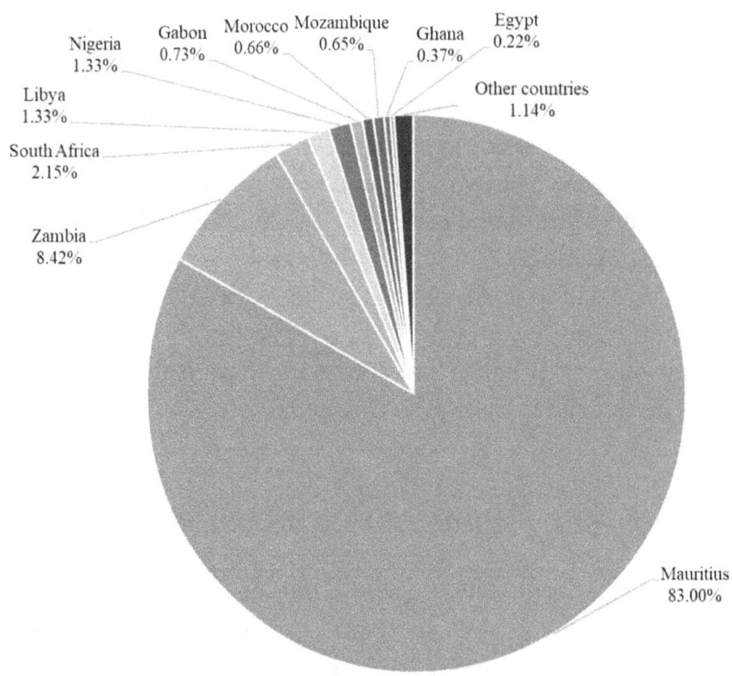

Technology Transfer

The importance of technology has been recognized by all nations of the world as it is an over-riding factor in the determination of international relations and world peace. The possession of sophisticated technology has been recognized by the world powers as a tool of leadership. National security of a state depends on the wise application of nation's science and technological capability. Diplomacy of technology transfer, usually tanned as techno-diplomacy, refers to the global communication process by which scientific and other organized knowledge is systematically applied by power politics. It has emerged as an important phenomenon and strategic factor for economic development in the contemporary world

The cooperation for technology transfer between the countries of the South was required because direct application western technologies may not be appropriate for developing countries due to complex challenges. The technology gap between the Southern countries was very small. So, Indian technologies were more suitable for the needs of African countries, particularly, in agriculture and renewable energy. However, till early 1990s, India itself was a large aid recipient. So that, the scope of India-Africa cooperation was limited. Since the early 2000s, however, rapid growth of Indian economy has been achieved due to an increase in the role of information technology in India's growth story. African countries have a potential to grow very fast in the world. The scope of technological cooperation between India and Africa has now widened.

Capacity Building: India providing scholarships to African students to promote cultural and educational relationships. India focused on three main components: to provide training, by sending experts team to partner countries and to provide equipment for project sites. India has taken up larger issues at various multilateral forums including the WTO and the World Intellectual Property Organization for capacity building in Africa.

India has been providing multiple fellowships and training programs to the rejuvenation of the civilian training programs like Indian Technical & Economic Cooperation Program (ITEC) and Special Commonwealth Assistance for Africa Program (SCAAP) to assist African countries. Indian government provides different educational scholarships under 21 schemes. Indian engineers have been providing their services for development projects in terms of (Figure 11).

SOLUTIONS AND RECOMMENDATIONS

The study explains the various factors, external and internal, that enhance economic relations between the African continent and India. Africa-India trade and investment undoubtedly has more potential. The governments of India and Africa should relax the regulations for better bilateral relations in trade and investment for development. Both India and Africa provide proper information for trade, investment and technology transfer that will be helpful for India and Africa.

FUTURE RESEARCH DIRECTIONS

The directions of trade and investment from both side is stats decreasing 2015 onwards that requires corrective initiatives for India and African countries require thorough study. The importance of technology has been recognized by all nations of the world as it is an over-riding factor in the determination of

Figure 11. Number of students from Africa in India in 2011-2018, people
Source: Ministry of Human Resource Development of India (n.d.)

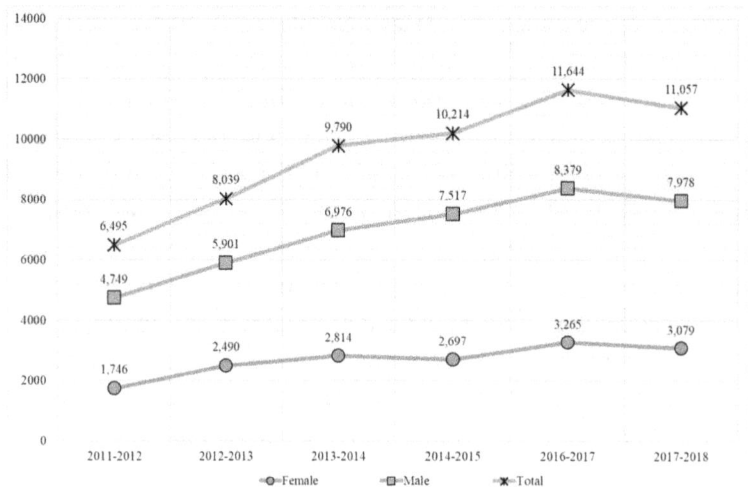

international relations and world peace. The possession of sophisticated technology has been recognized by world powers as a tool of leadership. National security of a state is dependent on the wise application of nation's science and technological capability. Diplomacy of technology transfer, usually tanned as techno-diplomacy, refers to the global communication process by which scientific and other organized knowledge is systematically applied by power politics. It has emerged as an important phenomenon and strategic factor for economic development in the contemporary world.

CONCLUSION

Foreign direct investments and trade can play an important role in connecting India with Africa. The bilateral trade and investment between India and Africa was increased up to 2014 and after that it starts diminishing. This is not good signal for India and Africa because both have big potential to contribute for each other. Africa has large sources of natural resources and workable manpower but they have shortage of capital and technological knowhow. In this aspect India can help African countries in there development process by investing in Africa's dream project, second by importing natural resources as raw material and then export to Africa after converting in finished goods for African peoples, third India is providing the support in capacity building for African people by providing different sponsorship and scholarship to acquire technological and professional knowledge.

REFERENCES

Chakrabarty, M. (2018). *Indian Investments in Africa: Scale, Trends, and Policy Recommendations*. New Delhi, India: Observer Research Foundation.

Erokhin, V. (2015). Contemporary Reshaping of Eurasian Integration: Russia's Policies and their Implication for the EU and EurAsEC. *Procedia Economics and Finance*, *22*, 402–411. doi:10.1016/S2212-5671(15)00313-5

Erokhin, V. (2016). Rising Economic Powers among Economies in Transition: Is There Enough Space on the Global Market? In V. Erokhin (Ed.), *Global Perspectives on Trade Integration and Economies in Transition* (pp. 1–25). Hershey, PA: IGI Global. doi:10.4018/978-1-5225-0451-1.ch001

Government of India. (n.d.). *Directorate General of Commercial Intelligence and Statistics.* Retrieved October 1, 2019, from http://dgciskol.gov.in/

International Monetary Fund. (n.d.). *Coordinated Direct Investment Survey.* Retrieved October 1, 2019, from http://data.imf.org/site_moved.html

Ministry of Human Resource Development of India. (n.d.). *All India Survey on Higher Education.* Retrieved October 1, 2019, from https://www.india.gov.in/all-india-survey-higher-education-ministry-human-resource-development

Nayyar, R., & Aggarwal, P. (2014). *Africa-India's New Trade and Investment Partner.* Retrieved October 1, 2019, from https://papers.ssrn.com/sol3/papers.cfm?abstract_id=2757798

Prabhakar, A. (2005). Globalisation, Poverty & Inequality: A Study of India, China, the USA and OECD, *VIKLP*.

Roy, S. (2013). *India and Africa Ties: Challenges and Opportunities.* Retrieved October 1, 2019, from https://blogs.lse.ac.uk/africaatlse/2013/07/03/india-and-africa-ties-challenges-and-opportunities/

United Nations Conference on Trade and Development. (2019). *World Investment Report 2019: Special Economic Zones*. Geneva: United Nations Conference on Trade and Development.

ADDITIONAL READING

Alden, C. (2007). *China in Africa? Partner, Competitor or Hegemon?* London: Zed Books.

Anusree, P. (2014). Indian Foreign Direct Investment: A Way to Africa. *Procedia: Social and Behavioral Sciences*, *157*, 183–195. doi:10.1016/j.sbspro.2014.11.021

Arkhangelskaya, A. (2010). *India, Brazil and South Africa Dialogue Forum: A Bridge between Three Continents: Challenges, Achievements and Policy Options.* Retrieved October 1, 2019, from http://nai.diva-portal.org/smash/record.jsf?pid=diva2:371853

Beri, R. (2011). *Evolving India-Africa Relations: Continuity and Change*. Johannesburg: South African Institute of International Affairs.

Buhlungu, S., Daniel, J., Southall, R., & Lutchman, J. (2006). *State of the Nation: South Africa 2005-2006*. Cape Town: HSRC Press.

Buhlungu, S., Daniel, J., Southall, R., & Lutchman, J. (2007). *State of the Nation: South Africa 2007.* Cape Town: HSRC Press.

Draper, P., & Le Pere, G. (2005). *Enter the Dragon: Towards a Free Trade Agreement between China and Southern African Customs Union.* Cape Town: South African Institute of International Affairs.

Goldstein, A. (2007). *Multinational Companies from Emerging Economies.* London: Palgrave Macmillan UK. doi:10.1057/9780230206335

Government of India. (2017). *Towards Sustainable and Lasting Growth. Annual Report 2016-2017.* New Delhi: Government of India.

Kohli, A. (Ed.). (2001). *The Success of India's Democracy.* Cambridge: Cambridge University Press.

Kuada, J. (2006). Cross-Cultural Interactions and Changing Management Practices in Africa: A Hybrid Management Perspective. *African Journal of Business and Economic Research, 1*(1), 96–113.

Le Pere, G. (Ed.). (2007). *China in Africa: Mercantilist Predator or Partner in Development? Mildrand.* Institute for Global Dialogue.

MacLean, S., Black, D., & Shaw, T. (2006). *A Decade of Human Security: Global Governance and New Multilateralisms.* Aldershot: Ashgate Publishing Limited.

Mawdsley, E., & McCann, G. (Eds.). (2011). *India in Africa: Changing Geographies of Power.* Oxford: Pambazuka Press.

McKay, V. (1963). *Africa in World Politics. New York, NY.* New York: Harper & Row.

Naidu, S. (2008). India's Growing African Strategy. *Review of African Political Economy, 115*(35), 116–128. doi:10.1080/03056240802021435

Park, R. L. (1965). Indian-African Relations. *Asian Survey, 5*(7), 350–358. doi:10.2307/2642294

Singh, S. K. (2007). *India and West Africa: A Burgeoning Relationship.* London: Chatham House.

Smith, D. (2007). *The Dragon and The Elephant: China, India and the New World Order.* London: Profile Books.

Stubbs, R., & Underhill, G. R. D. (1994). *Political Economy and the Changing Global Order.* London: The Macmillan Press Ltd. doi:10.1007/978-1-349-13497-7

Villares, F. (Ed.). (2006). *Perspectives and Alliances. San Paolo.* India, Brazil and South Africa: San Paolo State University.

KEY TERMS AND DEFINITIONS

Development Cooperation: A type of cooperation that has three major tasks: supporting and complementing efforts of developing countries to guarantee the provision of universal social basic standards to their citizens, as a means for people to exercise their basic human rights; promoting the convergence of the developing (and particularly the poorest) countries to higher levels of income and wellbeing, correcting extreme international inequalities; supporting efforts of developing countries to participate actively in the provision of international public goods.

Developing Country: A country that has low levels of industrialization and fares poorly on the Human Development Index (HDI). A low HDI score means that the citizens of a particular country have lower life expectancy, lower educational attainment, lower per capita incomes, and higher fertility rates than found in other countries.

Economic Integration: A process of regional integration that often occurs among neighboring nations. Itincludes seven stages: a preferential trading area, a free trade area, a customs union, a common market, an economic union, an economic and monetary union, and complete economic integration.

Free Trade Agreement: A pact between two or more nations to reduce barriers to imports and exports among them.

Investment: an asset or item that is purchased with the hope that it will generate income or appreciate in the future; an act of putting money to work to start or expand a business or project or the purchase of an asset, with the goal of earning income or capital appreciation.

Regional Trade Agreement: A treaty that is signed by two or more countries to encourage free movement of goods and services across the borders of its members.

South-South Cooperation: A term used to describe the technical cooperation, exchange of resources, supporting local capabilities, institutes, expertise, and human capital, in contribution of national development policies, of the Global South.

Chapter 6

India's Trade and Development Strategies With BRCS, EAC, and SCO in the Era of Globalization

Sandip Solanki
https://orcid.org/0000-0002-9455-5263
Symbiosis International University, India

Krishna Murthy Inumula
https://orcid.org/0000-0002-4556-549X
Symbiosis International University, India

ABSTRACT

India's trade with the major economic groups BRCS, EAC, and SCO revealed that there exists a long-run equilibrium relation between BRCS and SCO group of countries trade with India's economic growth, whereas EAO group of countries does not show any long-run equilibrium relation. It is concluded that 1% change in imports from BRCS countries causes the economic growth to increase by about 0.84% meaning that in the long run, imports from BRCS countries tend to have a significant impact on economic growth, similarly a 1% change in exports to BRCS countries causes the economic growth to decrease by about 0.53%, meaning that in the long run, exports to BRCS countries tend to have a significant impact on economic growth. Similar to BRCS co-integration model, the SCO group of countries' imports are positively affecting, whereas exports are negatively affecting economic growth. The exported items to SCO countries are negatively affecting the economy meaning that exports are not contributing.

INTRODUCTION

The relationship between foreign trade and economic growth in developing countries has continued to dominate the debate in trade and development economics. The results to examine the nature of a causal relationship between foreign trade and economic growths are also mixed. Some researchers have found a positive association between foreign trade and economic growth while others saw opposite conclusions.

DOI: 10.4018/978-1-7998-1730-7.ch006

Van den Berg and Schmidt (1994) presented that there is a positive relationship between export growth and aggregate economic growth over time for the majority of the 17 Latin American economies, while Abhayaratne (1996) rejected the hypothesis that foreign trade stimulates economic growth in Sri Lanka.

It is well known that foreign trade has accelerated under globalization, and developing countries have captured a growing share of that trade, including by trading more with each other. The share of BRICS in global output increased from 5.4% in 1990 to 22.2% in 2016. Excluding China, the aggregated share of Russia, Brazil, India, and South Africa in global output went up from 3.7% to around 7.4% – an increase, but not a spectacular one. This is mirrored in global export shares, where China significantly outpaces the others in the group. Indeed, in most of the developing countries outside East and Southeast Asia, export shares remained roughly constant and in some cases even declined, other than during the rising phase of the commodity price super-cycle, when major commodity exporters registered a temporary increase of their market shares (United Nations Conference on Trade and Development [UNCTAD], 2018).

Since the topic impact of foreign trade on economic growth remained a key subject of debate in research and policy discourses, this chapter studies causal relationship between India's foreign trade with the four remaining member countries of BRICS (referred to as BRCS (Brazil, Russia, China, and South Africa) in this study), East African Community (EAC), and Shanghai Cooperation Organization (SCO).

BACKGROUND

The increase of reciprocal trade agreements between pairs and groups of countries over the past few decades has resulted in a plethora of literature addressing the causes of regionalism, their effects of members and non-members, as well as their effects towards promoting global free trade. This study makes a contribution to the literature with reference to investigate the relationship between foreign trade of India with three groups of countries namely BRCS, EAC, and SCO and its impact on India's economic growth.

Fajana (1979) analyzed the impact of trade on Nigeria's economic growth. Using a two-gap model, it estimates the relationships between exports, foreign capital, and economic growth. The results of the analysis provided empirical support for the hypothesis that trade has been an important engine of growth in Nigeria.

Feder (1983) investigated the sources of growth in the period of 1964-1973 for a group of semi-industrialized less developed countries. The result found that growth could be generated not only by increases in the aggregate levels of labor and capital but also by the reallocation of existing resources from the less efficient non-export sector to the higher productive export sector.

Kavoussi (1984) examined the relationship between export expansion and economic growth in a sample of 73 developing countries using data for the period of 1960-1978. The study highlighted that in both groups of low- and middle-income countries, export expansion was associated with better economic performance and that an important cause of that association was the favorable impact of exports on total factor productivity. Kavoussi (1984) also demonstrated that the effect of commodity composition of exports on the relationship between export expansion and economic growth was substantial in more advanced developing economies.

Jung and Marshall (1985) performed causality tests between exports and growth for 37 developing countries. The results cast considerable doubt on the validity of the export promotion hypothesis.

Fan (1992a) explored the regional implications of China's recent open-door policy. The results suggested that foreign trade was more readily translated into economic development in the most well developed and industrialized eastern coastal provinces. Fan (1992b) indicated that foreign trade benefited core provinces and major industrial regions more than other parts of China.

Dodaro (1993) employed individual country time-series analysis to test the contemporaneous relationship between real export growth and real GDP growth as well as to establish the direction of causality between them. The causality test offers a very weak support for the contention that export growth promotes GDP growth. Support for the alternate contention that GDP growth promotes export growth is also weak although somewhat stronger than the former. The results challenged the notion that exports promoted growth and that export promotion was the best strategy for the least developed countries (LDCs) – even if that was taken to mean simply neutrality of effective exchange rates (EERs).

Van den Berg and Schmidt (1994) confirmed a positive relationship between export growth and aggregate economic growth over time for the majority of 17 Latin American economies. Abhayaratne (1996) observed the relationship between export and economic growth in Sri Lanka in 1960-1992 using the techniques of causality and co-integration. The hypothesis that foreign trade stimulates economic growth was rejected by the findings of the study. Harrison (1996) revealed that the correlation across different types of openness was not always strong, but there was generally a positive association between growth and different measures of openness. Henriques and Sadorsky (1996) in the case of Canada found that, first, real exports, real terms of trade, and real GDP were co-integrated. That implied that there existed a long-run steady relationship between those three variables. Second, Henriques and Sadorsky (1996) found that a one-way Granger causal relationship existed in Canada whereby changes in GDP preceded the changes in exports.

Begum and Shamsuddin (1998) studied the effect of export on economic growth in Bangladesh using annual data for the period of 1961-1992. The results suggested that export growth significantly increased economic growth through its positive impact on total factor productivity in the economy.

Ekanayake (1999) highlighted the causal relationship between export growth and economic growth in eight Asian developing countries using annual data for the period of 1960-1997. The empirical results confirmed that bi-directional causality existed between export growth and economic growth in India, Indonesia, South Korea, Pakistan, the Philippines, Sri Lanka, and Thailand. There was also an evidence of export-led growth in Malaysia. Furthermore, there was an evidence of short-run Granger causality running from economic growth to export growth in all countries included in the study except Sri Lanka. However, there was no strong evidence for short-run causality running from export growth to economic growth.

Beatty (2000) inspected the relationship between trade and the early growth of domestic industry for Mexican economy. The study revealed a development process in which trade growth and the spread of domestic manufacturing were highly complimentary for the economy.

Hatemi-J (2002) examined bi-directional Granger-causality for the period of 1960-1999 and suggested that the expansion of export was an integral part of the economic growth process in Japan. Liu, Burridge, and Sinclair (2002) confirmed the causal links between trade, economic growth, and inward foreign direct investment (FDI) in China at the aggregate level. Long-run relationships between growth, exports, imports, and FDI were identified in a co-integration framework in which the study found bi-directional causality between economic growth, FDI, and exports. Economic development, exports, and FDI appeared to be mutually reinforcing under the open-door policy.

Lewer and van den Berg (2003) revealed that many empirical studies were surprisingly consistent in terms of the size of the relationship: a 1%-point increase in the growth of exports is associated with a 0.2%-point increase in economic growth. Given the power of compounding, the effect of trade on growth is very important for human welfare.

Dritsaki, Dritsaki, and Adamopoulos (2004) analyzed the relationship between trade, FDI, and economic growth in Greece in the period of 1960-2002. The co-integration analysis suggested that there was a long-run equilibrium relationship. The results of Granger causality test confirmed a causal relationship between the examined variables. Economic growth, trade, and FDI appear to be mutually reinforcing under the open-door policy.

Dollar and Kraay (2004) discussed that evidence from individual cases and cross-country analysis supported the view that globalization led to faster growth and poverty reduction in poor countries. Makki and Somwaru (2004) confirmed that FDI and trade had a positive impact on economic growth. The size of such impact may varied across the countries depending on the level of human capital, domestic investment, infrastructure, macroeconomic stability, and trade policies. Awokuse (2007) investigated the impact of export and import expansion on growth in three transition economies (CEEC). The empirical results suggested that trade stimulated economic growth.

Awokuse (2008) examined the relationship between trade and economic growth in Argentina, Colombia, and Peru with emphasis on both the role of exports and imports. Granger causality tests and impulse response functions were used to examine whether growth in trade stimulated economic growth (or vice versa). The results suggested that the singular focus of past studies on exports as the engine of growth might be misleading. Although there was some empirical evidence supporting export-led growth, the empirical support for import-led growth hypothesis was relatively stronger. In some cases, there was also evidence for reverse causality from GDP growth to exports and imports.

Awokuse and Christopoulos (2009) re-examined the relationship between exports and economic growth in five industrialized economies (Canada, Italy, Japan, the UK, and the USA) with emphasis on the effect of nonlinearities on the causal relationships. Results from linearity tests justified that nonlinearities existed in the dynamic relationship between exports and GDP growth. Nonlinear smooth transition autoregressive (STAR) model results suggested that nonlinear Granger causality flew from exports to output growth and vice versa.

Jayachandran and Seilan (2010) investigated the relationship between trade, FDI, and economic growth for India over the period of 1970-2007. The co-integration analysis suggested that there was a long-run equilibrium relationship. The results of Granger causality test demonstrated an existence of a causal relationship between the examined variables. Economic growth, trade, and FDI appeared to be mutually reinforcing under the open-door policy.

Heidari, Katircioglu, and Davoudi (2012) studied the long-run relationship between exports, imports, and economic growth in Iran using annual data over the period of 1960-2007. The results revealed that while there was a significant and positive relationship between exports and economic growth, the effect of imports was insignificant and also human capital had a negative effect on growth both in short and long-term periods.

Caleb, Mazanai, and Dhoro (2014) confirmed an existence of a long-run relationship between various trade and other macroeconomic variables in Zimbabwe in 1975-2005. The results of the study indicated that trade and economic growth were co-integrated. The relationship was strengthened by the stability of macroeconomic policy since negative macroeconomic drivers such as rising inflation could constrain economic growth. Openness to trade was also deemed to play a crucial role, where reduction and elimination of barriers to trade promoted growth in trade and ultimately economic growth.

Were (2015) highlighted that in general, the results were largely consistent with positive impact of trade on economic growth as found in the literature. However, the empirical results based on different categories of countries demonstrated that whereas trade positively impacted economic growth in developed and developing countries, its effect was insignificant for LDCs which largely included African countries.

Musila and Yiheyis (2015) revealed that controlling for a number of factors, aggregate trade openness was found to have positively affected the level of investment and the rate of economic growth in the case of Kenya. Balasubramaniam, Mansor, and Puah (2016) explored regional trade among ASEAN-5 countries (Indonesia, Malaysia, the Philippines, Singapore, and Thailand). The study applied ARDL bound testing approach with instrumental variables to explore the relationship and found that estimates was in range of 0.27-0.55%. The study concluded that trade integration should be promoted in order to stimulate economic growth in each country.

Semančíková (2016) indicated a positive effect of trade and trade openness on macroeconomic variables. Temiz Dinç, Gökmen, Nakip, and Azari (2017) investigated the correlation between foreign trade and economic growth in some developing countries, including Iran and Turkey, by using econometrics applications (panel co-integration method and E-views software), also resting on credible national and international publications. The study found that foreign trade had a positive impact on economic growth, resource allocation, energy and green energy consumption, human capital development, and physical capital consumption.

Mishra, Gadhia, Kubendran, and Sahoo (2015) in case of the BRICS countries and Raza, Sbia, Shahbaz, and Rousan (2018) in the case of the United Arab Emirates observed the relationship between trade and economic growth. The empirical analysis highlighted the presence of co-integration between trade and economic growth. Furthermore, exports had positive effect on economic growth while that of imports was negative. The rolling window approach confirmed the stability of long-run estimates.

Tah, Czerniak, Levine, Wiggin, and Osondu (2019) discussed the effects of foreign trade (economic openness) on economic growth in South Africa. The empirical evidence indicated that foreign trade was a significant catalyst of growth in both the short- and long-run period. The evidence also indicated that human and physical capital were significant catalyst of growth in the long run.

MAIN FOCUS OF THE CHAPTER

Data and Methods

Data and Scope

This study uses annual time series data for the period of 1995-2017 collected from the United Nations Conference on Trade and Development (UNCTAD) database on three key macroeconomic variables namely GDP, imports, and exports expressed in current price in the US dollar denomination. Three groups of countries, namely BRCS (representing Brazil, Russia, China, and South Africa), EAC (representing Burundi, Rwanda, Kenya, Tanzania, and Uganda), and SCO (representing China, Kazakhstan, Kyrgyzstan, Russia, Uzbekistan, and Tajikistan) are considered to evaluate the impact of trade on India's economic growth.

Business relations and trade partnerships are important for country's economic growth in the contemporary era of globalization. Keeping up the development strategies for regional trade is at most important in current global scenario. India as a developing nation and major consumer market imports and exports diversified commodities to neighboring nations and maintains economic cooperation among different member nation in the elite groups. In general, economic theory suggests that exports should exceed imports to facilitate surplus of foreign exchange reserve in safeguarding and promotion of foreign trade with globalized world. This study focuses on the relationship between economic growth and foreign trade, long-run and short-run relation, and how innovations and shock to one variable change the other variables. In this study, the economic growth is considered as the study variable to see the long-run relationship between economic growth and trade with BRCS, EAC, and SCO.

Econometric Methods

The above time series variables are tested for stationarity by using the Augmented Dicky Fuller (ADF) test in which the unit root hypothesis assumes that the series under consideration is nonstationary and alternative hypothesis is the series is stationary. Selection of lag length is important for the model building as it affects the size of the data, the more the lag length the more the loss of information. For selecting the lag length, the standard information criterions like Akaike Information criterion (AIC), Schwarz Bayesian criterion (BIC), and Hannan-Quinn criterion (HQC) were used. Johansen's co-integration test is used to determine the long-run relationship between the variables. Stationarity of the data variables is the pre-condition for co-integration, once the data variables are found to be co-integrated which implies that there exists a long-run equilibrium relationship among the variables, then after testing for the short-run relations by using the vector error correction model (VECM).

The purpose of the co-integration test is to determine whether a set of non-stationary series is co-integrated or not. In addition to the Engle-Granger causality technique, Johansen procedure of co-integration is also employed. Johansen's approach begins with unrestricted vector autoregressive framework (VAR) involving non-stationary variables, which allows to deal with models having several endogenous variables. A key aspect of Johansen's co-integration approach is isolating and identifying the r co-integrating combinations among a set of k integrated variables and incorporate them into an empirical model. The co-integration rank divides the data into r relations, towards which the process is adjusting (equilibrium errors), and k-r (k, number of non-stationary $I(1)$ variables) relations, which are pushing the process (common driving trends).

The presence of a co-integrating relation forms the basis of VECM specification. The authors estimate the following system of equations formulated in a VECM:

$$\Delta X_t = \Pi \Delta X_t\text{-}1 + \ldots + \Pi_{k-1} \Delta X_{t-k-1} + \Pi X_t\text{-}1 + \mu + \varepsilon_t;\ t = 1, \ldots, N \tag{1}$$

where:

Δ – first difference operator;

X – vector of variables in logarithmic form;

ε_t – error term (normal, independent and identically distributed random variable with mean zero and standard deviation Σ);

μ – drift parameter;

Π – (pxp) long run matrix of the form $\Pi = \alpha \times \beta$.

If the data variables are not co-integrated meaning that there exists no long-run relationship, then VAR is used to study the direction of causality between the variables. VAR is commonly used for forecasting the systems of interrelated time series and for analyzing the dynamic impact of random disturbances on the system of variables. VAR approach sidesteps the need for conventional structural modeling by treating every variable as endogenous in the system as a function of the lagged values of all the other endogenous variables.

Results and Discussion

Trend of Variables

Over the study period, India's GDP has increased consistently from $355 billion in 1995 to $2.6 trillion in 2017. Trade with the BRCS countries shows an uptrend with minor fluctuations. In 2013-2016, there was a drop in the exports whereas the imports have been continually increased from $212 billion in 1995 to $905 billion in 2017. Trade with the EAC and the SCO member countries has shown a steady increase with minor fluctuations at the end of the time period of study. Over the study period, India's GDP had a compound annual growth rate (CAGR) of 10.42%, its imports from BRCS countries had an annual growth rate of 23.24%, and exports registered CAGR of 17.38%. For the EAC group of countries, imports registered a CAGR of 13.20% and exports stood at CAGR of 20.05%. The import with the SCO registered a CAGR of 23.63% and exports saw an annual growth rate of 15.05%. For both the BRCS and the SCO, annual growth rate of imports is higher than that of the exports. For the EAC group of countries, annual growth rate of exports is higher than that of the imports (Figure 1).

Figure 1. Time series graph
Source: Authors' development

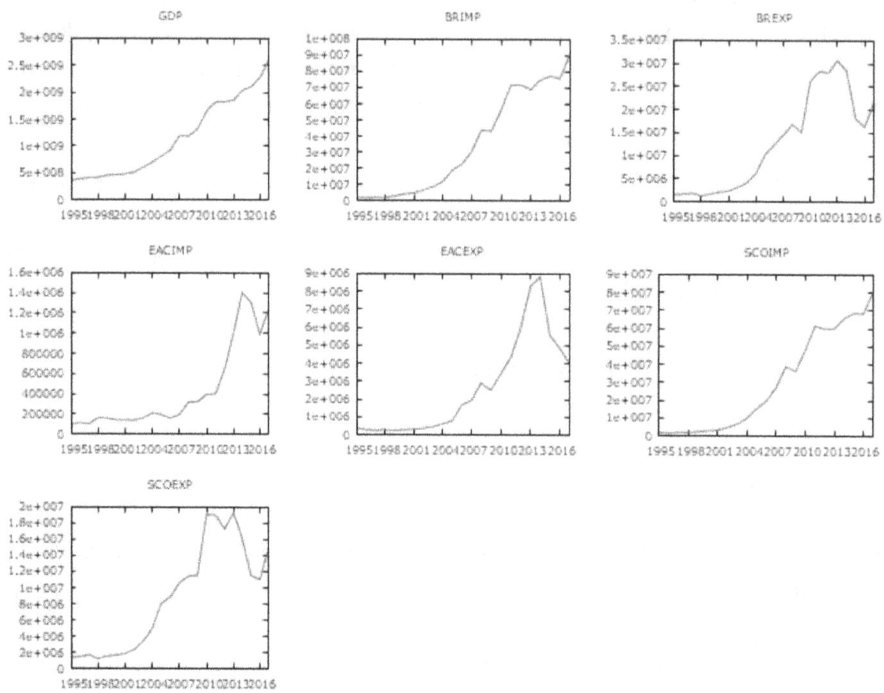

Stationary Variables

All the data variables in log level and after first difference are tested for stationarity by using the ADF test. The unit root hypothesis assumes that the series under consideration is non-stationary and alternative hypothesis is the series is stationary. Since the data variables are non-stationary in log level and stationary in first difference, there exists at least one linear combination of the non-stationary variables (in level form) (Table 1).

The next step is to see whether the variables are co-integrated or not, that is, whether economic growth and foreign trade have long-term equilibrium relationship between them or not.

Test for Co-Integration in the BRCS

The results show that there exists a co-integrating equation which confirms the long-run relation between India's economic growth and foreign trade with the BRCS (Table 2; Table 3).

It is concluded that 1% change in imports from BRCS countries causes the economic growth to increase by about 0.84% meaning that in the long-run, imports from BRCS countries tends to have a significant impact on economic growth. Similarly, a 1% change in exports to BRCS countries causes the economic growth to decrease by about 0.53% meaning that in the long-run, exports to BRCS countries trends to have a significant impact on economic growth. For the BRCS, imports positively affects whereas exports negatively affects economic growth meaning that the items which are meant for imports are crucial in India's economy. India is not self-sufficient in those import items and therefore imports them. The export items negatively affect the economy meaning that export does not contribute to the economic growth. Therefore, proper care should be taken to realign and balance both the imports and exports.

Table 1. ADF tests for stationary

Variables in log level	Test	ADF test – *p*-values	Variables in first difference	Test	ADF test – *p*-values
I_GDP	with constant with constant and trend	0.564 0.468	d_GDP	with constant with constant and trend	0.001 0.050
I_BRIMP	with constant with constant and trend	0.457 0.265	d_I_BRIMP	with constant with constant and trend	0.003 0.008
I_BREXP	with constant with constant and trend	0.874 0.451	d_ I_BREXP	with constant with constant and trend	0.008 0.045
I_EACIMP	with constant with constant and trend	0.124 0.356	d_ I_EACIMP	with constant with constant and trend	0.000 0.000
I_EACEXP	with constant with constant and trend	0.478 0.578	d_ I_EACEXP	with constant with constant and trend	0.002 0.001
I_SCOIMP	with constant with constant and trend	0.354 0.214	d_ I_SCOIMP	with constant with constant and trend	0.012 0.002
I_SCOEXP	with constant with constant and trend	0.452 0.248	d_ I_SCOEXP	with constant with constant and trend	0.000 0.000

Source: Authors' development

Table 2. Johansen's co-integration test (co-integration rank test), unrestricted co-integration rank tests, trace and maximum Eigen (L_{max}) value

No. of co-integrating equations or rank	Eigen values (λ_i)	Trace test	*P*-value	L_{max} test	*P*-value
0	0.73377	41.774	0.0011	27.791	0.0037
1	0.45168	13.983	0.1826	12.619	0.1888
2	0.06291	1.3646	0.2427	1.3646	0.2427

Note: Both the Trace test and L_{max} test indicates one co-integrating equation at both 5% and 1%
Source: Authors' development

Table 3. Johansen's co-integration test, normalized co-integrating β and adjustment α coefficients

Coefficients	Values			
β-coefficients	1_GDP	1_BRIMP	1_BREXP	Constant
	1.00 (0.00)	-0.84** (0.101)	0.53** (0.123)	5.08** (1.59)
α-coefficients	d_I_GDP	d_I_BRIMP	d_I_BREXP	
	-0.33** (0.00)	-0.68** (0.00)	-1.42** (0.00)	
Short-run coefficients				
d_1_GDP_1	0.25 (0.30)	1.38** (0.00)	1.53* (0.02)	
d_1_BRIMP_1	-0.25* (0.04)	-0.58* (0.02)	-1.11** (0.00)	
d_1_BREXP_1	0.08 (0.35)	0.21 (0.21)	0.36 (0.11)	

Note: Standard errors in parenthesis; * 5% level of significance; **1% level of significance
Source: Authors' development

The VECM shows that the error correction term (-0.33) is negative and significant which means that there exists a long-run causality running from exports and imports to economic growth. The speed of adjustment to the long-run equilibrium is restored by around 33%. In the short run, there is a significant (coefficient (-0.25) with *p*-value 0.04) causal relationship between imports and economic growth. In the context of the BRCS' imports as a study variable, (-0.68**) in the long-run (*p*-value 0.00) and 1.38 in the short-run (*p*-value 0.02) demonstrate a significant relationship between imports and economic growth at 5% level of significance. In case of BRCS' exports as a study variable, (-1.42**) in the long-run (*p*-value 0.00) and 1.53 in the short-run (*p*-value 0.02) demonstrate a significant relationship between exports and economic growth at 5% level of significance. The residual and diagnostic checks of VECM model is found to be satisfactory (Figure 2).

It is found that one standard deviation shock to economic growth results in immediate decrease in economic growth, negative imports and exports over the period of ten years, whereas a shock to the imports results in an increase in economic growth, imports, and exports. One standard deviation shock to the exports results in a decrease in economic growth, imports, and exports over the next ten years' time period.

Figure 2. Impulse response of the BRCS
Source: Authors' development

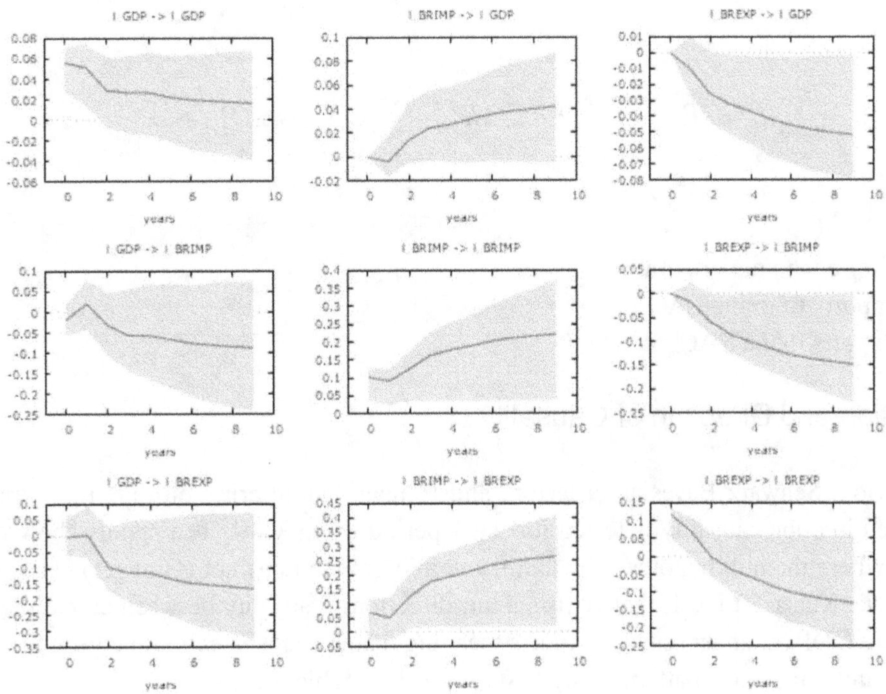

Test for Co-Integration in the EAC

For the EAC, there exists no co-integrating equation in the system, which confirms that there exists no long-run equilibrium relation between India's economic growth and trade with the EAC (Table 4).

Using VAR framework, the authors check the short-run relation in terms of the direction causality running between economic growth and foreign trade with the EAC:

$$GDP_t = C_1 + \sum_{i=1}^{k} a_{1i} GDP_{t-i} + \sum_{i=1}^{k} b_{1i} EACIMP_{t-i} + \sum_{i=1}^{k} c_{1i} EACEXP_{t-i} + e_{1t} \quad (2)$$

Table 4. Johansen's co-integration rank tests Unrestricted co-integration rank tests, trace and maximum Eigen (L_{max}) value

No. of co-integrating equations or rank	Eigen values (λ_i)	Trace test	*P*-value	L_{max} test	*P*-value
0	0.3850	15.347	0.7613	10.211	0.7286
1	0.2148	5.1353	0.7931	5.0791	0.7327
2	0.0026	0.0561	0.8127	0.0561	0.8127

Note: Both the Trace test and L_{max} test indicates no co-integrating equation at both 5% and 1%
Source: Authors' development

$$EACIMP_t = C_2 + \sum_{i=1}^{k} a_{2i} GDP_{t-i} + \sum_{i=1}^{k} b_{2i} EACIMP_{t-i} + \sum_{i=1}^{k} c_{2i} EACEXP_{t-i} + e_{2t} \quad (3)$$

$$EACEXP_t = C_3 + \sum_{i=1}^{k} a_{3i} GDP_{t-i} + \sum_{i=1}^{k} b_{3i} EACIMP_{t-i} + \sum_{i=1}^{k} c_{3i} EACEXP_{t-i} + e_{3t} \quad (4)$$

Where:
GDP: Proxy for economic growth.
EACIMP: Imports from the EAC.
EACEXP: Exports to the EAC.

Lag Selection and Direction of Causality

Akaike criterion, Schwarz Bayesian criterion, and Hannan-Quinn criterion give the optimum period of lag 1. The direction causality is tested for lag 1 period using VAR. The results show the direction of causality where the null hypothesis is that economic growth does not (Granger) cause imports and exports and vice versa. At lag 1, there exists a uni-directional causality between economic growth and exports, where GDP (Granger) causes exports meaning that changes in economic growth are useful for predicting changes in export pattern to the EAC countries (Table 5).

There exists a uni-directional causality between imports and exports, where imports (Granger) causes exports meaning that changes in import patterns are useful for predicting changes in export pattern to the EAC. The hypothesis that economic growth does not (Granger) cause exports is rejected (Table 6).

There exists a co-integrating equation which confirms the long-run relation between India's economic growth and foreign trade with the SCO. It is concluded that 1% change in imports from the SCO causes the economic growth to increase by about 0.72% meaning that in the long-run, imports from the SCO tends to have a significant impact on economic growth. Similarly, a 1% change in exports to the SCO causes economic growth to decrease by about 0.43% meaning that in the long-run, the exports to the SCO tends to have a significant impact on economic growth (Table 7).

Similar to the BRCS co-integration model, the SCO's imports positively affect economic growth, whereas exports negatively affect economic growth (Table 8). The exported items to the SCO negatively affect the economy. Therefore, proper care should be taken to realign and balance the import and export items.

Table 5. Direction of causality among economic growth, imports, and exports

Lags	loglik	p(LR)	AIC	BIC	HQC
1	35.53462		-2.353462*	-1.756023*	-2.236835*
2	38.79246	0.68740	-1.779246	-0.733727	-1.575150
3	50.24982	0.00639	-2.024982	-0.531384	-1.733416

Note: The asterisks indicate the best (that is, minimized) values of the respective information criteria; AIC – Akaike criterion; BIC – Schwarz Bayesian criterion; HQC – Hannan-Quinn criterion

Source: Authors' development

Table 6. Causality: directions and decisions

Direction of causality	Number of lags	F-value	p-value	Decision
1_GDP → 1_EACIMP	1	0.1285	0.7241	Accept
1_GDP → 1_EACEXP		13.688	0.0016	Reject
1_EACIMP → 1_GDP		0.9506	0.3425	Accept
1_EACIMP → 1_EACEXP		11.507	0.0032	Reject
1_EACEXP → 1_GDP		0.0980	0.7578	Accept
1_EACEXP → 1_EACIMP		1.0349	0.3225	Accept

Source: Authors' development

Test for Co-Integration in the SCO

Table 7. Johansen's co-integration test (co-integration rank test), unrestricted co-integration rank tests, trace and maximum Eigen (L_{max}) value

No. of co-integrating equations or rank	Eigen values (λ_i)	Trace test	*P*-value	L_{max} test	*P*-value
0	0.79628	46.500	0.0002	33.411	0.0003
1	0.42730	13.089	0.1116	11.705	0.1228
2	0.063761	1.3836	0.2395	1.3836	0.2395

Note: Both the Trace test and L_{max} test indicates one co-integrating equation at both 5% and 1%

Source: Authors' development

Table 8. Johansen's co-integration test, normalized co-integrating β and adjustment α coefficients

Coefficients	Values			
β-coefficients	1_GDP	1_SCOIMP	1_SCOEXP	Constant
	1.00 (0.00)	-0.72** (0.05)	0.43** (0.08)	7.94** (2.32)
α-coefficients	d_I_GDP	d_I_SCOIMP	d_I_SCOEXP	
	-0.51** (0.00)	-1.10** (0.00)	-2.13** (0.00)	
Short-run coefficients				
d_1_GDP_1	0.29 (0.25)	1.60** (0.00)	1.50* (0.01)	
d_1_SCOIMP_1	-0.27* (0.04)	-0.80** (0.00)	-1.36** (0.00)	
d_1_SCOEXP_1	0.12 (0.21)	0.38* (0.02)	0.51* (0.02)	

Note: Standard errors in parenthesis; * 5% level of significance; **1% level of significance

Source: Authors' development

The VECM shows that the error correction term (-0.51) is negative and significant which means that there exists a long-run causality running from the exports and imports to economic growth. The speed of adjustment to the long-run equilibrium is restored by around 51%. In the short run, there is a significant (coefficient (-0.27) with *p*-value 0.04) causal relationship between the imports and economic growth. In the context of the SCO's imports as a study variable, (-1.10**) in the long-run (*p*-value 0.00) and 1.60 in the short-run (*p*-value 0.02), economic growth 0.38 (*p*-value 0.02), exports has its significant impact on the SCO's imports at 5% level of significance. For the SCO's exports as a study variable, (-2.13**) in the long-run (*p*-value 0.00) and 1.50 in the short-run (*p*-value 0.01), economic growth (-1.36) (*p*-value 0.0), imports has its significant impact on the SCO's exports at 5% level of significance. The residual and diagnostic checks of VECM model is found to be satisfactory (Figure 3).

Impulse responses generated for the forecast horizon of ten years by Cholesky ordering keeping the order from economic growth, imports, and exports, it is found that one standard deviation shock to economic growth results in immediate decrease in economic growth and results in negative imports and exports over the period of ten years, whereas shock to imports results in increase in economic growth, imports, and exports. One standard deviation shock to the exports results in a decrease in economic growth, imports, and exports over the next ten years' time period. The finding is similar to that obtained for the BRCS.

SOLUTIONS AND RECOMMENDATIONS

Based on the findings of the current study, India and developing countries of the BRCS, the EAC, and the SCO can increase economic growth through regional integration, and support each other at all levels: investment, technological transfer, trade, and economic cooperation. In all of the collaboration frameworks, including the BRICS, the EAC, and the SCO, policymakers need to formulate appropriate and effective policy in order to encourage FDI, expand trade volume and further stimulate economic growth (Prabhakar, 2016, 2017, 2018). The recommendation is to continue conducting cross-country analysis,

Figure 3. Impulse response of the SCO
Source: Authors' development

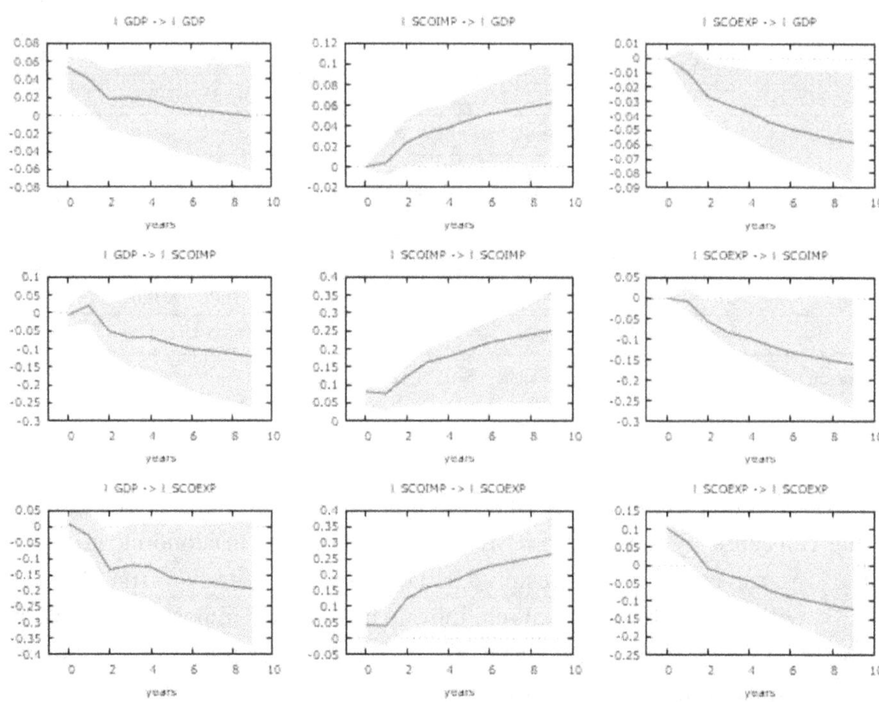

long-period data, and more sophisticated econometric techniques, covering the main determinants of FDI, investment, trade, technical and production cooperation will certainly give more robust results and largely help policymakers in the context of the BRICS, the EAC, and the SCO.

FUTURE RESEARCH DIRECTIONS

In relation to the discovery of the relationships between foreign trade and economic growth in the region of East and Southeast Asia, the major trend of research activities should be aimed at facing new global challenges. Until the present time, developing economies of the BRICS, the EAC, and the SCO have been focused on their domestic developments, but in order to be competitive on the global market, they will have face new global challenges. Investigations have to be directed on exploration of economic and trade cooperation in the formats of the BRICS, the EAC, and the SCO, as well as their relations with the international community (Erokhin, 2016a, 2016b, 2017).

CONCLUSION

The study has revealed that in case of India's trade with the BRCS, the EAC, and the SCO, there exists a long-run equilibrium relationship between the BRCS' and the SCO's trade with India's economic growth, whereas the EAC does not show any long-run equilibrium relation. It is concluded that 1% change in the imports from the BRCS causes the economic growth to increase by about 0.84% meaning that in the long-run, the imports from the BRCS tends to have a significant impact on economic growth. Similarly, a 1% change in the exports to the BRCS causes economic growth to decrease by about 0.53% meaning that in the long-run, the exports to the BRCS tends to have a significant impact on economic growth. Similar to the BRCS co-integration model, the SCO's imports positively affects, whereas the exports negatively affects economic growth. The exported items to the SCO countries negatively affect the economy meaning that the exports is not contributing. Therefore, proper care should be taken to realign and balance the import and export items for sustainable trade practices.

REFERENCES

Abhayaratne, A. S. P. (1996). Foreign Trade and Economic Growth Evidence from Sri Lanka, 1960-1992. *Applied Economics Letters*, *9*(3), 567–570. doi:10.1080/135048596355961

Awokuse, T. O. (2007). Causality between Exports, Imports, and Economic Growth: Evidence from Transition Economies. *Economics Letters*, *94*(3), 389–395. doi:10.1016/j.econlet.2006.08.025

Awokuse, T. O. (2008). Trade Openness and Economic Growth: Is Growth Export-Led or Import-Led? *Applied Economics*, *40*(2), 161–173. doi:10.1080/00036840600749490

Awokuse, T. O., & Christopoulos, D. K. (2009). Nonlinear Dynamics and the Exports-Output Growth Nexus. *Economic Modelling*, *26*(1), 184–190. doi:10.1016/j.econmod.2008.06.009

Balasubramaniam, A., Mansor, S. A., & Puah, C.-H. (2016). The Relationship between Trade Integration and Economic Growth: Case of ASEAN-5 Countries. *Global Economy Journal*, *16*(4), 745–768. doi:10.1515/gej-2016-0024

Beatty, E. (2000). The Impact of Foreign Trade on the Mexican Economy: Terms of Trade and the Rise of Industry 1880-1923. *Journal of Latin American Studies*, *32*(2), 399–433. doi:10.1017/S0022216X00005794

Begum, S., & Shamsuddin, A. F. M. (1998). Exports and Economic Growth in Bangladesh. *The Journal of Development Studies*, *35*(1), 89–114. doi:10.1080/00220389808422556

Caleb, G., Mazanai, M., & Dhoro, N. L. (2014). Relationship between International Trade and Economic Growth: A Cointegration Analysis for Zimbabwe. *Mediterranean Journal of Social Sciences*, *20*(5), 621–627.

Dodaro, S. (1993). Exports and Growth: A Reconsideration of Causality. *Journal of Developing Areas*, *27*(2), 227–244.

Dollar, D., & Kraay, A. (2004). Trade, Growth, and Poverty. *Economic Journal (London)*, *493*(114), F22–F49. doi:10.1111/j.0013-0133.2004.00186.x

Dritsaki, M., Dritsaki, C., & Adamopoulos, A. (2004). A Causal Relationship between Trade, Foreign Direct Investment and Economic Growth for Greece. *American Journal of Applied Sciences*, *3*(1), 230–235.

Ekanayake, E. M. (1999). Exports and Economic Growth in Asian Developing Countries: Cointegration and Error-Correction Models. *Journal of Economic Development*, *24*(2), 43–56.

Erokhin, V. (Ed.). (2016a). *Global Perspectives on Trade Integration and Economies in Transition*. Hershey, PA: IGI Global. doi:10.4018/978-1-5225-0451-1

Erokhin, V. (2016b). Rising Economic Powers among Economies in Transition: Is There Enough Space on the Global Market? In V. Erokhin (Ed.), *Global Perspectives on Trade Integration and Economies in Transition* (pp. 1–25). Hershey, PA: IGI Global. doi:10.4018/978-1-5225-0451-1.ch001

Erokhin, V. (2017). How to Shape the Market: China's One Belt One Road Initiative. In M. Malovic, & K. Roy (Eds.), *The State and the Market in Economic Development: In Pursuit of Millennium Development Goals* (pp. 144–156). Brisbane, Australia: The IIDS Australia Inc.

Fajana, O. (1979). Trade and Growth: The Nigerian Experience. *World Development*, *7*(1), 73–78. doi:10.1016/0305-750X(79)90009-3

Fan, C. C. (1992a). Foreign Trade and Regional Development in China. *Geographical Analysis*, *24*(3), 240–256. doi:10.1111/j.1538-4632.1992.tb00264.x

Fan, C. C. (1992b). Regional Impacts of Foreign Trade in China, 1984-1989. *Growth and Change*, *23*(2), 129–159. doi:10.1111/j.1468-2257.1992.tb00576.x

Feder, G. (1983). On Exports and Economic Growth. *Journal of Development Economics*, *12*(1-2), 59–73. doi:10.1016/0304-3878(83)90031-7

Harrison, A. (1996). Openness and Growth: A Time-Series, Cross-Country Analysis for Developing Countries. *Journal of Development Economics*, *48*(2), 419–447. doi:10.1016/0304-3878(95)00042-9

Hatemi-J, A. (2002). Export Performance and Economic Growth Nexus in Japan: A Bootstrap Approach. *Japan and the World Economy*, *14*(1), 25–33. doi:10.1016/S0922-1425(01)00071-8

Heidari, H., Katircioglu, S., & Davoudi, N. (2012). Trade and Growth Nexus in Iran: An Application of Bounds Test Approach to Level Relationship. *Economic Computation and Economic Cybernetics Studies and Research*, *46*(3), 241–254.

Henriques, I., & Sadorsky, P. (1996). Export-Led Growth or Growth-Driven Exports? The Canadian Case. *The Canadian Journal of Economics. Revue Canadienne d'Economique*, *29*(3), 540–555. doi:10.2307/136249

Jayachandran, G., & Seilan, A. (2010). A Causal Relationship between Trade, Foreign Direct Investment and Economic Growth for India. *International Research Journal of Finance and Economics*, *42*, 74–88.

Jung, W. S., & Marshall, P. J. (1985). Exports, Growth and Causality in Developing Countries. *Journal of Development Economics*, *18*(1), 1–12. doi:10.1016/0304-3878(85)90002-1

Kavoussi, R. M. (1984). Export Expansion and Economic Growth. *Journal of Development Economics*, *14*(1), 241–250. doi:10.1016/0304-3878(84)90052-X

Lewer, J. J., & van den Berg, H. (2003). How Large Is International Trade's Effect on Economic Growth? *Journal of Economic Surveys*, *17*(3), 363–396. doi:10.1111/1467-6419.00198

Liu, X., Burridge, P., & Sinclair, P. J. N. (2002). Relationships between Economic Growth, Foreign Direct Investment, and Trade: Evidence from China. *Applied Economics*, *34*(11), 1433–1440. doi:10.1080/00036840110100835

Makki, S. S., & Somwaru, A. (2004). Impact of Foreign Direct Investment and Trade on Economic Growth: Evidence from Developing Countries. *American Journal of Agricultural Economics*, *86*(3), 795–801. doi:10.1111/j.0002-9092.2004.00627.x

Mishra, A. K., Gadhia, J. N., Kubendran, N., & Sahoo, M. (2015). Trade Flows between India and Other BRICS Countries: An Empirical Analysis Using Gravity Model. *Global Business Review*, *16*(1), 107–122. doi:10.1177/0972150914553523

Musila, J. W., & Yiheyis, Z. (2015). The Impact of Trade Openness on Growth: The Case of Kenya. *Journal of Policy Modeling*, *37*(2), 342–354. doi:10.1016/j.jpolmod.2014.12.001

Prabhakar, A. (2016). Trade and Economic Integration in BRICS: Towards Multi-Polarity. In V. Erokhin (Ed.), *Global Perspectives on Trade Integration and Economies in Transition* (pp. 45–57). Hershey, PA: IGI Global. doi:10.4018/978-1-5225-0451-1.ch003

Prabhakar, A. (2017). *The Current Global Recession: A Theoretical and Empirical Investigation into Developed and BRICS Economies*. London, UK: Emerald Group.

Prabhakar, A. (2018). *Comparative Economic Systems and Welfare Economics*. New Delhi, India: ISARA.

Raza, S. A., Sbia, R., Shahbaz, M., & Rousan, S. (2018). Trade-Growth Nexus and the Rolling Window Analysis in United Arab Emirates. *Journal of Asia Business Studies*, *12*(4), 469–488. doi:10.1108/JABS-07-2016-0098

Semančíková, J. (2016). Trade, Trade Openness and Macroeconomic Performance. *Procedia: Social and Behavioral Sciences*, *220*, 407–416. doi:10.1016/j.sbspro.2016.05.515

Tah, K. A., Czerniak, C., Levine, A., Wiggin, K., & Osondu, I. N. (2019). Foreign trade and economic growth in South Africa. *Asia-Pacific Journal of Accounting & Economics*, *17*(1), 1–10. doi:10.1080/16081625.2019.1567352

Temiz Dinç, D., Gökmen, A., Nakip, M., & Azari, N. M. (2017). The Impact of Foreign Trade Issues on Economic Growth in Some Developing Countries Including Iran and Turkey. *Journal of Transnational Management*, *22*(3), 171–202. doi:10.1080/15475778.2017.1346455

United Nations Conference on Trade and Development. (2018). *Trade and Development Report 2018*. Geneva, Switzerland: United Nations Conference on Trade and Development.

Van den Berg, H., & Schmidt, J. R. (1994). Foreign Trade and Economic Growth: Time Series Evidence from Latin America. *The Journal of International Trade & Economic Development*, *3*(3), 249–268. doi:10.1080/09638199400000016

Were, M. (2015). Differential Effects of Trade on Economic Growth and Investment: A Cross-Country Empirical Investigation. *Journal of African Trade*, *2*(1-2), 71–85. doi:10.1016/j.joat.2015.08.002

ADDITIONAL READING

Agrawal, G. (2013). Foreign Direct Investment & Economic Growth in BRICS Economies: A Panel Data Analysis. *Journal of Economics. Business and Management*, *4*(3), 421–424.

Emery, R. F. (1967). The Relation of Exports and Economic Growth. *Kyklos*, *20*(4), 470–486. doi:10.1111/j.1467-6435.1967.tb00859.x

Gelb, S. (2014). *South Africa's Foreign Direct Investment Links with the BRIC Countries*. Bern: World Trade Institute, University of Bern.

Ho, C. S. F., Ahmad, N., & Dahan, H. M. (2013). Economic Freedom, Macroeconomic Fundamentals and Foreign Direct Investment in Fast Emerging BRICS and Malaysia. *International Journal of Banking and Finance*, *10*(1), 57–73.

Morazan, P., Knoke, I., Knoblauch, D., & Schafer, T. (2012). *The Role of BRICS in the Developing World*. Brussels: European Parliament, Directorate-General for External Policies.

Nandi, S. (2012). Comparative Analysis of Foreign Direct Investment Trends in Emerging Economies. *Procedia: Social and Behavioral Sciences*, *37*, 230–240. doi:10.1016/j.sbspro.2012.03.289

Sajal, M. (2013). *From BRIC to BRICS: An Overview*. New Delhi: Swati Communications.

Sharma, N., & Nishant, M. (2014). Co-Integration and Casualty between FDI and GDP: A Study of BRICS Nations. *International Journal of Information Technology and Business Management*, *25*(1), 71–78.

Sridharan, P., Vijayakumar, N., & Chandra Sekhara Rao, K. (2009). Causal Relationship between Foreign Direct Investment and Growth: Evidence from BRICS Countries. *International Business Research*, *4*(2), 198–203.

Vijayakumar, N., Sridharan, P., & Chandra Sekhara Rao, K. (2010). Determinants of FDI in BRICS Countries: A Panel Analysis. *International Journal of Business and Applied Management*, *5*(3), 1–13.

KEY TERMS AND DEFINITIONS

Augmented Dicky Fuller Test: A test that tests the null hypothesis that a unit root is present in a time series sample. The alternative hypothesis is different depending on which version of the test is used but is usually stationarity or trend-stationarity. It is an augmented version of the Dickey-Fuller test for a larger and more complicated set of time series models.

BRICS: The set of countries comprising Brazil, Russia, India, China, and South Africa, especially viewed as an emerging market.

Developing Country: A country with a less developed industrial base and a low Human Development Index relative to other countries.

East African Community: An intergovernmental group which includes Kenya, Uganda, Burundi, Rwanda, and Tanzania that promotes social and economic cooperation.

Economic Growth: An increase in the inflation-adjusted market value of the goods and services produced by an economy over time. It is conventionally measured as the percent rate of increase in real gross domestic product, or real GDP.

Foreign Trade: A combined form of commercial transactions between two or more countries in the form of sales, investments, and transportation.

Shanghai Cooperation Organization: An intergovernmental organization that currently comprises eight Member States (China, India, Kazakhstan, Kyrgyzstan, Russia, Pakistan, Tajikistan, and Uzbekistan), four Observer States interested in acceding to full membership (Afghanistan, Belarus, Iran, and Mongolia), and six "Dialogue Partners" (Armenia, Azerbaijan, Cambodia, Nepal, Sri Lanka, and Turkey).

Chapter 7
India-BIMSTEC Bilateral Trade Activities:
A Gravity Model Approach

Gurpreet Kaur
https://orcid.org/0000-0001-9259-2709
Lovely Professional University, India

Akriti Gupta
Lovely Professional University, India

ABSTRACT

The Bay of Bengal Initiative for Multi-Sectoral Technical and Economic Cooperation (BIMSTEC) is one of the solutions to converge the economic interests of India's Look East Policy and Thailand's Look West Policy. Its objective is to integrate the regions on both sides of the Bay of Bengal. The development of BIMSTEC countries is indispensable for the forward march of Asia as a whole. This chapter analyzes the India-BIMSTEC trade activities after the establishment of BIMSTEC bloc. Gravity model and Auto-Regressive Integrated Moving Average (ARIMA) are used. The model estimates the sets of regression equations to measure the effects of regional trade agreements using ordinary least squares with nation dummies to capture country-specific fixed effects. The study reveals that all coefficients of regional dummy variables are mostly positive and significant, indicating the agreements that tend to enhance more trade than bilateral trade agreements. The authors state that based on India's trade with the BIMSTEC region, there exists a scope for intraregional trade in the future.

INTRODUCTION

The most significant feature in the economic development activities of BIMSTEC is the proposed Free Trade Area (FTA) amongst the member countries which expected to expand it later to involve other countries as well as other regional trading blocs. At the BIMSTEC Economic Ministerial Meeting held

DOI: 10.4018/978-1-7998-1730-7.ch007

on August 1988, there was concluded a decision that BIMSTEC should aim to develop a free trade agreement. At the BIMSTEC Trade, Commerce and Economic Ministerial meeting held on February 8, 2004, in Phuket, Thailand, member countries jointly signed a framework agreement to establish an FTA by 2013 to create a conducive environment for trade between member countries without any barriers. Initially, Bangladesh did not sign the agreement due to prevailing domestic issues, but later the country joined the framework agreement. The objective of the agreement is to strengthen and enhance economic, trade, and investment cooperation among the members, progressively liberalize and promote trade in goods and services, and explore new areas. The Trade Negotiating Committee (TNC) was set up in 2004 to continue the negotiations on the implementation of the FTA. Trade negotiations mainly cover all trade in goods and outline the reduction and elimination of tariffs with more flexibility granted to the least developed countries (LDCs). The Committee is required to start deliberations on general rules focusing on the preparation of positive and negative lists.

India's keen desire to promote regional cooperation in the South Asia had been fulfilled after obtaining the membership in BIMSTEC. India's role is pivotal in the evolution and growth of BIMSTEC regional group. India and Thailand play a proactive role in forging a meaningful cooperation in the region. The Bay of Bengal space has emerged as an integral and inseparable part of India's evolving Look East policy. East of India bordering the Bay of Bengal has been a traditional gateway to the hinterland of the Southeast Asia and beyond. There is strong civilization, ethnic, cultures, linguistic, economic, and political link with Southeast Asia which has developed as an imperative of interdependence through ages. The security, strategic, and economic interest of Indian Ocean region, including the Andaman and Nicobar group of Island, are also very closely linked to the Southeast Asian region surrounding it. India is now growing, while a considerable commerce with East and Southeast Asia passes through sea lanes in this sub-region. About the two-thirds of India's exclusive economic zone and economic space in this region is estimated to be excess of the combined size of BIMSTEC economies. The Bay of Bengal sub-region accounts about 10% of India's external economic relation. India has to anchor the peace and prosperity of sub-region for common good and interdependent destiny. India as the largest country has the responsibility to initiate more effective and proactive measures to hasten cooperation, including by developing enduring and mutually beneficial trade, infrastructure, investment, and other linkage, which alone has created and sustained a vested interest in sub-regional cooperation. BIMSTEC, nevertheless, is a modest experiment in pragmatic politics and realistic economics in a fiercely competitive globalized and rapidly changing environment. It is an experiment aimed at the achievement of incrementality without redefinition or reordering existing arrangements. It is an experiment to forge an arrangement to optimize step by step, opportunities through cooperation in selected identified areas and make up for missed opportunities. It is an experiment in moving forward without waiting all political or economic challenges to be overcome. It is above all a modest experiment in promoting sub-regional cooperation, optimizing synergies, complementarities, and advantages of shared geography and history. India and Thailand are among the rapidly growing economies of Bay of Bengal region which could together pilot the sub-region towards greater prosperity through cooperation, interdependence, and sub-regional common approach on crucial issues. Ultimately, the Bay of Bengal community has to be seen as a sub-regional building block of a larger Asian economic community and the emerging macro-level integration process.

Being the leading country in the group, India draws attention in the BIMSTEC framework and its functioning in the backdrop of the fast-changing global economic environment. India is the fast-emerging global power and dynamic economic player in the region responsible for peace and stability. India with its recent economic clout, capacity building measure and IT prowess, together with the gradual shift in the foreign policy outlook to suit to be rapid change in global geo-political issues deserve a special status in the BIMSTEC region.

The most of available literature is basically focused on the issues related with investment, economic integration, economic development, social, political, and geo-politics issues (Erokhin, 2016). To overcome this gap, this study sheds light on bilateral trade flow between India and BIMSTEC countries and attempts to make a forecast for the trade of BIMSTEC nations by employing gravity model of trade and Auto-Regressive Integrated Moving Average model (ARIMA).

BACKGROUND

Literature Review

Being a founding member and the largest country in terms of the population as well as territory, India despite being preoccupied with the idea of getting its partnership with the Association of Southeast Asian Nations (ASEAN) enhanced made the efforts to live up to the expectation of its partners in the BIMSTEC and to carry forward the BIMSTEC vision of mutually beneficial regional cooperation. Mutual cooperation in numbers of areas in the BIMSTEC region are more or less covered by India's bilateral economic relations with individual economies and this fosters the rate of economic growth by tapping regional synergies.

Mehta (2002) explored some issues related with the establishment of free trade arrangement among BIMSTEC countries. Study exposed that the FTA between BIMSTEC nations led to trade creation rather than trade diversion, particularly, between member countries rather than non-members of the FTA. In the case of demand and supply responsiveness, trade creation was superior. In economic terms, some countries were more open, but few BIMSTEC nations still follow the quantitative restrictions (QR) regime. Under the FTA, India's exports from Sri Lanka accelerated after 1990. India's exports to Bangladesh had been moderately diversified but the share of some particular products was very large. Myanmar was a single country among BIMSTEC group with which India had a trade deficit. India's trade relations with Thailand had been diversified but India had been exporting more than importing from Thailand. India had export competitiveness as compared to other BIMSTEC countries.

Banik (2006) stated that the BIMSTEC promised to form an FTA and analyzed some important indicators such as price, income, geographical characteristics, trade, and economic structure. There were constructive indications for the BIMSTEC economies to thrive into a successful RTA. To form an FTA, it was expected to generate relative advantage for the member nations. Better economic cooperation between BIMSTEC member nations has vital implication in the form of bigger market economies of level of production and better resource distribution.

Bhattacharya and Bhattacharya (2006) empirically analyzed the prospects of regional cooperation in trade, investment, and finance in Asia for BIMSTEC countries and Japan. The study focused on BIMSTEC seven nations' trade, investment, and finance trends and patterns with Japan and also analyzed the trends and patterns of bilateral and sub-regional economic cooperation in Asia as well as BIMSTEC-Japan trade. Japan is the second-biggest trading partner for BIMSTEC countries. Being a part of regional agreements trade and investment among the members of BIMSTEC together with Japan increased appreciably over the years. The study concluded that Japan being the part of the FTA with BIMSTEC, increased its exports to BIMSTEC countries in a greater degree compared to imports, which indicated that Japan benefited being the part of free trade area with BIMSTEC. BIMSTEC-Japan cooperation encourages a suitable financial integration procedure that takes into account diverse states of growth of associated economies, predominantly, banking and financial sectors, capital account systems, exchange rate systems, and bond markets.

Bhattacharya (2007) discussed the case of free trade arrangement between BIMSTEC and Japan for promoting intra-regional trade and economic corporation. With the formation of Preferential Trade Agreement (PTA) and FTA between BIMSTEC and Japan, the intra-industry trade has been growing much faster to catch the level of ASEAN trading bloc. The intra-industry trade among BIMSTEC nations has been increased but the intra-industry trade of Nepal has decreased with the establishment of the FTA with Japan.

Leela (2007) conducted a study on the evolution of BIMSTEC towards a Bay of Bengal economic community. The study pointed out that BIMSTEC's FTA was a comprehensive arrangement covered the trade in goods and services and investment and provided a framework for trade liberalization in all sectors. The FTA has also exploited the potential of economic integration in the Bay of Bengal region. The study suggested that successful promotion of mutual cooperation in the BIMSTEC region required speedy development of transport and communication linkage, exchange of information, progress in science and technology, and enhanced technical cooperation.

Rao and Rao (2007) studied a re-envisioning on India and Myanmar relations. The study stated that India made several efforts towards sub-regional, cross-regional, and bilateral regional trading arrangements. Myanmar builds the bridge to Southeast Asia, while India hopes to transform northeast from security into land of economic opportunity. Among the BIMSTEC nations, India is the fourth-largest trading partner of Myanmar and Myanmar's largest export market accounting for nearly one-fourth of its exports. Myanmar is the only Southeast Asian nation with which India shares both land and maritime boundaries. India has emerged as the largest market for Myanmar. The study revealed that economic cooperation with Myanmar led to economic development of India's northeastern states because Myanmar provided the shortest links to Southeast Asian markets by air, land, and sea that promoted the intra-regional trade among BIMSTEC nations.

Strutt (2008) described a dynamic analysis of probable impact on BIMSTEC with Japan's FTA. The study revealed that the BIMSTEC economies were predictable to considerably raise their share in global GDP as well as global exports and imports. If BIMSTEC free trade area included Japan as the member then it would lead to momentous gains of output, welfare, and exports for both BIMSTEC and Japan.

Data Sources and Research Methodology

The study is based on secondary data compiled from a wide variety of sources such as yearbooks publishing statistical data on trade, particularly, the World Bank, the United Nations Conference on Trade and Development (UNCTAD), United Nations Comtrade, the International Monetary Fund (IMF), the Asian Development Bank (ADB), and the World Trade Organization (WTO). A diverse online data sources, textbooks, magazines, and websites have been explored as well. To fulfill the purpose of the study, panel data has been used by employing econometric models, i.e. gravity model and autoregressive integrated moving average model.

Gravity Model

To examine the bilateral trade flow between BIMSTEC and India, gravity model has been used. Gravity models relate trade flows among the nations to the size of their markets and the cost of moving goods among them. The gravity approach to modeling trade had extensive history, initially used in the 1960s by Tinbergen (1962). The technique acquires its name from the equivalent with the physical energy of gravity determined by the joint accumulation of two bodies and the inverse square of the distance among them. In economics, the gravity approach was primarily essentially a theoretical but has proved awfully successful empirically in amplification a huge proportion of trade flows. The technique was also used to clarify other types of international flows, notably, migration. The gravity approach was located on a firmer theoretical base by Anderson (1979) and Bergstrand (1985). These derivations of the gravity model exhibit that it is not merely an ad hoc data process but a reduced-form version of a theoretical demonstration of world trade. Ekanayake, Mukherjee, and Veeramacheneni (2010) used gravity model to measure economic integration between the Asian developing nations. Gravity model estimates trade creation and trade diversion effects of different RTAs on trade flows inside and across member groups of ASEAN. Rahman (2003) used gravity model to evaluate Bangladesh's trade flow with its main trading partner nations. Results showed that Bangladesh's trade was optimistically determined by the size of the economies, per capita GNP disparity of the nations concerned, and openness of the trading nations. Tripathi and Leitao (2013) described India's trade flows using a gravity model for the period of 1998-2012. The study revealed that political globalization and cultural closeness had optimistic influence in bilateral trade and economic size, common border proxies confirming a positive impact of bilateral trade.

The gravity model can explain the pattern of bloc's trade.

$$\text{Trade}_{ij} = {}^{2}\,\frac{GDPi*GDPj}{Distanceij} \quad (1)$$

The equation for gravity model is:

$$TF_{ij} = \beta_0 + \beta_1(TGDP)_{ij} + \beta_2(REF)_{ij} + \beta_3(SIM)_{ij} + \beta_4(DIS)_{ij} + \beta_5(BOR)_{ij} +$$

$$\beta_6(CMLG)_{ij} + \beta_7(BTA)_{ij} + \beta_8(BIM)_{ij} + \beta_9(PCGDP)_{ij} + \varphi_i + \gamma_i + \lambda_t + (\varphi\gamma)I + (\gamma\lambda)_j + \varepsilon_{ij} \quad (2)$$

where:

TF_{ij}: Value of trade flow of *i* and *j* nations.
TGDP: Sum of total gross domestic product.
REF: Relative factor endowment.
SIM: Similarity index.
DIS: Distance between *i* and *j* nations.
BOR: Border.
CMLG: Common language.
BTA: Bilateral trade agreements.
BIM: BIMSTEC member.

PCGDP: Per capita income.
e_{ij}: Error or random term.

$$RFE_{ij} = | In\ PGDP_i - In\ PGDP_j | \quad (3)$$

$$SIM_{ij} = 1 - \{In\ (GDP_i / (GDP_i + GDP_j))^2 + In\ (GDP_j / (GDP_i + GDP_j))^2\} \quad (4)$$

RFE_{ij} takes a minimum of zero if both countries exhibit equal GDP or production. The range of *SIM* is given by $0 < SIM_{ij} < 0.5$, where 0.5 means "equal" and zero implies "absolute divergence" in country size. In Equation (2), the following binary or dummy variables are included:

BTA_{ij} = 1 if a country pair (*ij*) has a bilateral trade agreement at period *t*; = 0 if otherwise.
BOR_{ij} = 1 if a country pair (*ij*) has a common border; = 0 if otherwise.
$CMLG_{ij}$ = 1 if a country pair (*ij*) has a common language; = 0 if otherwise.
BIM_{ij} = 1 if the exporter (*ij*) is a member of BIMSTEC; = 0 if otherwise.

In Equation (2), φ, γ, and λ are exporter, importer, and time or business cycle effects, respectively. The interaction effects are exporter-by-importer ($\varphi\gamma$), exporter-by-time ($\varphi\lambda$), and importer-by-time ($\gamma\lambda$).

Hypothesis:

H1: The larger economic dimension increases trade.
H2: Trade increases when the partners are geographically close to each other.

According to Kabir and Salim (2010) and Tripathi and Leiato (2013), GDP helps to increase trade. The distance between India and BIMSTEC member nations excepted to be negative. Ghatak, Silaghi, and Daly (2009) found a negative relationship between the distance and bilateral trade. In case of India, Tharakan, Beveren, and Ourti (2005), De (2013), and Batra (2010) examined a negative relationship between the distance and India's bilateral trade.

Auto-Regressive Integrated Moving Average (ARIMA)

A projection of trade flow has been made with the help of Auto-Regressive Integrated Moving Average (ARIMA). These projections have been made with the help of Box-Jenkins' ARIMA model. Keck and Raubold (2006) developed the set of time series models that provided the short-term forecasts (6-18 months) for international trade both at the global level and for selected regions. Khan (2011) identified the suitable forecasting model for forecasting total import of Bangladesh. An attempt has been made to develop a distinctive and appropriate forecasting model of total import of Bangladesh and helped to find forecasts with minimum forecasting error. Mehmood (2012) examined a study to make an attempt to forecast Pakistan's exports to South Asian Association for Regional Cooperation (SAARC) for coming years by using Box-Jenkins' methodology of univariate ARIMA model. The study found ARIMA (1,1,4) as most appropriate model among other ARIMA models to make forecasts. Kongcharoen and Kruangpradit (2013) supported the Autoregressive Integrated Moving Average with Explanatory Variable (ARIMAX) Model for Thailand's export with its major trade partners. A projection has been made on the following assumptions.

- Relative price structure remains the same.
- The growth rate of income assumed to be constant.
- The trade (X+M) prices remain either competitive or favorable to the world export prices.

Box-Jenkins' ARIMA model is given as:

$$ARIMA(1,1,1)$$
$$(1-\phi B)(1-B)X_t = (1+\theta B)Z_t$$
$$(1-\phi B - B + \phi B^2)X_t = (1+\theta B)Z_t$$
$$(1-B-\phi B + \phi B^2)X_t = (1+\theta B)Z_t$$
$$X_t - X_{t-1} - \phi X_{t-1} + \phi X_{t-2} = Z_t + \theta Z_{t-1}$$
$$\Rightarrow X_t = X_{t-1} + \phi X_{t-1} - \phi X_{t-2} + Z_t + \theta Z_{t-1}$$

Time Series Modeling Using ARIMA Models

These are special type of regression model where dependent variable is considered to be stationary and independent variable is lags of dependent variable and lags of errors. An ARIMA process is a combination of an Auto-Regressive and a Moving Average Process. A time series can follow an ARIMA process only when it is stationary. A time series is said to be stationary only when it exhibits mean reversion around a constant long-run mean, has a finite variance and decreasing correlogram as lag length increases. Stationary is important because if the series is non-stationary then all the typical results of the classical regression analysis are not valid.

Autoregressive Model

An autoregressive model of order p is represented as:

$$\boldsymbol{Y_t = \varphi_1 Y_{t-1} + \varphi_2 Y_{t-2} + \ldots\ldots \varphi_p Y_{t-p} + u_t} \tag{5}$$

Where $|\phi|<1$ and u_t is a gaussian (white noise) error term. For the *AR(p)* model to be stationary is that the summation of the p autoregressive coefficients should be less than 1:

$$\sum_{i=1}^{p} \varphi_i < \mathbf{1} \tag{6}$$

If the observations are generated by an *AR(p)* process, then the theoretical partial autocorrelations will be high and significant for up to p lags and zero for lags beyond p. This rule is generally utilized to define which process the series is following and is incorporated in the ARIMA model.

Moving Average Model

A moving average model of order q can be written as:

$$Y_t = u_t + \theta_1 u_{t-1} + \theta_2 u_{t-2} + \dots + \theta_q u_{t-q} \quad (7)$$

Moving average $MA(q)$ process is an average of q stationary white noise process, hence it is always stationary as long as q has a finite value. A time series is said to be invertible if it can be represented by a finite order *MA* or convergent autoregressive process. Invertibility is an important property for identifying the order of *MA* process using autocorrelation and partial autocorrelation function as in this case it is assumed that Y_t sequence is well approximated by autoregressive model. An $MA(1)$ process can be inverted to an infinite order *AR* process with geometrically declining weights if the necessary condition $|\theta|<1$ is met. The mean of the *MA* process will be clearly equal to zero as it is the mean of white noise terms. For a $MA(q)$ model correlogram, *ACF* is expected to have q spikes for $k=0$ and then go down immediately. Auto covariance of a *MA* process is equal to zero.

ARMA Models

These models are the combinations of the two processes and usually represented by $ARMA(p,q)$. The general form of $ARMA(p,q)$ models is represented by:

$$\begin{aligned} Y_t = \varphi_1 Y_{t-1} + \varphi_2 Y_{t-2} + \dots + \varphi_p Y_{t-p} + u_t \\ + \theta_1 u_{t-1} + \theta_2 u_{t-2} + \dots + \theta_q u_{t-q} \end{aligned} \quad (8)$$

The equation can be rewritten as:

$$Y_t = \sum_{i=1}^{p} \varphi_i Y_{t-i} + u_t + \sum_{i=1}^{q} \theta_j u_{t-j} \quad (9)$$

For stationarity of *ARMA* process, only *AR* part of the model needs to be stationary as *MA* part by default is stationary.

Integrated Processes and the ARIMA Models

ARMA models can only be applied on a stationary time series. If a series is not stationary, then stationarity needs to be induced into it by differencing it in such a way that differenced time series ΔY_t is represented by:

$$\Delta Y_t = Y_t - Y_{t-1} \quad (10)$$

Generally, time series need to be difference at least once to make them stationary. After differencing once the series hence obtained is said to integrated to order one and denoted by *I(1)*. Hence a series which needs to be differenced *d* times to make it stationary and then follows *ARMA(p,q)* model then the series is said to be following *ARIMA(p,d,q)* process.

MAIN FOCUS OF THE CHAPTER

In the past five decades, the gravity equation of trade has been widely used to predict trade flows. After the controversies concerning its theoretical foundation in the 1980s and the specification of its use in the 1990s, the estimation of gravity models has gone through an intense debate about estimations techniques in recent years. As pointed by Silva and Tenreyro (2006), in presence of heteroscedasticity, the Pseudo Poisson Maximum Likelihood (PPML) estimator performs better since ordinary least squares (OLS) is not efficient. Another challenge the literature concerns is the zero values. Helpman, Melitz, and Rubinstein (2008) renewed this debate by proposing a theoretical foundation of the zero values based on a model with heterogeneity of firms la Melitz and an adapted Heckman's procedure to predict trade taking into account these features. Pham and Martin (2008) obtained some divergent results when comparing alternative estimators to deal with the heteroscedasticity and zero values problems. Gravity models were first applied to international trade by Tinbergen (1962) and Poyhonen (1963). Tinbergen (1962) developed the model to determine the normal or standard pattern of international trade that prevailed among 42 countries in the absence of trade barriers. Besides the standard gravity model, Tinbergen (1962) also estimated other models including dummy variables for trade agreements and the presence of a common border among trading countries. Later, Anderson (1979) used Armington's preferences in a model of homogenous goods to derive a role for transport costs.

The gravity equation of trade is highly effective at explaining bilateral flows. However, this model threw several controversies. Theoretical framework was put into doubt and afterward justified by Bergstrand (1985) for the factorial model, Anderson (1979) for the goods differentiated according to their origin, and Helpman et al. (2008) in the context of heterogeneity of firms.

GDP is included to capture the factors associated with the level of economic development. It also captures the productive capacity of the exporting country and the purchasing power of the importing country. The coefficients of the real GDP variables are expected to be positive.

The distance variable ($Dist_{ij}$) is expected to be negative. This is a proxy for transportation costs and time, access to market information, access to markets, and other factors that make it difficult for the nations to engage in trade. The anticipated sign on all the ten dummy variables is positive, reflecting the idea that proximity, common language, historical links, and regional trading agreements are trade-creating networks. However, the expected sign of the dummy variable *RTA(O)* can either be positive or negative.

The relative factor endowment variable (RFE_{ij}) is defined as the absolute value of the difference between natural logarithm of per capita GDPs between country *i* and country *j*. The choice of this variable as an explanatory variable is based on the standard comparative advantage explanation of trade. This variable aims to capture technology differences between the countries in explaining trade patterns. Though this variable is generally measured as the absolute value of the difference between natural logarithm of capital-labor ratio, due to the unavailability of data, per capita GDP is used in place of capital-labor ratio. The expected sign of this variable is positive.

The expected sign of the similarity index variable is positive. This is due to the fact that similarity with respect to GDP per capita implies increased similarity in size of country-specific product diversity in the differentiated goods sector and that leads to an increased trade volume (Ekanayake et al., 2010).

Empirical Results of Gravity Model

In this study, the model is estimated with panel data for seven BIMSTEC countries, including Bangladesh, Bhutan, India, Myanmar, Nepal, Sri Lanka, and Thailand. It measures trade flows between them. The model estimated four sets of regression to measure the effects of regional trade agreements in BIMSTEC in 1997-2017. The model was estimated using OLS with country dummies to capture country-specific fixed effects.

The conventional variables behave very much the same way as the model predicts, and the estimated coefficients are statistically significant. The adjusted R_2 values lies between 0.544 and 0.604. These values are acceptable for a cross-sectional study and are comparable to those obtained in other studies employing the gravity model to examine intra-regional trade flows. All coefficients of regional dummy variables are mostly positive and significant, indicating that multilateral trade agreements tend to enhance more trade than bilateral trade agreements.

The conventional variables behave very much the same way as the model predicts, and the estimated coefficients are statistically significant. The adjusted R_2 values range between 0.544 and 0.604. These values are acceptable for a cross-sectional study and are comparable to those obtained in other studies employing the gravity model to examine intra-regional trade flows. R_2 has a high value that implies that the coefficients are highly significant. The values of R_2 is 0.9849 within the model, 0.9567 between the models, while the overall value of R_2 is 0.9327 (Table 1).

The results of estimation for each nation of BIMSTEC are shown in Table 2. The result for ordinary gravity trade model for trade flow is significant. The model was estimated using OLS with country dummies to capture country-specific fixed effects. Market size variables: GDP per capita of India's bilateral trade partners (*GDP*) and India's GDP per capita (GDP_i), both have the positive and significant (at 1%) effect on India's bilateral trade. The coefficient of joint GDP is significant and positive, and from results, it is proven that the larger economic dimension increase trade. GDP per capita of India's trade partners (or India's GDP per capita) is associated with 7.6% increase in India's bilateral trade and supports the positive effect of market size on India's bilateral trade. This indicates that market size promotes India's bilateral trade.

Table 1. Gravity model estimation for BIMSTEC countries

Group variable	Year	Number of groups	19
R-square: within	0.9849	Obs. per group: minimum	6
between	0.9567	average	6.0
overall	0.9327	maximum	6
F(5,90)		1174.26	
Corr (u_i, Xb)	0.0862	Prob > F	0.0000

Source: Authors' development based on United Nations Conference on Trade and Development [UNCTAD] (2019)

Table 2. Gravity model estimation for India and BIMSTEC countries

	Lngdp	Coef.	Std. Err.	t	P>|t|	95% Conf. Interval
Distance	-0.0003967	0.0000851	-4.66	0.000	-0.0005659	-0.0002276
Sim	65.13144	2.1334320	30.53	0.000	60.89301	69.36988
Rfe	1.76752	0.2603625	-6.79	0.000	2.284775	-1.250264
Border	-2.172587	0.1160684	-18.72	0.000	-2.403177	-1.941997
Land-locked	-0.7784701	0.1145500	-6.80	0.000	-1.006044	-0.5508966
Constant	-18.15614	1.1219040	-16.18	0.000	-20.385	-15.92729
sigma_u	0.43911723					
sigma_e	0.24117654					
Rho	0.76825328 (fraction of variance due to u_i)					
F test that all u_i	0					
F(18, 90)	18.72					
Prob > F	0.0000					

Source: Authors' development based on UNCTAD (2019)

Geographical distance between India and partner country (distance) and border dummy (border), both have the positive and statistically significant effect on India's bilateral trade in both the models. Coefficient of distance is negative and significant, supporting the basic idea of gravity model. This proved the hypothesis is accepted that the trade increase when partners are geographically close. Though the sign of the coefficient of border dummy supports the expected hypothesis, and the sign of the coefficient of distance variable support the predicted hypothesis and indicate that geographical proximity matter for India's bilateral trade. The results for the distance variable provide strong support for the hypothesis that transportation and other distance-related costs are an important determinant of trade flows.

Furthermore, the significant of *SIM* (similarity) is also significant and positive. Similarity with respect to GDP per capita implies increased similarity in size of country-specific product diversity in the differentiated goods sector and leads to an increased trade volume.

The coefficient on relative factor endowment variable is statistically significant in four of the six cases and has the expected sign in three time periods. Its positive sign suggests that bilateral trade flows are related positively to inter-country differences in the level of technological advancement.

The coefficient of the land-locked dummy is statistically insignificant in the three cases. It has the unexpected negative sign in the three of the six cases. In sum, all coefficients of regional dummy variables are mostly positive and significant, indicating agreements tend to enhance more trade than bilateral trade agreements.

Auto-Regressive Integrated Moving Average Model (ARIMA) – Analysis

Forecasting future values of economic variables are some of the most critical tasks of a country. Especially the values related to foreign trade are to be forecasted efficiently as the need for planning is great in this sector.

Table 3 analyzed the Autoregressive Integrated Moving Average or *ARIMA(p,d,q)* models are the extension of the *AR* model that use three components for modelling the serial correlation in the time-series data. The first component is the Auto Regressive (*AR*) term. The *AR(p)* model uses the *p* lags of the time series in the equation. An *AR(p)* model has the form: $y(t) = a(1) * y(t-1) +...+ a(p) * y(t-p) + e(t)$. The second component is the integration (*d*) order term. Each integration order corresponds to differencing the time series. *I(1)* means differencing the data once. *I(d)* means differencing the data *d* times. The third component is the moving average *MA* term. The *MA(q)* model uses the *q* lags of the forecast errors to improve the forecast. An *MA(q)* model has the form: $y(t) = e(t) + b(1) * e(t-1) +...+ b(q) * e(t-q)$. Finally, an *ARMA(p,q)* model has the combined form: $y(t) = a(1) * y(t-1) +...+ a(p) * y(t-p) + e(t) + b(1) * e(t-1) +...+ b(q) * e(t-q)$.

The R_2, or coefficient of determination, indicates the percent variation in the dependent variable that can be explained and accounted for by the independent variables in this regression analysis (Table 4). However, in a multiple regression, the adjusted R_2 takes into account the existence of additional independent variables or regressors and adjusts this R_2 value to a more accurate view the regression's explanatory power. However, under some ARIMA modeling circumstances (e.g., with non-convergence models), the R_2 tends to be unreliable. Multiple correlation coefficient (multiple *R*) measures the correlation between the actual dependent variable (*Y*) and the estimated or fitted (*Y*) based on the regression equation. This correlation is also the square root of the coefficient of determination (R_2). Standard error of the estimates (SE_y) describes the dispersion of data points above and below the regression line or plane. This value is used as part of the calculation to obtain the confidence interval of the estimates later. The *AIC* and *SC* are often used in model selection. *SC* imposes a greater penalty for additional coefficients. Generally, the user should select a model with the lowest value of the *AIC* and *SC*. The Durbin-Watson statistic measures the serial correlation in the residuals. Generally, *DW* less than 2 (<2) implies positive serial correlation.

Table 3. AUTO-ARIMA (Autoregressive Integrated Moving Average)

Models	Adjusted R-squared	Akaike information criterion (AIC)	Schwarz criterion (SC)	Durbin-Watson statistic (DW)	Number of iterations	Model rank
P=1, D=0, Q=0	0.9590	12.3914	12.7247	2.6578	0	1
P=2, D=0, Q=0	0.9584	13.0892	13.6090	2.3275	0	2
P=0, D=0, Q=2	0.8090	14.6500	15.1318	0.4975	27	3
P=0, D=0, Q=1	0.5707	15.5244	15.8456	0.4873	17	4
P=2, D=2, Q=0	0.5079	13.3587	13.9242	2.3651	0	5
P=0, D=1, Q=0	0.0000	12.5719	12.7385	1.9892	0	6
P=0, D=2, Q=0	0.0000	14.1023	14.2756	3.0483	0	7
P=0, D=1, Q=1	-0.0660	12.5713	12.9046	1.9381	5	8
P=1, D=1, Q=0	-0.0708	13.3784	13.7249	2.0212	0	9
P=2, D=1, Q=0	-0.1603	12.4921	13.0337	2.0209	0	10

Source: Authors' development based on UNCTAD (2019)

Table 4. Regression statistics

Parameter	Value	Parameter	Value
R-squared (coefficient of determination)	0.961	Akaike information criterion (*AIC*)	42.731
Adjusted R-squared	0.959	Schwarz criterion (*SC*)	11.274
Multiple R (multiple correlation coefficient)	0.980	Log likelihood	-36.54
Standard error of the estimates (*SEy*)	919.28	Durbin-Watson (*DW*) statistic	2.657
Number of observations	17	Number of iterations	0

Source: Authors' development based on UNCTAD (2019)

The coefficients provide the estimated regression intercept and slopes (Table 5). For instance, the coefficients are estimates of the true population *b* values in the following regression equation $Y = b_0 + b_1X_1 + b_2X_2 + ... + b_nX_n$. The standard error measures how accurate the predicted coefficients are, and the *t*-statistics are the ratios of each predicted coefficient to its standard error.

The analysis of variance (ANOVA) provides an *F*-test of the regression model's overall statistical significance (Table 6). Instead of looking at individual regressors as in the *t*-test, the *F*-test looks at all the estimated coefficients' statistical properties. The *F*-statistic is calculated as the ratio of the regression's mean of squares to the residual's mean of squares. The numerator measures how much of the regression is explained, while the denominator measures how much is unexplained. Hence, the larger the *F*-statistic, the more significant the model. The corresponding *p*-value is calculated to test the null hypothesis (H0) where all the coefficients are simultaneously equal to zero, versus the alternate hypothesis (Ha) that they are all simultaneously different from zero, indicating a significant overall regression model. If the *p*-value is smaller than 0.01, 0.05, or 0.10 alpha significance, then the regression is significant. The same approach can be applied to the *F*-statistic by comparing the calculated *F*-statistic with the critical *F* values at various significance levels.

If autocorrelation *AC(1)* is nonzero, it means that the series is first-order serially correlated. If *AC(k)* dies off more or less geometrically with increasing lag, it implies that the series follows a low-order autoregressive process. If *AC(k)* drops to zero after a small number of lags, it implies that the series follows a low-order moving-average process (Table 7).

Partial correlation *PAC(k)* measures the correlation of values that are *k* periods apart after removing the correlation from the intervening lags (Figure 1). If the pattern of autocorrelation can be captured

Table 5. Regression results

Parameter	Intercept	AR (1)
Coefficients	568,648,791.20	1.1012
Standard error	749,759,420.46	0.0569
t-statistic	0.7584	19.3701
p-value	0.4599	0.0000
Lower 5%	1,883,014,787.94	1.2009
Upper 95%	-745,717,205.54	1.0016

Source: Authors' development based on UNCTAD (2019)

Table 6. Analysis of variance

	Sums of squares	Mean of squares	F-statistic	p-value	Hypothesis test	
Regression	1.300	1.300	375.2	0.0000	Critical *F*-statistic (99% confidence with *df* of 1 and 15)	8.6831
Residual	5.197	3.465			Critical *F*-statistic (95% confidence with *df* of 1 and 15)	4.5431
Total	1.352				Critical *F*-statistic (90% confidence with *df* of 1 and 15)	3.0732

Source: Authors' development based on UNCTAD (2019)

Table 7. Autocorrelation

Time lag	AC	PAC	Lower bound	Upper bound	Q-Stat	Prob
1	0.8126	0.8126	(0.4714)	0.4714	13.3316	0.0003
2	0.6340	(0.0778)	(0.4714)	0.4714	21.9857	0.0000
3	0.4724	(0.0581)	(0.4714)	0.4714	27.1349	0.0000
4	0.2933	(0.1609)	(0.4714)	0.4714	29.2717	0.0000
5	0.1579	(0.0044)	(0.4714)	0.4714	29.9428	0.0000
6	0.0709	0.0255	(0.4714)	0.4714	30.0902	0.0000
7	(0.0684)	(0.2406)	(0.4714)	0.4714	30.2414	0.0001
8	(0.1797)	(0.0680)	(0.4714)	0.4714	31.4005	0.0001
9	(0.2589)	(0.0540)	(0.4714)	0.4714	34.1074	0.0001
10	(0.3289)	(0.0602)	(0.4714)	0.4714	39.0991	0.0000
11	(0.3702)	(0.0639)	(0.4714)	0.4714	46.4761	0.0000
12	(0.3733)	(0.0359)	(0.4714)	0.4714	55.4792	0.0000
13	(0.3767)	(0.0561)	(0.4714)	0.4714	66.9391	0.0000
14	(0.3554)	(0.0216)	(0.4714)	0.4714	80.5346	0.0000
15	(0.2942)	0.0374	(0.4714)	0.4714	94.5178	0.0000
16	(0.2169)	0.0339	(0.4714)	0.4714	109.7202	0.0000

Source: Authors' development based on UNCTAD (2019)

by an autoregression of order less than k, then the partial autocorrelation at lag k will be close to zero. Ljung-Box Q-statistics and their p-values at lag k has the null hypothesis that there is no autocorrelation up to order k. The dotted lines in the plots of the autocorrelations are the approximate two standard error bounds. If the autocorrelation is within these bounds, it is not significantly different from zero at (approximately) the 5% significance level.

Table 8 explains the prospects of intraregional trade among India and BIMSTEC in coming years. Projections has been made for the intraregional trade on the basis of their actual performance from 1997 to 2017. India's potential trade volume with BIMSTEC is \$6,535.57 million in 2025. Thus, based on India's trade with BIMSTEC region, there exists a scope for intraregional trade in the future. Therefore, the efforts at the international level are required to be made to increase intraregional trade to earn a fair name for BIMSTEC in the world trade.

Figure 1. Autocorrelation and partial autocorrelation
Source: Authors' development

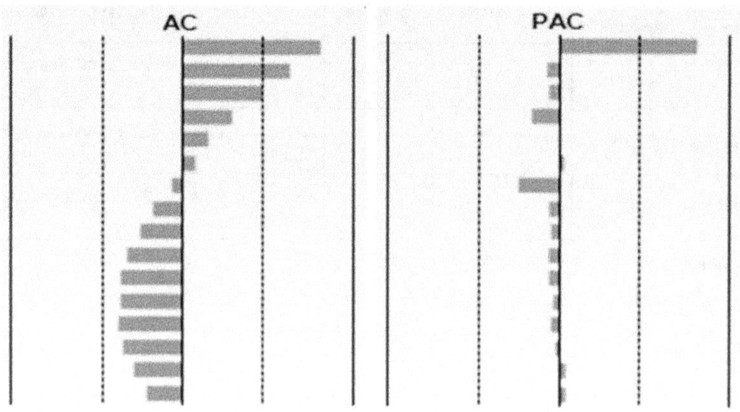

Figure 2 illustrates the actual vs. forecast of intraregional trade among India and BIMSTEC nations in coming years.

SOLUTIONS AND RECOMMENDATIONS

The three key issues in BIMSTEC region are development, connectivity, and economic integration. Though the BIMSTEC nations are rich in resources, they remain underdeveloped and disconnected from Asia's growth story. Even though the member states are connected via regional cooperative processes, they have remained on the margins of Asian market integration. Each individual member of the region needs to exhibit different capabilities for economic cooperation among the member countries. Cooperation across the world may take an added interest in respect of the Southeast Asian region. India has to

Figure 2. Actual vs. forecast of trade between India and BIMSTEC
Source: Authors' development

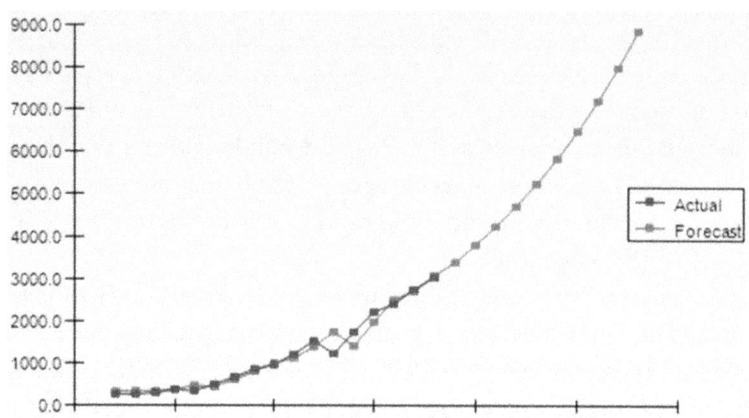

Table 8. Projections of intraregional trade among India and BIMSTEC till 2025, $ million

Period	Actual values	Forecast values
1997	249.09	259.70
1998	261.36	263.39
1999	262.12	256.78
2000	298.75	263.49
2001	379.38	290.41
2002	343.43	360.67
2003	506.24	388.84
2004	677.09	496.60
2005	861.12	676.14
2006	965.41	908.08
2007	1,215.00	1,110.88
2008	1,536.79	1,358.75
2009	1,233.50	1,681.52
2010	1,742.84	1,661.06
2011	2,218.89	1,849.36
2012	2,404.35	2,240.37
2013	2,743.40	2,604.15
2014	3,027.91	2,997.49
2015	3,113.56	3,135.03
2016	3,294.39	3,360.93
2017	3,701.48	3,713.67
Forecast 2018		4,066.40
2019		4,419.14
2020		4,771.88
2021		5,124.62
2022		5,477.36
2023		5,830.10
2024		6,182.83
2025		6,535.57

Source: Authors' development based on UNCTAD (2019)

take the lead in BIMSTEC and reorient by delivering on promises made in timely manner. BIMSTEC is also an intergovernmental organization of some South Asian and Southeast Asian countries whose main priories are tourism and economic development.

FUTURE RESEARCH DIRECTIONS

The authors have identified the following future research directions:

- The study is limited to India's trade performance with BIMSTEC countries only. There will be another perspective from other member countries still uncover;
- The study is based on secondary data only;
- Another macro-economic factors such as investment, foreign exchange, and stock exchange will have a scope for further study in BIMSTEC region.

CONCLUSION

The conventional variables behave very much the same way as the model predicts, and the estimated coefficients are statistically significant. The adjusted R_2 values range from a low of 0.544 to a high of 0.604. These values are acceptable for a cross-sectional study and are comparable to those obtained in other studies employing the gravity model to examine intra-regional trade flows. R_2 has a high value which means that the coefficients are highly significant. The result for ordinary gravity trade model for trade flow is significant. The model was estimated using OLS with country dummies to capture country-specific fixed effects. The projections of intraregional trade among India and BIMSTEC are made for the intraregional trade on the basis of their actual performance from 1997 to 2017. India's potential trade volume with BIMSTEC is $6,535.57 million in 2025. Thus, based on India's trade with BIMSTEC region, there exists a scope for intraregional trade in the future. Therefore, the efforts at the international level are required to be made to increase intraregional trade to earn a fair name for BIMSTEC in the world trade. Given the geostrategic location of India's North-Eastern Region (NER) in BIMSTEC, multiple expositions about its economic potential have been made in terms of trade and investment. Yet, the purported economic remedies to the North-Eastern region through greater infrastructural connectivity remain low.

REFERENCES

Anderson, J. E. (1979). A Theoretical Foundation for the Gravity Equation. *The American Economic Review*, *69*(1), 106–116.

Banik, N. (2006). How Promising Is BIMSTEC? *Economic and Political Weekly*, *41*(51), 5264–5268.

Batra, A. (2010). Asian Economic Integration and Sub-Regionalism: A Case Study of the BIMSTEC. *International Studies*, *47*(1), 1–25. doi:10.1177/002088171104700101

Bergstrand, J. H. (1985). The Gravity Equation in International Trade: Some Microeconomic Foundations and Empirical Evidence. *The Review of Economics and Statistics*, *67*(3), 474–481. doi:10.2307/1925976

Bhattacharya, S. K. (2007). *Does BIMSTEC-Japan Economic Cooperation Promote Intra-Regional Trade? The Case for Free Trade Arrangement*. Delhi, India: Centre for Studies in International Relations and Development.

Bhattacharya, S. K., & Bhattacharya, B. N. (2006). *Prospects of Regional Cooperation in Trade, Investment and Finance in Asia: An Empirical Analysis on BIMSTEC Countries and Japan*. Retrieved October 4, 2019, from https://ssrn.com/abstract=905761

De, P. (2013). Assessing Barriers to Trade in Services in India: An Empirical Investigation. *Journal of Economic Integration*, *28*(1), 108–143. doi:10.11130/jei.2013.28.1.108

Ekanayake, E. M., Mukherjee, A., & Veeramacheneni, B. (2010). Trade Blocks and the Gravity Model: A Study of Economic Integration among Asian Developing Countries. *Journal of Economic Integration*, *25*(4), 627–643. doi:10.11130/jei.2010.25.4.627

Erokhin, V. (2016). Rising Economic Powers among Economies in Transition: Is There Enough Space on the Global Market? In V. Erokhin (Ed.), *Global Perspectives on Trade Integration and Economies in Transition* (pp. 1–25). Hershey, PA: IGI Global. doi:10.4018/978-1-5225-0451-1.ch001

Ghatak, S., Silaghi, M., & Daly, V. (2009). Trade and Migration Flows between Some CEE Countries and the UK. *The Journal of International Trade & Economic Development*, *18*(1), 61–78. doi:10.1080/09638190902757426

Helpman, E., Melitz, M., & Rubinstein, Y. (2008). Estimating Trade Flows: Trading Partners and Trading Volumes. *The Quarterly Journal of Economics*, *123*(2), 441–487. doi:10.1162/qjec.2008.123.2.441

Kabir, M., & Salim, R. (2010). Can Gravity Model Explain BIMSTEC's Trade? *Journal of Economic Integration*, *25*(1), 143–165. doi:10.11130/jei.2010.25.1.144

Keck, A., & Raubold, A. (2006). *Forecasting Trade*. Geneva, Switzerland: World Trade Organization.

Khan, T. (2011). Identifying an Appropriate Forecasting Model for Forecasting Total Import of Bangladesh. *International Journal of Trade, Economics, and Finance*, 2(3), 242–246.

Kongcharoen, C., & Kruangpradit, T. (2013). Autoregressive Integrated Moving Average with Explanatory Variable (ARIMAX) Model for Thailand Export. In *Proceedings of the 33rd International Symposium on Forecasting*. Seoul, South Africa: International Institute of Forecasters.

Leela, P. (2007). Evolution of BIMSTEC: Towards a Bay of Bengal Economic Community. In T. Nirmala Devi (Ed.), *India and Bay of Bengal Community: The BIMSTEC Experiment* (pp. 172–178). New Delhi, India: Gyan Publishing House.

Mehmood, S. (2012). Forecasting Pakistan's Exports to SAARC: An Application of Univiriate Arima Mode. *Journal of Contemporary Issues in Business Research*, *3*(1), 96–110.

Mehta, R. (2002). *Establishment of Free Trade Arrangement among BIMSTEC Countries Some Issues*. New Delhi, India: Research and Information System for Developing Countries.

Pham, C. S., & Martin, W. (2008). *Estimating the Gravity Equation when Zero Trade Flows Are Frequent*. Washington, DC: World Bank.

Poyhonen, P. (1963). A Tentative Model for the Volume of Trade between Countries. *Weltwirtschaftliches Archiv*, *90*, 93–100.

Rahman, M. M. (2003). *A Panel Data Analysis of Bangladesh's Trade: The Gravity Model Approach*. Sydney, Australia: University of Sydney.

Rao, B. M., & Rao, S. S. (2007). Re-Envisioning India-Myanmar Relations. In T. Nirmala Devi (Ed.), *India and Bay of Bengal Community: The BIMSTEC Experiment* (pp. 218–234). New Delhi, India: Gyan Publishing House.

Silva, J. S., & Tenreyro, S. (2006). The Log of Gravity. *The Review of Economics and Statistics*, *88*(4), 641–658. doi:10.1162/rest.88.4.641

Strutt, A. (2008). Dynamic Analysis of a BIMSTEC-Japan Free Trade Area. In *Proceedings of 11th Annual Conference in Global Trade Analysis*. Helsinki, Finland.

Tharakan, P. K. M., Beveren, I. V., & Ourti, T. V. (2005). Determinants of India's Software Exports and Goods Exports. *The Review of Economics and Statistics*, *87*(4), 776–780. doi:10.1162/003465305775098161

Tinbergen, J. (1962). *An Analysis of World Trade Flows in Shaping the World Economy*. New York, NY: Twentieth Century Fund.

Tripathi, S., & Leitao, N.C. (2013). India's Trade and Gravity Model: A Static and Dynamic Panel Data. *MPRA Paper 45502*.

United Nations Conference on Trade and Development. (2019). *Statistics Database* [Data file]. Retrieved October 4, 2019, from http://unctad.org/en/Pages/Statistics.aspx

ADDITIONAL READING

Anderson, J. E. (2011). The Gravity Model. *Annual Review of Economics*, *3*(1), 133–160. doi:10.1146/annurev-economics-111809-125114

Erokhin, V. (Ed.). (2016). *Global Perspectives on Trade Integration and Economies in Transition*. Hershey, PA: IGI Global. doi:10.4018/978-1-5225-0451-1

Lynch, D. A. (2010). *Trade and Globalization: An Introduction to Regional Trade Agreements*. Plymouth: Rowman & Littlefield Publishers.

Palit, A., Choudhury, R., & Tieri, S. (2018). *BIMSTEC: Relevance and Challenges*. Singapore: Institute of South Asian Studies.

Rahman, M. M., & Bari, E. (2018). *Value Chains in BIMSTEC Region. Current Status, Possibilities and Challenges*. Dhaka: Centre for Policy Dialogue.

Rahman, M. M., & Kim, C. (2015). BIMSTEC Regional Integration: Prospects and Challenges. *Advanced Science and Technology Letters, 114*, 90–95. doi:10.14257/astl.2015.114.18

Rasul, G., Neupane, N., & Hussain, A. (2018). *Mountain Economies in BIMSTEC Countries: An Agenda for Regional Cooperation and Shared Prosperity*. Kathmandu: International Centre for Integrated Mountain Development.

KEY TERMS AND DEFINITIONS

Autoregressive Model: A type of random process which is often used to model and predict various types of natural phenomena. The autoregressive model is one of a group of linear prediction formulas that attempt to predict an output of a system based on the previous outputs.

Autoregressive Moving Average Process Model: A model of a differenced time series (one that has been rendered stationary by the elimination of “drift”) whose output needs to be anti-differenced to forecast the original series. ARIMA models can represent a wide range of time-series data and are used generally in computing the probability of a future value lying between any two limits.

Gravity Model: A model of international trade in international economics that predicts bilateral trade flows based on the economic sizes and distance between two units.

Moving Average Model: A common approach for modeling univariate time series which specifies that the output variable depends linearly on the current and various past values of a stochastic (imperfectly predictable) term.

Multiple Correlation Coefficient: A measure of how well a given variable can be predicted using a linear function of a set of other variables. It is the correlation between the variable’s values and the best predictions that can be computed linearly from the predictive variables.

The Bay of Bengal Initiative for Multi-Sectoral Technical and Economic Cooperation: (BIMSTEC): An international organization of seven nations of South Asia and South East Asia, namely, Bangladesh, India, Myanmar, Sri Lanka, Thailand, Nepal, and Bhutan.

Time Series: A series of data points indexed (or listed or graphed) in time order. Most commonly, a time series is a sequence taken at successive equally spaced points in time.

Chapter 8
India's Export Competitiveness With BIMSTEC Countries

Gurpreet Kaur
https://orcid.org/0000-0001-9259-2709
Lovely Professional University, India

ABSTRACT

This chapter analyzes the export competitiveness of India against BIMSTEC countries. To identify the comparative advantage/disadvantage of India's exports with BIMSTEC countries, revealed comparative advantage (RCA) approach is used at HS 6-digit. It provides an understanding of challenges and opportunities that India's export sector faces as it becomes rapidly integrated into global markets. The study identifies those export categories in which India loses, gains, or maintains its comparative advantage with following the stages of comparative advantages. The study concludes that India's export sectors witnessed competitive positioning of some of its product, and these trends have not been uniform across all Industries. Rapid export growth of some sector does not imply that the sector is displaying high demand growth in BIMSTEC markets. In an ideal situation, there would be the emergence of an export structure that has a heavy concentration in those industries that exhibit high growth in the BIMSTEC market.

INTRODUCTION

Economic integration within regional trading blocs adds the significant value to economic growth, trade, and investment. Being a founder member of the Association of Southeast Asian Nations (ASEAN) and the largest member country in terms of population as well as territory, India despite being preoccupied with the idea of getting its partnership with ASEAN enhanced made efforts to live up to the expectation of its colleagues in the Bay of Bengal Initiative for Multi-Sectoral Technical and Economic Cooperation (BIMSTEC) and to carry forward the BIMSTEC vision of mutually beneficial regional cooperation. In BIMSTEC region, mutual cooperation in various areas is more or less covered by India's bilateral economic relations with other countries. It fosters the rate of economic growth by tapping regional synergies (Devi, 2007).

DOI: 10.4018/978-1-7998-1730-7.ch008

BIMSTEC is an international organization linking a cluster of nations in South Asia and Southeast Asia, including India, Thailand, Bangladesh, Myanmar, Sri Lanka, Bhutan, and Nepal. The Bay of Bengal is a bay that forms the north-eastern part of the Indian Ocean. It resembles a triangle bordered by India, Sri Lanka, Bhutan, Bangladesh, Myanmar, Thailand, Malaysia, and Indonesia. On June 6, 1997, a new sub-regional alliance was established in Bangkok and received the name BIST-EC (Bangladesh, India, Sri Lanka, and Thailand Economic Cooperation). Myanmar participated the foundational gathering as a spectator and joined the organization as a full member at the Special Ministerial conference held in Bangkok on December 22, 1997, upon which the name of the alliance was changed to BIMSTEC. This new organization was established with the objective to merge the "West Look" policy of Thailand and ASEAN with the "East Look" policy of India and South Asia. Therefore, BIMSTEC can be explained as association among ASEAN and South Asian Association for Regional Cooperation (SAARC) (Uperti, 2007).

It is generally recognized that trade is essential for growth and that growth is useful for economic development. The composition and volume of global trade has witnessed significant changes during the last two decades. Trade liberalization, rising income, and technological advancements have been the main determinants (Erokhin, 2016a, 2016b). Against the backdrop of a rapidly changing global export pattern, and the success of Southeast Asian economies, there is strong case for India to pursue an export-led growth strategy that ultimately leads to the improvement of economic conditions in a country. However, given India's recent macroeconomic performance and its current export structure, such a turnaround would require major structural transformation of the economy and changes in its export specialization patterns.

Openness in trade and patterns of specialization are, however, interconnected variables (Mahmood, 2005). In the context of on-going multilateral trade negotiations, the study analyses the comparative advantage/disadvantage of India's exports with BIMSTEC countries, by using the revealed comparative advantage (RCA) approach at HS 6-digit. This is to provide a unique understanding of challenges and opportunities that India's export sector faces, as it becomes rapidly integrated into global markets.

It is important to note that supply and demand-side conditions play a crucial role in changing the comparative advantage profile of a country. The objective of this study is to identify export categories, in which India is losing, gaining, or maintaining its comparative advantage with following the stages of comparative advantages given by Balassa (1965) and technological classification of products given by Lall (2000). The effort is also taken to examine the extent to which India's leading export product lines have witnessed a shift in their comparative advantage away from traditional labor-intensive production to export of technology-based production activities. This insight is important to envision if past specialization patterns have witnessed any change, or if they have been reinforced over time due to internal and external forces. Specifically, the chapter investigates whether India has succeeded in moving from low value-added to technology-intensive high-value manufacturing with BIMSTEC countries. While identifying the dominance of certain sectors and a lack of shift in the revealed comparative advantage pattern of export structure provides a broad picture of country's export competitiveness, it falls short of identifying industries that, though exhibit revealed comparative advantage, are under threat.

This chapter highlights the RCA ranking of product lines based upon their technological classification at examines the extent to which India's export specialization in export sector has shifted away from labor and natural resource-intensive products to high value-added knowledge and technology-intensive products during 1997-2017. The author attempts to throw light on RCA ranking product lines for exported commodities at HS 6-digit level by India to BIMSTEC countries.

BACKGROUND

BIMSTEC strategies has been made with such a way that encouraging national and regional interests at a multilateral level. Through this platform, BIMSTEC economies attract international support and cooperation for developmental projects and productive economic strategies. Chakraborty (2007a) stated that India had taken holistic view about the emergence of BIMSTEC in the context of new global order, particularly, its Look East thrust. Thailand plays important role to speed up the pace of trade liberalization and economic cooperation within BIMSTEC. India's outward orientation process lead to increase trade with Asia-Pacific Economic Cooperation (APEC) economies.

Chakraborty (2007b) analyzed trade performance and integration experience of BIMSTEC. The study observed that the intra-block trade in final products and trade in intermediate products increased within BIMSTEC nations which increased possible production integration among BIMSTEC nations. The study revealed that removal of tariff and non-tariff barriers and implementation of trade facilitation significantly contributed to the increase in trade among BIMSTEC economies.

Kumari (2007) stated that system for trade development and governance in BIMSTEC insisted the centrality of market forces above person, communities, and government and promoted the rights of business sector overthrow the people, communities, and states. Women played a significant role in trade liberalization but trade policies trends for women still debatable in these nations.

Devi (2007) examined the emerging trends and prospects of economic cooperation in BIMSTEC. The study revealed significant change in trade orientation of BIMSTEC nations since the 1990s and most of them exhibited a higher outward orientation, the relevance of the regional bloc in enhancing trading and investment patterns, as well as analyzed the existing socio-economic performance of member nations. With the formation of BIMSTEC trading bloc, majority of South Asian countries were able to improve their export competitiveness to some extent in international market and free trade agreements (FTAs) under BIMSTEC umbrella helped to expand market size in international market of member nations.

Mukherji and Paswan (2007) explored trade and investment opportunities of India in BIMSTEC trading bloc. The study highlighted that trade liberalization induced the growth of intra-regional trade and trade potential at sectoral and product levels. Manufacturing units added the impetus to India's intra-industry trade. For the growth of India trade in BIMSTEC manufacturing units play a vital role by expanding trade volumes.

Nag and De (2007) stated that BIMSTEC made the bridge between South Asia and Southeast Asia. BIMSTEC had a potential to increase trade among member countries by enchanting gain of their geological location in the state of the Bay of Bengal and the Eastern coast of the Indian Ocean. Foreign direct investment (FDI) from Asian countries, including Japan, may help to overcome many problems in a bloc. Key sectors were recognized by BIMSTEC for the encouragement of trade, while trade facilitation took serious concentration by BIMSTEC nations. In the field of transport and infrastructure, BIMSTEC helps integration process in Asia by giving important focus on cross-border infrastructure growth and also makes investment demand in key sectors preferred by BIMSTEC nations.

Wijayasiri and Mel (2008) examined BIMSTEC-Japan economic cooperation in trade and investment from Sri Lankan perspective. Sri Lanka continues to look for increased diversification of export market which presently concentrated in Europe and the USA. Japan is a chief trading partner for BIMSTEC as a source of imports and destination of exports. Japan acts as a channel that enhances rivalry in BIMSTEC region and promotes quality of products and services in the country. High transaction costs to trade in the state necessitate enhanced infrastructure, reduction of non-tariff barriers (NTBs). The coverage of the agreement included main issues for BIMSTEC-Japan corporation. But Japan still may play a key role in boosting economic cooperation in BIMSTEC.

Kabir and Salim (2010) revealed that the share of intra-BIMSTEC trade in world trade was rather modest. Main import sources and export destinations of the majority of BIMSTEC countries are still outside the bloc. The study revealed that the GDP and governance of both importers and exporters positively influenced bilateral trade in BIMSTEC which indicated a strong evidence of positive trade response to the bloc even before the forming an FTA.

Kalirajan and Bhattacharya (2011) empirically measured export potentials among BIMSTEC and Japan. The study pointed that BIMSTEC was expected to be more successful in enhancing intraregional trade because of its proximity of demand and strong historical, cultural, political, and economic ties with member countries. As Japan is the second-largest trading partner and given Japan's technological development status, it is beneficial for BIMSTEC countries to have closer economic cooperation in terms of sustained trade and investment. It is also beneficial to Japan to cater for the dynamic emerging economies such as India in BIMSTEC.

Saxena and Bhadauriya (2012) tried to identify the areas of improvement in Indo-BIMSTEC trade relations. Sri Lanka and Thailand were the leading partners of India in the context of both import and export. India's biggest trading partner among BIMSTEC nations is Sri Lanka because Thailand has adverse trade with India. For the growth of export, India must identify the potential products which can drive Indian export to export market. In context of imports, India imports from Thailand were high. Stronger relation between India-BIMSTEC means steadier and more affluent Asia.

Chowdhury and Neogi (2014) estimated trade complementarity and similarity between India and BIMSTEC countries in the context of regional trade agreement (RTA). The study revealed that BIMSTEC was an important element in India's "Look East" strategy and adds a new dimension to India's economic cooperation with Southeast Asian countries. India-BIMSTEC free trade agreement promotes trade and greater connectivity between India, Nepal, Bangladesh, Myanmar, Sri Lanka, Bhutan, and Thailand. Trade structure between India and BIMSTEC exposed that there were complementary sectors and products available for enhancing trade cooperation between trading partners. India, with trade cooperation with some BIMSTEC nations, in all product categories can be a vital player in the region. India's average tariff is higher than that in BIMSTEC countries. Reduction of tariffs has a short term crash on India's exports but can unite in the medium term through productivity gains and efficiency. Also, emerging economic structure warrants greater cooperation from India in the regionalization efforts in Asia.

Rahman and Kim (2016) analyzed trade and investment potential under the ambit of regional co-operation comprising the seven contiguous countries of Bangladesh, India, Sri Lanka, Nepal, Bhutan, Thailand, and Myanmar. The potential economic impact of economic cooperation in BIMSTEC, as well as FTAs, promote the growth for the region. One of the major findings of the study was that a large part of BIMSTEC's trade had remained unrealized and the trade transaction cost was one of the major trading barriers prohibiting the growth of BIMSTEC intra-regional trade. The study reinforced that improvement in infrastructure and connectivity led to less trade transportation costs. It should be a necessary step in order to realize BIMSTEC's trade and investment potential and liberalization of non-policy barriers and spur trade and economic cooperation in BIMSTEC format.

MAIN FOCUS OF THE CHAPTER

Competitiveness of BIMSTEC: The Use of RCA

To analyze the India's export competitiveness with BIMSTEC countries, secondary data has been used from various authentic sites such United Nations Commodity Trade Statistics and Trade map at HS code 6-digit classification. Revealed Comparative Advantage (RCA) has been used for calculating export competitiveness. The revealed comparative advantage approach is most important methodology to measure a country's intensity of comparative advantage and disadvantage in a particular industry. Revealed comparative advantage is usually used to investigate shifts over time in comparative advantage of industries. This approach, however, is not meant to capture the potential future comparative advantage of a country, as RCA indices are based on actual trade data. However, RCA indices estimated across time can point to the general direction in which the pattern of comparative advantage is moving. The RCA index compares a country's world export share of a commodity, with the country's total export share in total world exports. If a country's share of world exports of a particular commodity is greater than its share of world exports of all commodities, the RCA will be greater than one. A country has a revealed comparative advantage only in those products for which its market share of world exports is above its average share of world exports (Mahmood, 2005).

To calculating comparative advantages in trade, RCA has been used more frequently in research. RCA firstly used by Balassa (1965). The conception of RCA was originated on conventional trade theory. Balassa (1965) defined RCA as:

$$RCA= [\ (X_{ij}/X_{nj})\ /\ (X_{it}/X_{nt})\ ]\ (1)$$

where,

X_{ij} – export of *i* product of *j* country,
X_{it} – world export of *i* product,
X_{nj} – total export of *j* country of *i* product,
X_{nt} – total world export.

RCA index measures a comparative advantage in *i* goods export of *j* country. If the value is higher than 1, then the analyzed country has RCAs in export of various goods. If the value is lower than 1, then there is an obvious comparative disadvantage in export of various goods. RCA index presents the status of a certain economy, together with the expansion of certain products which have market potential. The choice of this methodology has been properly chronicled and there are many instances which prove the strength of this method. Batra and Khan (2005) identified the pattern of RCA using the Balassa (1965) index for export data and found broad similarities in the structure of comparative advantage for India and China that help to enjoy comparative advantage for labor and resource-intensive sectors in the global market for both countries. Shohibul (2013) measured RCA for ASEAN and China trade flows using Balassa index and found that China had more established patterns of trade, while ASEAN trade patterns were very dynamic.

It is important to note that RCA indices are quite robust and insensitive to the changes in growth and business cycle differences across trading partners. These changes influence the numerator and denominator in the RCA formula. Similarly, the indices are not sensitive to the height of market access barriers, as long as these barriers are across the board, against all exporters of a particular product line. Yet, they are sensitive to discriminatory market access barriers against exports of a particular country. The RCA indices can also be used gain further insight to target those industries that currently exhibit revealed comparative disadvantage, but have potential to achieve export competitiveness over time. This can be achieved by categorizing a country's export structure, based upon HS 2-digit and HS 6-digit product lines, into six broader product groups based upon their relative RCA profile. In the order of their relative comparative advantage position, these groups are competitively positioned product lines, threatened product lines, emerging products, and weakly positioned products (Table 1).

Table 1. Product lines based on their relative comparative advantage position

Groups	Description	Decision criteria
Competitively positioned product lines	These product lines have RCAs greater than unity and show consistent improvement over time owing to favorable external and internal conditions.	RCA index of a product line *i* is > 1 in RCA Average (2015, 2016, 2017), i.e. RCA_i 2015, 2016, 2017 > 1. Difference between RCA index of product line *i* RCA Average (2015, 2016, 2017) and its last three years average RCA is positive, i.e. RCA_i 2015, 2016, 2017 – RCA_i Average 1997, 1998, 1999 > 0.
Threatened products lines	These product lines have RCAs greater than unity, but indices are declining over time, due to an adverse domestic environment and/or global competitive pressures.	RCA index of a product line *i* RCA Average is > 1 in 2015, 2016, 2017, i.e. RCA_i 2015, 2016, 2017 > 1. Difference between RCA index of product line *i* in RCA_i Average 2015, 2016, 2017 and its last three years' average RCA is negative, i.e. RCA_i 2015, 2016, 2017 – RCA_i Average 1997, 1998, 1999 < 0.
Emerging products – Tier I and Tier II	These product lines exhibit RCA indices that are less than unity, (revealed comparative disadvantage) but their relative global position in the exports market is improving. These product lines signal promise for future export potential. To provide a meaningful analysis, the "Emerging Product Group" is sub-divided into two groups in terms of their RCA position within this broader group.	Tier I: < 1 and equal to or > 0.5. Difference between RCA of product line *i* in 2017 and its last three years' average RCA is positive, i.e. RCA_i 2015, 2016, 2017 – RCA_i Average 1997, 1998, 1999 > 0. Tier II: RCA of a product line *i* is < 0.5 in 2017, i.e. RCA_i 2015, 2016, 2017 < 0.5. Difference between RCA of product line *i* in 2015, 2016, 2017 and its last three years' average RCA is positive, i.e. RCA_i 2015, 2016, 2017 – RCA_i Average 1997, 1998, 1999 > 0.
Weakly positioned products – Tier I and Tier II	RCA indices of these product lines are less than unity and declining due to non-conducive global and domestic factors. The "Weakly Positioned Product Group" is subdivided into two groups based on their relative level of revealed comparative disadvantage.	Tier I: RCA of a product line *i* is < l but equal to or > 0.5 in 2015, 2016, 2017, i.e. RCA 2015, 2016, 2017 < 1 and equal to or > 0.5. Difference between RCA of product line *i* in 2015, 2016, 2017 and its last three years' average RCA is negative, i.e. RCA_i 2015, 2016, 2017 – RCA_i Average 1997, 1998, 1999 < 0. Tier II: RCA of a product line *i* is < 0.5 in 2015, 2016, 2017, i.e. RCA_i 2015, 2016, 2017 < 0.5. Difference between RCA of product line *i* in 2015, 2016, 2017 and its last three years' average RCA is negative, i.e. RCA_i 2015, 2016, 2017 – RCA_i Average 1997, 1998, 1999 < 0.

Source: Author's development

Shifting Comparative Advantage of India's Export Products to BIMSTEC Countries: Aggregate Analysis for Leading Products

The lists of top exported with RCA ranking product lines in their technological orientation and relative factor intensities such as (a) resource-intensive; (b) scale intensive/technological intensive- low, medium and high; (c) labor-intensive; and (d) differentiation-based (Lall, 2000). According to H-O model, an FTA creates a large free trade area with common factor prices. It increases the economic power of the area and promotes its culture, also increases factor mobility.

Table 2 shows the analysis of product categories at 2-digit HS code that leads to interesting observations. The list is dominated by technological (including low, medium, and high) and resource-intensive production activities, operating at the lower end of the technology spectrum and requiring relatively low technical skills. Table 2 also illustrates that six product categories out of the fifteen industries, RCA ranking exports in 2017 were resource-intensive and eight product categories out of fifteen, RCA ranking exports in 2017 were technological intensive. One industry (98-99 HS classification) was not specified.

Resource-based (RB) products tend to be simple and labor-intensive, e.g. simple food or leather processing, but there are segments using capital, scale, and skill-intensive technologies (petroleum refining or modern processed foods). Since competitive advantages in these products arises generally

Table 2. Technological classifications and RCA of India trade with BIMSTEC at HS-2 digit level in 2017

HS code	Product categories	Technological classification	Bangladesh	Bhutan	Nepal	Myanmar	Sri Lanka	Thailand
01-05	Animals and animal products	RI	2.11	3.14	10.44	8.01	8.81	19.34
06-15	Vegetable products	RI	9.36	1.44	70.40	2.29	62.18	43.63
16-24	Foodstuffs	RI	12.50	17.14	83.15	43.51	89.64	37.04
25-27	Mineral products	RI	0.58	2.16	18.85	0.15	21.72	1.63
28-38	Chemical and allied industries	MTI	1.87	0.56	9.23	6.57	12.29	17.06
39-40	Plastic / rubbers	RI	0.37	1.40	50.95	6.45	41.46	30.24
41-43	Raw hides, skins, leathers and furs	LTI	14.09	20.17	2.36	7.43	21.55	65.06
44-49	Wood and wood products	LI	4.96	5.12	17.61	7.80	23.89	58.04
50-63	Textiles	LTI	0.43	0.05	5.33	4.64	32.84	9.10
64-67	Footwear / headgear	LTI	12.06	4.33	17.68	5.70	27.36	11.18
68-71	Stone / glass	RI	1.75	1.06	2.84	0.16	3.24	32.20
72-83	Metals	LTI	3.81	5.57	32.31	3.79	13.89	21.57
84-85	Machinery / electrical	HTI	9.92	0.37	5.40	2.11	5.54	5.90
86-89	Transportation	MTI	3.28	1.71	14.77	2.10	89.73	9.19
90-97	Miscellaneous	HTI	4.16	1.00	12.45	4.68	17.07	19.65
98-99	Service	Not specified	3.95	2.59	4.73	1.33	5.60	25.26

Note: RI – resource-intensive; HTI – high technological intensive; MTI – medium technological intensive; LTI – low technological intensive; LI – labor-intensive.

Source: Author's development based on United Nations Commodity Trade Statistics [COMTRADE] (n.d.) and Lall (2000)

but not always from the local availability of natural resources, they do not raise important issues for competitiveness (Lall, 2000). The effective and efficient application of all useful resources that the economy can muster helps determine its competitive advantage. From the observation, it has been clear that Bangladesh manufacturing moving from resource-based and labor-intensive to technological-based manufacturing of products (Figure 1). In case of Bhutan, it now moved for low intensive and medium intensive technology manufacturing of products.

Low technology (LT) products tend to have stable and well-diffused technologies. The technologies are primarily embodied in the capital equipment, the low end of the range has relatively simple skill requirements. Medium technology (MT) products, comprising the bulk of skill and scale-intensive technologies in capital goods and intermediate products, are the heartland of industrial activity in mature economies. They tend to have complex technologies, with moderately high levels of R&D, advanced skill needs and lengthy learning periods. Those in the engineering and automotive sub-groups are very linkage-intensive and need considerable interaction between firms to reach "best practice" technical efficiency (Lall, 2000).

The third less developed country economy in BIMSTEC region is Nepal. It uses resource-based, technological-based, and labor-intensive techniques in products manufacturing. In case of Myanmar, more focus is required on technological intensive manufacturing as compared to resource-based or labor-intensive. Sri Lanka uses labor-intensive techniques but side by side switching toward the technology-intensive products manufacturing. In case of Thailand and India, manufacture includes almost all the classification of products but more toward high technology. High technology (HT) products have advanced and fast-changing technologies, with high R&D investments and prime emphasis on product design. The most advanced technologies require sophisticated technology infrastructures, high levels of specialized technical skills, and close interactions between firms, and between firms and universities or research institutions.

Figure 1. Technological classification of BIMSTEC (1997-2015) using RCA approach
Source: COMTRADE (n.d.)

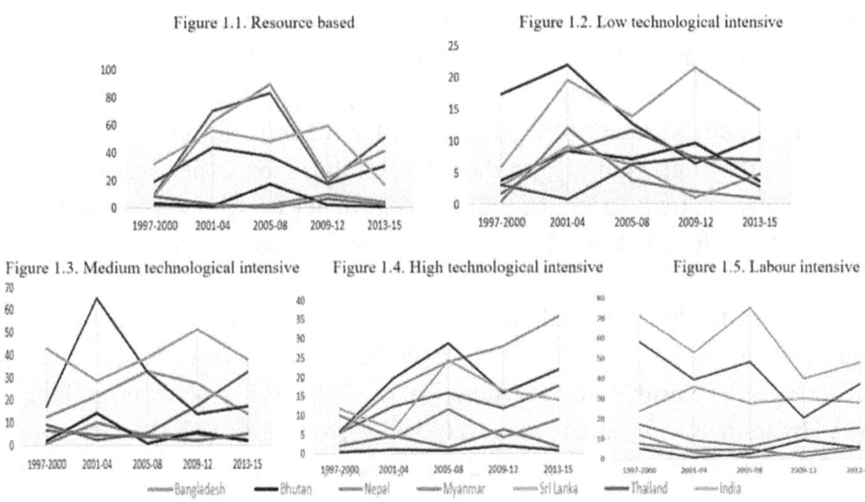

Out of 339 HS 6-digit level product lines, 97 (28.6%) have RCAs greater than unity (Table 3). This places them in the category of Competitively Positioned Products in first category, i.e. animals and animal products. In case of foodstuffs, 64 commodities from 420 commodities are Competitively Positioned Products. Other industries fall in Competitively Positioned Product group (wood and wood products). From 304 products, 118 (38.82%) products have been competitively positioned in product group followed by machinery/electrical, metal, and transportation with 35.64%, 40.94%, and 40.29% share in exports, respectively. The profile of Competitively Positioned Products highlights the lack of inroads made by some unskilled and skilled labor-intensive and resource-intensive industries, which draw their competitive strength from low wages and the availability of raw material. This included industries such as animals and animal products, foodstuffs, machinery/electrical, metals, transportation, and wood and wood products. Lack of headway made by the transportation equipment industry has been a reflection of its narrow production base and cost disadvantage, due to a higher share of imported inputs, absence of forward and backward linkages, and lack of economies of scale and scope.

In the case of Threatened Product group, there are six industrial products which fall under that category. These products exhibit revealed comparative advantage, but have experienced a declining share in trade during 1997-2017 between India and Bangladesh. It was important to note that 51.21% of chemical and allied industries, 39.39% of mineral products, 51.77% of plastic/rubbers, 35.29% of stone/glass, 37.03% of miscellaneous products, and 100% of services fall under Threatened Product group, which has been the driving force of India's export structure. In view of their significance to India's RCA profile, there has been a need for determined efforts to ensure that India should sustain and enhance its export competitiveness by reversing the above trends. As a part of BIMSTEC, it is not difficult to formulate product-specific policy responses, there is a strong economic rationale for targeting those Threatened Products that have significant comparative advantage, but losing their competitiveness.

Emerging Product Group is sub-divided into two groups to draw a distinction between two types of product lines: (a) product lines that demonstrate underlying trends to join the Competitive Group, but exhibit a comparative disadvantage at present; (b) Tier II products. There were three industry lines under Tier I. In case of India and Bangladesh, raw hides, skins, leathers, and furs industry with the highest, i.e. 53.40% of product lines covered under Emerging Product Group followed by footwear/headgear (38.18%) and vegetable products (37.50%), which are relatively labor-intensive sectors. This result highlights the comparative advantage dynamics of India's manufacturing sector, where momentum is developing to move towards relatively high value-added technology-intensive production activities.

Weakly Positioned products are categorized into Tier I and Tier II sub-groupings. The RCAs of Tier I product lines are less than unity but greater than 0.5 and thus have experienced negative growth. In case of India and Bangladesh trade, only one industry falls under weakly positioned Tier I category i.e. textile industry. 44.12% of these industrial products were weakly positioned under RCA classification, i.e. 398 out of 902.

The profile of Competitively Positioned Products between India and Bhutan covered five industries, including animals and animal products, foodstuffs, metals, rawhides, skins, leathers, and furs, and service (Table 4). The highest contribution is registered in raw hides, skins, leathers, and furs product lines (62.50%) followed by animals and animal products (33.33%), foodstuffs (42.19%), metals (30.89%), and services (100%). Most of the lines in competitively positioned products are resource and technological-based ones.

In Threatened Product group between India and Bhutan, there are only two industries: (1) vegetable products contributing 50%, i.e. total 32 products out of 72 ones exported by India and (2) wood and

Table 3. RCA profile and product grouping: India and Bangladesh in 1997-2017

HS code	Product categories	CP	TP	EP (TI)	EP (TII)	WP (TI)	WP (TII)	Grand total
01-05	Animals and animal products	97	32	79	21	57	53	339
		(28.6)	(9.43)	(23.3)	(6.19)	(16.81)	(15.63)	(100)
06-15	Vegetable products	113	70	157	42	23	15	420
		(26.90)	(16.67)	(37.38)	(10.00)	(5.48)	(3.57)	(100)
16-24	Foodstuffs	64	43	27	12	59	16	221
		(28.96)	(19.46)	(12.22)	(5.43)	(26.70)	(7.24)	(100)
25-27	Mineral products	28	65	27	13	07	25	165
		(16.97)	(39.39)	(16.36)	(7.88)	(4.24)	(15.15)	(100)
28-38	Chemical and allied industries	205	464	73	52	88	24	906
		(22.63)	(51.21)	(8.06)	(5.74)	(9.71)	(2.65)	(100)
39-40	Plastic/ rubbers	48	117	-	29	19	13	226
		(21.24)	(51.77)	-	(12.83)	(8.41)	(5.75)	(100)
41-43	Raw hides, skins, leathers and furs	-	21	55	17	08	02	103
		-	(20.39)	(53.40)	(16.50)	(7.77)	(1.94)	(100)
44-49	Wood and wood products	118	29	14	46	71	26	304
		(38.82)	(9.54)	(4.61)	(15.13)	(23.36)	(8.55)	(100)
50-63	Textiles	233	82	64	59	398	66	902
		(25.83)	(9.09)	(7.10)	(6.54)	(44.12)	(7.32)	(100)
64-67	Footwear / headgear	17	2	21	8	2	5	55
		(30.91)	(3.64)	(38.18)	(14.55)	(3.64)	(9.09)	(100)
68-71	Stone/ glass	21	78	46	35	19	22	221
		(9.50)	(35.29)	(20.81)	(15.84)	(8.60)	(9.95)	(100)
72-83	Metals	253	107	42	85	62	69	618
		(40.94)	(17.31)	(6.80)	(13.75)	(10.03)	(11.17)	(100)
84-85	Machinery / electrical	314	28	89	115	209	126	881
		(35.64)	(3.18)	(10.10)	(13.05)	(23.72)	(14.30)	(100)
86-89	Transportation	56	9	17	31	7	19	139
		(40.29)	(6.47)	(12.23)	(22.30)	(5.04)	(13.67)	(100)
90-97	Miscellaneous	35	157	113	37	14	68	424
		(8.25)	(37.03)	(26.65)	(8.73)	(3.30)	(16.04)	(100)
98-99	Service	-	1	-	-	-	-	1
		-	(100)	-	-	-	-	(100)

Note: CP – competitive positioned product; TP – threatened product; EM (TI) – emerging product Tier I; EM (TII) – emerging product Tier II; WP (TI) – weakly positioned product (TI); WP (TII) – weakly positioned product (TII)

Source: Author's development based on COMTRADE (n.d.)

Table 4. RCA profile and product grouping: India and Bhutan in 1997-2017

HS code	Product categories	CP	TP	EP (TI)	EP (TII)	WP (I)	WP (II)	Grand total
01-05	Animals and animal product	14	4	5	8	8	3	42
		(33.33)	(9.52)	(11.90)	(19.05)	(19.05)	(7.17)	(100)
06-15	Vegetable products	13	36	5	3	11	4	72
		(18.06)	(50.00)	(6.94)	(4.17)	(15.28)	(5.56)	(100)
16-24	Foodstuffs	27	7	18	5	2	5	64
		(42.19)	(10.94)	(28.13)	(7.81)	(3.13)	(7.81)	(100)
25-27	Mineral products	13	9	26	6	4	5	63
		(20.63)	(14.29)	(41.27)	(9.52)	(6.35)	(7.94)	(100)
28-38	Chemical and allied industries	12	45	2	9	26	68	162
		(7.41)	(27.78)	(1.23)	(5.56)	(16.05)	(41.98)	(100)
39-40	Plastic / rubbers	3	12	51	16	5	9	96
		(3.13)	(12.50)	(53.13)	(16.67)	(5.21)	(9.38)	(100)
41-43	Raw hides, skins, leathers, and furs	05	-	-	-	-	03	08
		(62.50)	-	-	-	-	(37.50)	(100)
44-49	Wood and wood products	1	56	-	6	31	-	94
		(1.06)	(59.57)	-	(6.38)	(32.98)	-	(100)
50-63	Textiles	68	90	32	59	201	109	559
		(12.16)	(16.10)	(5.72)	(10.55)	(35.96)	(19.50)	(100)
64-67	Footwear / headgear	-	7	19	5	14	8	53
		-	(13.21)	(35.85)	(9.43)	(26.42)	(15.09)	(100)
68-71	Stone / glass	-	-	-	-	21	-	21
		-	-	-	-	(100)	-	(100)
72-83	Metals	117	67	21	56	75	43	379
		(30.89)	(17.68)	(5.54)	(14.78)	(19.79)	(11.35)	(100)
84-85	Machinery / electrical	-	69	85	-	48	205	407
		-	(16.95)	(20.88)	-	(11.79)	(50.37)	(100)
86-89	Transportation	-	-	-	-	64	11	75
		-	-	-	-	(85.33)	(14.67)	(100)
90-97	Miscellaneous	15	9	27	33	146	2.95	237
		(6.33)	(3.80)	(11.39)	(13.92)	(61.60)	(2.95)	(100)
98-99	Service	1	-	-	-	-	-	01
		(100)	-	-	-	-	-	(100)

Note: CP – competitive positioned product; TP – threatened product; EM (TI) – emerging product Tier I; EM (TII) – emerging product Tier II; WP (TI) – weakly positioned product (TI); WP (TII) – weakly positioned product (TII)

Source: Author's development based on COMTRADE (n.d.)

wood products contributing 59.57%. These industries exhibit revealed comparative advantage, but have experienced a declining share in trade between both the countries in 1997-2017. The most significant decline in the revealed comparative advantage occurred in vegetable products industry including live trees and other plants; bulbs, roots and the like; cut flowers and ornamental foliage, edible vegetables and certain roots and tubers, edible fruit and nuts; peel of citrus fruits or melons, coffee, tea, mate and spices, cereals, products of the milling industry; malt; starches; inulin; wheat gluten, oil seeds and oleaginous fruits; miscellaneous grains, seeds and fruit; industrial or medicinal plants; straw and fodder, lac; gums, resins and other vegetable saps and extracts, vegetable plaiting materials; vegetable products not elsewhere specified or included and animal or vegetable fats and oils and their cleavage products; prepared edible fats; animal or vegetable wax. In view of their significance to India's revealed comparative advantage profile with Bhutan, there is a need to determined efforts that lead to grow the healthy trade relations between India and Bhutan as a part of BIMSTEC region.

In case of India and Bhutan, three industries (footwear/headgear, plastic/rubbers, and mineral products) include emerging products (Tier I) with positive RCA value throughout the study period. Their contribution is 35.85% for footwear/headgear, 53.13% for plastic/rubbers, and 41.27% for mineral products, respectively.

India and Bhutan faced weak position under Tier I for four industries, i.e. textiles (35.96%), stone/glass (100%), transportation (85.33%), and miscellaneous products (61.60%). The RCAs of Tier I product lines are less than unity but greater than 0.5 and thus have experienced negative growth. As far as Tier II is concerned between India and Bhutan trade, only two industries fall under category, i.e. chemical and allied industries and machinery/electrical. 41.98% of chemical and allied industries products and machinery/electrical (50.37%) have been weakly positioned under RCA classification.

In the profile of Competitively Positioned Products between India and Nepal, India enjoys trade competitiveness in fifteen industries except raw hides, skins, leathers, and furs. This group comes under Threatened Product category with 51.06% contribution. Overall, India has a revealed comparative advantage over Nepal. Under Competitively Positioned Products, the highest contributing industries are wood and wood products (79.38%) followed by footwear/headgear (76.19%) and mineral products (73.79%) (Table 5).

Competitive Products from India's perspective cover a broad spectrum of production activities with Myanmar. This involves a range of product lines with varying degrees of manufacturing sophistication, indicating the presence of backward and forward linkages within this industrial cluster. These industries are animals and animal products (33.01%), vegetable products (37.31%), foodstuffs (44.78%), chemical and allied industries (33.76%), plastic/rubbers (50%), rawhides, skins, leathers, and furs (45.45%), footwear/headgear (52.89%), machinery/electrical (34.08%), and miscellaneous products (34.84%) that include optical, photographic, cinematographic, measuring, checking, precision, medical or surgical instruments and apparatus; parts and accessories thereof, clocks and watches and parts thereof, musical instruments; parts and accessories of such articles, arms and ammunition; parts and accessories thereof, furniture; bedding, mattresses, mattress supports, cushions and similar stuffed furnishings; lamps and lighting fittings, not elsewhere specified or included; illuminated signs, illuminated name-plates and the like; prefabricated buildings, toys, games and sports requisites; parts and accessories thereof, miscellaneous manufactured articles, works of art, collectors' pieces and antiques (Table 6).

Table 5. RCA profile and product grouping: India and Nepal in 1997-2017

HS code	Product categories	CP	TP	EP (TI)	EP (TII)	WP (I)	WP (II)	Grand total
01-05	Animals and animal product	119	89	-	32	52	4	296
		(40.20)	(30.07)	-	(10.81)	(17.57)	(1.35)	(100)
06-15	Vegetable products	146	84	26	12	32	67	367
		(39.78)	(22.89)	(7.08)	(3.27)	(8.72)	(18.26)	(100)
16-24	Foodstuffs	84	06	55	21	11	10	187
		(44.92)	(3.21)	(29.41)	(11.23)	(5.88)	(5.35)	(100)
25-27	Mineral products	76	3	15	-	10	-	103
		(73.79)	(2.91)	(14.56)	-	(9.71)	-	(100)
28-38	Chemical and allied industries	329	89	32	105	60	127	742
		(44.34)	(11.99)	(4.31)	(14.15)	(8.09)	(17.12)	(100)
39-40	Plastic / rubbers	18	-	7	13	-	-	38
		(47.37)	-	(18.32)	(34.21)	-	-	(100)
41-43	Raw hides, skins, leathers, and furs	15	48	6	10	6	9	94
		(15.96)	(51.06)	(6.38)	(10.64)	(6.38)	(9.57)	(100)
44-49	Wood and wood products	204	22	7	9	11	4	257
		(79.38)	(8.56)	(2.72)	(3.50)	(4.28)	(1.56)	(100)
50-63	Textiles	390	89	93	79	69	143	863
		(45.19)	(10.31)	(10.78)	(9.15)	(8.00)	(16.57)	(100)
64-67	Footwear / headgear	16	-	1	4	-	-	21
		(76.19)	-	(4.76)	(19.05)	-	-	(100)
68-71	Stone / glass	32	5	11	11	21	18	98
		(32.65)	(5.10)	(11.22)	(11.22)	(21.43)	(18.37)	(100)
72-83	Metals	148	38	89	57	40	116	538
		(36.80)	(7.06)	(16.34)	(10.59)	(7.43)	(21.56)	(100)
84-85	Machinery / electrical	207	79	84	95	142	128	715
		(28.95)	(11.05)	(8.95)	(13.29)	(19.86)	(17.90)	(100)
86-89	Transportation	15	8	10	9	2	8	52
		(28.85)	(15.58)	(19.23)	(17.31)	(3.85)	(15.38)	(100)
90-97	Miscellaneous	120	39	56	71	-	75	361
		(33.24)	(10.80)	(15.51)	(19.67)	-	(20.78)	(100)
98-99	Service	1	-	-	-	-	-	01
		(100)	-	-	-	-	-	(100)

Note: CP – competitive positioned product; TP – threatened product; EM (TI) – emerging product Tier I; EM (TII) – emerging product Tier II; WP (TI) – weakly positioned product (TI); WP (TII) – weakly positioned product (TII)

Source: Author's development based on COMTRADE (n.d.)

Table 6. RCA profile and product grouping: India and Myanmar in 1997-2017

HS code	Product categories	CP	TP	EP (TI)	EP (TII)	WP (I)	WP (II)	Grand total
01-05	Animals and animal products	68	45	35	21	17	20	206
		(33.01)	(21.84)	(16.99)	(10.19)	(8.25)	(9.71)	(100)
06-15	Vegetable products	122	78	54	29	11	33	327
		(37.31)	(23.85)	(16.51)	(8.87)	(3.36)	(10.09)	(100)
16-24	Foodstuffs	30	14	4	-	2	17	67
		(44.78)	(20.90)	(5.97)	-	(2.99)	(25.37)	(100)
25-27	Mineral products	6	29	0	-	13	45	93
		(6.45)	(31.18)	-	-	(13.98)	(48.39)	(100)
28-38	Chemical and allied industries	210	78	36	64	149	85	622
		(33.76)	(12.54)	(5.79)	(10.29)	(23.95)	(13.67)	(100)
39-40	Plastic / rubbers	39	6	1	8	3	21	78
		(50.00)	(7.69)	(1.28)	(10.26)	(3.85)	(26.92)	(100)
41-43	Raw hides, skins, leathers, and furs	45	5	12	16	8	13	99
		(45.45)	(5.05)	(12.12)	(16.16)	(8.08)	(13.13)	(100)
44-49	Wood and wood products	64	89	12	10	31	25	231
		(27.71)	(38.53)	(5.19)	(4.33)	(13.42)	(10.82)	(100)
50-63	Textiles	167	98	354	69	63	51	802
		(20.82)	(12.22)	(44.14)	(8.60)	(7.86)	(6.360	(100)
64-67	Footwear / headgear	64	8	12	21	10	6	121
		(52.89)	(6.61)	(9.92)	(17.36)	(8.26)	(4.96)	(100)
68-71	Stone / glass	7	4	14	56	10	23	114
		(6.14)	(3.51)	(12.28)	(49.12)	(8.77)	(20.18)	(100)
72-83	Metals	73	187	62	19	58	116	515
		(14.17)	(36.31)	(12.04)	(3.69)	(11.260	(22.52)	(100)
84-85	Machinery / electrical	153	78	61	45	23	89	449
		(34.08)	(17.37)	(13.59)	(10.02)	(5.12)	(19.82)	(100)
86-89	Transportation	5	2	14	10	-	1	32
		(15.63)	(6.25)	(43.75)	(31.25)	-	(3.13)	(100)
90-97	Miscellaneous	146	72	15	69	83	34	419
		(34.84)	(17.18)	(3.58)	(16.47)	(19.81)	(8.11)	(100)
98-99	Service	-	1	-	-	-	-	01
		-	(100)	-	-	-	-	(100)

Note: CP – competitive positioned product; TP – threatened product; EM (TI) – emerging product Tier I; EM (TII) – emerging product Tier II; WP (TI) – weakly positioned product (TI); WP (TII) – weakly positioned product (TII)

Source: Author's development based on COMTRADE (n.d.)

In the case of Threatened Products Group, product lines lose their competitive position at an increasing rate are tin-related items. In India-Myanmar trade, there are three industries, namely, metals, services, and wood and wood products. For metals, 187 out of 515 products are under Threatened Products Group followed by wood and wood products with 38.53% and services (one product). There is a need to undertake industry-specific steps to highlight the issues concerning these product lines.

The presence of Emerging Product Group for both the tiers between India and Myanmar points to a need to look at the impact of the current tariff regime on the cost competitiveness of exports for textiles. This industry covered 44.14% of India's exports to Myanmar under Emerging Product Group I. Transportation industry with 43.75% also falls under Emerging Product Group I. Stone/glass industry with 49.12% goes under Emerging Product Group II.

There are 48.39% of product lines from mineral industry that are Weakly Positioned, including salt; sulfur; earths and stone; plastering materials, lime and cement, ores, slag and ash, mineral fuels, mineral oils, and products of their distillation; bituminous substances; mineral waxes. This industry requires time-bound assistance or protection to those segments that are technological-based and have positioning to achieve export competitiveness.

With Sri Lanka, India has a 44% of competitively positioned export products (Table 7) from seven industries: vegetable products (28.45%), footwear/headgear (70.59%), rawhides, skins, leathers, and furs (39.77%), textiles (36.88%), miscellaneous products (43.44%), transportation (82.76%), and services. All these industries were resource and technological-based. Vegetable products are the most competitively positioned segment. It includes live trees and other plants; bulbs, roots and the like; cut flowers and ornamental foliage, edible vegetables and certain roots and tubers, edible fruit and nuts; peel of citrus fruits or melons, coffee, tea, mate and spices, cereals, products of the milling industry; malt; starches; inulin; wheat gluten, oil seeds and oleaginous fruits; miscellaneous grains, seeds and fruit; industrial or medicinal plants; straw and fodder, lac; gums, resins and other vegetable saps and extracts, vegetable plaiting materials; vegetable products not elsewhere specified or included and animal or vegetable fats and oils and their cleavage products; prepared edible fats; animal or vegetable wax.

In the case of Threatened Product group, there are seven lines. From chemical and allied industries, 359 out of 862 products considered as Threatened Product followed by foodstuffs, animals and animal products, wood and wood products, metals, plastic/rubbers, and mineral products. According to the observation, India's revealed comparative advantage profile with Sri Lanka needs more efforts to ensure that India's economic growth enhances export competitiveness.

The presence of Emerging Product Group for Tier I between India and Sri Lanka was 47.40% for stone/glass and 49.34% for machinery/electrical industry. These industries are relatively resource and technological intensive.

In trade with Thailand, India enjoys competitive position in eleven industries from total exports as a member of BIMSTEC. After Nepal, India has good export competitiveness with Thailand in some industries that includes industries such as foodstuffs (45.65%), machinery/electrical (57.90%), plastic/rubbers (58.11%), rawhides, skins, leathers, and furs (69.88%), vegetable products (37.57%), textiles (42.84%), wood and wood products (60%), footwear/headgear (64.52%), miscellaneous products (44.79%), transportation (57.76%), and services (100%). In the case of Threatened Product group, there are four lines (25% of the total). These products exhibit revealed comparative advantage, but have experienced a declining share in trade in 1997-2017 between India and Thailand. These industries are metals with 43.10%, stone/glass with 56.52%, chemical and allied industries (33.19%), and animals and animal products with 31.95%, respectively (Table 8).

Table 7. RCA profile and product grouping: India and Sri Lanka in 1997-2017

HS code	Product categories	CP	TP	EP (TI)	EP (TII)	WP (I)	WP (TII)	Grand total
01-05	Animals and animal products	48	117	53	30	61	28	337
		(14.24)	(34.72)	(15.73)	(8.90)	(18.10)	(8.31)	(100)
06-15	Vegetable products	113	53	51	48	61	71	397
		(28.46)	(13.35)	(12.85)	(12.09)	(15.37)	(17.88)	(100)
16-24	Foodstuffs	20	31	7	5	1	11	75
		(26.67)	(41.33)	(9.33)	(6.67)	(1.33)	(14.67)	(100)
25-27	Mineral products	8	49	15	10	-	9	91
		(8.79)	(53.85)	(16.48)	(10.99)	-	(9.89)	(100)
28-38	Chemical and allied industries	95	359	73	60	119	156	862
		(11.02)	(41.65)	(8.47)	(6.96)	(13.81)	(18.10)	(100)
39-40	Plastic / rubbers	18	64	9	5	21	8	125
		(14.40)	(51.20)	(7.20)	(4.00)	(16.80)	(6.40)	(100)
41-43	Raw hides, skins, leathers, and FURS	35	12	4	7	10	15	88
		(39.77)	(19.32)	(4.55)	(7.95)	(11.36)	(17.05)	(100)
44-49	Wood and wood products	7	214	-	47	-	-	268
		(2.61)	(79.85)	-	(17.54)	-	-	(100)
50-63	Textiles	274	111	82	51	83	142	743
		(36.88)	(14.94)	(11.04)	(6.86)	(11.17)	(19.11)	(100)
64-67	Footwear / headgear	12	-	5	-	-	-	17
		70.59	-	29.41	-	-	-	(100)
68-71	Stone / glass	12	24	82	17	12	26	173
		(6.94)	(13.87)	(47.40)	(9.83)	(6.94)	(15.03)	(100)
72-83	Metals	51	196	69	73	18	87	494
		(10.32)	(39.68)	(13.97)	(14.78)	(3.64)	(17.61)	(100)
84-85	Machinery / electrical	67	185	371	59	52	18	752
		(8.91)	(24.60)	(49.34)	(7.85)	(6.91)	(2.39)	(100)
86-89	Transportation	48	-	-	6	-	4	58
		(82.76)	-	-	(10.34)	-	(6.90)	(100)
90-97	Miscellaneous	139	72	40	26	33	10	320
		(43.44)	(22.50)	(12.50)	(8.13)	(10.31)	(3.13)	(100)
98-99	Service	1	-	-	-	-	-	01
		(100)	-	-	-	-	-	(100)

Note: CP – competitive positioned product; TP – threatened product; EM (TI) – emerging product Tier I; EM (TII) – emerging product Tier II; WP (TI) – weakly positioned product (TI); WP (TII) – weakly positioned product (TII)

Source: Author's development based on COMTRADE (n.d.)

Table 8. RCA profile and product grouping: India and Thailand in 1997-2017

HS code	Product categories	CP	TP	EP (TI)	EP (TII)	WP (I)	WP (TII)	Grand total
01-05	Animals and animal products	48	77	43	7	61	5	241
		(19.92)	(31.95)	(17.84)	(2.90)	(25.31)	(2.07)	(100)
06-15	Vegetable products	127	31	18	21	53	88	338
		(37.57)	(9.17)	(5.33)	(6.21)	(15.68)	(26.04)	(100)
16-24	Foodstuffs	84	25	31	8	25	11	184
		(45.65)	(13.59)	(16.85)	(4.35)	(13.59)	(5.98)	(100)
25-27	Mineral products	3	37	76	13	7	9	145
		(2.07)	(25.52)	(52.41)	(8.97)	(4.83)	(6.21)	(100)
28-38	Chemical and allied industries	278	349	-	12	24	145	808
		(34.41)	(43.19)	-	(1.49)	(2.97)	(17.95)	(100)
39-40	Plastic / rubbers	86	30	02	17	-	13	148
		(58.11)	(20.27)	(1.35)	(11.49)	-	(8.78)	(100)
41-43	Raw hides, skins, leathers, furs	58	-	-	25	-	-	83
		(69.88)	-	-	(30.12)	-	-	(100)
44-49	Wood and wood products	156	19	1	53	18	13	260
		(60.00)	(7.31)	(0.38)	(20.38)	(6.92)	(5.00)	(100)
50-63	Textiles	308	69	26	82	172	62	719
		(42.84)	(9.60)	(3.62)	(11.40)	(23.92)	(8.62)	100)
64-67	Footwear / headgear	20	11	-	-	-	-	31
		(64.52)	(35.48)	-	-	-	-	(100)
68-71	Stone / glass	23	117	-	41	15	11	207
		(11.11)	(56.52)	-	(19.81)	(7.25)	(5.31)	(100)
72-83	Metals	69	228	49	31	120	32	529
		(13.04)	(43.10)	(4.26)	(5.86)	(22.68)	(6.05)	(100)
84-85	Machinery / electrical	447	40	-	-	113	172	772
		(57.90)	(5.18)	-	-	(14.64)	(22.28)	(100)
86-89	Transportation	67	21	9	5	11	3	116
		(57.76)	(18.10)	(7.76)	(4.31)	(9.48)	(2.59)	(100)
90-97	Miscellaneous	146	68	31	26	45	10	326
		(44.79)	(20.86)	(9.51)	(7.98)	(13.80)	(3.07)	(100)
98-99	Service	1	-	-	-	-	-	01
		(100)	-	-	-	-	-	(100)

Note: CP – competitive positioned product; TP – threatened product; EM (TI) – emerging product Tier I; EM (TII) – emerging product Tier II; WP (TI) – weakly positioned product (TI); WP (TII) – weakly positioned product (TII)

Source: Author's development based on COMTRADE (n.d.)

In case of India and Thailand, out of sixteen industries, only mineral products industry relatively resource-intensive has been emerging product under Tier I with 52.41% product lines in 1997-2017.

Table 9 shows the common products exported that India has a revealed comparative advantages with BIMSTEC at HS 2-digit and 6- digit level.

SOLUTIONS AND RECOMMENDATIONS

In order to achieve high level of economic cooperation among BIMSTEC countries, it is very important to understand and appreciate the structures of individual economies as well as identify the potential areas of trade and economic cooperation.

- A major thrust of BIMSTEC is connecting South Asia with Southeast Asia via Myanmar. The participation of ASEAN countries in BIMSTEC connectivity projects would speed that process up while also promoting intra-BIMSTEC and ASEAN connectivity.
- The geographical composition of BIMSTEC has remained overwhelmingly South Asian. The presence of Malaysia would give more legitimacy to the idea of a community that covers the entire arch of the Bay of Bengal.
- The need to identify the areas of cooperation and competition in intra-state trade base on production complementarities and on the other hand, here is requirement of rule simplification with a motive to increase trade liberalization between member states.

Table 9. Common products > RCA value between India and BIMSTEC

HS code	Product description	RCA>1
01-05	Animals and animal products	16.59
06-15	Vegetable products	21.80
16-24	Foodstuffs	33.20
25-27	Mineral products	5.63
28-38	Chemical and allied industries	8.34
39-40	Plastic / rubbers	17.43
41-43	Raw hides, skins, leathers, and furs	19.88
44-49	Wood and wood products	26.58
50-63	Textiles	6.94
64-67	Footwear / headgear	10.67
68-71	Stone / glass	10.60
72-83	Metals	13.96
84-85	Machinery / electrical	3.32
86-89	Transportation	14.70
90-97	Miscellaneous	8.46
98-99	Service	16.07

Source: Author's development based on COMTRADE (n.d.)

- A serious effort to provide infrastructure support is essential especially in terms of connectivity, cheaper transport system specifically maritime transport, simple banking system, and better border trade management
- Direct involvement of stakeholders is of prime importance and thus business communities, technocrats, and representatives of the knowledge community must interact to identify new avenues of BIMSTEC cooperation
- A need to create BIMSTEC's own identity bereft of its image as a restricted trade liberalization arrangement or as an interface between SAARC and ASEAN and in order to do so it must consider a minimal level of political engagement
- Security considerations of this region ought to be taken into account and an extended arm of BIMSTEC could address emerging security issues taken into account the greater geopolitical relevance of the region, particularly the maritime dimension and the emerging non-traditional security threats

FUTURE RESEARCH DIRECTIONS

The scope of study is limited only to export competitiveness between India and BIMSTEC. India's possibility of emerging as a regional energy hub in South Asia depends on its likely setting up of bilateral grids in the coming years. Moving from BIMSTEC towards the Bay of Bengal Economic Community will have long-run advantages of fully exploiting the potential of economic integration in the Bay of Bengal region. Poor communication and transport facilities, lack of information regarding capabilities and resources across the countries are important stumbling blocks, along with tariff and non-tariff barriers to the evolution of the Bay of Bengal Economic community. In future, there is possibility to work on role of geo-politics for the promotion of trade and investment among the BIMSTEC regions that would help the successful promotion of mutually beneficial cooperation in the Bay of Bengal region.

CONCLUSION

Trade liberalization and market access is a necessary, but not a sufficient condition, to achieve competitive advantage at the enterprise and industry level. Achieving export competitiveness in the rapidly globalize markets would require efforts at micro and macro levels. More than twenty years of partnership between India and BIMSTEC is sufficient enough to capture the comparative advantage of trade taking place among themselves. On the ride of India's Look East Policy, which is now rechristened as Act East Policy, provide ample reasOn to strengthen trade with BIMSTEC nations. India's export competitiveness vis-à-vis BIMSTEC does not lay on equal kneel, while competitiveness varied across the nations in 1997-2017. Like Bangladesh manufacturing moving from resource-based and labor-intensive to technology-based manufacturing of products. In case of Bhutan, it now moved for low intensive and medium intensive technology manufacturing of products. In case of Nepal, it uses resource-based, technological-based, and labor-intensive techniques in manufacture. Myanmar focuses on technological intensive manufacturing as compared to resource-based or labor-intensive. Sri Lanka uses labor-intensive techniques but side by side switches toward the technology-intensive products manufacturing. In Thailand and India, there is a manufacturing of almost all kinds of products with a growing share of hi-tech goods.

From export competitiveness analysis of India and BIMSTEC countries, it is clear that India loses its competitiveness in some products and shifts to the category of threatened and weakly positioned products. The result highlights comparative advantage dynamics of India's manufacturing sector, where momentum is developing to move towards relatively high value-added technology-intensive production activities. In view of their significance to India's revealed comparative advantage profile, there is a need in determined efforts to ensure that India sustains and enhances its export competitiveness. As a part of BIMSTEC, it is not difficult to formulate product-specific policy responses for India. There is a strong economic rationale for targeting those Threatened Products that have significant comparative advantage but lose their competitiveness. However, India's narrow low value-added export base has failed to create a solid foundation for an export-led growth. In the current climate of trade liberalization, India's export sector has come under increasing competitive pressure from lower-cost producers such as China. India's economic well-being depends on the extent to how the country enhances export competitiveness within BIMSTEC region and investment in potential sectors that contribute more to trade.

Given the present profile of India's revealed comparative advantage in BIMSTEC region, these outcomes depend on (a) industrial restructuring of India that enables it to contest high growth sectors of BIMSTEC as well as world trade and (b) ability of the manufacturing sector to create, sustain and enhance its export competitiveness. While India's export sectors witnessed competitive positioning of some of its product, these trends have not been uniform across all the industries. Rapid export growth in some sectors does not imply that the sector displays high demand growth in BIMSTEC markets. A need is to more assertive on pursue India's Look East Policy and make the road connectivity for encouraging trade among BMSTEC nations. In an ideal situation, there would be the emergence of export structure that has a heavy concentration in those industries that exhibit high growth in BIMSTEC market.

REFERENCES

Balassa, B. (1965). Trade Liberalization and Revealed Comparative Advantage. *The Manchester School of Economic and Social Studies*, *33*(2), 99–123. doi:10.1111/j.1467-9957.1965.tb00050.x

Batra, A., & Khan, Z. (2005). *Revealed Comparative Advantage: An Analysis for India and China*. New Delhi, India: Indian Council for Research on International Economic Relations.

Chakraborty, D. (2007a). India's New Regionalism in Asia: Look East and BIMSTEC Interface. In T. Nirmala Devi (Ed.), *India and Bay of Bengal Community: The BIMSTEC Experiment* (pp. 106–121). New Delhi, India: Gyan Publishing House.

Chakraborty, D. (2007b). *Trade Performance and Integration Experience of BIMSTEC: A Review of Issues*. Kolkata, India: Centre for Studies in International Relations and Development.

Chowdhury, A. B., & Neogi, D. (2014). Trade Complementarity and Similarity between India and BIMSTEC Countries in the Context of the Regional Trade Agreement (RTA). [IJRESS]. *International Journal of Research in Economics & Social Sciences*, *4*(6), 5–14.

Devi, T. N. (2007). Economic Cooperation in BIMSTEC: Emerging Trends and Prospects. In T. Nirmala Devi (Ed.), *India and Bay of Bengal Community: The BIMSTEC Experiment* (pp. 128–154). New Delhi, India: Gyan Publishing House.

Erokhin, V. (Ed.). (2016a). *Global Perspectives on Trade Integration and Economies in Transition*. Hershey, PA: IGI Global. doi:10.4018/978-1-5225-0451-1

Erokhin, V. (2016b). Rising Economic Powers among Economies in Transition: Is There Enough Space on the Global Market? In V. Erokhin (Ed.), *Global Perspectives on Trade Integration and Economies in Transition* (pp. 1–25). Hershey, PA: IGI Global. doi:10.4018/978-1-5225-0451-1.ch001

Kabir, M., & Salim, R. (2010). Can Gravity Model Explain BIMSTEC's Trade? *Journal of Economic Integration*, *25*(1), 143–165. doi:10.11130/jei.2010.25.1.144

Kalirajan, K., & Bhattacharya, S. K. (2011). Export Potentials among BIMSTEC and Japan: An Empirical Measurement. *The Journal of World Economic Review*, *6*(2), 173–188.

Kumari, B. R. (2007). Gender Mainstreaming in Trade Policies in BIMSTEC. In T. Nirmala Devi (Ed.), *India and Bay of Bengal Community: The BIMSTEC Experiment* (pp. 348–354). New Delhi, India: Gyan Publishing House.

Lall, S. (2000). *The Technological Structure and Performance of Developing Country Manufactured Exports, 1985-1998*. Oxford, UK: University of Oxford.

Mahmood, A. (2005). Export Competitiveness and Comparative Advantage of Pakistan's Non-agricultural Production Sectors: Trends and Analysis. *Pakistan Development Review*, *43*(4), 541–561.

Mukherji, I. N., & Paswan, N. K. (2007). India's Trade and Investment Opportunities in BIMSTEC. In T. Nirmala Devi (Ed.), *India and Bay of Bengal Community: The BIMSTEC Experiment* (pp. 60–105). New Delhi, India: Gyan Publishing House.

Nag, B., & De, D. (2007). *Asian Integration Process and BIMSTEC*. Kolkata, India: Centre for Studies in International Relations and Development. doi:10.2139srn.2819875

Rahman, M. M., & Kim, C. (2016). Prospects for Economic Integration of BIMSTEC: Trade and Investment Scenario. *International Journal of u- and e- Service. Science and Technology*, *9*(4), 235–248.

Saxena, S., & Bhadauriya, S. (2012). India and BIMSTEC: An Analysis of India's Trade Performance & Prospects. *Business Analyst: A Refereed Journal of Shri Ram College of Commerce, 33*(1), 103-114.

Shohibul, A. (2013). Revealed Comparative Advantage Measure: ASEAN-China Trade Flows. *Journal of Economics and Sustainable Development*, *4*(7), 136–145.

United Nations Commodity Trade Statistics. (n.d.). *UN Comtrade Database*. Retrieved September 29, 2019, from https://comtrade.un.org/

Uperti, B. C. (2007). Development of BIMSTEC: Nature, Direction, Challenges and Issues. In T. Nirmala Devi (Ed.), *India and Bay of Bengal Community: The BIMSTEC Experiment* (pp. 184–196). New Delhi, India: Gyan Publishing House.

Wijayasiri, J., & Mel, D. D. (2008). *BIMSTEC-Japan Cooperation in Trade and Investment: A Sri Lankan Perspective*. Kolkata, India: Centre for Studies in International Relations and Development.

ADDITIONAL READING

Batra, A. (2010). Asian Economic Integration and Sub-Regionalism: A Case Study of the BIMSTEC. *International Studies*, *47*(1), 1–25. doi:10.1177/002088171104700101

Erokhin, V. (2016). *Global Perspectives on Trade Integration and Economies in Transition*. Hershey, PA: IGI Global. doi:10.4018/978-1-5225-0451-1

Faheem, M. (2019). Strengthening India's Act East Policy through Sub-Regional Organization BIMSTEC: New Regional Cooperation Approach. In M. Banu, U. S. Singh, & M. Faheem (Eds.), *Evolving Narratives in Humanities and Management* (pp. 30–37). New Delhi: New Delhi Publishers.

Ghosh, I., & Chakrabarti, S. (2016). Inward and Outward Foreign Investments of the Asian Economies in Transition and India: Determinants of FDI and India's Prospects in CLMV. In V. Erokhin (Ed.), *Global Perspectives on Trade Integration and Economies in Transition* (pp. 212–237). Hershey, PA: IGI Global. doi:10.4018/978-1-5225-0451-1.ch011

Kumari, D., & Malhotra, N. (2014). Export-Led Growth in India: Cointegration and Causality Analysis. *Journal of Economics and Development Studies*, *2*(2), 297–310.

Prabhakar, A. C. (2016). Trade and Economic Integration in BRICS: Towards Multi-Polarity. In V. Erokhin (Ed.), *Global Perspectives on Trade Integration and Economies in Transition* (pp. 45–57). Hershey, PA: IGI Global. doi:10.4018/978-1-5225-0451-1.ch003

Rahman, M. M., & Kim, C. W. (2015). BIMSTEC Regional Integration: Prospects and Challenges. *Advanced Science and Technology Letters*, *114*, 90–95. doi:10.14257/astl.2015.114.18

Ray, S. (2011). A Causality Analysis on the Empirical Nexus between Export and Economic Growth: Evidence from India. *International Affairs and Global Strategy*, *1*, 24–38.

KEY TERMS AND DEFINITIONS

ASEAN: An international organization established by the governments of Indonesia, Malaysia, the Philippines, Singapore, and Thailand in 1967 to accelerate economic growth, social progress, and cultural development and to promote peace and security in Southeast Asia.

BIMSTEC: An international organization of seven nations of South Asia and South East Asia, including Bangladesh, India, Myanmar, Sri Lanka, Thailand, Nepal, and Bhutan, the countries dependent on the Bay of Bengal.

Economic Integration: An arrangement among nations that typically includes the reduction or elimination of trade barriers and the coordination of monetary and fiscal policies.

Export Competitiveness: An ability of a country/region to export more in value-added than it imports.

Free Trade Agreement: A pact between two or more nations to reduce barriers to imports and exports among them. Under a free trade policy, goods and services can be bought and sold across international borders with little or no government tariffs, quotas, subsidies, or prohibitions to inhibit their exchange.

Globalization: The tendency of businesses, technologies, people or philosophies to spread throughout the world, or the process of making this happen.

Revealed Comparative Advantage: An index used in international economics for calculating the relative advantage or disadvantage of a certain country in a certain class of goods or services as evidenced by trade flows.

Chapter 9
Indian Ocean Rim Association:
India's Trade Potential With Member Nations

Jasdeep Kaur Dhami
CT University, India

Manbir Singh
CT University, India

ABSTRACT

The Indian Ocean Rim Association (IORA) is a regional forum that focuses on bringing together representatives of government, business, and academia, for promotion purposes. It depends on the principles of open regionalism for strengthening trade facilitation and investment, promotion, and social development of the region. Social, cultural, political, geographical, and economic linkages exist between 22 member nations. The main objective of this chapter is analyzing India's trade potential with IORA member nations. The main outcome of this chapter is that India should concentrate on ammonium dihydrogen orthophosphate for Australia, gold and semi-manufactured for Singapore, mineral or chemical fertilizers for Thailand, tankers for Malaysia, warp knit fabrics of synthetic fibers for Indonesia, ammonium dihydrogen orthophosphate for South Africa, palm oil and fractions for Sri Lanka, Bangladesh, Mozambique, Tanzania, the United Republic of Yemen, crude palm oil for Kenya, bigeye tunas, frozen for Mauritius, and carded yarn of fine animal hair for Madagascar.

INTRODUCTION

Regionalism is a new concept and it is a mid-way between Nationalism and universalism, depending on a certain degree of shared economic, political and ideological interests. Regionalism is a collective action at regional level to achieve national objectives. The variety's regional financial provisions, now more widely acknowledged, arose and were continuously developed in multiple areas of the developing world under colonial rule between 1870-1950. Regional cooperation arrangements existed under British

DOI: 10.4018/978-1-7998-1730-7.ch009

and French colonial rule in South Asia, East Asia, and the Middle East as well as in various sub-regions of Africa and Caribbean. The world witnessed simultaneous formation of political regional groupings (Erokhin, 2016). Most important among political regional arrangements have been Arab League, Organization of African Unity (OAU), Organization of Islamic Conference (OIC), South Asia Association for Regional Cooperation (SAARC), and ASEAN Regional Forum (ARF). Onset of economic regionalism began right back from the 1950s. But first forceful appearance was that of the OPEC. Many other economic regional formations like SADC, ASEAN, NAFTA, G-15, and SAFTA are the representatives of progressively changing version of economic regionalism. Earlier, these were formed with the basic objective of bargaining with developed nations as far as the prices of raw materials and other commodities are concerned. In 1996, 88 regional integration agreements were counted by the World Trade Organization (WTO). Regional integration agreements cover motive statements (APEC), preferential trade agreements, free trade treaties, custom unions, to the common market with its freedom movement for labor and capital.

The 1990s have witnessed significant changes in the world's economic environment. A number of steps have been taken towards formation of mega blocks in Europe, western hemisphere, and Pacific basin. The process of formation of new trading blocs is called new regionalism. Moreover, regionalism has become universal phenomena on the one hand and a reality on other hand. It induced the different playing partners to achieve their common goal and to reach to a particular agreement. The regionalism as a concept has been perpetuating through a large number of regional blocs like ASEAN, Caribbean Community and Common Market (CARICOM), Central American Common Market (CACM), Common Market for Eastern and Southern Africa (CAMESA), NAFTA, OPEC, MERCOSUR, WTO, and Indian Ocean Rim Association – Association for Regional Cooperation (IOR-ARC).

Gamage (2016) stated that in the case of international trade, oceans were an essential source for export and import. First, over 80% of world trade is conducted via the seas; maritime transport is the backbone of international trade and, by extension, the global economy. The primary objective of the blue economy is recognizing the oceans as the latest frontier of economic development – essentially as a strategy to explore the ocean's potential as a source of resources, livelihood, and services. There are two main elements of this economic development model which warrant further elaboration. The first is that of sustainable development. Blue economy considers the sustainable utilization of oceanic resources to be significant, albeit as a secondary priority.

BACKGROUND

The Indian Ocean Rim Association (IORA) was started with the purpose of strengthening regional co-operation and sustainable development significantly in the Indian Ocean Region. It is a regional forum which focuses on bringing together representatives of government bodies, business, and academia, for promotion purposes and to create co-operation and healthy relationship among them. It relies largely on the region's trade facilitation and investment, promotion and social development on the values of open regionalism to strengthen economic cooperation.

Kelegama (1998) argues that in ancient times seaborne commerce in the Indian Ocean had generated a thriving network of trade and people-to-people links. But with the arrival of the Europeans in the fifteenth century, the Indian Ocean economies, which were earlier tightly interdependent, were restructured to meet extra-regional imperatives. And this erosion of regional cohesion continued even after the European presence faded away from IOR countries in the post-Second World War years. But now the environment is conducive to resurrect the past glory of the Indian Ocean. IOR-ARC has a long way to go to achieve some meaningful economic integration. Meanwhile, IOR-ARC should become a forum to build up the spirit of economic co-operation and induce a commitment by member nations to implement a dialogue to promote a regional environment conducive for growth in trade and investment. Such a move would lay the foundation for more ambitious economic activities in the IOR-ARC in the future.

Kalirajan (2000) states that APEC has been recognized as an effective and dynamic economic collaboration mostly represented by market powers with no formal exchanging or local courses of action. Acknowledgment of its achievement regarding advancing in general financial development in part nations has as of late prompted a noteworthy activity towards the formation of local monetary joining inside the Indian Ocean Rim. As a portion of the APEC part nations are additionally Indian Ocean Rim nations, the inquiries tended to in this paper are: regardless of whether the APEC-style showcase driven monetary coordination is practical with IOR-ARC and how successful are the exchange linkages among Australia and IOR-ARC part nations. Exchange power measures show that a lion's share of IOR-ARC part nations are exchanging with one another seriously as of late and the positive pattern is empowering.

Attri (2016) explained that India, Mauritius, Seychelles, Thailand, and Bangladesh instigated progression of mutual cooperation to promote and strengthen the Blue Economy. It was suggested that this course might be included at regional as well as at sub-regional level. Research has focused on chief Blue Economy subdivisions like fishing and aquaculture, ocean renewable force, tourism, seaports and shipping, and seabed journeying and minerals (developing a cautious approach). The Blue Economy is said to be pioneering, thus, the foremost fence to innovation embraces, financial access, predicament amongst inventor and investor. Deficiency of entrepreneurship ethnicity, authoritarian indecisiveness, and incorporation of industries needs elimination through the development of Blue Economy approach based policy-framework at regional, national as well as at international level.

Mittra (2017) stated that regional focus has turned towards the Indian Ocean as the new frontier for sustainable economic development, alongside concerns of security issues. India should build on the momentum it has created thus far and take on a larger responsibility in developing and securing the Indian Ocean by developing ideas, norms and road maps for an inclusive and collaborative ocean governance society. Developing a normative framework for doing business and harnessing the ocean's potential in a sustainable manner is another area where India could demonstrate leadership. This framework must ensure a just and equitable environment for seizing the business opportunities in the IOR. India should start by creating robust mechanisms for knowledge creation. For instance, diverse platforms for interaction between sectoral experts, professionals, scientists, and the business community could be envisaged. The existing and new multilateral trading agreements should also be modified and defined in a way that enables the creation of sustainable infrastructure to meet the demands of future economic activities.

Elisabeth (2017) states that the situation of the common workshop implied one of the IORA need regions that fuse (1) ocean prosperity and safety, (2) fisheries the officials, (3) exchange and theory help, (4) catastrophe hazard enterprise, (5) technology and academic interest, (6) social exchanges and the motion commercial enterprise. The others are blue economic system and women's fortifying. Since the established order of IORA in 1997, social troubles had never been academically discussed. Regardless, fact does now not advise that the area has consideration regarding social differences that could have positive or bad elements for shape up to the close by economic coordination inside the Indian Ocean.

Yu and Bai (2017) mentioned that there are four on a totally simple level incredible coordinated effort fashions among the Indian shoreline the front nations. The first is the GCC model with normally excessive affirmations measures. The second type is the ASEAN model, wherein exclusive countries with balanced powers work collectively because of traditional budgetary and political functions. In any case, the improvement of this version will moreover be attempted through international locations like Australia, India, and so forth. Who have quite lately been convincing in the IORA? The 1/3 is the SAARC model. These versions, in light of nonappearance of accept as true with and the closeness of adversary international locations, they preserve their correspondence by means of an unprecedented joint effort in limited districts. Regardless, this circumstance is not proper for the whole Indian Ocean vicinity. The fourth is the SADC, COMESA, and IORA version. Regardless of the manner that SADC and COMESA have moreover created money related compromise than IORA, differentiated and the past three types, those three affiliations are not primary as some distance as issues its states.

Doyle (2018) has expressed the Indian Ocean as a site of common however distinguishing errands transcending national welfare – wherever excessive fishing, illegitimate activities, coastal progression, climate transformation, and long-term development involves that ordered international support corroborates all facets of a maritime economy. It is revealed that IORA is superlatively positioned to offer this regional leadership and synchronization in the Rim for the twenty-first century.

Main FOCUS OF the CHAPTER

Linkages Among Indian Ocean Countries

Geographical Linkages

The Indian Ocean covers a 74 million km^2, including, among others, the Red Sea, the Persian Gulf, the Arab Sea, the Bay of Bengal and the Andaman Sea, some 20% of the world's total water area. The geographical linkages among different countries of Indian Ocean could be evident from the farming patterns and dependence of the region on the monsoon. Monsoon brings rain in the region on which the economy of the region depends primarily due to agriculture-based economy in the region. Moreover, the abundant natural resources which are available in the Indian Ocean region countries are another factor for linkage.

Historical Linkages

A large amount of historical evidence shows that the Indians and Africans next shore neighbors as they have close and friendly relations. The evidences show that much before Vasco de Gama discovered the route to India via Cape of Hope, Indians and east Africans were in continuous contact with the whole Indian Ocean Complex. The end of apartheid system in South Africa and the establishment of transitional government of National Unity at Pretoria have abolished the political gap between the Indian Ocean coast countries and increased opportunities for the creation of an Indian Ocean Rim trading group with South and South Africa getting nearer to South Asia in aspects of trade, ideology and economic ties in the post-Cold War age, the Indian Ocean coastal raw materials exporting areas have the chance to unite to contest post-Cold War super-power condominium. Thus since the ancient era the bond and linkages among the Indian Ocean countries people and society is very formidable and strong.

Cultural Linkages

There seems to be cultural linkages in the Indian Ocean countries since the long time. The ancient linkages between India and other East Asian states are known. The spread of Buddhism outside India is the evidence of cultural linkages with other Indian countries. Moreover, India's linkages with Vietnam, Cambodia, and Laos are well known. Indeed, ethnic-religious differences divide the population of the Indian Ocean Region. However, most of the sea is simultaneously tied together by followers of the same faith, culture and often also language. Thus these linkages and bonds played a very significant role in order to unite the people of the Indian Ocean Region.

Political Linkages

The dawn of the XIX century witnessed Industrial revolution in Europe, which led to spread of British colonialism in Asia and African continents. The supremacy of British Empire and proliferation of the British colonies compelled the scholars to call the Indian Ocean as the British lake for more than three consecutive centuries. The anti-colonial movement which was almost started in all the colonies was interlinked. Mahatma Gandhi experimented his struggle against imperial power in South Africa through his unique way of Satyagraha, which he applied in India successfully. This shows the similarity between the existing political situations in colonial countries. Thus at political level too, there was in-depth relations among Indian Ocean countries. These strong bonds are the main cause for the evolution and emergence of the IOR-ARC.

Economic Linkages

The old trading waterway of the world is the Indian Ocean. India maintained commercial contacts with China, South-East Asia, West Asia, and Roman Empire. Moreover, Indian sent its missionaries, conquerors, and traders to the neighboring countries where they founded settlements. There is complementarity of natural resources in Indian Ocean Region countries. The petroleum oil-rich Gulf region requires human resources and technology from the other countries. The gold diamond and coal are in abundance in South Africa which requires other raw materials from the other countries of the region. Moreover, the food grain production in the entire region is somewhat dependent on the monsoon, which led to linkages in the agricultural production also. The evidences show that in a heterogeneous structure of countries of regional trading bloc there could be substantial trade cooperation among them.

Emergence of Indian Ocean Rim-Association for Regional Cooperation

The IOR-ARC is the product of persistent discourse and deliberation among the Rim countries for more than three years and four months. During this long gap, the concept passed through different phases and lastly it was transformed into reality. The idea of IOR-ARC was first mooted by the former Foreign Minister of South Africa, Pik Botha when he visited India in 1993. He proposed an economic grouping of the Indian Ocean Rim countries. According to news report, such a grouping could effectively meet the challenge posed by emerging economic grouping such as NAFTA, ASEAN, and APEC. The next milestone in the formation of the IOR-ARC was South African President Nelson Mandela visit to India and his formidable support to the cause of the IOR-ARC. The IOR-ARC was one of the latest initiatives in the establishment of regional arrangements for economic co-operation.

The birth of the IOR-ARC in March 1997 is the culmination of long-lasting linkages among the member countries. These linkages cover almost every walk of life, geographical, social, cultural, economic, and political. The countries of Indian Ocean Region have been connected with one another since long time. The spurt of regionalism, demise of apartheid in South Africa, completion of Uruguay Round of the GATT, establishment of the WTO, demise of the USSR, establishment of unipolar world, and above all liberalization of India in 1990, are some of the important causes for the initiative taken in the field of Indian Ocean Region for some regional groupings. India, Sri Lanka, Bangladesh, Singapore, Australia, Iran, Thailand, Indonesia, Malaysia, South Africa, Tanzania, Kenya, Mauritius, UAE, Yemen, Seychelles, Somalia, Comoros, Mozambique, Republic of Maldives, Madagascar, and Oman are among the members of the IORA.

According to Attri (2016), it is well known for people that the India Ocean is the world's third-largest ocean which carries around half of the world's ships along with bulk cargo traffic, etc. This ocean is also known as a lifeline for international trade and transport, further, this region is woven together for making a trade route or commands the major sea lanes. The region mentioned above has cultural diversity and is considered to be much cultural diversity and richness. Based on population, these peoples are divided into a number of sub-regions i.e. Australia, southeast, etc. and considered as a group of countries like ASEAN, SAARC, GCC, and COMESA, SADC, and BIMSTEC.

Analysis of Trade Relations

The products with the finest export potential from India to the world are diamonds, jewelry, precious metals, and medicaments such as mixed or unmixed products, for retail sale (Figure 1). Diamonds worked demonstrates the biggest absolute difference in price between prospective and real exports in value terms allowing space for further imports valued $27.0 billion.

In the year 2011, India took over as chair of the organization and it was marked as a turning point for the IORA. In keeping with the emerging geostrategic challenges, a major bolster, that challenged the Indian Ocean region commenced, with re-establishment of the IORA priorities taking center-stage.

In November 2011, at the 11th COM Meeting in Bengaluru, on the basis of an Indian proposal, six high subject regions have been recognized to focus cooperation amongst member states of IORA within the years yet to come back. These are consisting of trade and investment facilitation; maritime safety and security; fisheries management; disaster risk management; academic, science and technology; tourism and cultural exchange. India has processed its contribution of $100,000 for the IORA Special Fund. To the IORA Special fund, India is the topmost contributor.

In 2000-2018, IOR-ARC's trade with India and the world has increased, including export and import volumes (Table 1).

IOR-ARC's exports to India increased from $7.9 billion in 2000 up to almost $107.0 billion in 2018 (Table 2; Figure 2).

H0: The coefficient is equal to zero.

P value is less than 0.05 which indicates that the null hypothesis is rejected. The predictor has a small p-value meaning that modifications in the predictor variable are associated with medications in the response variable. R2 value is discovered to be quite large and

Figure 1. India's product potential with rest of the world
Source: International Trade Centre [ITC] (2019)

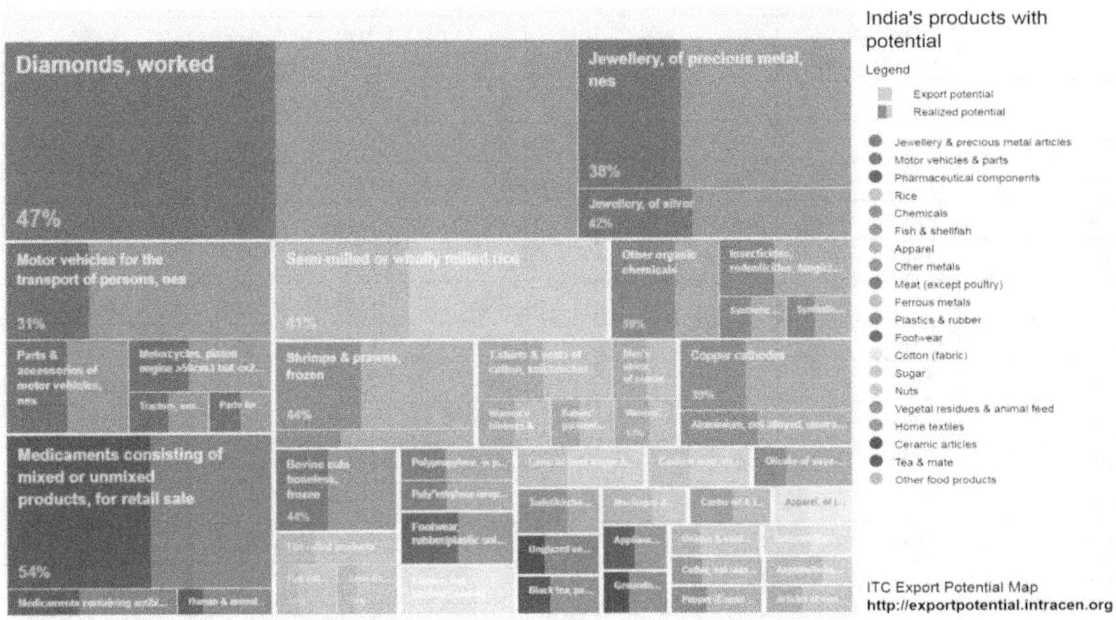

Table 1. Trade of IOR-ARC, $ billion

Year	IOR-ARC's exports to India	IOR-ARC's exports to the world	IOR-ARC's imports from India	IOR-ARC's imports from the world
2001	7.863	514.993	6.396	468.979
2002	8.323	537.198	7.436	506.558
2003	11.237	632.715	9.223	584.775
2004	16.582	780.414	12.732	754.840
2005	28.844	1,046.504	23.730	983.813
2006	29.527	1,083.969	19.306	1,050.789
2007	47.074	1,400.505	37.347	1,346.330
2008	62.877	1,698.465	50.863	1,727.653
2009	42.475	1,228.430	25.436	1,239.143
2010	58.489	1,612.888	34.023	1,587.682
2011	70.665	1,992.047	47.788	1,952.611
2012	84.883	2,301.486	73.996	2,309.449
2013	74.965	2,324.532	76.084	2,311.264
2014	69.910	2,267.348	65.770	2,230.390
2015	63.527	1,931.958	60.219	1,971.372
2016	61.751	1,884.134	58.205	1,855.192
2017	76.098	2,125.467	69.309	2,112.338
2018	106.961	2,111.731	84.960	2,217.918

Source: ITC (2019)

Table 2. Trend analysis of IOR-ARC's exports to India, $ billion

Year	IOR-ARC's exports to India	Predicted values
2001	7.863	9.204
2002	8.323	14.147
2003	11.237	19.091
2004	16.582	24.035
2005	28.844	28.979
2006	29.527	33.922
2007	47.074	38.866
2008	62.877	43.810
2009	42.475	48.753
2010	58.489	53.697
2011	70.665	58.641
2012	84.883	63.584
2013	74.965	68.528
2014	69.910	73.472
2015	63.527	78.415
2016	61.751	83.359
2017	76.098	88.303
2018	106.961	93.246

Source: ITC (2019)

Table 3. Trend analysis of IOR-ARC's exports to the world, $ billion

Year	IOR-ARC's exports to the world	Predicted values
2001	514.992	602.292
2002	537.198	711.008
2003	632.715	819.724
2004	780.414	928.440
2005	1,046.504	1,037.156
2006	1,083.969	1,145.871
2007	1,400.505	1,254.587
2008	1,698.465	1,363.303
2009	1,228.430	1,472.019
2010	1,612.888	1,580.735
2011	1,992.047	1,689.451
2012	2,301.486	1,798.166
2013	2,324.532	1,906.882
2014	2,267.348	2,015.598
2015	1,931.958	2,124.314
2016	1,884.134	2,233.030
2017	2,125.467	2,341.746
2018	2,111.731	2,450.461

Source: ITC (2019)

Figure 2. Trend analysis of IOR-ARC'S exports to India
Source: Authors' development based on ITC (2019)

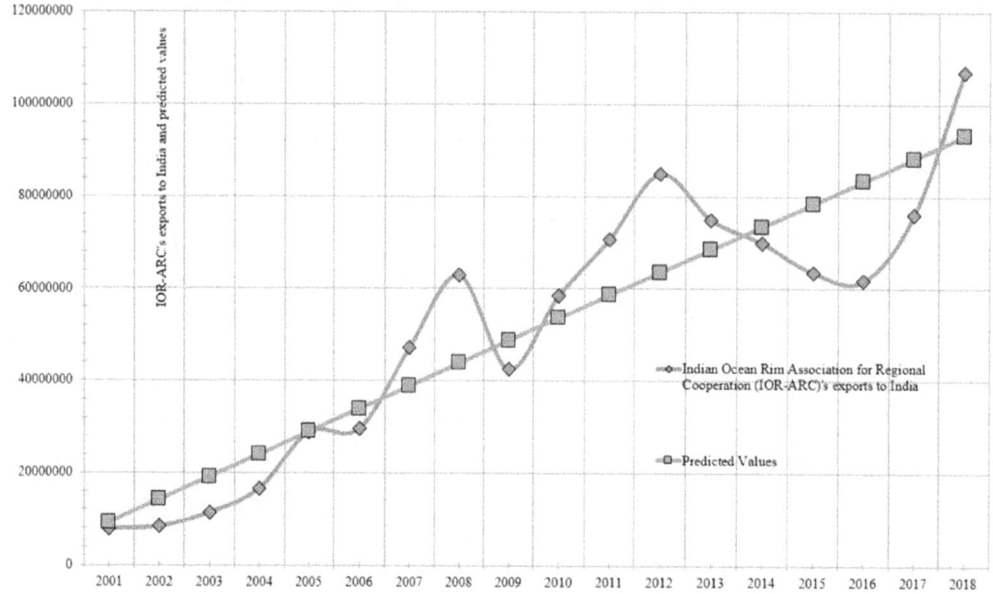

Number of XY pairs18.
Equation Y = 4.944e+006*X – 9.883e+009.
The P value is < 0.0001, R square is 0.8348.
Y-intercept is -9.883e+009 ± 1.105e+009 and X-intercept is 1999.
The value of R2 is found to be quite high and statistically important at 5% meaning stage.

IOR-ARC's exports to the world increased from $515.0 billion in 2000 up to over $2.1 trillion in 2018 (Table 3; Figure 3).

H0: The coefficient is equal to zero.
Equation Y = 1.087e+008*X – 2.169e+011.
R square is 0.8273.
Slope is 1.087e+008 ± 1.242e+007.
Y-intercept is -2.169e+011 ± 2.496e+010.
X-intercept is 1995.

P value is less than 0.05 which indicates that the null hypothesis is rejected. The predictor has a small p-value meaning that modifications in the predictor variable are associated with medications in the response variable. R2 value is discovered to be quite large and statistically important at 5% level of significance.

IOR-ARC's imports from India increased tremendously from $6.4 billion in 2000 up to over $84.9 billion in 2018 (Table 4; Figure 4).

Figure 3. Trend analysis of IOR-ARC'S exports to the world
Source: Authors' development based on ITC (2019)

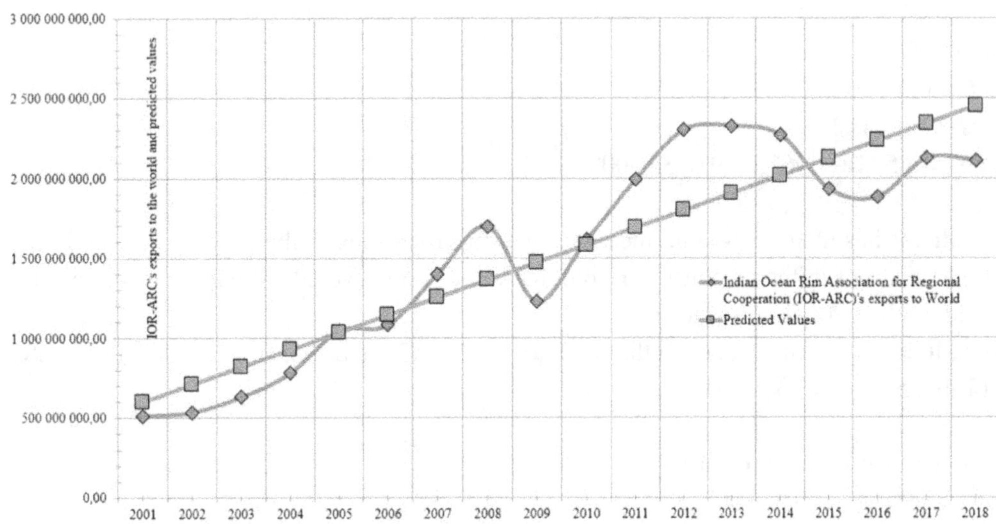

Table 4. Trend analysis of IOR-ARC'S imports from India, $ billion

Year	IOR-ARC's imports from India	Predicted values
2001	6.396	3.947
2002	7.436	8.469
2003	9.223	12.990
2004	12.732	17.511
2005	23.730	22.033
2006	19.306	26.554
2007	37.347	31.076
2008	50.863	35.597
2009	25.436	40.118
2010	34.023	44.640
2011	47.788	49.161
2012	73.996	53.682
2013	76.085	58.204
2014	65.770	62.725
2015	60.219	67.247
2016	58.205	71.768
2017	69.309	76.289
2018	84.960	80.811

Source: ITC (2019)

Table 5. Trend analysis of IOR-ARC's imports from the world, $ billion

Year	IOR-ARC's imports from the world	Predicted values
2001	468.979	550.347
2002	506.558	663.450
2003	584.775	776.554
2004	754.840	889.657
2005	983.813	1,002.761
2006	1,050.789	1,115.865
2007	1,346.330	1,228.968
2008	1,727.653	1,342.072
2009	1,239.143	1,455.176
2010	1,587.682	1,568.279
2011	1,952.611	1,681.383
2012	2,309.449	1,794.487
2013	2,311.264	1,907.590
2014	2,230.390	2,020.694
2015	1,971.372	2,133.798
2016	1,855.192	2,246.901
2017	2,112.338	2,360.005
2018	2,217.918	2,473.109

Source: ITC (2019)

H0: The coefficient is equal to zero.
Slope 4.521e+006 ± 474175, Y-intercept-.043e+009 ± 9.529e+008
X-intercept 2000
R square 0.8504
Number of XY pairs 18
Equation Y = 4.521e+006*X - 9.043e+009

The predictor has a small p-value meaning that modifications in the predictor variable are associated with medications in the response variable. R2 value is discovered to be quite large and statistically important at 5% level of significance.

In 2018, IOR-ARC's imports from the world exceeded $2.2 trillion, an increase from $468.9 billion in 2000 (Table 5; Figure 5).

H0: The coefficient is equal to zero.
Slope 1.131e+008 ± 1.219e+007.
Y-intercept-2.258e+011 ± 2.450e.
X-intercept 1996+010.

Figure 4. Trend analysis of IOR-ARC'S imports from India
Source: Authors' development based on ITC (2019)

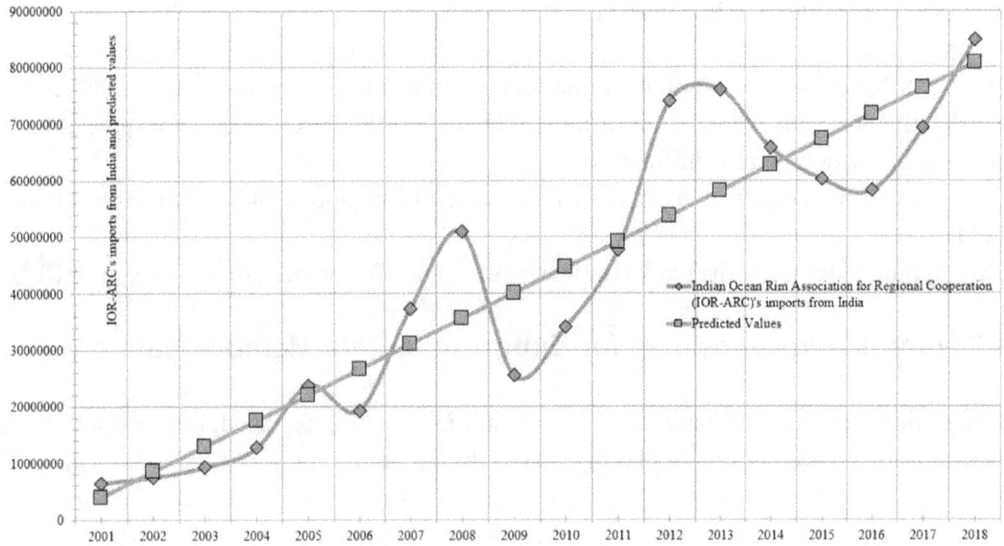

Figure 5. Trend analysis of IOR-ARC'S imports from the world
Source: Authors' development based on ITC (2019)

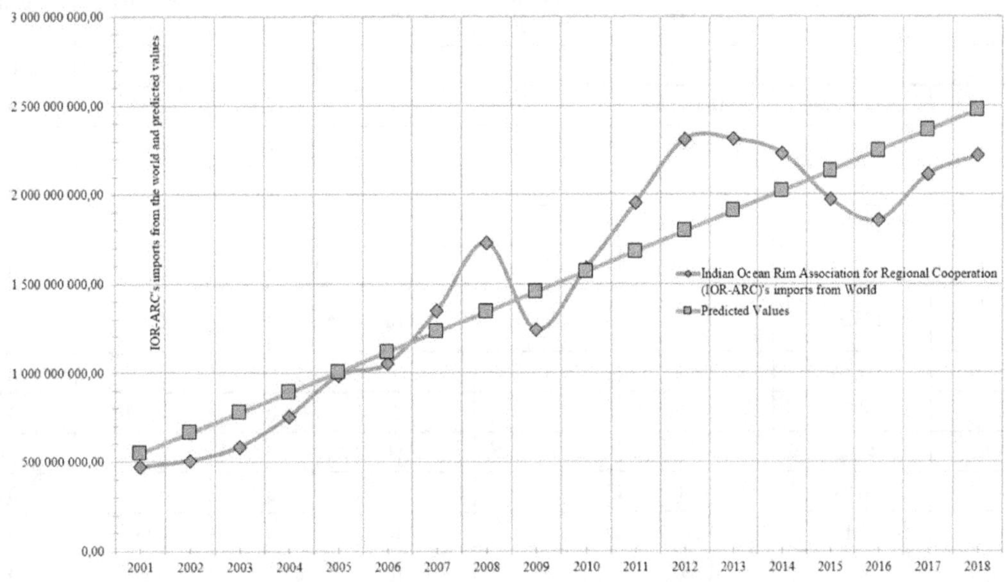

R square 0.8432.
Number of XY pairs 18.
Equation Y = 1.131e+008*X - 2.258e+011.

The predictor has a low p-cost approach that modifications inside the predictor variable are associated with adjustments inside the reaction variable. The fee of R2 is determined to be quite excessive and statistically big at 5% degree of significance.

Total share in world's export is more than 1% in case of Singapore, India, Australia, Thailand, and Malaysia (Table 6).

Iran, India, Bangladesh, and Sri Lanka imposed more than 10% of tariff on imports in 2018 (Table 7).

India's Diversification Products for Export to IORA's Member Nations

India's best options for export diversification in Australia are apricots, dried, basketwork, wickerwork and other articles from non-vegetable plaiting materials and grains leather of hides and skins of bovine

Table 6. Exporters of selected products in 2018

Exporters	Value exported in 2018, $ billion	Trade balance in 2018, $ billion	Annual growth in value in 2014-2018, %	Annual growth in value in 2017-2018, %	Share in world exports, %	Average distance to importers, km	Concentration of importers
Singapore	411.742	41.252	1	10	2.1	4,750	0.07
India	323.056	-184.524	1	9	1.7	6,379	0.05
Australia	253.828	26.544	2	10	1.3	8,633	0.14
Thailand	249.777	-1.114	3	6	1.3	5,485	0.05
Malaysia	247.286	29.834	2	14	1.3	5,080	0.07
Indonesia	180.215	-8.496	2	7	0.9	6,274	0.07
United Arab Emirates	173.348	-7.981	0	18	0.9	5,543	0.08
South Africa	94.422	0.998	1	7	0.5	7,859	0.04
Iran	66.612	25.558	7	2	0.3	4,710	0.17
Bangladesh	42.469	-10.901	6	11	0.2	8,187	0.08
Oman	36.933	16.780	-4	38	0.2	5,890	0.29
Sri Lanka	11.167	-7.561	2	8	0.1	8,909	0.10
Mozambique	5.161	-1.658	6	10	0.0	6,389	0.14
Kenya	5.078	-10.760	-4	11	0.0	6,289	0.07
Tanzania	3.796	-4.715	-11	-9	0.0	4,758	0.09
Madagascar	2.999	-0.929	9	5	0.0	9,730	0.11
Mauritius	1.964	-3.294	-7	-7	0.0	8,253	0.07
Yemen	1.232	-5.059	-35	6	0.0	6,819	0.36
Seychelles	0.646	-0.161	6	5	0.0	7,360	0.10

Source: ITC (2019)

Table 7. Importers of selected products in 2018

Importers	Value imported in 2018, $ billion	Trade balance in 2018, $ billion	Annual growth in value in 2014-2018, %	Annual growth in value in 2017-2018, %	Share in world imports, %	Average distance from supplying countries, km	Concentration of supplying countries	Average tariff (estimated) applied by the country, %
India	507.580	-184.524	3	14	2.6	5,847	0.05	12.7
Singapore	370.489	41.252	1	13	1.9	6,234	0.07	0.0
Thailand	250.891	-1.114	3	11	1.3	5,054	0.08	7.1
Australia	227.284	26.544	1	3	1.2	10,210	0.09	1.5
Malaysia	217.452	29.834	2	12	1.1	5,147	0.08	4.5
Indonesia	188.711	-8.496	2	20	1.0	5,770	0.10	5.0
United Arab Emirates	181.329	-7.981	-4	-6	0.9	5,774	0.08	5.2
South Africa	93.424	0.998	-2	13	0.5	8,992	0.06	6.5
Bangladesh	53.370	-10.901	9	14	0.3	4,067	0.15	12.5
Iran	41.054	25.558	-4	-20	0.2	5,227	0.14	25.5
Oman	20.153	1.6780	0	-2	0.1	6,144	0.07	5.3
Sri Lanka	18.728	-7.561	-1	5	0.1	4,509	0.13	11.4
Kenya	15.838	-10.760	-6	4	0.1	7,150	0.14	9.6
Tanzania	8.511	-4.715	-13	10	0.0	6,645	0.09	9.6
Mozambique	6.819	-1.658	-8	18	0.0	6,283	0.11	7.9
Yemen	6.291	-5.059	-8	9	0.0	6,320	0.13	6.9
Mauritius	5.258	-3.294	0	0	0.0	7,373	0.09	0.6
Madagascar	3.927	-0.929	5	7	0.0	7,238	0.08	8.6
Seychelles	0.807	-0.161	3	6	0.0	6,720	0.06	1.4

Source: ITC (2019)

or equine animals (Figure 6). India finds basketwork, wickerwork and other articles from non-vegetable plaiting materials easiest to reach. ammonium dihydrogen orthophosphate is a product that faces the highest demand potential in Australia.

India's best options for export diversification in Singapore are basketwork, wickerwork and other articles from non-vegetable plaiting materials, fixed electrical capacitors, aluminum electrolytic and ornamental ceramic articles, of porcelain (Figure 7). India finds basketwork, wickerwork and other articles from non-vegetable plaiting materials easiest to reach. Gold, semi-manufactured, for non-monetary purposes is the product that faces the highest demand capacity in Singapore.

India's best options for export diversification in Thailand are grains leather of hides and skins of bovine or equine animals, mineral or chemical fertilizers and pears and quinces, fresh (Figure 8). India finds single yarn of jute easiest to reach. Mineral or chemical fertilizers are the product that faces the highest demand capacity in Thailand.

India's best options for export diversification in Malaysia are tankers, single yarn of jute and adzuki beans dried and shelled (Figure 9). India finds single yarn of jute easiest to reach. Product facing Malaysia's highest demand potential are tankers.

Figure 6. India's diversification products for exports to Australia
Source: ITC (2019)

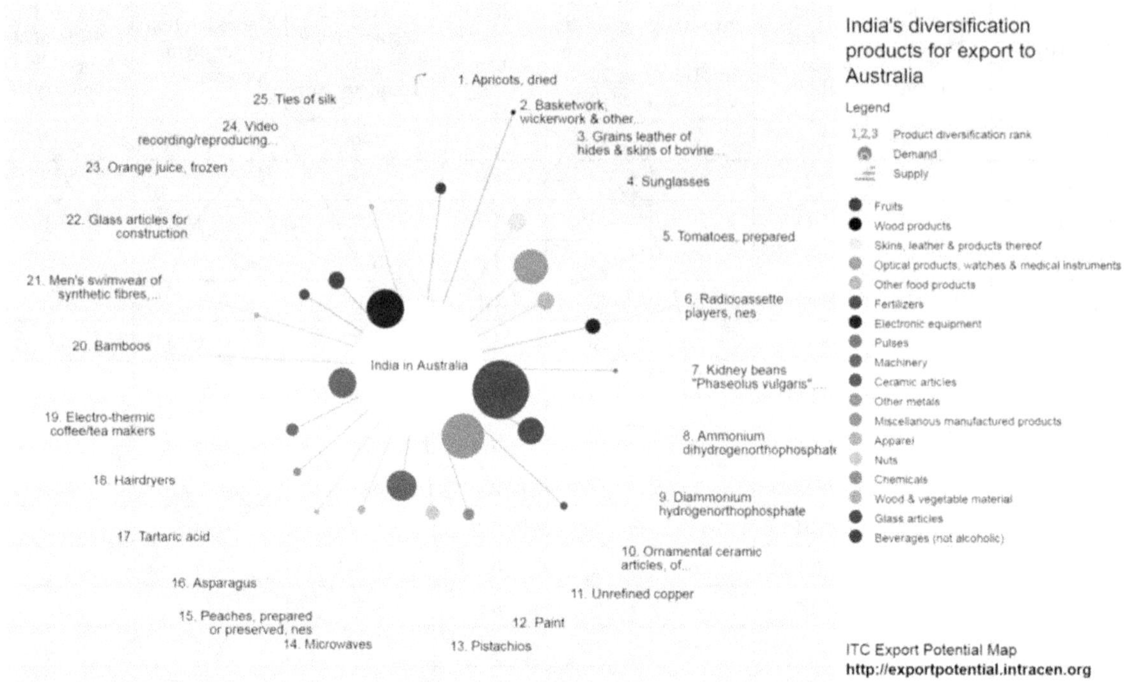

Figure 7. India's diversification products for exports to Singapore
Source: ITC (2019)

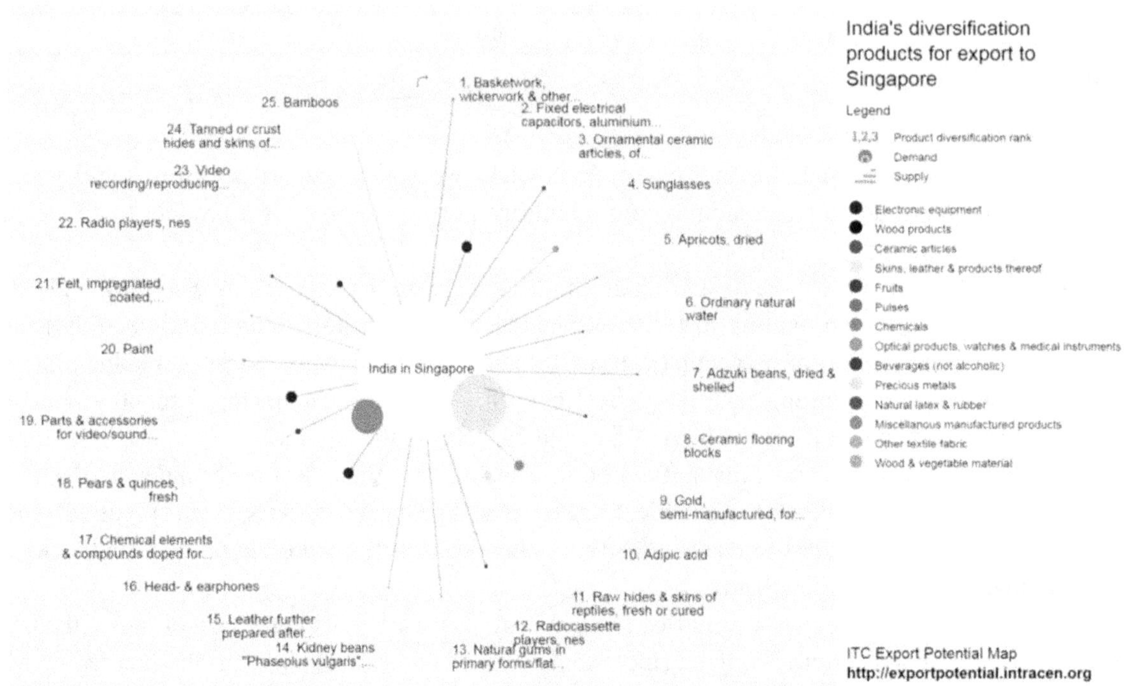

Figure 8. India's diversification products for exports to Thailand
Source: ITC (2019)

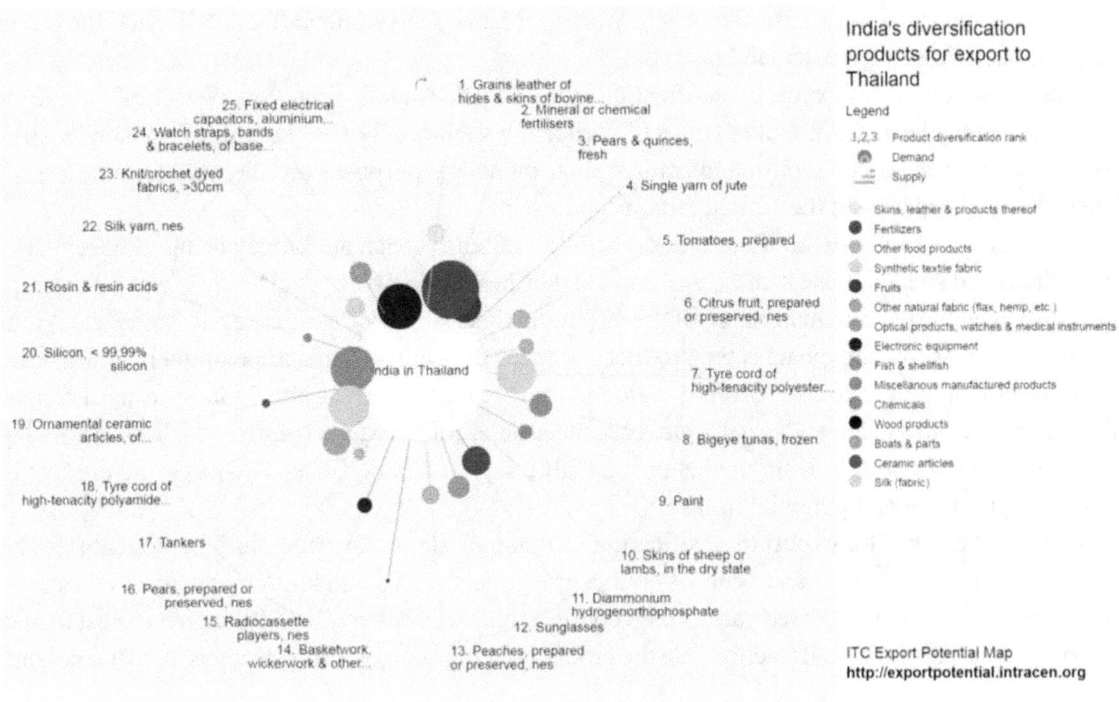

Figure 9. India's diversification products for exports to Malaysia
Source: ITC (2019)

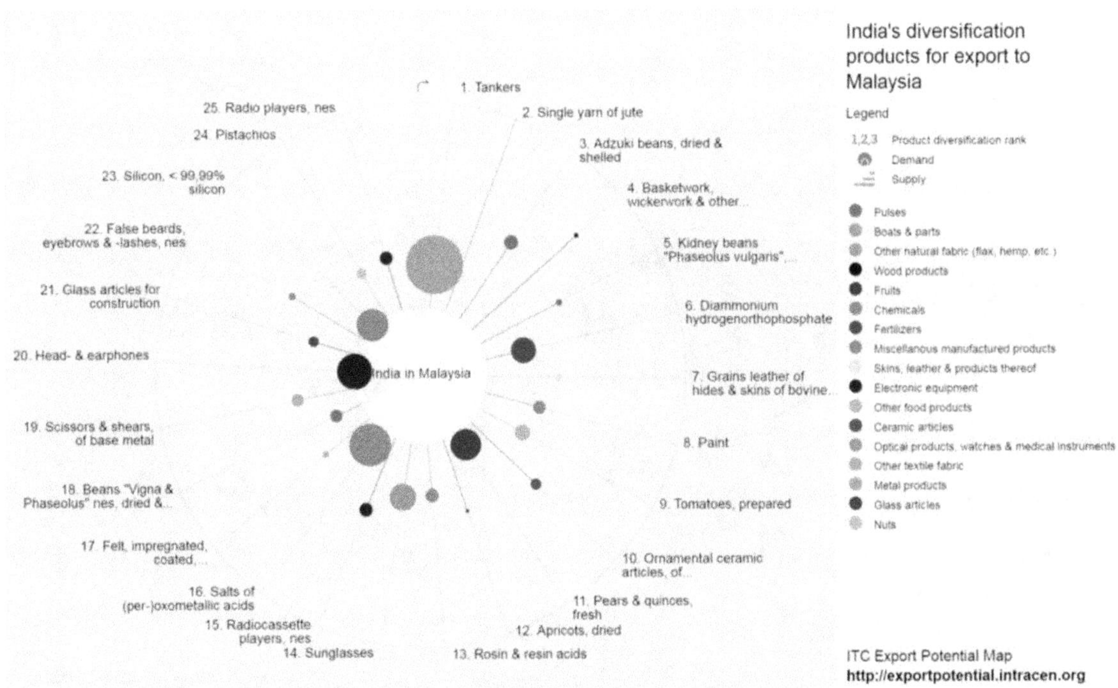

India's best options for export diversification in Indonesia are single yarn of jute, Diammonium hydrogenorthophosphate and grains leather of hides and skins of bovine or equine animals (Figure 10). India finds single yarn of jute easiest to reach. Warp knit fabrics of synthetic fibers >30 cm is the product facing Indonesia's strongest demand potential.

India's best options for export diversification in the United Arab Emirates are pistachios, single yarn of jute and kidney beans "Phaseolus vulgaris", dried and shelled (Figure 11). India finds single yarn of jute easiest to reach. Gold, semi-manufactured, non-monetary purposes are the product that faces the highest demand capacity in the United Arab Emirates.

India's greatest export diversification alternatives in South Africa are kidney beans "Phaseolus vulgaris", dried and shelled, false beards, eyebrows and lashes, basketwork, wickerwork, and other articles from non-vegetable plaiting materials (Figure 12). India finds single yarn of jute easiest to reach. Ammonium dihydrogen orthophosphate is the product that faces the highest demand potential in South Africa.

India's best options for export diversification in Iran are single yarn of jute, kidney beans "Phaseolus vulgaris", dried and shelled and ornamental ceramic articles, of porcelain (Figure 13). India finds single yarn of jute easiest to reach. Knit/crochet printed fabrics, of synthetic fibers >30 cm is the product that faces the highest demand potential in Iran.

India's best options for export diversification in Bangladesh are Diammonium hydrogenorthophosphate, grains leather of hides and skins of bovine or equine animals and knit/crochet dyed fabrics, >30 cm (Figure 14). India finds cabled yarn, <85% cotton, combed fibres >=714,29 dtex per easiest to reach. Palm oil (excluding crude) and fractions are the products facing Bangladesh's strongest demand potential.

Figure 10. India's diversification products for exports to Indonesia
Source: ITC (2019)

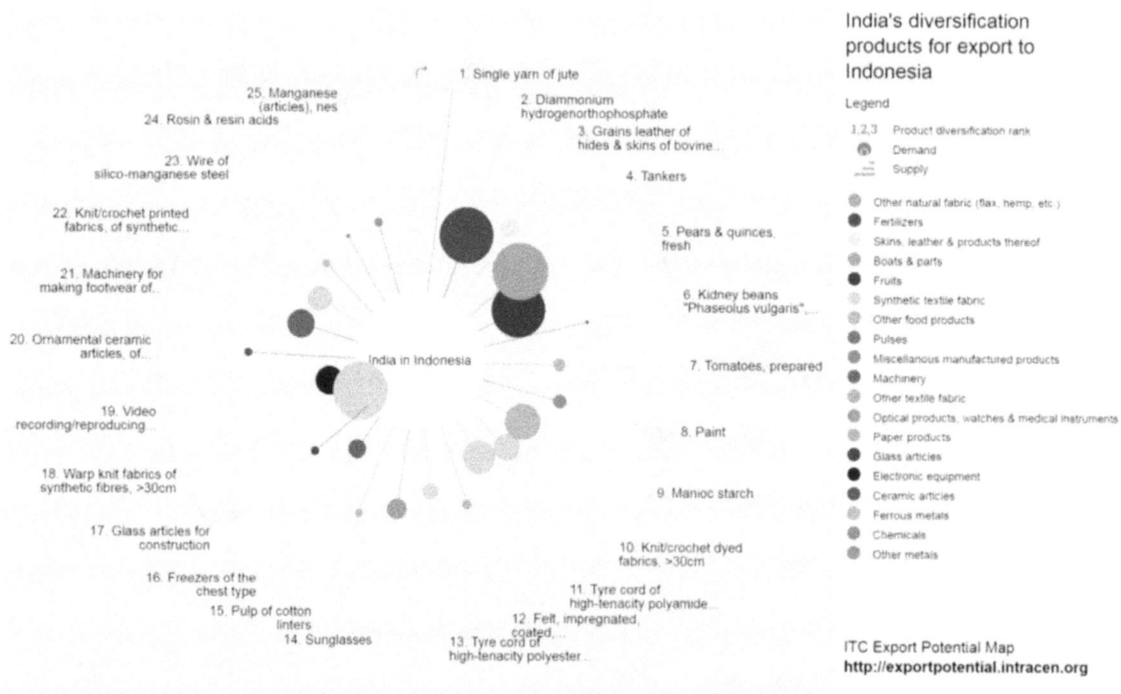

Figure 11. India's diversification products for exports to the United Arab Emirates
Source: ITC (2019)

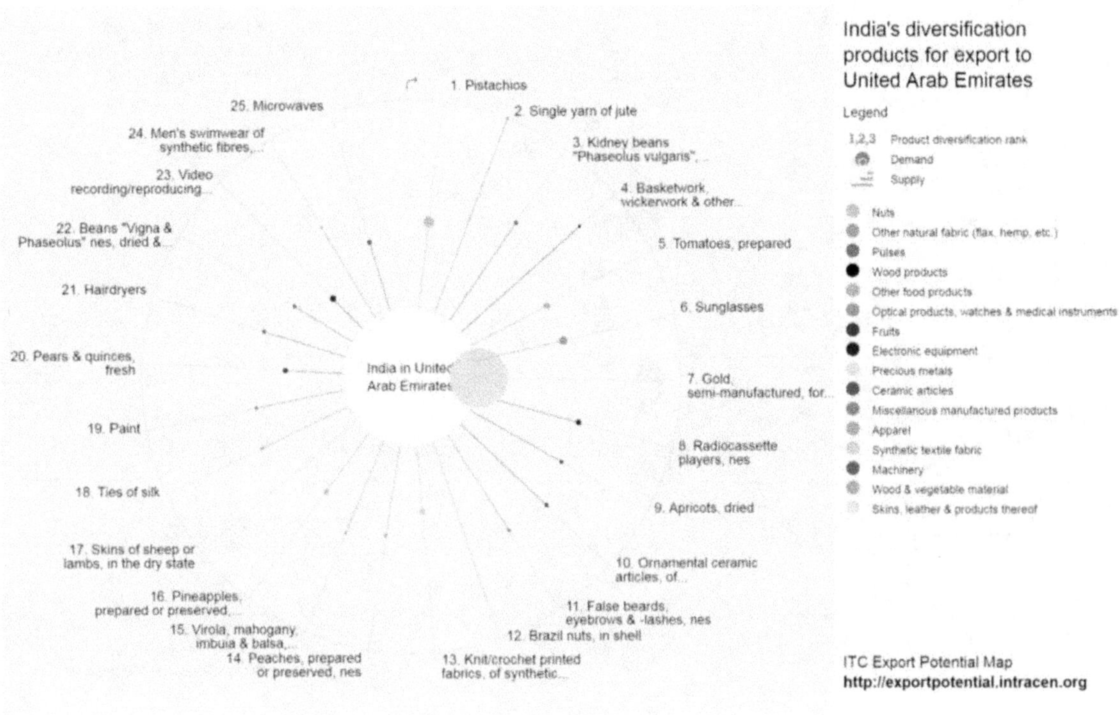

Figure 12. India's diversification products for exports to South Africa
Source: ITC (2019)

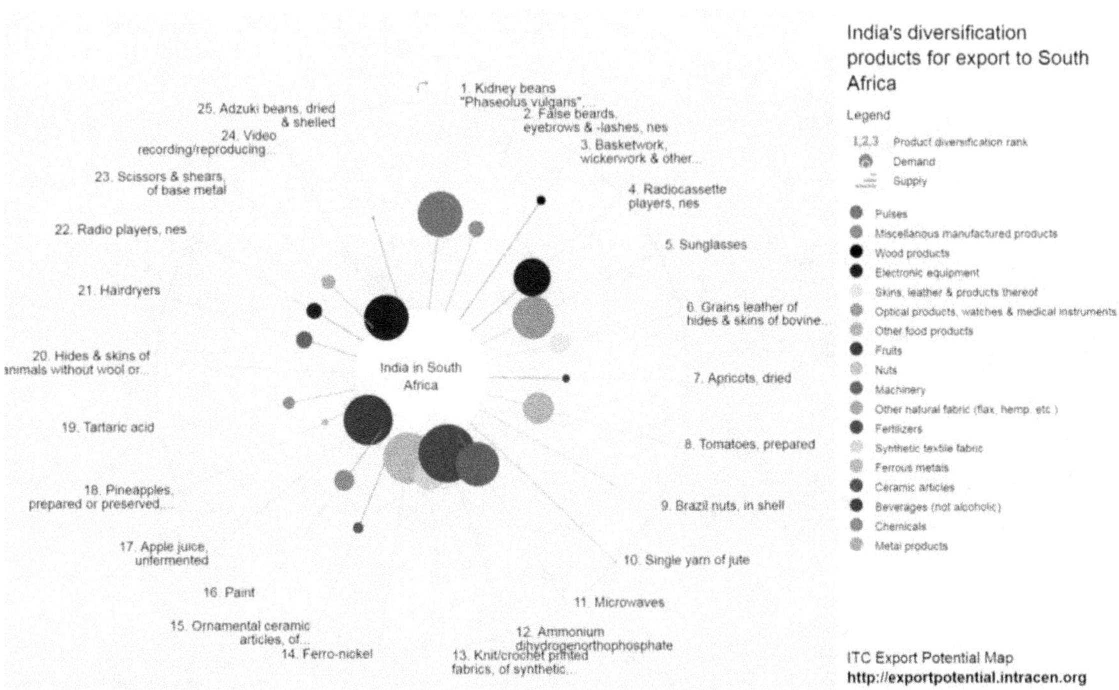

Figure 13. India's diversification products for exports to Iran
Source: ITC (2019)

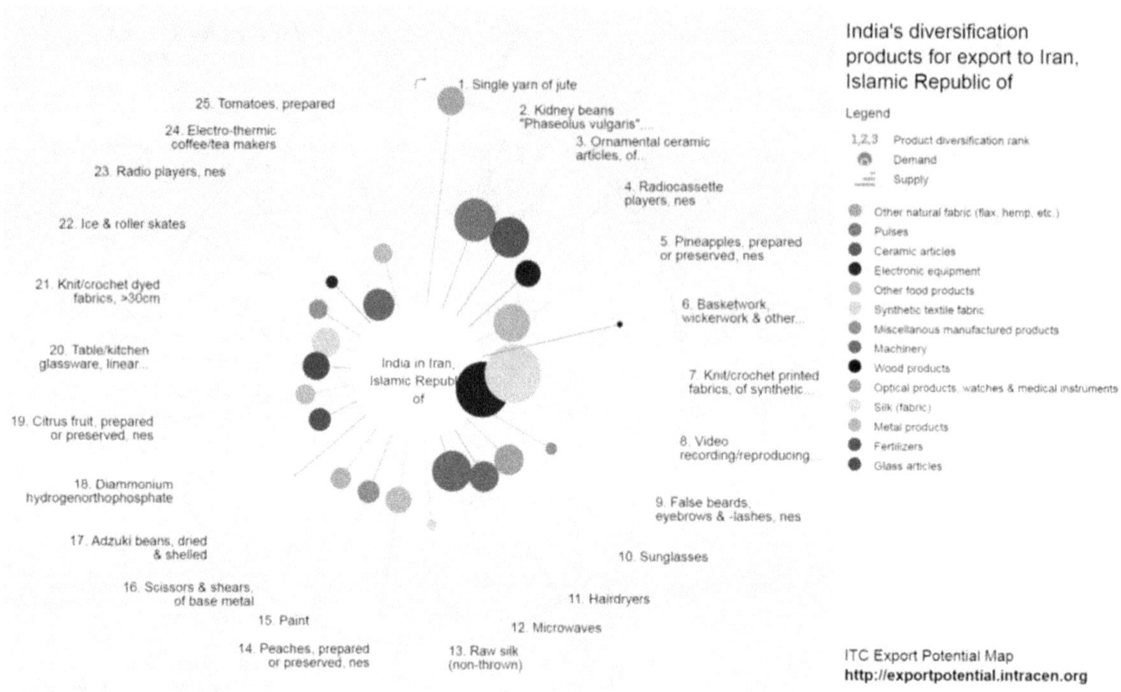

Figure 14. India's diversification products for exports to Bangladesh
Source: ITC (2019)

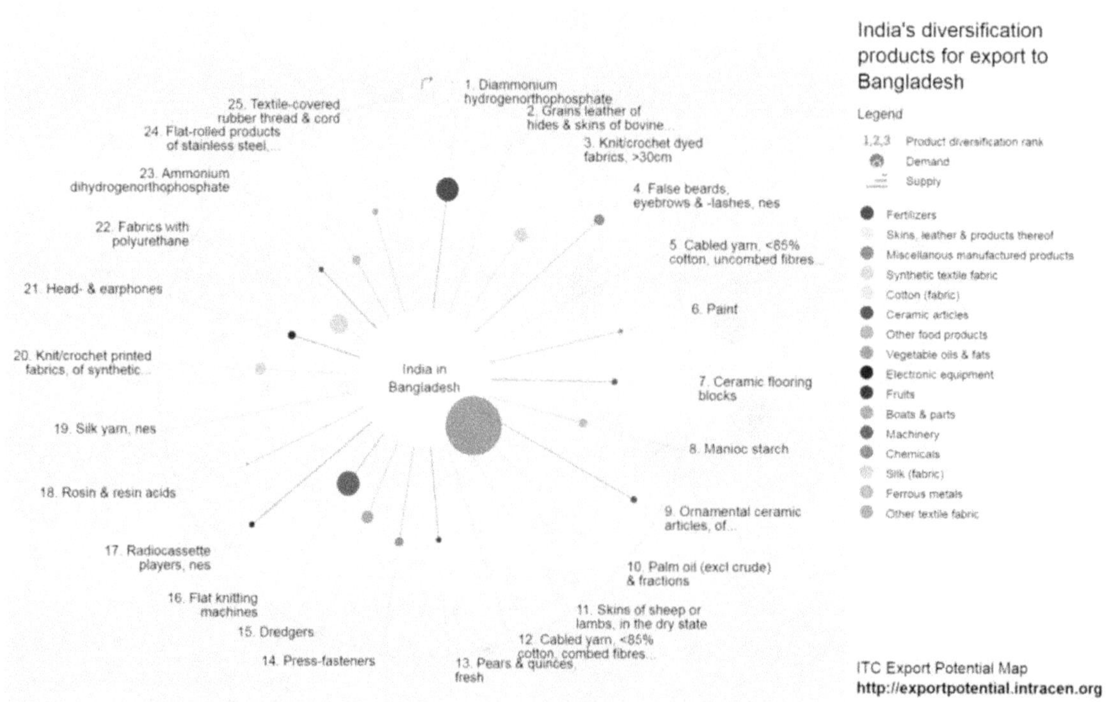

India's greatest export diversification alternatives in Oman are tomatoes, prepared, kidney beans "Phaseolus vulgaris", dried and shelled, and virola, mahogany, imbuia, and balsa, sawn/chipped lengthwise (Figure 15). India finds single yarn of jute easiest to reach. Tomatoes, prepared are the products that aces Oman's highest demand potential.

India's best options for export diversification in Sri Lanka are single yarn of jute, kidney beans "Phaseolus vulgaris", dried and shelled and knit/crochet dyed fabrics, >30 cm (Figure 16). India finds single yarn of jute easiest to reach. In Sri Lanka, Palm oil (excluding crude) and fractions are the products facing the highest demand potential.

India's greatest export diversification alternatives in Mozambique are kidney beans "Phaseolus vulgaris", dried and shelled Ammonium dihydrogen orthophosphate and mineral or chemical fertilizers (Figure 17). India finds single yarn of jute easiest to reach. In Mozambique, palm oil (excluding crude) and fractions are the products facing the highest demand potential.

India's greatest export diversification alternatives in Kenya are kidney beans "Phaseolus vulgaris", frozen and shelled beans, Diammonium hydrogenorthophosphate and crude palm oil (Figure 18). India finds single yarn of jute easiest to reach. In Kenya, crude palm oil are the products that faces the highest demand potential.

India's best options for export diversification in Tanzania are Diammonium hydrogenorthophosphate, crude palm oil, and tomatoes, prepared (Figure 19). India finds basketwork, wickerwork and other articles from non-vegetable plaiting materials easiest to reach. In Tanzania, palm oil (excluding crude) and fractions are the products facing the highest demand potential.

Figure 15. India's diversification products for exports to Oman
Source: ITC (2019)

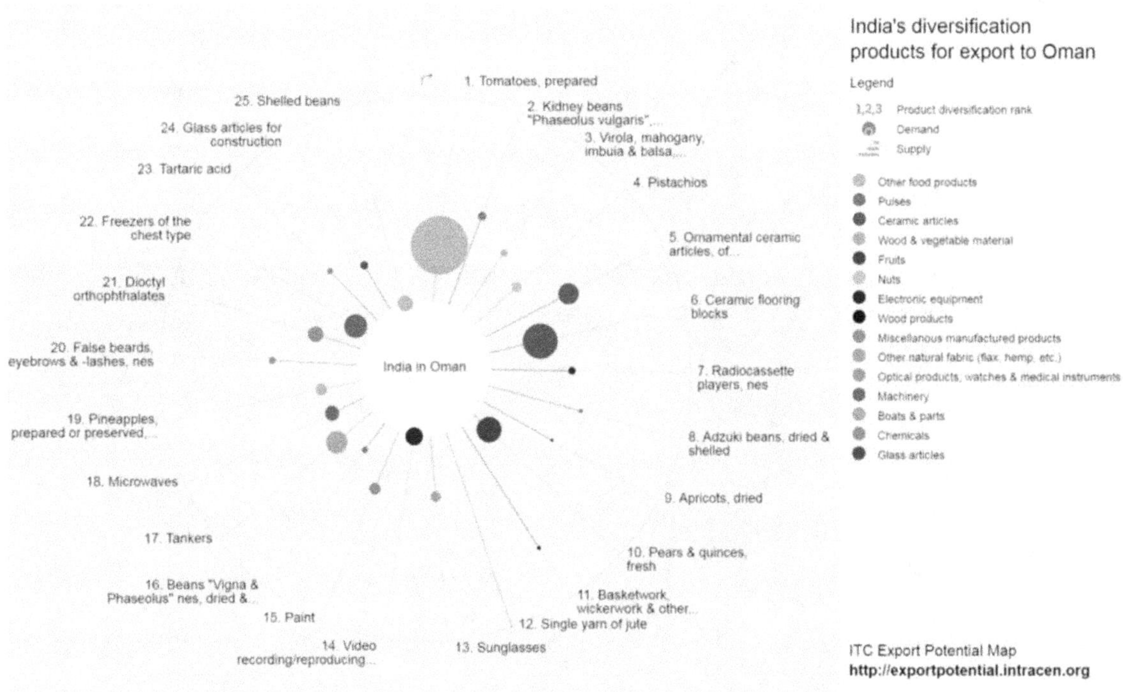

Figure 16. India's diversification products for exports to Sri Lanka
Source: ITC (2019)

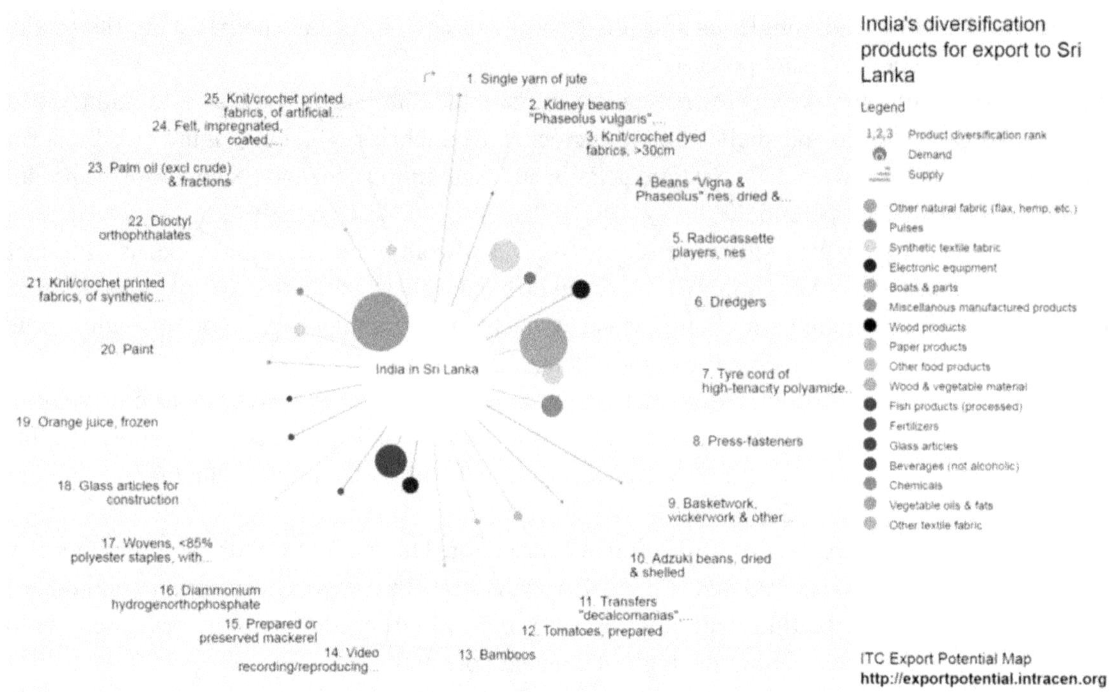

Figure 17. India's diversification products for exports to Mozambique
Source: ITC (2019)

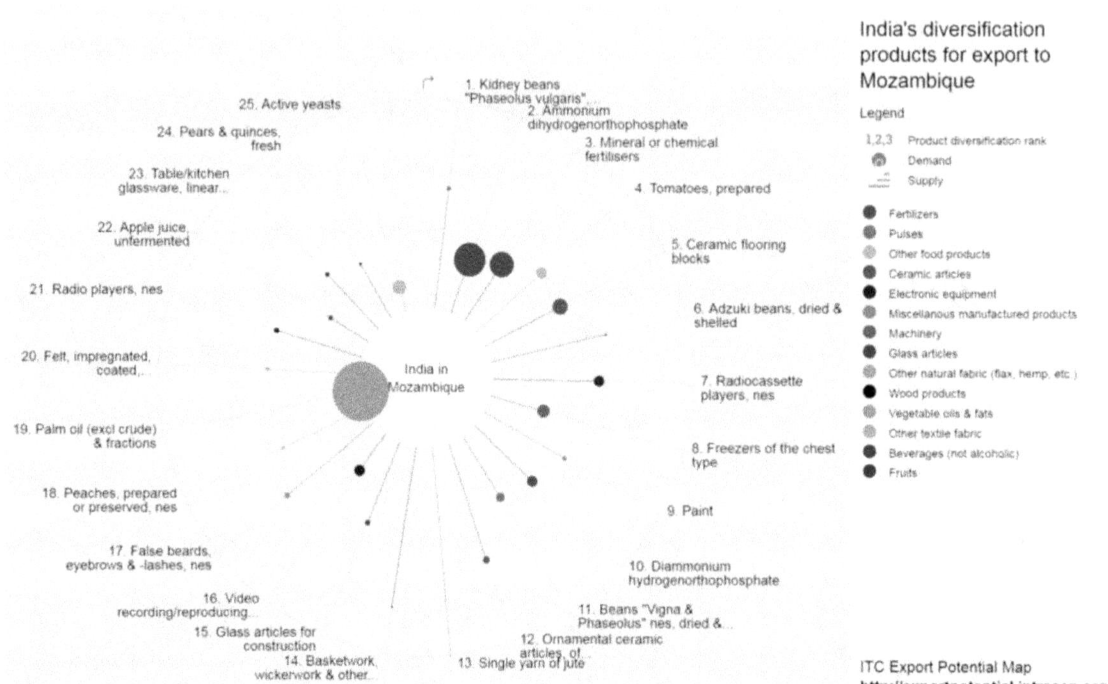

Figure 18. India's diversification products for exports to Kenya
Source: ITC (2019)

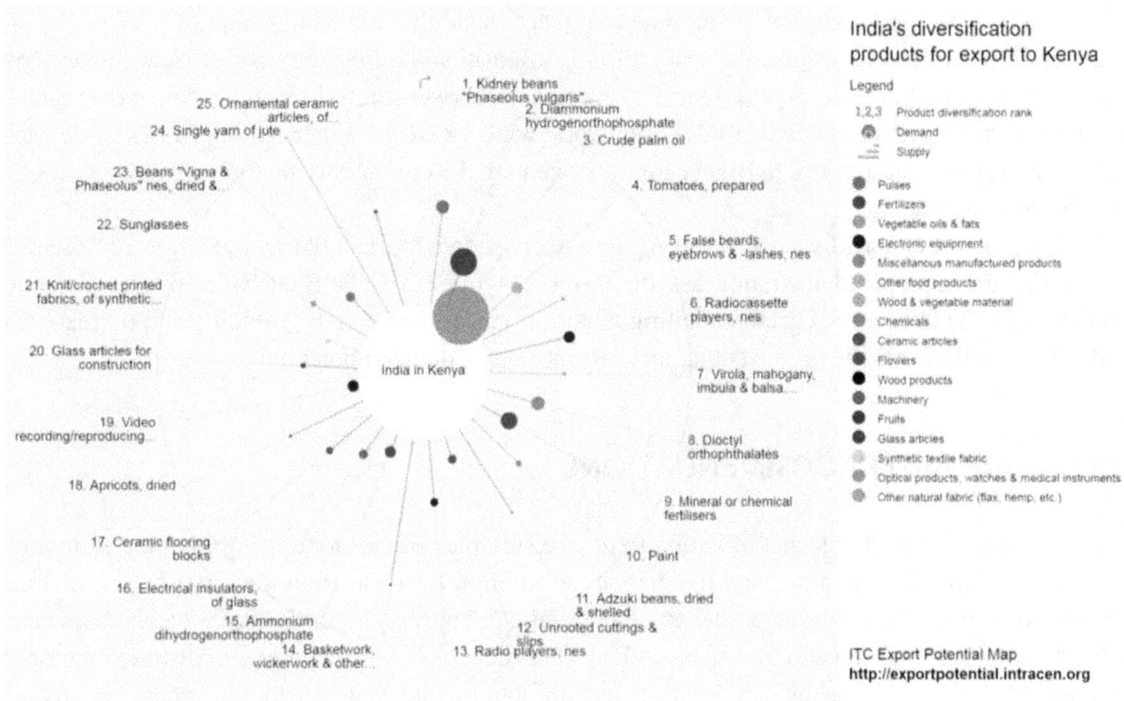

Figure 19. India's diversification products for exports to Tanzania
Source: ITC (2019)

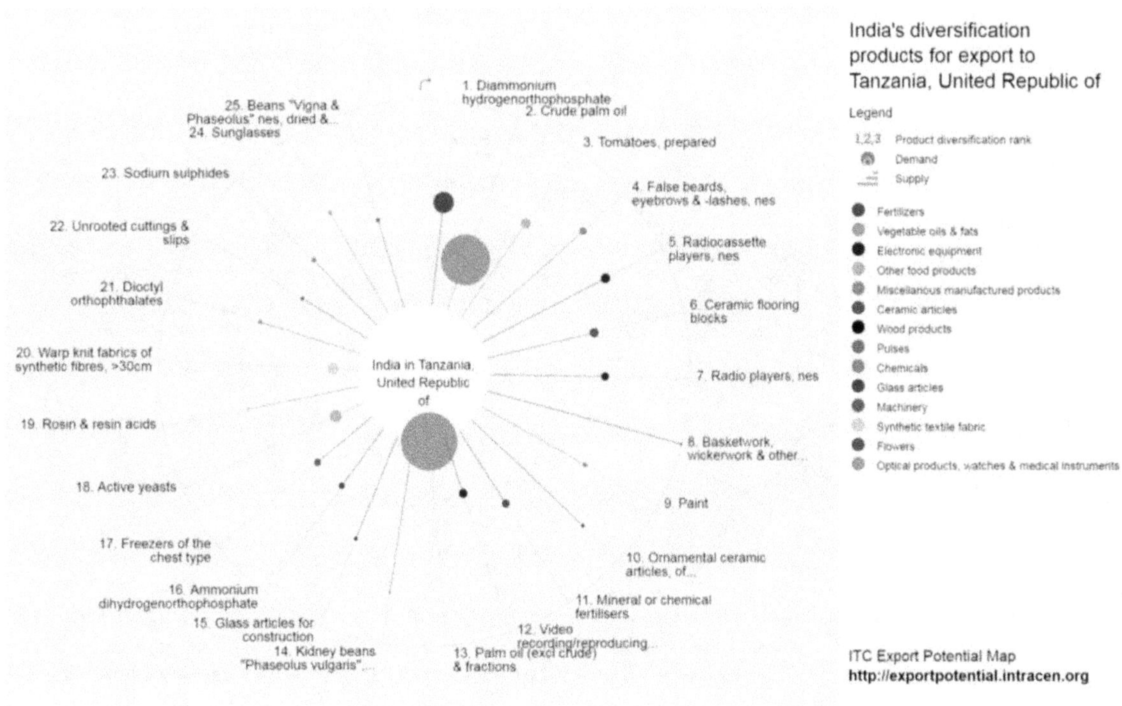

India's best options for export diversification in Madagascar are carded yarn of fine animal hair, bigeye tunas, frozen and radio cassette players (Figure 20). India finds silk yarn, easiest to reach. In Madagascar, fine animal hair Carded yarns are the product that faces the highest demand potential.

India's best options for export diversification in Mauritius are bigeye tunas, frozen, kidney beans "Phaseolus vulgaris", dried and shelled and basketwork, wickerwork and other articles from non-vegetable plaiting materials (Figure 21). India finds basketwork, wickerwork and other articles from non-vegetable plaiting materials easiest to reach. Bigeye tunas, frozen are the commodity that faces Mauritius's greatest demand potential.

India's greatest export diversifications in Yemen are kidney beans "Phaseolus vulgaris", dried and shelled, tomatoes, prepared and radio cassette players (Figure 22). India finds basketwork, wickerwork and other articles from non-vegetable plaiting materials easiest to reach. In Yemen, palm oil (excluding crude) and fractions are the products that faces the strongest demand potential.

SOLUTIONS AND RECOMMENDATIONS

India should evolve a reliable classification to devise suitable policies for developing blue economy in the IORA region. There is a demand of financial evaluation for measuring the contribution of Indian blue economy the IORA nations wishes to be devised. An appropriate institutional mechanism can be evolved on the regional stage to formulate and observe the size of blue economy in distinct member international locations. India should concentrate on Ammonium dihydrogen orthophosphate for Australia,

Figure 20. India's diversification products for exports to Madagascar
Source: ITC (2019)

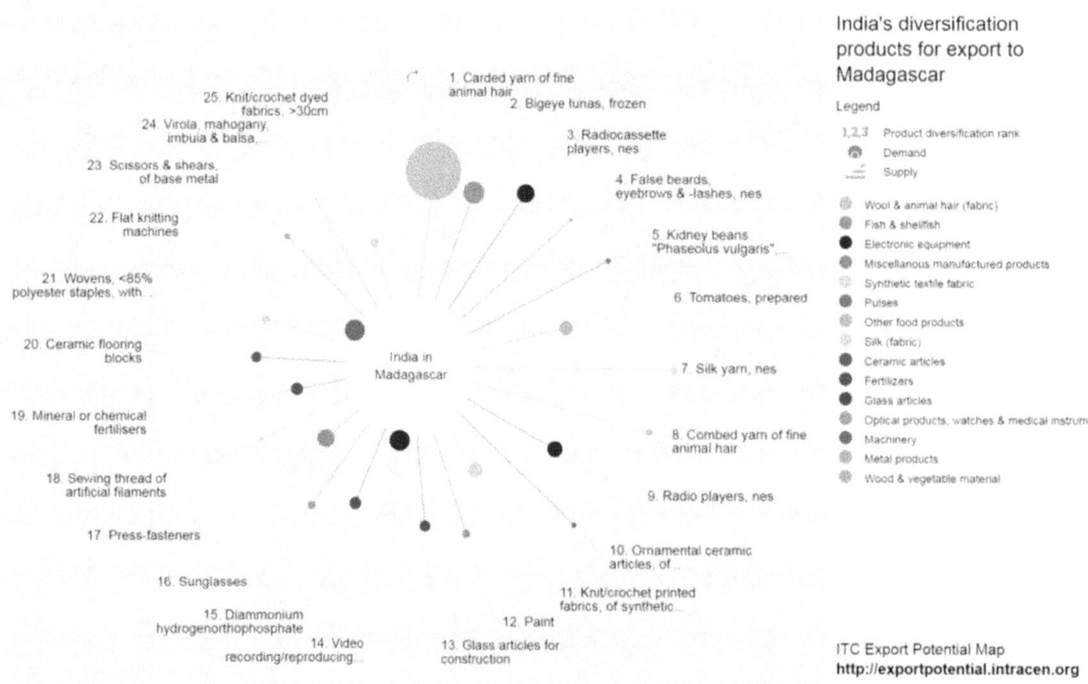

Figure 21. India's diversification products for exports to Mauritius
Source: ITC (2019)

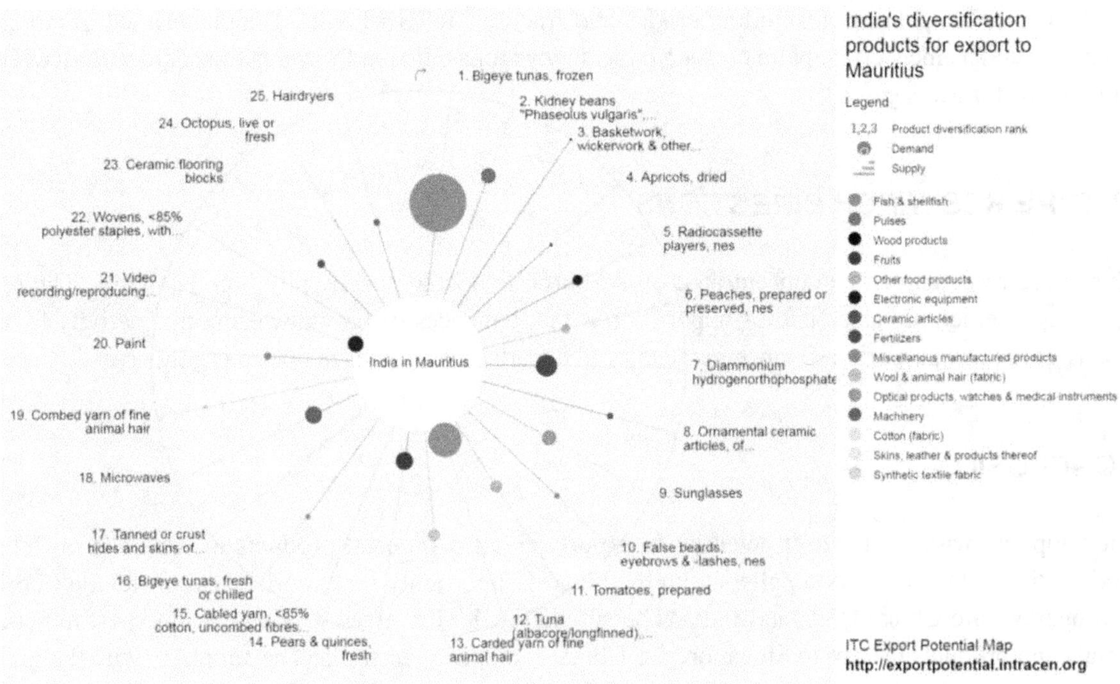

Figure 22. India's diversification products for exports to Yemen
Source: ITC (2019)

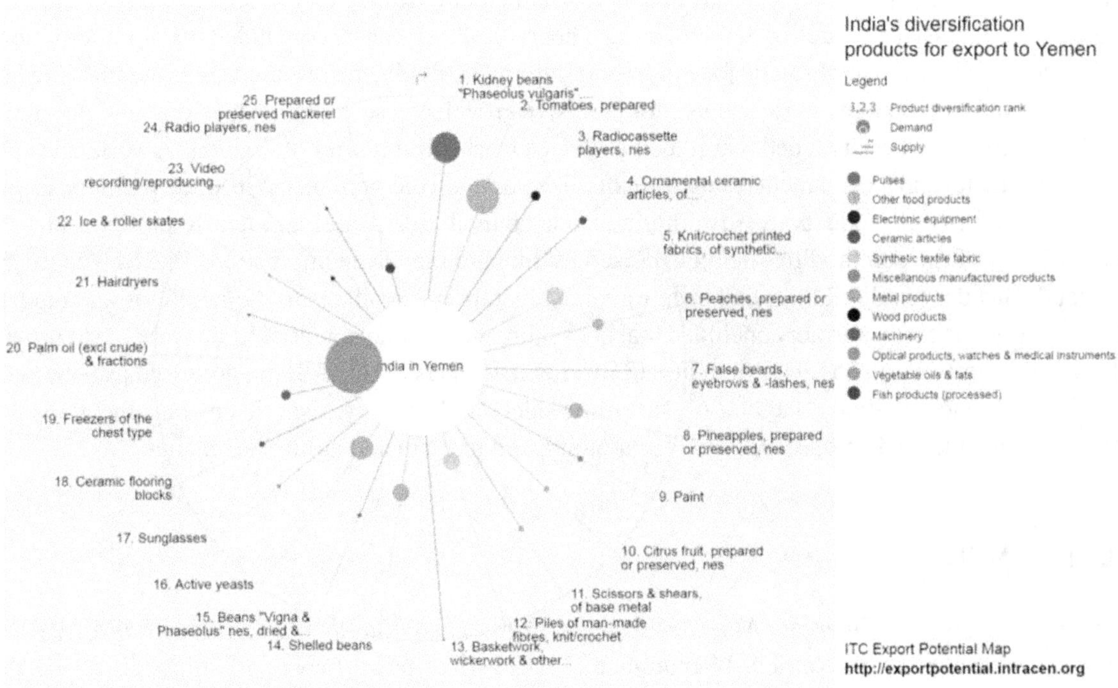

gold, semi-manufactured for Singapore, mineral or chemical fertilizers for Thailand, tankers for Malaysia, warp knit fabrics of synthetic fibres, >30 cm for Indonesia, Ammonium dihydrogen orthophosphate for South Africa, palm oil (excluding crude) and fractions for Sri Lanka, Bangladesh, Mozambique, Tanzania, and Yemen, crude palm oil for Kenya, bigeye tunas, frozen for Mauritius, carded yarn of fine animal hair for Madagascar.

FUTURE RESEARCH DIRECTIONS

The future research can be concentrated on seaborne trade and specifically blue economy. The blue economy is emerging as a field of opportunities that enhances or provides economic activity by the means of the ocean. Carbon finance markets or blue carbon is another major emerging area.

CONCLUSION

The suppliers with the greatest potential to export cereals and cereal products to Australia are Thailand, India, and China. The suppliers with the biggest opportunity for exporting export textile (fabric) to Singapore are China, USA, and India. The suppliers with the greatest potential to export minerals, metals and products thereof to Singapore are China, India, and Australia. The suppliers with the greatest potential to export cereals and cereal products to Singapore are India, Thailand, and Vietnam. India demonstrates the greatest absolute difference in value between prospective and actual exports, leaving space for further exports worth $51.9 million. The suppliers with the greatest potential to export apparel and textile products to Singapore are China, India, and Indonesia. The suppliers with the greatest potential to export apparel and textile products to Thailand are China, Vietnam, and India.

From the extensive research of the primary and heuristic data it can be concluded that for international trade, oceans are an essential source for export and import. Similarly, the researchers have pinpointed the emergence of blue economy as rich source for inclusive growth and sustainable development. Pertaining to all the facts it can be concluded that India has been a markable exporter of diamonds, worked jewelry of precious metal and medicaments consisting of mixed or unmixed products to its trade partners. Export of cereals and cereal products to Australia is also accountable. Apparel and textile products are also in the big list of the commodities being exported by India to the advancing nations like Singapore and Thailand. Besides textile (fabric) and even minerals, metals and products to the neighboring countries like Singapore. It can be further concluded that encashing the oceanic potential India was able to provide additional exports worth $51.9 million. For all the member states of IORA India proposed a cooperation pact for trade and investment facilitation, maritime safety and security, fisheries management, disaster risk management, academic, science and technology, and tourism and cultural exchange.

REFERENCES

Attri, V. N. (2016). *An Emerging New Development Paradigm of the Blue Economy in IORA; A Policy Framework for the Future.* Retrieved September 27, 2019, from https://www.iora.int/media/23838/the-blue-economy-and-iora-2016.pdf

Doyle, T. (2018). Blue Economy and the Indian Ocean Rim. *Journal of the Indian Ocean Region, 14*(1), 1–6. doi:10.1080/19480881.2018.1421450

Elisabeth, A. (2017). Diversity, Community, Cooperation: Cultural Intersections in the Indian Ocean Region. *Journal of the Indian Ocean Region, 13*(3), 277–280. doi:10.1080/19480881.2017.1374674

Erokhin, V. (Ed.). (2016). *Global Perspectives on Trade Integration and Economies in Transition*. Hershey, PA: IGI Global. doi:10.4018/978-1-5225-0451-1

Gamage, R. N. (2016). Blue Economy in Southeast Asia: Oceans as the New Frontier of Economic Development. *Maritime Affairs: Journal of the National Maritime Foundation of India, 12*(2), 1–15.

International Trade Centre. (2019). *Trade Map*. Retrieved September 27, 2019, from https://www.trademap.org/Index.aspx

Kalirajan, K. P. (2000). Indian Ocean Rim Association for Regional Cooperation (IOR-ARC): Impact on Australia's Trade. *Journal of Economic Integration, 15*(4), 533–547. doi:10.11130/jei.2000.15.4.533

Kelegama, S. (1998). Can Open Regionalism Work in the Indian Ocean Rim Association for Regional Co-operation? *ASEAN Economic Bulletin, 15*(2), 153–167. doi:10.1355/AE15-2D

Mittra, S. (2017). *Blue Economy: Beyond an Economic Proposition*. New Delhi, India: Observer Research Foundation.

Yu, Z., & Bai, X. (2017). From Southeast Asia to the Gulf: Analysis of the Prospect of Indian Ocean Integration. *Asian Journal of Middle Eastern and Islamic Studies, 11*(3), 90–106. doi:10.1080/25765949.2017.12023312

ADDITIONAL READING

Bateman, S., Gamage, R., & Chan, J. (2017). *ASEAN and the Indian Ocean: The Key Maritime Links*. Singapore: S. Rajaratnam School of International Studies.

Campbell, G. R., & Scerri, M. (1994). The Prospects for an Indian Ocean Rim (IOR) Economic Association. *South African Journal of International Affairs, 2*(2), 11–37. doi:10.1080/10220469409545134

Dowdy, W. L. (1985). The Indian Ocean Region as Concept and Reality. In W. L. Dowdy & R. B. Trood (Eds.), *The Indian Ocean: Perspectives on a Strategic Arena* (pp. 3–23). Durham, NC: Duke University Press.

Ghosh, R., Gabbay, R., & Siddique, A. (1999). *Good Governance Issues and Sustainable Development: The Indian Ocean Region*. New Delhi: Atlantic.

Kelegama, S. (2000). Open Regionalism in the Indian Ocean: How Relevant is the APEC Model for IOR-ARC? *Journal of the Asia Pacific Economy, 5*(3), 255–274. doi:10.1080/13547860050175044

Kelegama, S. (2002). Indian Ocean Regionalism: Is There a Future? *Economic and Political Weekly*, 2422–2425.

Panchamukhi, V. R. (1996). *Indian Ocean Region: Prospects for Economic and Scientific Cooperation. The Making of the Indian Ocean Community*. Delhi: New Age.

Sakhuja, V. (2015). Harnessing the Blue Economy. *Indian Foreign Affairs Journal, 10*(1), 39.

Smith, J. (1984). *Dictionary of Geography*. New Delhi: Arnold-Heinemann.

Tiwari, S. K. (2004). *Indian Ocean Rim-Association for Regional Cooperation (IOR-ARC): Problems and Prospects*. Delhi: Abhijeet Publications.

Voyer, M., Schofield, C., Azmi, K., Warner, R., McIlgorm, A., & Quirk, G. (2018). Maritime Security and the Blue Economy: Intersections and Interdependencies in the Indian Ocean. *Journal of the Indian Ocean Region, 14*(1), 28–48. doi:10.1080/19480881.2018.1418155

Wagner, C. (2013). The Indian Ocean Rim–Association for Regional Co-operation (IOR–ARC): The Futile Quest for Regionalism? *Journal of the Indian Ocean Region, 9*(1), 6–16. doi:10.1080/19480881.2013.793909

KEY TERMS AND DEFINITIONS

APEC: Asia-Pacific Economic Cooperation.
ASEAN: Association of Southeast Asian Nations.
CACM: Central American Common Market.
CAMESA: Common Market for Eastern and Southern Africa.
CARICOM: Caribbean Community and Common Market.
IORA: India Ocean Rim Association.
NAFTA: North American Free Trade Agreement.
SAARC: South Asia Association for Regional Cooperation.
WTO: World Trade Organization.

Chapter 10
Factors Influencing International Institutional Investments:
A Case Study of the 21st Century India

Akriti Gupta
Lovely Professional University, India

Gurpreet Kaur
https://orcid.org/0000-0001-9259-2709
Lovely Professional University, India

Mahesh Sarva
Lovely Professional University, India

ABSTRACT

At the turn of the 21st century, globalization of developed and developing countries in the world witnessed institutional inflows from international investors which became the main characteristic of global capital markets. The current research has assessed time-series data from 2000 to 2017 to understand how the different elements that have influenced the foreign institutional investments and helped India become a global market for such investors. The results revealed that political risk, financial market development, trade openness of the country, size of the economy, and rate of return on investment are the important determinants in attracting foreign institutional investments in India. The chapter also found economic risk and financial market risk played an insignificant role in determining foreign institutional investment in India. The findings of the research help the present government and market regulators to introduce policies aimed at increasing the flow of funds from international institutional investors.

DOI: 10.4018/978-1-7998-1730-7.ch010

INTRODUCTION

International trade had created pathways among countries but in the beginning of the twenty-first century, true globalization took birth as the world witnessed institutional capital flows from investors irrespective of geography, which became the main characteristic of global capital markets. Earlier the international capital markets were narrow in scope due to geographical limitations but with the technological and institutional developments, the capital markets matured both locally and globally. The wave of globalization was experienced by India in the 1990s when the financial crisis in Indian economy forced the country to open its gates to foreign portfolio investors in September 1992. Since the globalization of Indian economy, international institutional investors have been playing a major role in the Indian economy and are the prime source to foreign portfolio investments. These international institutional investors are often referred as foreign institutional investors and are defined as those entities which are based outside Indian Territory and invest in securities and other financial assets of the country. These entities can be pension funds, university funds, endowments and charitable trusts etc. and are regulated by the Securities and exchange board of India (SEBI) and the Reserve bank of India (RBI). Foreign institutional investors have been able to give an upward thrust to the prices of the domestic stock market and boost the quantitative as well as qualitative developments. Foreign investors help to reduce the cost of capital for firms in host country as they increase the demand for domestic stocks. This increase in demand for domestic stocks causes an upsurge in equity prices thereby lowering the cost of capital for firms (Fischer, 1995). Literature substantiates the positive influence of FIIs trading behaviour on stock markets of different countries (Dornbusch and Park, 1995; Banaji, 2000; Richards, 2002; Mohan, 2006; Upadhyay, 2006).

The international finance theory states that inflows from foreign institutional investors are an outcome of the risk diversification by portfolio managers holding investments in different countries. The foreign investors while investing in a country take into consideration multiple factors before making an investment. Factors, such as country risk and currency risk in the host country other than the risk related to the company have to be taken into consideration by foreign investors before channeling their investments. Country risk is the risk related to investing in a particular country and the country's ability or inability to repay its financial obligations. (Taffler and Abassi, 1984) have defined country risk as the inability of a country to repay its' external debt. External debt is the debt in the form of sovereign debt or loans given to public sector or private sector by non-residents which have to be repaid by the borrower country's government in foreign currency, goods and services. International Country Risk Guide (2012), has encapsulated country risk into three types - economic, political and financial risk. If a country is rated with a high risk it implies a risk in its political, economic and social environment. The risks in home and host country can lead to new problems on the macroeconomic front and cause sudden exit of foreign flows from a country, thereby altering its balance of payment position and destabilizing its exchange rate. The Asian crisis is an example of the adverse impact of volatile foreign investments on the balance of payment position of major Asian countries.

Some governments have blamed FIIs for the increase in market volatility and disruption in their capital markets. Previous studies have demonstrated that the influx of FIIs have led to higher volatility in the markets (Rai and Bhanumurthy, 2004; Porwal et al., 2005; Chittedi, 2008). The entry of FIIs resulted in the increased uncertainty in the markets of host country as FIIs are more speculative and may have huge unfavorable impact on the markets of developing countries (Pal, 1998). Thus, FIIs have been criticized for their short-term nature and are notoriously called "Hot Money".

Despite their treacherous nature, foreign inflows are crucial from the perspective of a developing country like India as they help to bridge the gap between savings and investments and provide necessary foreign exchange. Also, foreign institutional investments spur the economic growth and development of the capital markets. It is due to these reasons that majority of the developing countries frame policies to attract investments from foreign institutional investors. In the view of the increasing relevance of FIIs and their ability to influence the capital market of a country, it is important to examine the determinants of these foreign institutional investors into emerging countries especially India.

The current chapter looks to make significant contribution to literature by analyzing an extensive set of probable determinants influencing FIIs flows into India. Previously studies have looked at inflation, exchange rate, rate of return, index of industrial production (IIP) and domestic growth as the major macroeconomic determinants influencing FIIs into India. However, the current research examines the elements of country risk- economic, political and financial play any significant role in determining foreign inflows in India. The study also aims to explore the importance of size of the economy, trade openness of the country, development of the financial market and rate of return on investment in determining FII investments in India. Due to lack of continuous data on the variables undertaken in the study, much work has not been done to understand the factors that determine foreign institutional investment in India. Thus, the study looks to bridge this research gap by identifying the factors determining the flow of FIIs that enables the government to frame policies and introduce immediate measures to control foreign inflows and outflows, to meet the demand of sufficient foreign exchange reserves and reduce the gap between savings and investments and keeping the current account deficit in check. Since all economies in the world have become interdependent, it is vital to understand how different factors affect a country's foreign inflows as it not only impacts the local economy but stretches to different parts of the global economy.

The chapter is organized as follows: Section II "Background" encapsulates the existing studies on the topic. Section III "Main Focus of Chapter" presents an outline of the chapter problem and hypothesis development. Section IV "Solutions and Recommendations" presents and analyses the results and provides the recommendations, Section V "Future Research Direction" discusses the scope for future research, section VI "Conclusion" concludes the chapter and its findings.

BACKGROUND

Studies have been conducted in the past to assess a broad range of factors responsible for determining the foreign flows to developed and emerging countries. One strand of literature, has studied factors like stock market return, inflation and risk as probable determinants of foreign inflows in India. (Chakarbarti, 2001) established that returns in domestic stock market had a causal impact on FII flows in India. (Rai and Bhanumurthy, 2004) investigated the influence of return and risk on stock market as a possible determinant of foreign institutional investments. (Saraogi, 2008) found positive influence of Sensex and inflation and negative influence of S&P 500 and exchange rate on FIIs in India. (Kaur and Dhillon, 2010) explored different macroeconomic and stock market related factors to ascertain their impact on FIIs investment decisions in India and found a positive association between stock market turnover and market capitalization in the short-run and corroborated significant influence of macroeconomic factor-inflation on FII investments in the long-run. (Srinivasan and Kalaivani, 2013) employed Autoregressive Distributed Lag Bound testing approach to ascertain a significant influence of exchange rate, domestic inflation, equity returns in domestic market, returns and risk in US equity market on FIIs in India. (Garg and Dua, 2014) researched the importance of currency risk, domestic stock market, interest rate differential and exchange rate in determining the foreign portfolio flows to India and concluded currency risk posed a negative influence on foreign inflows, implying higher the risks, higher the outflows from foreign investors.

The current study looks to examine the influence of different risk factors, specifically economic, political and financial risk along with different macroeconomic variables like size of the economy, trade openness of the country, development of the financial market and rate of return on investment, have in determining the extent of foreign institutional investments in India.

Country Risk

Country risk is the risk related to investing in a particular country and the country's ability or inability to repay its financial obligations. (Taffler and Abassi, 1984) have defined country risk as the inability of a country to repay its' external debt. (Cosset and Roy, 1991) explain the ratings of a country's risk signal towards the probability with which the government of a particular country might default on its debt. The instances like countries defaulting on their debt payments, Mexican crisis in 1994-95, Asian crisis of 1997-98, Banking crisis in 2005, debt crisis in European countries have made financial investors cautious about the current market situation in the world. The reckless flow of capital and opening of capital markets by developing and developed countries pose serious threats to the financial institutions across the globe (Al-Khouri, 2015). Foreign investors before making an investment decision into a multinational company analyse the environment in which the companies operate especially the environment of the host country. This additional information on the risk environment of a country arising from the political institutions, construct of the economy, currencies and geographical location helps understand country risk. (Harvey, 2004) established, country risk measures are more important and beneficial when calculated on emerging markets compared to developed markets, as markets in emerging economies are less integrated with the world capital market than markets of developed countries. Since, foreign institutional investors are looking to make gains from diversifying their portfolio to different countries, a higher risk reduces the chances of foreign investments due to poor or low profit earnings for investors. The research has employed the International Country Risk Guide's elements of country risk- political, economic and financial risks to understand the influence exerted on foreign institutional investors. (Cosset and Roy, 1991) state that economic and political variables are an indicator of a country's credit worthiness. (Basu et al., 2011) used the Country Beta Approach based on several macroeconomic variables to estimate the country risk of India.

Economic Risk

The risk related to the macroeconomic conditions of a country which has the likelihood to deter the foreign investments of the host country and decrease profit potential owing to sudden changes in a market is called economic risk. (Azam and Lukman, 2010) opined that a stable economic and political environment will help to boost FDI in Indian Territory. (Alguacil et al., 2011) found macroeconomic instability had a detrimental impact on the growth of countries while economic freedom had a significantly positive and external debt and inflation had a significantly negative influence on growth of an economy. (Singhania and Gupta, 2011) found GDP and inflation as the important and significant macroeconomic variables explaining the variation in FDI flows in India. The literature review shows the absence of considerable work conducted to examine the role of economic risk in influencing foreign institutional investments in India.

The International Country Risk Guide assesses a country's economic strengths and weakness which implies an economically strong country will have low economic risk and an economically weak country will have high economic risk. Points are assigned to each economic risk component- GDP per head, real GDP growth, annual inflation rate, budget balance as percent of GDP and current account as percent of GDP. A high score indicates low economic risk and a low score indicates high economic risk.

Political Risk

Political risk is defined as the risk to foreign investors' investments due to the political instability or disruptions in state policies making it difficult for the host country to enable a conducive business environment to its investors. (Diamonte et al., 1996) examined the influence of political risk on returns in stock markets of developed and emerging economies and concluded that political risks had a strong impact on stock market returns of emerging economies compared to market returns of developed economies. Study by (Jun and Singh, 1996) found political risk as a significant determinant in attracting FDI to countries, implying higher political risks draws low FDIs. (Busse and Hefeker, 2007) established political risk as one of the crucial determinants in influencing foreign direct investment to countries and found political risk indicators as essential element in influencing foreign direct investment. (Hayakawa et al., 2013) propounded a decrease in the political risk of developing countries helped in attracting more FDI inflows. The above literature suggests most of the studies have focused on analyzing the influence of political risk in determining FDI in different countries but few researches has been conducted to understand the impact of political risk in influencing international institutional investments to different countries, especially emerging countries given the huge inflows from portfolio investors. Therefore, it is required to understand the impact of political risk and its role in influencing foreign institutional investments in India.

The current research assumes a negative relationship between political risk and foreign institutional investments in India. The study has incorporated the political risk index of International country risk guide (ICRG) which has 12 risk components – government stability, socioeconomic conditions, investment profile, internal conflict, external conflict, corruption, military in politics, religious tensions, law and order, ethnic tensions, democratic accountability and bureaucracy quality. If the political score is high it indicates towards less political risk in a country and if the total score on political risk is low it indicates a high political risk in a country.

Financial Risk

Financial risk is the risk that the foreign investors might stand to lose their investments made in a host country due to the country's inability to repay or default on its sovereign debt. Developing countries like India require foreign capital to meet their investment demands and finance their current account deficit. If the financial debt on a country increases beyond its repaying capacity, chances of an impending financial crisis increases. (Kim and Wu, 2008) propounded that an improvement in a country's short-term currency rating proved to be an unfavorable element to international capital flows as foreign investors tend to alter their long-term investment strategies to short term which can cause liquidity risks and outflow of foreign capital. Long-term ratings on foreign currency were established as the most crucial factor to encourage foreign capital flows. (Hayakawa et al., 2013) found a low level of financial risk in developing countries failed to draw more FDI inflows in the countries.

The study assumes a positive role of financial risk in influencing foreign institutional investments in India. Indicators of financial risk have been taken from the International country risk guide (ICRG)- foreign debt as percentage of GDP, foreign debt as percentage of exports of goods and services, current account as a percentage of exports of goods and services, net international liquidity as months of import cover and exchange rate stability. Lower the risk point total higher the financial risk and higher the risk point total, lower the financial risk in a country.

Trade Openness of the Country

Trade openness is defined as the extent to which the host country is receptive to international trade. (Pistoresi, 2000; Deichmann, 2001; Asiedu, 2002; Hill, 2005; Li & Filer, 2007; Al-Khouri, 2015) opined trade openness plays a significant role in promoting foreign investment in host countries. (Janicki and Wunnava, 2004) found empirically international trade as the most important determinant of foreign investment in a country. The trade openness of a country is estimated by sum of exports and imports of the country divided by the GDP of the country. The current research expects a positive relationship between trade openness and foreign institutional investments in India.

Size of Economy

While the size refers to absolute size, a growth of an economy means a rise in the demand for the goods and services and increase in productivity of the country. The study has proxied growth of size of the economy with the GDP per capita growth of the host country. (Shamsuddin, 1994; Tsai, 1994; Billington, 1999; Pistoresi, 2000; Janicki and Wunnava, 2004; Parletun, 2008; Al-Khouri, 2015) propounded with the increase in the market size of the economy foreign investment increases. Further, (Wheeler and Mody, 1992) found market size of the economy as an essential factor in gauging the investments from international investors. The study expects positive relationship between the growth of the size of the economy and foreign institutional investments.

Development of the Financial Market

Foreign investments are high in countries that have an established and developed financial market (Portes and Rey, 2005). To capture the effect of financial market development, the study has used stock market capitalization to GDP as a proxy for financial market development. The research expects positive association between development in the financial market and foreign institutional investments in the country.

Rate of Return on Investment

Investments in countries having scarce capital yield higher returns while, the countries with higher per capita income yield lower returns (Asiedu, 2002). The current study has used the inverse of real GDP per capita to denote the return on investments. Based on the work of (Asiedu, 2002), the study has proxied the rate of return on investment with the log of the inverse of real GDP per capita.

MAIN FOCUS OF CHAPTER

The research assesses the determinants of foreign institutional investments in India from the period 2000 to 2017. Time series data has been collected to fulfil the purpose of the study. Based on the literature discussed in the previous section seven variables have been identified as the probable determinants of foreign institutional investments in India- economic risk, political risk, financial risk, trade openness, size of the economy, development of the financial market and rate of return on investment. To determine the data on risks for India, the study has collected data from International country risk guide (ICRG) which is provided by PRS group. The research has analysed the impact of risk factors- economic, political and financial risk and also determined the influence of trade openness, size of the economy, development of the financial market and rate of return on investment on net foreign institutional investments in India. The ratio of net foreign institutional investments to GDP is taken as the dependent variable to avoid the problem of non-stationary and normalize flows of foreign institutional investments in terms of GDP.

Since the study seeks to examine the influence of the lagged value of the dependent variable acting as a regressor, a Distributed Lag model has been employed. (Arellano and Bond, 1991) used the lagged value of the dependent variable as an instrument and the present study has followed the same for the purpose of estimation. To investigate the influence of independent variables – economic risk, political risk, financial risk, trade openness, size of the economy, financial market development and rate of return on investment in determining foreign institutional investments in India following equation has been assumed:

$$Y_{it} = \alpha + \delta Y_{it} - 1 + \beta X1_{it} + \beta X2_{it} + \beta X3_{it} + \beta X4_{it} + \beta X5_{it} + \beta X6_{it} \beta X7_{it} + \varepsilon_{it} \quad (1)$$

$\varepsilon_{it} \sim iid(0,\sigma^2\varepsilon)$

where:

Y_t – net foreign institutional investment flows to GDP in India;
X_1 – economic risk;
X_2 – political risk;
X_3 – financial risk;
X_4 – trade openness of a country;
X_5 – size of an economy;
X_6 – financial market development of a country;
X_7 – rate of return on investment;
ε_{it} –composite error;
t – time dimension;
ε_{it} – white noise error term (serially uncorrelated and independent) with zero mean and constant variance.

To control for autocorrelation in the model, lagged dependent variable has been employed. The study expects a negative relationship between political risk and foreign institutional investment flow as political uncertainty in a country is likely to dissuade foreign investors who are looking to make gains from their investment strategies. The study also expects negative relationship of economic risk on foreign institutional investment flows implying an increase in economic risk will lead to a decrease in foreign inflows. Moreover, the impact of financial risk on foreign institutional flows is likely to be less significant as foreign institutional investors can easily withdraw their money at the very hint of financial trouble in a country. Financial market development, rate of return on investment, the size of the economy and trade openness are expected to bear a positive relationship on foreign institutional investments.

The study uses Difference Generalized Method of Moments model to examine the influence of the different independent variables in determining foreign institutional investments in India. The Generalized Method of Moments was introduced by (Hansen, 1982) after he made improvements to the Method of Moments model by defining the properties of econometric estimators in terms of orthogonality conditions. The GMM model is suitable to assess the issue of endogeneity in the lagged dependent variable. (Bajpai and Sharma, 2018) used the Generalized Method of Moments to address the issue of endogeneity in their study. (Al-Khouri, 2015) used GMM model to control for unobserved heterogeneity and endogeneity with the help of the instrumental variable matrix. The study undertook to analyse the impact of political risk and its variables in influencing foreign direct investment and foreign portfolio investment in MENA countries. (Anwar and Sun, 2011) employed GMM model and found contribution of financial development towards the growth of domestic capital stock in Malaysia. The study revealed that rise in the foreign investment in Malaysia has further enhanced the stock of domestic capital. (Fanta, 2017) applied GMM model to introduce different combination of control variables to understand the importance of finance growth by using financial development indictors in developed and emerging economies.

For the model to be a good fit two essential conditions are required to be satisfied. Firstly, the error term should follow AR (1) but should be insignificant at AR (2) i.e. the error term should be serially correlated at first difference but should be uncorrelated at second difference. The second condition that needs to be checked is absence of correlation between our error term and instruments used. To ensure unbiased and consistent estimators the study has used difference GMM model which converts the equation (1) of the model as follows:

$$\Delta Y_{it} = \Delta\delta Y_{it} - 1 + \Delta\beta X1_{it} + \Delta\beta X2_{it} + \Delta\beta X3_{it} + \Delta\beta X4_{it} + \Delta\beta X5_{it} + \Delta\beta X6_{it}\ \Delta\beta X7_{it} + \Delta\varepsilon_{it} \quad (2)$$

SOLUTIONS AND RECOMMENDATIONS

Table 1 shows the descriptive statistics and Table 2 shows the correlation matrix of the data undertaken in the study. Correlation matrix in Table 2 indicates towards a strong association between the variables undertaken in the study and significant correlation is found foreign institutional investments, political risk, economic risk, financial risk, financial market development and size of the economy. Negative association is found between foreign institutional investments, trade openness of the country and rate of return on investment. To check for the presence of multicollinearity between the independent variables the study has used VIF (Variance Inflation Factor) statistics. The results of VIF statistics have values less than 10 which points that the model is free from the issue of multicollinearity.

UNIT ROOT

The first step in estimating time series equation is to determine whether the variables are stationary having a constant mean and variance or non-stationary. If the series are found non-stationary and incorporated in the study it will distort the results (Libanio, 2005). To check the condition of stationarity and pres-

Table 1. Descriptive statistics

Variables	Mean	S.D	Minimum	Maximum
FII/GDP	1.039603	.9076158	-.8414	2.7751
ER	33.937778	1.1113085	32.5400	35.6700
FR	42.498333	1.5431071	39.1300	44.5400
PR	60.2294	2.77037	54.92	63.71
Fm_Dev	63.979672	23.3533968	22.8935	113.3330
Size	5.104179	1.8320106	1.5827	7.0247
TO	261.637267	239.8132292	94.7908	960.5886
ROI	-4.698662	.2689854	-5.1060	-4.3079

Table 2. Correlation matrix

Variables	FII/GDP	ER	FR	PR	Fm_Dev	Size	TO	ROI
FII/GDP	1.00							
ER	0.126	1.00						
FR	0.395	0.334	1.00					
PR	0.309	0.389	0.817	1.00				
Fm_Dev	0.225	-0.061	0.559	0.638	1.00			
Size	0.597	0.320	0.686	0.747	0.388	1.00		
TO	-0.119	0.007	0.150	0.088	-0.050	0.322	1.00	
ROI	-0.117	0.441	-0.269	-0.297	-0.510	-0.450	0.853	1.00

Notes: FII/GDP is the net foreign institutional investment as percentage of GDP, ER is the economic risk, FR is the financial risk, PR is the political risk, Fm_Dev is the financial market development of the country, size is the growth of the GDP per capita capturing the size of the economy, TO is the trade openness of the country which is estimated by the total of exports and imports of the country to GDP, ROI is the rate of return on investment in the country

ence of unit root in the variables Augmented Dicky- Fuller Test is conducted and results are shown in Table 3. The null hypotheses are tested at 1 percent, 5 percent and 10 percent level of significance for acceptance or rejection. The results in table 3 show that the independent variable size of the economy and trade openness of the country are stationary at level while, foreign institutional investments, financial market development, financial risk and economic risk are stationary at first difference and rate of return on investment and political risk are found to be stationary at their second difference.

Once the series are checked for presence of stationarity the next step is to check for autocorrelation for which Durbin-Watson test is used. The Durbin-Watson value for the variables is around 2 which shows the series is free from the problem of autocorrelation. However, the presence of lagged dependent variable as one of the regressor in the equation might lead to deceptive results suspecting the validity of Durbin-Watson test. To remove this limitation of Durbin-Watson test, the study has also applied Q-statistic test to check for the presence of autocorrelation. The results indicate towards an insignificant p value which attest to the results of Durbin-Watson of no serial correlation.

Table. 3 Results of augmented dickey fuller test for determinants of FII in India

Variables	Test Statistics	Critical Value[a]	Critical Value[b]	Conclusion
FII/GDP	-5.394[A]	-3.081	-2.681	No unit root
ER	-5.028[B]	-3.733	-3.310	No unit root
FR	-3.200[A]	-3.119	-2.701	No unit root
PR	-4.055[A]	-3.081	-2.681	No unit root
Fm_Dev	-3.946[A]	-3.065	-2.673	No unit root
Size	-3.268[A]	-3.052	-2.666	No unit root
TO	-4.889[A]	-3.052	-2.666	No unit root
ROI	-4.398[B]	-3.791	-3.342	No unit root

Ho: FII/GDP, ER, FR, PR, Fm_Dev, Size, TO and ROI have unit root
[A] indicates ADF model with constant and no trend
[B] indicates ADF model with constant and trend
[a] indicates at 5 percent level of significance
[b] indicates at 10 percent level of significance

After meeting the condition of no unit root and no serial correlation amongst the variables the next step is to check the cointegration amongst the variables. Cointegration is applied to check whether there exits any long run correlation between the variables in the study. For testing of cointegrating relationship amongst the variables the study has used Johansen- Juselius cointegration technique. To estimate the number of cointegrating vectors Trace test statistics and Max-Eigenvalue test are used which help to validate the long run relationship between the variables. The results of Johansen-Juselius cointegration technique are shown in Table 4. The result of cointegration amongst the variables is shown in the table along with the null hypothesis test for the same. First cointegration test was run to check presence of a long run association between FII/GDP, size and trade openness. The probability value for trace test statistics and Max-Eigen Value is more than the significance value of 0.05 which leads to the acceptance of null hypothesis and concludes that there exists long run relationship between FII/GDP, size and trade openness.

The probability value of trace test statistics and Max-Eigen Value for testing cointegrating relationship between FII/GDP, financial risk, economic risk and financial market development is greater than the significance value of 0.05 signaling towards presence of long run relationship between our variables and acceptance of null hypothesis for the same. Further, long run correlation was found between FII/GDP, political risk and rate of return on investment as the probability value of trace test statistics and Max-Eigen Value was more than 5 percent level.

To check the model is free from problem of serial correlation Breusch-Godfrey serial correlation LM test have been conducted. The null hypothesis framed is stated as- no serial correlation is present in the residuals. The results of Breusch-Godfrey test show that the probability chi-square value is greater than 0.05 percent which leads to the acceptance of the null hypothesis and confirms that the residuals do not suffer from any serial correlation. Further, Breusch-Pagan-Godfrey test has been conducted to check for heteroscedasticity amongst the residuals in the model. The null hypothesis framed is homoscedastic errors are present in the residual. The probability chi-square value is greater than the accepted value of 0.05 percent thus, leading to acceptance of null hypothesis of homoscedastic errors. The test results show that our model is free from the problem of multicollinearity, serial correlation and heteroscedasticity.

Table 4. Unrestricted cointegration rank test (trace) and unrestricted cointegration rank test (maximum eigenvalue)

Hypothesized No. of CE(s)	Trace Statistic	0.05 critical value	Prob[b]	Max-Eigen Statistic	0.05 critical value	Prob[b]
None	27.0184	29.797	0.101	13.9216	21.131	0.371
At most 1	13.0967	15.494	0.111	10.0075	14.264	0.211
At most 2	3.0892	3.841	0.078	3.0892	3.841	0.078
None	47.730	47.856	0.051	20.418	27.584	0.312
At most 1	27.311	29.797	0.094	15.626	21.131	0.247
At most 2	11.684	15.494	0.172	8.644	14.264	0.316
None	38.447	29.797	0.004	24.161	21.131	0.018
At most 1	14.285	15.494	0.075	13.224	14.264	0.072
At most 2	1.060	3.841	0.303	1.060	3.841	0.303

Ho: FII/GDP, Size of Economy and Trade Openness are correlated
Ho: FII/GDP, FR, ER and Fm_Dev are correlated
Ho: FII/GDP, PR and ROI are correlated
Trace test denotes 1 cointegrating eqn (s) at the level 0.05 and Max-Eigenvalue test denotes 1 cointegrating eqn (s) at the level 0.05.
[b] MacKinnon-Haug-Michelis (1999) p-values

Table 5. Results of GMM regression to identify determinants of FII in India

Variables	Coefficient	t-statistics	Probability Value
ER	-0.356	-1.945	0.083
FR	0.190	1.215	0.255
PR	-0.305	-5.132	0.000
Fm_Dev	0.013	3.643	0.005
Size	0.786	13.537	0.000
TO	-0.002	-6.100	0.000
ROI	2.372	2.623	0.027

H_1: Higher Economic Risk (ER) decreases the flow of FII
H_2: Higher Financial Risk (FR) decrease the flow of FII
H_3: Higher Political Risk (PR) decreases the flow of FII
H_4: Financial Market Development (Fm_Dev) and FII are positively related
H_5: Size of economy (Size) and FII are positively related
H_6: Trade Openness (TO) attracts more FII
H_7: Return on Investment (ROI) and FII are positively related

Further, results of difference GMM are shown in table 5. The R-squared is calculated at 0.7821 indicating towards good-fit of the model and determined 78.21 percent of variation in the dependent variable that is foreign institutional investments is explained by the independent variables undertaken in the study. The probability value of F-statistic is also significant at 0.05 percent which further attests towards the goodness of the model. Political risk, financial market development, trade openness of the country, the size of the economy and rate of return on investment are identified as important determinants of foreign institutional investments in India. However, the study found economic risk and financial market risk to be insignificant in determining foreign institutional investment in India. Political risk has a negative and significant influence on foreign institutional investments in India indicating higher the political risk, lower are the investments from foreign institutional investors. The finding is consistent with the results of (Al-Khouri, 2015) that political risk is one of the most crucial elements in influencing foreign portfolio investments. If the country has a stable political environment it increases the confidence of foreign investors in the investment profile of the country as a stable government is more likely to work towards the upliftment of the economy and have a functioning government with less corruption and lower chances of religious and ethnic tensions. Also, foreign institutional investors look to make investment in the long run to earn greater returns and if any correction in the stock market occurs due to changes in political environment of the country FIIs are likely to take advantage of the said correction and invest their money to enhance their gains. Thus, decrease in political risk increases foreign money inflow and increase in political risk is likely to decrease the money flow from foreign institutional investors. The results of the GMM regression also show development in the financial market bear a positive and significant influence on FIIs establishing the fact that a well-developed financial market draws investments from foreign institutional investors. Thus, the developed financial market of India acts as an important element for boosting activities in the stock market and foreign institutional investments. Further, a well-developed financial market signals towards the development of well-regulated institutions and assures the government's commitment to continue with the reforms in the market strengthening the confidence of international institutional investors and increase their participation in the stock markets. Also, development in the financial market hints towards an efficient managerial performance increasing the attractiveness of local companies for foreign institutional investors. The results also show that the negative bearing of trade openness has slight significant influence on FII which indicates towards the fact that India being an emerging country the trade policy of the country is less open restricting the flow of foreign inflows from international institutional investors. Moreover, the results also show foreign investors' hesitation to capitalize India as their source of international trade. To overcome this problem, the government should look to frame policies that help to further open the trade and remove barriers for firms that are involved in trade of goods and services. Enhancement of trade promotes exports of a country and increasing exports strengthen the prospects of the firms and companies involved in export which in turn creates bright prospects for investments by local and global investors. India being an emerging economy requires to modify its trade policies and build a comprehensive environment to enhance the development of the traders and businesses. Increase in business activity of companies involved in international trade will boost their growth and profits which in turn will attract foreign investors looking to make gains from their investments. Also, improved economic growth will further help to attract more investment from international investors. The results of the study are consistent with (Al-Khouri, 2015) which suggest trade openness is a critical factor in determining international institutional investments. Thus, it is established that trade openness of the country and financial market development are the major factors in influencing foreign inflows from international institutional investors. Also, rate of return on investment shows positive association with FII which signals higher return on investments attract more foreign institutional investments. FIIs invest outside their country of origin in search of more profits and those countries that have a high rate of return on investment are likely to be FIIs favorable destination. Thus, FIIs park their money in India on account of earning a higher rate of return on their investments. Further, the size of the economy positively influences FIIs into India signalling larger economic size draws more inflows into the country. (Chakarbarti, 2001) established that market size of an economy acted as a crucial factor in determining funds from foreign investors. In terms of risk, political risk has key role in influencing investments from international institutional investors than economic risk or financial risk in Indian economy.

Since, political risk has a significant influence on FIIs the Indian government should lay emphasis on stabilizing the political climate of the country and reduce political uncertainties. Government should ensure freedom of speech and absence of discriminating business policies to boost a healthy business and investment environment. Also, stable governments are more welcomed by foreign investors which is likely to benefit the businesses. The government should constantly upgrade and examine their political environment to sustain the foreign inflow. Also, the government needs to further liberalize its trade regime to attract more investments from institutional investors investing into the country. If the Indian government wants to reap the benefits of the foreign institutional investments it continuously needs to regulate and monitor is trade policies, political environment and financial markets that benefit the foreign investors and Indian economy. Policies should be made to sustain the existing investment environment and incorporate new measures that help foreign investors earn a higher rate of return on their investments. The results of the study persuade the current government and market regulators to introduce policies that intend to increase the fund flows from international institutional investors. Also, elimination of restrictions that limit the inflow should be encouraged to enable more participation from foreign investors. A market that appeals to international institutional investors attracts more inflows and thus has a higher probability of making efficient use of financial resources and boost economic development of the country.

FUTURE RESEARCH DIRECTION

The research can be further extended to new areas with the addition of new variables to understand the factors influencing foreign institutional investments. The current chapter has limited its discussion to examine the determinants of foreign institutional investments in India however the study can be enhanced by conducting a comparative analysis of determinants of FII investment in other Asian and developed countries. The model undertaken in the current research explains 78 percent of the variation in the foreign institutional investments is due to economic risk, political risk, financial risk, size of the economy, trade openness, development of the financial market and rate of return on investment however, 22 percent of the variation in foreign institutional investments remains unexplained. Further, study can be undertaken to a broader aspect and include more variables like index of industrial production, inflation volatility etc. to determine factors affecting FIIs in India and other emerging economies.

CONCLUSION

The purpose of the study is to determine the factors that impact and influence foreign institutional investments into India. Time series data from the period 2000 to 2017 has been undertaken for the study. The research undertook factors like political risk, financial risk, economic risk, financial market development, size of the economy, trade openness and rate of return on investment in determining foreign institutional investments. The results highlighted political risk has a significant influencer on FIIs in India. A healthy political environment reduces the fear of unstable government, corruption, religious and ethnic tensions and builds confidence in the investment profile, democratic accountability and law and order in the country and hence attracts investments. The study also revealed that trade openness of the country plays a small but significant role in determining foreign institutional investments thus the government should look to frame policies that help to further open the trade and remove barriers for firms that are involved in trade of goods and services. Enhancement of trade promotes exports of a country and increasing exports strengthen the prospects of the firms and companies involved in export which in turn creates bright prospects for investments by local and global investors. Since, trade openness has significant positive relationship with the economic growth of a country and India being an emerging economy it could improve its trade policies and build a comprehensive environment to enhance the development of the traders and businesses. The study also illustrated positive influence of a liberalized and developed financial market in attracting investments from international institutional investors. Finally, the study showed rate of return on investment and size of the economy positively influencing foreign institutional investments in the country.

REFERENCES

Alguacil, M., Cuadros, A., & Orts, V. (2011). Inward FDI and Growth: The Role of Macroeconomic and Institutional Environment. *Journal of Policy Modeling*, *33*(3), 481–496. doi:10.1016/j.jpolmod.2010.12.004

Anwar, S., & Sun, S. (2011). Financial Development, Foreign Investment and Economic Growth in Malaysia. *Journal of Asian Economics*, *22*(4), 335–342. doi:10.1016/j.asieco.2011.04.001

Arellano, M., & Bond, S. (1991). Some Tests of Specification for Panel Data: Monte Carlo Evidence and an Application to Employment Equations. *The Review of Economic Studies*, *58*(2), 277–297. doi:10.2307/2297968

Asiedu, E. (2002). On the Determinants of Foreign Direct Investment to Developing Countries: Is Africa Different? *World Development*, *30*(1), 107–119. doi:10.1016/S0305-750X(01)00100-0

Azam, M., & Lukman, L. (2010). Determinants of Foreign Direct Investment in India, Indonesia and Pakistan: A Quantitative Approach. *Journal of Managerial Sciences*, *4*(1), 31–43.

Bajpai, S., & Sharma, A. K. (2018). An Empirical Test of the Select Multifactor Asset Pricing Models with GMM. *International Journal of Business Innovation and Research*, *15*(3), 357–380. doi:10.1504/IJBIR.2018.089753

Banaji, J. (2000). *Foreign Portfolio Investment in Indian Equity Markets: Has the Economy Benefited?* Oxford, UK: Queen Elizabeth House.

Basu, S., Deepthi, D., & Reddy, J. (2011). *Country Risk Analysis in Emerging Markets: The Indian Example*. Bangalore, India: Indian Institute of Management Bangalore.

Billington, N. (1999). The Location of Foreign Direct Investment: An Empirical Analysis. *Applied Economics*, *31*(1), 65–76. doi:10.1080/00036846.2019.12067087

Busse, M., & Hefeker, C. (2007). Political Risk, Institutions and Foreign Direct Investment. *European Journal of Political Economy*, *23*(2), 397–415. doi:10.1016/j.ejpoleco.2006.02.003

Chakrabarti, A. (2001). The Determinants of Foreign Direct Investments: Sensitivity Analyses of Cross-Country Regressions. *Kyklos*, *54*(1), 89–114. doi:10.1111/1467-6435.00142

Chakrabarti, R. (2001). FII Flows to India: Nature and Causes. *Money and Finance, 2*(7). Retrieved October 2, 2019, from https://papers.ssrn.com/sol3/papers.cfm?abstract_id=649852

Chittedi, K. R. (2008). Volatility of Indian Stock Market and FIIs. *European Business Review*, *15*(31), 22–34.

Cosset, J. C., & Roy, J. (1991). The Determinants of Country Risk Ratings. *Journal of International Business Studies*, *22*(1), 135–142. doi:10.1057/palgrave.jibs.8490296

Deichmann, J. I. (2001). Distribution of Foreign Direct Investment among Transition Economies in Central and Eastern Europe. *Post-Soviet Geography and Economics*, *42*(2), 142–152. doi:10.1080/10889388.2001.10641167

Diamonte, R. L., Liew, J. M., & Stevens, R. L. (1996). Political Risk in Emerging and Developed Markets. *Financial Analysts Journal*, *52*(3), 71–76. doi:10.2469/faj.v52.n3.1998

Dornbusch, R., & Park, Y. C. (1995). *Financial Integration in a Second Best World: Are We Still Sure About Our Classical Prejudices*. Seoul, South Korea: Korea Institute of Finance.

Fanta, A. B. (2017). Bond Markets, Stock Markets, Banks and Growth: A System GMM Analysis. *Global Business and Economics Review*, *19*(1), 1–14. doi:10.1504/GBER.2017.080779

Fischer, B. (1995). Foreign Portfolio Equity Investment in Emerging Markets: A Panacea for Economic Development. *Savings and Development*, *19*(2), 149–173.

Garg, R., & Dua, P. (2014). Foreign Portfolio Investment Flows to India: Determinants and Analysis. *World Development*, *59*, 16–28. doi:10.1016/j.worlddev.2014.01.030

Harvey, C. H. (2004). Country Risk Components, the Cost of Capital, and Returns in Emerging Markets. In S. Wilkin (Ed.), *Country and Political Risk: Practical Insights for Global Finance* (pp. 71–102). London, UK: Risk Books. doi:10.2139srn.620710

Hayakawa, K., Kimura, F., & Lee, H. H. (2013). How Does Country Risk Matter for Foreign Direct Investment? *The Developing Economies*, *51*(1), 60–78. doi:10.1111/deve.12002

Hill, C. (2008). International Business: Competing in the Global Market Place. *Strategic Direction*, *24*(9). doi:10.1108d.2008.05624iae.001

Janicki, H. P., & Wunnava, P. V. (2004). Determinants of Foreign Direct Investment: Empirical Evidence from EU Accession Candidates. *Applied Economics*, *36*(5), 505–509. doi:10.1080/00036840410001682214

Jun, K., & Singh, H. (1996). The Determinants of Foreign Direct Investment in Developing Countries. *Transnational Corporations*, *5*(2), 67–105.

Kaur, M., & Dhillon, S. S. (2010). Determinants of Foreign Institutional Investors Investment in India. *Eurasian Journal of Business and Economics*, *3*(6), 57–70.

Kim, S. J., & Wu, E. (2008). Sovereign Credit Ratings, Capital Flows and Financial Sector Development in Emerging Markets. *Emerging Markets Review*, *9*(1), 17–39. doi:10.1016/j.ememar.2007.06.001

Li, S., & Filer, L. (2007). The Effects of the Governance Environment on the Choice of Investment Mode and the Strategic Implications. *Journal of World Business*, *42*(1), 80–98. doi:10.1016/j.jwb.2006.11.006

Libanio, G. A. (2005). Unit Roots in Macroeconomic Time Series: Theory, Implications and Evidence. *Nova Economia*, *15*(3), 145–176. doi:10.1590/S0103-63512005000300006

Mohan, T. T. R. (2006). Neither Dread nor Encourage Them. *Economic and Political Weekly*, *41*(2), 95–99.

Pal, P. (1998). Foreign Portfolio Investment in Indian Equity Markets: Has the Economy Benefited? *Economic and Political Weekly*, *33*(11), 589–598.

Parletun, J. (2008). *The Determinants of Foreign Direct Investment: A Regional Analysis with Focus on Belarus.* Retrieved October 2, 2019, from http://lup.lub.lu.se/luur/download?func=downloadFile&recordOId=1336912&fileOId=1646641

Pistoresi, B. (2000*). Investimenti diretti esteri e fattori di localizzazione: L'America Latina e il Sud Est asiatico.* Retrieved October 2, 2019, from http://www.rivistapoliticaeconomica.it/2000/feb.php

Portes, R., & Rey, H. (2005). The Determinants of Cross-Border Equity Flows. *Journal of International Economics*, *65*(2), 269–296. doi:10.1016/j.jinteco.2004.05.002

Porwal, A., Kumar, H., & Gupta, R. (2005). The Stock Market Volatility. *The Journal of Accounting and Finance*, *20*(1), 31–44.

Rai, K., & Bhanumurthy, N. R. (2004). Determinants of Foreign Institutional Investment in India: The Role of Return, Risk, and Inflation. *The Developing Economies*, *42*(4), 479–493. doi:10.1111/j.1746-1049.2004.tb00246.x

Richards, A. (2002). Big fish in small ponds: The momentum investing and price impact of foreign investors in Asian emerging equity markets. *Journal of Financial and Quantitative Analysis*, *40*(1), 1–27. doi:10.1017/S0022109000001721

Saraogi, R. (2008). *Determinants of FII Inflows: India.* Retrieved October 2, 2019, from https://mpra.ub.uni-muenchen.de/22850/

Shamsuddin, A. F. (1994). Economic Determinants of Foreign Direct Investment in Less Developed Countries. *Pakistan Development Review*, *33*(1), 41–51. doi:10.30541/v33i1pp.41-51

Singhania, M., & Gupta, A. (2011). Determinants of Foreign Direct Investment in India. *Journal of International Trade Law and Policy*, *10*(1), 64–82. doi:10.1108/14770021111116142

Srinivasan, P., & Kalaivani, M. (2013). Determinants of Foreign Institutional Investment in India: An Empirical Analysis. *Journal of Academic Research in Economics*, *5*(3), 361–375.

Taffler, R. J., & Abassi, B. (1984). Country Risk: A Model for Predicting Debt Servicing Problems in Developing Countries. *Journal of the Royal Statistical Society. Series A (General)*, *147*(4), 541–568. doi:10.2307/2981843

Tsai, P. L. (1994). Determinants of Foreign Direct Investment and Its Impact on Economic Growth. *Journal of Economic Development*, *19*(1), 137–163.

Upadhyay, S. (2006). FIIs in the Stock Market and the Question of Volatility. *Portfolio Organizer,* 22-30.

Wheeler, D., & Mody, A. (1992). International Investment Location Decisions: The Case of US Firms. *Journal of International Economics*, *33*(1-2), 57–76. doi:10.1016/0022-1996(92)90050-T

ADDITIONAL READING

Engle, R. F., & Granger, C. W. (1987). Co-Integration and Error-Correction: Representation, Estimation, and Testing. *Econometrica*, *55*(2), 251–276. doi:10.2307/1913236

Erokhin, V. (2016). *Global Perspectives on Trade Integration and Economies in Transition*. Hershey, PA: IGI Global. doi:10.4018/978-1-5225-0451-1

Greene, W. H. (2003). *Econometric Analysis*. Delhi: Pearson Education India.

Pesaran, M. H., & Pesaran, B. (1997). *Working with Micro Fit 4.0: Interactive Econometric Analysis*. Oxford: Oxford University Press.

Pesaran, M. H., & Shin, Y. (1999). An Autoregressive Distributed Lag Modelling Approach to Cointegration Analysis. *Econometric Society Monographs*, *31*, 371–413.

Pesaran, M. H., Shin, Y., & Smith, R. (2001). Bounds Testing Approaches to the Analysis of Level Relationships. *Journal of Applied Econometrics*, *16*(3), 289–326. doi:10.1002/jae.616

KEY TERMS AND DEFINITIONS

Corruption: Control of corruption weighs the influence exerted by private enterprises over public needs and inclination of public power in the hands of a few private individuals.

Country Risk: A risk related to investing in a particular country and the country's ability or inability to repay its financial obligations. It also highlights about the country's stability and profitability and lower risk of defaults on its payments.

Economic Risk: A risk related to the macroeconomic conditions of a country which has the likelihood to deter the foreign investments to the host country and decrease profit potential due to sudden changes in market.

Financial Risk: A risk that the foreign investors might lose their investments made in a host country due to the country's inability to repay or default on its sovereign debt.

Government Stability: It quantifies the government functioning in office and reduced risks of violence motivated by political interests. It also checks the independence of the government from social pressures from different political entities in the country.

Political Risk: A risk to foreign investors' investments which make it difficult for the host country to enable a conducive business environment due to the political instability or disruptions in state policies. Political risks make the investments of foreign investors unsafe due to the uncertain political prospects of the country of investment.

Trade Openness: An extent to which the host country is flexible and accessible to foreign investors for international trade.

Chapter 11
Empirical Analysis of Economic Cooperation:
An Evidence From MINT Economies

Kunal Dutta
https://orcid.org/0000-0003-3874-6126
Lovely Professional University, India

ABSTRACT

One of the crucial parts of globalization is the upsurge in the volume of Foreign Direct Investment (FDI) inflows across economies. Thus, it becomes inevitable for the mutual benefit of the countries among themselves as it promotes economic cooperation between them. Due to the favorable demography and increasing population size, MINT economies (Mexico, Indonesia, Nigeria, and Turkey) gain particular attention to FDI for GDP growth. Hence, this chapter analyzes the paramount determinants of GDP growth of MINT economies in the period of 2000-2019. To fulfill the purpose of the study, a linear regression model and pooled data analysis statistical technique are employed. GDP is taken as a dependent variable, while some key factors like inflation, unemployment, FDI, and trade openness are taken as independent variables.

INTRODUCTION

Immediate after the collapse of the Bretton woods system, a flexible or floating exchange system affects the entire world in both positive and negative aspects and seeks the attention of many researchers to investigate their impact over various economic trading blocs (Asteriou, Masatci, & Pılbeam, 2016). Regional Trade Agreement (RTA) covers more than half of international today, operating alongside global multilateral trade agreements under the World Trade Organization (WTO) in which there was an emergence of reducing the limits of tariffs and non-tariffs barriers among countries to boost the trade regarding tangible and non-tangible goods. The sole objective of creating RTA was to reduce the obstacles in the way of globalization and also to make trading nations benefited out of it. The instances of European

DOI: 10.4018/978-1-7998-1730-7.ch011

Union, NAFTA, ASEAN free trade agreements have shown the positive impact of promoting free trade among them and strengthen the economies in terms of socially, politically and economically (Erokhin, 2017; Prabhakar, 2016). Free trade has not only benefited in terms of boosting trade cooperation rather it also extends welfare in the society by removing the cap of high prices in terms of taxes imposed over products imported or exported (Erokhin, 2016a). On the contrary, considerably ignorance was faced by small or least developed economies of the world reason being finding themselves self-insufficient in terms of resources available for carrying out trade with rich countries (Erokhin, 2016b). Even though the RTA has contributed much to the overall growth among small and less developed countries due to removal or concessions on tariffs, which directly benefited them. Regional Trade Agreement ensures the deeper integration which can act as a model of sustained growth in terms of trade and GDP.

The current study aims at focusing on MINT which is an acronym stands for Mexico, Indonesia, Nigeria, and Turkey came into light during 2001 and was firstly coined by Fidelity Worldwide Investment. MINT economies, located at four different continents, are considering as an emerging powerhouse after the BRICS due to many favorable demographic features as well as political and economic stability. A fast-growing young population, natural resource availability, neighbor of developed countries and so on. These advantages drive them equally competitive to the rest of the economic or trading blocs by overpowering the BRICS in forthcoming.

In these economies Turkey has an advantage of having near boundaries to the edge of European economies which may give a boost in trade among them whereas, Mexico is also considered as strongest economy in Latin America strategically situated between South America and the US with ever-growing exports out of which 75 percent alone is towards the US alone which pushes the GDP of Mexican country. Indonesia and Nigeria are also considered to be ever fast-growing economies because of their natural raw material availability with them. In the case of Indonesia is well in the commodity production industry with ever-increasing demand, on contrary to this in case of Nigeria, is still well known and most notable economy among all African countries regarding geographical advantage over rest (Lenee & Oki, 2017). As per the current scenario, nowadays foreign direct investment (FDI) is more inclined towards developing and fast-moving economies than developed economies. There is a big shift of FDI to developing countries that have been witnessed in the last few years back due to several reasons. Since the MINT has emerged as a popular destination of FDI, investigating the indispensable factors involve in attracting FDI becomes a paramount priority.

The efforts have been made to identify the potential investment done by foreign companies among MINT nations and to predict the growth rate in the coming years, data for FDI inward between 1990 and 2019 is taken. Large population, market size, natural resource availability, trade openness are some prominent key factors used as an independent variable to estimate the value of dependent variables that is FDI inflow and helped in checking the trade pattern along with economic cooperation among MINT nations. For fulfilling the purpose of the study, the linear regression model and pooled data, the statistical technique has been employed and the nature of data is on a secondary basis gathered from the World Bank data set.

BACKGROUND

MINT has emerged as the powerful area after BRICS as per the data suggested in the world bank and there is unleashed potential which is yet to explore and moreover many pieces of literature suggested many views like, Asongu and Kodila-Tedika (2015) tried identifying the ever growth in emerging economies like BRICS and MINT due to inward FDI. In their findings, the first thing was FDI benefits of GDP growth which was more apparent in economies with higher levels of FDI. GDP output positively impacting FDI and the last one is the effect of trade-openness which has a Kuznets shape for Gross FDI and upsurge in a tendency for Net FDI. The data have Wiradanti been gathered from the United Nations Development Program (UNDP) and the World Bank websites for theory justification. Durotoye (2014) looked extensively into the economic prospects and potential for MINT economies by focusing on the youth of Mexico, Indonesia, Nigeria, and Turkey as the population of these economies may act as an asset for MINT as emerging economies if used productively. Accordingly, the demographic features of these four nations help them to gain the world's attention and may become the best destination for foreign companies. Francesco and Ardita (2015) discussed the major factors impacting MINT economies' growth. Trade, FDI, young population, strategic geographical position and a plentiful supply of raw material are the most convincing factors for pushing up the economies of Mexico, Indonesia, Nigeria, and Turkey. The data show the remarkable growth expected for the MINT over the forthcoming years. Kokotović and Kurečić (2016) investigated the study and found that MINT nations can never become an alternate of BRICS because of various reasons such as lack of geographical area, political, economic and military instability. Besides many hindrances, MINT countries emerged as powerful countries in terms of abundance of natural resource availability, favorable demography and to prove this a regression model, where GDP is considered as dependent variable and FDI, household consumption and government consumption are taken as independent variables and on the basis of that analysis it was found that FDI hasn't played a crucial role in the overall economic growth of MINT nations. Wiradanti, Pettit, Potter, Abouarghoub, and Beresford (2016) analyzed the prospective trade growth of developing countries with special emphasize over Mexico and Indonesia. The author identified the lack of trade-related infrastructure especially through ports as it could enhance the trade between the nations. The author tried fetching the results through trend patterns, focused more on their major trading partner and also identified their major ports and best possible solutions for better infrastructure. Asteriou et al. (2016) assessed the impact of exchange rate volatility on MINT economies international trade and found no linkage between each other and the results are proved with the help of GARCH models for both nominal and real effective exchange rate data. Indonesia and Mexico had witnessed the existing causal relationship between exchange rate volatility and international trade, unlike Nigeria and Turkey. Satoglu (2017) opined the role of Outward and Inward FDI into the MINT economies' overall growth apart from other factors responsible for development. In the study, it has been observed that during the years 1990-2013, there was ever an increase in the growth of MINT economies due to upsurge in FDI inflows. To identify the change, IDP (Investment Development Path) theory has been used for empirical analysis and found MINT at the 2nd stage of IDP theory and considered as the second most fast-growing economies after BRICS. A panel regression model has been employed for a more refined result. Lenee and Oki (2017) argued that the significant factor in improving the overall growth of MINT economies was development in the capital market. The study thus focuses on how capital market development as a subset of financial development has directly translated to the economic growth of the MINT from 2000 to 2012. Panel dataset comprising capital market activity variables of market capitalization ratio to gross domestic product (GDP), number of listed securities and value of transactions as ratios of GDP and gross fixed capital formation respectively; with key economic growth indicators of change in GDP, gross domestic savings relative to GDP and gross fixed capital formation relative to GDP has been used. The outcome shows that the amount of listed securities is the most impacting capital market development measure on the economic growth of the MINT as a group. Asongu and Odhiambo (2018) explored several other key factors playing a prominent role in the overall increase in the GDP of MINT and BRICS economies together. The result found that Net Foreign Direct Investment, Natural Resource availability, and Political Stability have a positive and important influence on the rate of growth of real GDP. To assess the determinants for the growth rate for the period 2001-2011, an instrumental variable (IV) quantile regression approach is applied along with Two-Stage-least Squares and IV Least Absolute deviations has been used.

Based on a study done, it has been observed that there were very few analytic papers have focused on the determinants of growth of MINT economies. The current study has filled the gap by providing evidence through empirical analysis done. To overcome these gaps, the trend and pattern of GDP as a measure of growth is carried out.

MAIN FOCUS OF THE CHAPTER

Research Methodology

This study aims at analyzing the economic cooperation among MINT economies for which, both primary and secondary data is used. The secondary data have been taken from various authentic sources like World Bank, World Trade Organization (WTO), United Nations Conference on Trade and Development (UNCTAD), UNComtrade, International Monetary Fund (IMF), and Trade Map. Diversification, similarity index of Mexico, Indonesia, Nigeria, and Turkey for exports and imports both and OLS regression model are employed and the empirical analysis statistical measure such as a Linear Regression model is used for ....

A descriptive and associative or explanatory type of research design has been used to identify the desired results. Descriptive research is conducted to describe the general statistical conditions of each variable for research purposes. The reason for employing associative research is to find how the changes in growth in terms of economic cooperation or overall development can be happened by analyzing the impact of independent variables on dependent variables. Thus, explanatory research targets to analyze and exaggerate the effect of FDI determinants (independent variables) on FDI (dependent variable) inflows to MINT countries.

Table 1 reveals various demographic features of four emerging economies i.e. Mexico, Indonesia, Nigeria, and Turkey. Various indicators have been gathered from various official websites like World Bank, UNESCO, and UNDP, etc.

In comparison to Mexico and Indonesia, Nigeria and Turkey hold lesser land surface areas whereas Turkey has the lowest population size on contrary to the three nations. The majority of the population are in the age between 15 to 64 belongs to the working group and contributes more to overall GDP. On the counterpart, the GDP is still less than the rest of the trading blocs like BRICS, BIMSTIC nations, etc., but Indonesia and Turkey have shown an upsurge in their overall GDP percentage growth n compared to the rest of the three.

In Table 2, the first column shows the contribution of agriculture and related sectors to the overall GDP of the four MINT economies. Accordingly, Nigeria has the largest contribution to the agriculture sector in comparison to the rest of the countries. Contrary to it, Mexico has the least contribution to GDP through the agriculture sector. Indonesia and Nigeria show more dependent on the agriculture sector for their growth. In the second column, the contribution of the manufacturing and industrial sector

Table 1. Different demographic features of MINT economies

Parameters	Year	Mexico	Indonesia	Nigeria	Turkey
Land area, km^2	2018	1,923,040	1,904,569	923,763	783,562
Population, thousand people	2018	126,190.79	267,663.43	195,874.74	82,319.72
Share of population in the age of 65 and above, percent of the total population	2018	7	5	3	8
Share of population in the age of 15-64, percent of the total population	2018	67	68	53	67
GINI Index	2018	45.90	45.70	39.00	39.80
Life expectancy, years	2018	77.30	69.40	53.90	76.00
Adult (15-24 years) literacy, percent of the total population	2016	99	100	76	100
HDI Rank	2018	74	116	157	64
HDI Value	2018	0.774	0.694	0.532	0.791
GDP growth rate, percent	2018	1.9	5.1	5.1	2.5
GDP per capita, current price	2018	9,698.1	3,893.6	2,028.2	9,311.4

Source: Author's development based on the United Nations Conference on Trade and Development [UNCTAD] (2019) and World Bank (2019)

is represented to the overall GDP of MINT economies. Indonesia is leading in this regard compared to next to its partners because of having more availability of raw materials followed by Mexico, Turkey, and Nigeria. In the case of the third column, the contribution of the service sector is the highest among all other sectors in all four MINT economies. Mexico has taken the lead because of boundaries with the USA and Canada which has given an advantage to this country. In general, all nations are getting more benefited in-service sector for the growth of their respective economies.

Table 3 shows the ratio of export and import to the overall GDP of Mexico, Indonesia, Nigeria and Turkey in 2013-2018. In the case of exports, Mexico has the highest rate whereas Nigeria has the fewest rates with ever falling. Indonesia and Turkey remain roughly the same. On the other hand, in the case of imports, again Mexico has the highest rate of imports with the least import rate partner, Nigeria.

Table 2. Sector-wise percentage share in GDP

Year	Agriculture, forestry, and fishing, value-added, percent of GDP				Industry (including construction), value-added, percent of GDP				Service, value-added, percent of GDP			
	Mexico	Indonesia	Nigeria	Turkey	Mexico	Indonesia	Nigeria	Turkey	Mexico	Indonesia	Nigeria	Turkey
2013	3.13	13.35	20.75	6.72	31.85	42.63	25.74	27.69	61.10	41.51	52.36	53.17
2014	3.13	13.33	19.99	6.58	31.49	41.92	24.64	28.19	60.19	42.24	54.15	53.65
2015	3.19	13.49	20.63	6.90	30.01	40.04	20.16	27.90	61.00	43.30	58.12	53.30
2016	3.34	13.47	20.98	6.18	29.50	39.30	18.17	28.18	60.88	43.64	59.78	53.76
2017	3.38	13.15	20.84	6.08	30.70	39.38	22.31	29.15	60.36	43.60	55.80	53.36
2018	3.34	12.80	21.19	5.76	31.15	39.73	23.88	29.43	60.24	43.41	52.00	54.31

Source: World Bank (2019)

Table 3. Overall trade of Mexico, Indonesia, Nigeria, and Turkey in 2013-2018

Year	Exports of goods and services, percent of GDP				Imports of goods and services, percent of GDP			
	Mexico	Indonesia	Nigeria	Turkey	Mexico	Indonesia	Nigeria	Turkey
2013	31.305	23.923	18.049	22.272	32.459	24.713	12.998	28.078
2014	31.892	23.665	18.435	23.764	33.071	24.414	12.450	27.649
2015	34.563	21.160	10.656	23.345	36.602	20.777	10.790	25.953
2016	37.101	19.088	9.218	21.965	39.072	18.332	11.504	24.850
2017	37.634	20.188	13.171	24.804	39.441	19.174	13.176	29.317
2018	39.223	20.965	-	29.612	41.099	22.055	-	30.790

Source: Author's development based on World Bank (2019) and UNCTAD (2019)

Turkey and Indonesia once again got a tie for import ratio in their overall GDP. Globalization of trade openness can be easily seen through the above data which ultimately shows the economic cooperation and emerging powers.

In Table 4, diverse indicators are taken into consideration to assess the status of economic development in Mexico, Indonesia, Nigeria, and Turkey.

In 2013, Turkey was at the top of the list for the highest GDP, 8.49 percent with a gradual fall till 2018 that is 2.56 percent. The reason behind the same was the excessive current account deficit in 2018. The same situation can be seen in the case of Nigeria. Since 2015, there has been a drastic fall in GDP due to lower oil revenues and a shortage of hard currencies. Whereas, Mexico's GDP remained very low between 1 percent to 3 percent only. Heavy reliance over the imports for machinery and agriculture makes economic growth a bit slow. In the case of inflation, Turkey has had the highest level of inflation since 2013. The inflation rate in Mexico has been increasing gradually and remaining almost under control. Nigeria and Turkey, on the contrary, were hit badly due to the consistent hike in the price level. Looking at the unemployment level, Turkey has the highest rate of unemployment due to slowing down of economic growth and the rise in the participation of the labor force, whereas, the remaining three nations remained roughly the same. Another growth indicator that is FDI also played a crucial role in the overall growth of MINT economies. Mexico and Nigeria got an advantage in terms of investment through

Table 4. Macroeconomic variables of MINT nations from 2013 to 2018

Years	GDP				Inflation				Unemployment				FDI			
	M	I	N	T	M	I	N	T	M	I	N	T	M	I	N	T
2013	1.35	5.55	6.67	8.49	1.52	4.96	4.96	6.26	4.91	4.33	3.70	8.73	4.73	2.32	5.56	1.35
2014	2.80	5.00	6.30	5.16	4.42	5.44	4.66	7.42	4.80	4.04	4.43	9.88	3.14	2.51	4.65	1.33
2015	3.28	4.87	2.65	6.08	2.78	3.98	2.86	7.82	4.31	4.51	5.31	10.23	3.71	1.97	3.13	1.92
2016	2.92	5.03	-1.6	3.13	5.35	2.43	9.54	8.09	3.85	4.30	6.23	10.83	3.6	4.54	4.44	1.39
2017	2.06	5.06	0.80	7.41	6.76	4.27	11.11	10.84	3.42	4.18	6.01	10.81	3.1	2.05	3.49	1.15
2018	1.99	5.17	1.93	2.56	5.29	3.83	10.23	16.15	3.28	4.30	6.02	10.89	3.46	2.01	-	1.30

Note: M – Mexico; I – Indonesia; N – Nigeria; T – Turkey
Source: World Bank (2019)

multinational companies, unlike Indonesia and Tukey. During 2018, there was no foreign investment in Nigeria due to widespread corruption, political instability, lack of transparency, and poor quality of infrastructure which restricted the country's FDI potential and witnessed the fall in foreign investment.

In Table 5, the schedule reveals the trade share of Mexico, Indonesia, Nigeria, and Turkey with the rest of the world in 2013-2018 since the concept of MINT was coined.

To find out the research gap, the correlation, linear regression, and descriptive statistics have been employed through statistical software (Table 6).

The value of mean and standard deviation is given for the selected macroeconomic variables like GDP, inflation, unemployment, FDI, and trade (Table 7).

In case of the coefficient of correlation, the values show the nature and strength of various economic factors among themselves. According to Karl Pearson's coefficient of correlation, as the authors tried establishing a relationship between GDP and the remaining variables, it can be seen that GDP and inflation have a moderate negative correlation (-0.637). In the case of unemployment, the rate is (-0.584) which again reveals a negative weak correlation between GDP and unemployment. When it comes to FDI and GDP, both demonstrate a positive trend but have a weak correlation between each other. Accordingly, FDI undoubtedly has a positive impact over MINT country's overall GDP but the strength of the relationship is not so strong and hence does not provide a solid justification for the growth of GDP of MINT economies. Lastly, the strength between the GDPs of MINT economies is showing a strong positive correlation between each other and proved as an important factor for the upsurge of GDP (Table 8).

Table 5. Trade share of MINT with the world

Year	Mexico's trade with the world		Indonesia's trade with the world		Nigeria's trade with the world		Turkey's trade with the world	
	Import	Export	Import	Export	Import	Export	Import	Export
2013	50.08	49.91	50.55	49.44	32.97	67.02	62.37	37.62
2014	50.19	49.8	50.3	49.69	31.02	68.97	60.57	39.42
2015	50.94	49.05	48.69	51.3	41.12	58.87	59.02	40.97
2016	50.86	49.13	48.42	51.57	51.69	48.3	58.22	41.77
2017	50.65	49.34	48.17	51.82	41.52	58.47	59.82	40.17
2018	50.75	49.24	51.15	48.84	40.79	59.2	57.04	42.95

Source: World Bank (2019)

Table 6. Descriptive statistics

Variables	Mean	Std. Deviation
GDP	15.7767	4.68419
Inflation	25.1617	7.66484
Unemployment	27.1783	5.66655
FDI	11.1417	2.73089
Trade	189.12700	6.953060

Source: Author's development

Table 7. Correlations between the GDP of MINT countries and other variables

		GDP	Inflation	Unemployment	FDI	Trade
Pearson Correlation	GDP	1.000	-0.637	-0.584	0.309	0.702
	Inflation	-0.637	1.000	0.952	-0.712	-0.041
	Unemployment	-0.584	0.952	1.000	-0.847	-0.109
	FDI	0.309	-0.712	-0.847	1.000	0.092
	Trade	0.702	-0.041	-0.109	0.092	1.000
Sig. (1-tailed)	GDP	0.000	0.087	0.112	0.275	0.060
	Inflation	0.087	0.000	0.002	0.056	0.469
	Unemployment	0.112	0.002	0.000	0.017	0.419
	FDI	0.275	0.056	0.017	0.000	0.431
	Trade	0.060	0.469	0.419	0.431	0.000

Source: Author's calculation and SPSS result

Table 8. Residuals statistics

	Minimum	Maximum	Mean	Standard deviation
Predicted value	9.97970	20.23990	15.77670	4.52995
Residual	-0.96941	1.82006	0.000000	1.19215
Standard predicted value	-1.28000	0.98500	0.000000	1.00000
Standard residual	-0.36400	0.68300	0.000000	0.44700

Source: Author's calculation and SPSS result

In case of linear regression analysis, GDP of Mexico, Indonesia, Nigeria, and Turkey is considered as a dependent variable whereas factors like trade, inflation, FDI, and unemployment are considered independent variables. Therefore, it is found that the value of R square represents the goodness of fit, which means the independent variables can explain the change in the dependent variable i.e. in GDP by 93.5 percent (table 9). Collectively all those independent variables are good enough for explaining the total variation independent variables. The value of Durbin-Watson is near to 2 and shows a positive auto-correlation among the variables. Accordingly, the data show less autocorrelation.

Table 10 represents the regression between GDP as predicted variable and inflation, unemployment, FDI, and trade being considered as predictors.

Table 9. Model summary (dependent variable: GDP)

Model	R	R Square	Adjusted R square	The standard error of the estimate	Durbin-Watson
1	0.967	0.935	0.676	2.66572	1.535

Source: Author's calculation and SPSS result

Table 10. Regression coefficients between GDP and other independent variables

Model		Unstandardized coefficients		Standardized coefficients	t	Sig.	95.0per cent confidence interval for B	
		B	standard error	Beta			lower bound	upper bound
1	(Constant)	-57.383	47.965		-1.196	0.443	-666.839	552.073
	Inflation	-0.622	0.650	-1.017	-0.957	0.514	-8.880	7.637
	Unemployment	0.160	1.164	0.194	0.138	0.913	-14.628	14.948
	FDI	-0.542	1.026	-0.316	-0.528	0.691	-13.581	12.497
	Trade	0.478	0.178	0.710	2.683	0.227	-1.787	2.744

Source: Author's calculation and SPSS result

According to the above, the following equation can be drawn.

$$GDP = \alpha - \beta 1\ (Inflation) + \beta 2\ (Unemployment) - \beta 3\ (FDI) + \beta 4\ (Trade) + \varepsilon \qquad (1)$$

GDP = -57.383 – (0.622) Inflation + (0.160) Unemployment – (0.542) FDI + (0.478) Trade + ε

The coefficient values of independent variables are given like (-0.622 percent) for inflation which reveals the inverse relation between GDP and inflation. With 1per cent change in inflation, GDP gets negatively affected by (-0.622 percent). In the case of unemployment, with 1per cent change, GDP is positively influenced by 0.160 percent. Likewise, in the case of FDI, the evidence shows that FDI inflow does not have enough impact on GDP growth. With a 1 percent change in FDI, GDP gets negatively impacted with (-0.542 percent) and shows the emergence of more of good FDI in MINT economies. In the last, increasing trade or trade openness has a positive impact as by assuming 1per cent change in trade will have 0.47 percent of a proportional relationship.

SOLUTIONS AND RECOMMENDATIONS

The study allowed to reveal the major strengths and weaknesses of MINT economies, as well as to forecast future opportunities and threats (Table 11).

FUTURE RESEARCH DIRECTIONS

The study highlights the scope of Mexico, Indonesia, Nigeria, and Turkey in terms of unleashed potential which is yet to explore. There are only a few analytical papers that can be found over the MINT economy's growth in comparison with BRICS and other major trading blocs. The current study has focused on the growth of GDP with few of its macro variable determinants like inflation, trade openness, FDI and unemployment. Accordingly, the current explanatory is very limited to directly reach over the final result. MINT is just an acronym realized in 2013 which means the majority of the literature has been done within the past few years. Therefore, the study finds its limitation with limited selected variables carried out for the study.

Table 11. MINTs aggregate SWOT analysis

Strengths	Weaknesses
Favorable climate for investments	Inadequate infrastructure supply
Customs union with the European Union	Crimes and thefts
Demographic features	Unskilled labor
Stability of the political, financial and economic system	Corruption
Number of industrial parks and technological centers - North American Management	Inefficient state bureaucracy
Young population	Access to funding
Strategic geographical position	Politically, economically instability
Natural raw materials	
Opportunities	**Threats**
Where to invest Transports and storage; Water supply, sewerage systems; Agricultural products, fishery, forestry; Building; Electric energy, gas, steam, air conditioning; Tourist flows, Motor-vehicles	Tariffs and non-tariff barriers
	Exchange rate
	Resort to protectionist measures in case of international crisis
	Corruption
	Infrastructure shortage
What to sell Furniture, food products; Machinery and appliances; Building; Motor-vehicles, trailers, semitrailers; Clothing and textile products; Information and communication services	Excessive dependence on the oil sector
	Credit access
	Market access
	Government/Parliament disagreement on policies and reforms adoption

Source: Author's development

CONCLUSION

The analysis done with various techniques for finding out the overall growth of GDP for MINT countries has made it possible for making concluding remarks. Initially, the importance of regional trade was discussed by looking at the best examples in the world on the international level i.e. BRICS – Brazil, Russia, India, China, and South Africa. There have been few pieces of evidence found in the rich literature proving MINT prospects and predictions scope of trade. As of now, MINT economies are considered as emerging powers but with the evidence gathered it can be notably observed that MINT cannot overpower BRICS easily due to many reasons, including the size of population and territory. Emerging superpowers like India and China are the biggest competitors of MINT countries. With the assistance of data gathered from various genuine websites and with statistical software SPSS, it became possible to conclude the importance of unexplored potential of Mexico, Indonesia, Nigeria, and Turkey. There are a plethora of opportunities available for MINT nations to survive for a longer period and gain competitive advantages over other trading blocs.

ACKNOWLEDGMENT

I acknowledge the great contribution made by my parents, Supreme Lord Krishna, and finally to Dr. Gurpreet Kaur who always stands behind me to guide me in every aspect of research. The words are just not enough to acknowledge all of the above mentioned hence I owe them respect and gratitude from the core of my heart.

REFERENCES

Asongu, S., & Kodila-Tedika, O. (2015). *Conditional Determinants of FDI in Fast Emerging Economies: An Instrumental Quantile Regression Approach.* Yaounde, Cameroon: African Governance and Development Institute.

Asongu, S., & Odhiambo, N. M. (2018). Drivers of Growth in Fast Emerging Economies: A Dynamic Instrumental Quantile Approach to Real Output and Its Rates of Growth in BRICS and MINT Countries, 2001-2011. *Applied Econometrics and International Development*, *18*(1), 5–22.

Asteriou, D., Masatci, K., & Pılbeam, K. (2016). Exchange Rate Volatility and International Trade: International Evidence from the MINT Countries. *Economic Modelling*, *58*, 133–140. doi:10.1016/j.econmod.2016.05.006

Durotoye, A. (2014). The MINT Countries as Emerging Economic Power Bloc: Prospects and Challenges. *Developing Country Studies*, *15*(4), 99–106.

Erokhin, V. (Ed.). (2016a). *Global Perspectives on Trade Integration and Economies in Transition.* Hershey, PA: IGI Global. doi:10.4018/978-1-5225-0451-1

Erokhin, V. (2016b). Rising Economic Powers among Economies in Transition: Is There Enough Space on the Global Market? In V. Erokhin (Ed.), *Global Perspectives on Trade Integration and Economies in Transition* (pp. 1–25). Hershey, PA: IGI Global. doi:10.4018/978-1-5225-0451-1.ch001

Erokhin, V. (2017). How to Shape the Market: China's One Belt One Road Initiative. In M. Malovic, & K. Roy (Eds.), *The State and the Market in Economic Development: In Pursuit of Millennium Development Goals* (pp. 144–156). Brisbane, Australia: The IIDS Australia Inc.

Francesco, S., & Ardita, T. (2015). Markets' Globalization and Emerging Economies. MINTs Economic Growth: Developments and Prospects. *International Journal of Business and Commerce*, *5*(2), 38–55.

Kokotović, F., & Kurečić, P. (2016). The MINT Countries: A Regression Analysis of the Selected Economic Features. *International Journal of Management Science and Business Administration*, *5*(2), 21–31.

Lenee, T. L., & Oki, J. (2017). Capital Market Development and Economic Growth: Evidence from the MINT Countries. *Journal of Economic and Sustainable Development*, *8*(2), 68–107.

Prabhakar, A. C. (2016). Trade and Economic Integration in BRICS: Towards Multi-Polarity. In V. Erokhin (Ed.), *Global Perspectives on Trade Integration and Economies in Transition* (pp. 45–57). Hershey, PA: IGI Global. doi:10.4018/978-1-5225-0451-1.ch003

Satoglu, E. B. (2017). Emerging through Foreign Investment: Investment Development Path Estimation of MINT Economies. *Advances in Economics and Business*, *5*(5), 256–264. doi:10.13189/aeb.2017.050503

United Nations Conference on Trade and Development. (2019). *Statistics Database* [Data file]. Retrieved October 3, 2019, from http://unctad.org/en/Pages/Statistics.aspx

Wiradanti, B., Pettit, S., Potter, A., Abouarghoub, W., & Beresford, A. (2016). Trends in Trade and Port Development of Rising Economies: Mexico and Indonesia. In *Proceedings of Logistics Research Network (LRN) Conference*. Hull: Chartered Institute of Logistics and Transport.

World Bank. (2019). *Global Economic Prospects, June 2019: Heightened Tensions, Subdued Investment*. Washington, DC: World Bank.

ADDITIONAL READING

Adeolu, D. (2013). The MINT Countries as Emerging Economic Power Bloc: Prospects and Challenges. *Developing Country Studies*, *15*(4), 99–106.

Barker, A. T. (2014). MINT Countries: How "Sweet" is Their Future? *California Business Review*, *2*(3), 39–46. doi:10.18374/CBR-2-3.6

Campanelli, G., Lee, J.-W., & Petri, P. (2009). *Developing Indicators for Regional Economic Integration and Cooperation*. Brugge: United Nations University.

Göstas Escobar, A., & Fanbasten, N. (2016). *Determinants of Foreign Direct Investment: A Panel Data Analysis of the MINT countries*. Uppsala: Uppsala University.

Gryczka, M. (2018). MINT Countries as Possible Rising Stars in the Global Economy – Benchmarking with BRICS Countries. *Acta Scientiarum Polonorum. Oeconomia*, *17*(3), 23–31.

Linn, J. F., & Pidufala, O. (2008). *The Experience with Regional Economic Cooperation Organizations: Lessons for Central Asia*. Washington, DC: Wolfensohn Center for Development.

Nnaji, C.E., Moses, N., Chimah, J., & Maduekwe, M.C. (2016). The Energy Intensity of Economic Sectors in MINT Countries: Implications for Sustainable Development. *IRA – International Journal of Management and Social Sciences*, *4*(1), 215-229.

KEY TERMS AND DEFINITIONS

BRICS: An acronym termed as Brazil, Russia, India, China, and South Africa. They are having a regional trade agreement with each other.

Foreign Direct Investment: The investment in the host economy for promoting trade among the nations of the globe.

Globalization: The openness of economies made it possible to improve their terms of trade and become more globalized and make counties together for mutual benefit.

Gross Domestic Product: A total money value of all goods and services produced within an accounting year within domestic territory.

Linear Regression: A model used for figuring out or to estimate the change independent variable and to get predicted values.

MINT: An acronym termed as Mexico, Indonesia, Nigeria, and Turkey.

Pooled Data: A mixture of cross-sectional and time-series data.

Regional Trade Agreement: An agreement between the regions to promote trade on a comparative advantage basis.

Chapter 12
Effects of Economic and Political Risks on Foreign Direct Investment:
A Panel Data Analysis in MENA Region

Souhaila Kammoun
University of Sfax, Tunisia

Youssra Ben Romdhane
University of Sfax, Tunisia

Marwa Ben Salem Fakhfakh
University of Sfax, Tunisia

ABSTRACT

The chapter identifies the main determinants of FDI and the factors that constitute the main obstacles to foreign investment attractiveness in a region affected by economic and political instability and even conflict and where investors may face a multitude of political, economic, and security risks. The sample includes 14 Arab countries over the period of 2003-2017. To determine the factors that explain the probability of attracting investment inflows in MENA countries, the study uses a multiple regression model to estimate data in a time series. The authors also use the World Bank's governance indicators to assess the quality of the Arab institutional framework. The results of the panel data estimates through three different regressions reveal that macroeconomic instability combined with political instability constitutes an obstacle to investment. On practical implications, the study suggests that, in general, economic managers should take some economic policy measures to reduce or mitigate risks to encourage foreign investors to invest in MENA countries.

DOI: 10.4018/978-1-7998-1730-7.ch012

INTRODUCTION

Since the 1980s, foreign direct investment (FDI) flows have become a key growth driver for developing countries. In this context, several studies have focused on the determinants of foreign direct investment and several questions have arisen to provide some clarification on this matter.

Many researches on the subject show that FDI has a positive overall effect on the economy (Alfaro, Chanda, Kalemli-Ozcan, & Sayek, 2004; Borensztein, De Gregorio, & Lee, 1998; Erokhin, 2016a, 2016b, 2017; Prabhakar, 2016, 2017, 2018; Gupta, Kangur, Papageorgiou, & Wane, 2014; Li & Liu, 2005). Indeed, the role of FDI is becoming increasingly important, since it contributes significantly to host countries' economic growth and development. Large flows of FDI are now a feature of the globalized economy and policymakers are competing to attract long-term investment. In recent decades, FDI flows to host countries have increased, particularly, in countries that have undertaken economic and political reforms and have seen their economies become more open to international trade. More specifically, FDI provides recipient countries with the capital flows, technological know-how, human capital development, and management skills necessary for sustainable economic development. FDI provides valuable capital to stimulate economic growth and development and thus enables the transfer of technology and knowledge to host countries.

Nevertheless, if several researchers have explained the determinants of FDI in stable and developing countries, only few studies have examined the relationship between FDI and macroeconomic aggregates in a context of political uncertainty, an issue which remains underexplored. In this context, some scholars have shown that there is a negative correlation between incoming FDI flows and the number of strikes, corruption, political stability and the quality of legislation (Schneider & Frey, 1985; Wheeler & Mody, 1992). Further, other studies have shown that political uncertainty has negative effects for some countries by discouraging savings and foreign direct investment by destroying trade with other countries (Ades & Chua, 1997). From the perspective of Arunatilake, Jayasuriya, and Kelegama (2001), political instability has economic costs such as lost income due to reduced domestic and foreign investment. Fosu (1992) also studied the effect of political instability on growth in Sub-Saharan African countries and the results of the study confirmed that political instability has a negative impact on economic growth. In the Franco-Prussian example of Devereux and Smith (2007), the effect of wars on production and consumption movements was considered mandatory to adapt to German and French macroeconomic history between 1871 and 1873.

Some other studies such as Abu-Bader and Abu-Qarn (2003), Aizenman and Glick (2006), and Deger (1986) have provided evidence of the negative effect of military spending on economic growth. Political uncertainty can lead to increased military spending, lower investment and also savings, which can hinder economic growth (Abu-Bader & Abu-Qarn, 2003; Arunatilake et al., 2001; Deger, 1986). In the Arab context, Ades and Chua (1997) noted that there were several countries that had suffered economic consequences due to political uncertainty, such as Jordan. Faced with political instability, the country suffered during the Gulf War (1990-1991) from the loss of tourism, falling exports, and a decline in gross domestic product (GDP). As a result, excessive government consumption reduces economic growth in the country (Barro, 1990; Grier & Tullock, 1989; Landau, 1983) and also excludes private investment (Argimón, González, & Roldán, 1997). FDI has increased significantly worldwide and that some emerging economies have been successful in attracting more FDI. Their empirical results confirm that a favorable institutional environment plays a key role in attracting foreign investment. In this context, such research on the economic, political, and institutional determinants of FDI is all the more relevant that many developing countries are generally characterized by economic and political instability, impunity for corruption, poor governance, and weak institutions. It can also be pointed out that the regional upheaval, which began in Tunisia and spread to some countries and left others in power such as Morocco and Jordan, is not without risk for the attractiveness of FDI. Nonetheless, if some of the MENA countries are not politically stable and suffer from corruption and poor governance quality, some others, in a politically stable area, have achieved a higher level of economic performance in recent years.

The overarching aim of this study is to identify the main determinants that influence the attractiveness of FDI in developing countries affected by economic and political instability. The empirical analysis purports to highlight the crucial barriers to foreign investment in order to help the economic managers to put in place economic policies that are of vital importance for attracting FDI in the MENA countries.

BACKGROUND

Literature review will provide a backdrop to the questions that have been raised in these research areas and will bring to the fore the relevance of economic and political stability related factors to explain the determinants of FDI in MENA region.

The first category of studies gives an economic explanation of FDI. Dunning (1973) focused on the relationship between FDI and several factors such as three types of explanatory factors: cost factors (inflation, labor, and production factors), business climate factors (political stability, democracy, debt levels), and market factors (size, growth). Sims (1994) and Laubach (2009) represented the FDI as a variable under the control of national decision-makers. According to these authors, fiscal policy plays a very important role in determining future levels of inflation, taxation, and interest rates. Further, Jensen (2003) found that fiscal discipline has a positive effect on the efficiency of foreign direct capital.

The second category of studies investigates the effect of the exchange rate on FDI. Some scholars find that high exchange rate volatility can penalize FDI. Nonetheless, there is no clear direction between exchange rate volatility and foreign direct investment (Kosteletou & Liargovas, 2000).

The last category of studies links the investment activity with economic and political factors. Schneider and Frey (1985) confirm that in estimating FDI flows in developing countries, it is necessary to take into account both economic and political factors in the host country of FDI. FDI is positively correlated with macroeconomic performance variables such as economic growth, inflation, and stock market performance. It is GDP that leads to FDI, but not the other way around. Asiedu (2002) uses panel data for 22 countries over the period 1984-2000 to examine the impact of natural resources, market size, government policies, political instability, and the quality of the host country's institutions on FDI to Africa. The study underlines that natural resources and large markets lower inflation, good infrastructure, an educated population, openness to FDI, less corruption, political stability, and a reliable legal system promote FDI. In the same vein, Sekkat and Veganzones-Varoudakis (2004) noted the relative importance of trade and exchange liberalization, infrastructure, and economic and political stability in the Euro-Mediterranean free trade area for FDI.

The importance of the FDI effect on economic growth has been supported by Alfaro et al. (2004) and Borensztein et al. (1998). Other research has shown that although foreign direct investment and domestic investment improve economic growth, FDI has a greater effect when it is reinforced by human capital capable of absorbing technologies provided by foreign investors (Borensztein et al., 1998; Li & Liu, 2005). Similarly, Dutta and Roy (2009) studied the interactive impact of corruption and human capital on

FDI and found that if a country's high corruption score becomes comparable to that of a low-corruption country, FDI inflows will increase by nearly 40% if the human capital stock increases.

Further, macroeconomic stability and the labour market of an economy have been identified in the literature as some of the main aspects that are analyzed by foreign investors before deciding for a future host country. The opposite impact is also mentioned by researchers who provide strong evidence supporting the hypothesis that FDI brings significant benefits to a country host. According to Jensen (2003), FDI facilitates the transfer of technological innovations and promotes employment and economic growth. There is an inverse relationship between the unemployment rate and the investment rate. The countries with higher unemployment rates have two major advantages for foreign investors, such as the abundance and availability of a low-wage labour force. However, other theories have confirmed that a high unemployment rate in a country is perceived by foreign investors as a signal of macroeconomic imbalance (Brozen, 1958). Botric and Škuflic (2006) used unemployment as macroeconomic indicator for countries and confirmed that foreign direct investment reduces the unemployment rate, recognizing that this relationship varies from country to country. As a result, the study of the interdependencies between FDI inflows and unemployment becomes of greatest importance for each country that shows increased interest in attracting FDI. In addition, FDI is represented as a very important source of management skills, jobs, and better-quality products and services. These investments improve the domestic market and export potential of their economy. FDI has been considered in recent years by developing countries as one of the best alternatives to fuel economic growth.

On the basis of the foregoing developments, the study will raise the two main questions: what are the implications of macroeconomic instability and political risks on FDI inflows in the MENA region? And what are the main determinants of FDI flows and the crucial barriers to FDI attractiveness in countries affected by economic instability and political and security risks?

MAIN FOCUS OF THE CHAPTER

Methodology and Econometric Model

This study uses multiple-regression model for the estimation of a time series data which represent both the dependent and independent variables. In order to identify the relevant explanatory variables of FDI in the MENA region in this context of macroeconomic and political instability, the authors use control variables such as macroeconomic variables, i.e. inflation rate, exchange rate, and unemployment rate. The authors also use the World Bank's governance indicators to assess the quality of the Arab institutional framework.

In the authors' econometric model, FDI inflows is modeled as a function of market size (*GDP*), GDP per capita (*GPDC*), exchange rate (*ExchR*), unemployment rate (*UnempR*), annual inflation rate (*InfR*), business freedom (*BusFree*), trade freedom (*TradFr*), financial freedom (*FinFr*), investment freedom (*InvFr*), monetary freedom (*MonFr*), political stability (*PolSt*), revolution index (*RevIn*), and corruption level (*CorrupL*). The study uses multiple-regression model to estimate the model by using ordinary least squared (OLS) technique. In order to normalize the distribution of the data, the authors take the natural logarithm (LN) of the following variables: FDI, GDP, GDP per capita, annual inflation rate, etc. The political risks related variables were used as either indexes or percentages. The multiple regression model to estimate the main determinants of FDI inflows has the following form:

$$LFDI_{i,t} = \beta_0 + \beta_1 LGPD_{i,t} + \beta_2 LGPDC_{i,t} + \beta_3 InfR_{i,t} + \beta_4 ExchR_{i,t} + \beta_5 UnempR_{i,t} +$$

$$\beta_6 BusFr_{i,t} + \beta_7 TradFr_{i,t} + \beta_8 FincFr_{i,t} + \beta_9 MonF_{i,t} + \beta_{10} InvFr_{i,t} + \beta_{11} PolSt_{i,t} +$$

$$\beta_{12} RevIn_{i,t} + \beta_{13} CorrpL_{i,t} + \varepsilon_t \qquad (1)$$

where:

β_0 – intercept or constant amount;

$\beta_1 - \beta_{13}$ – coefficients of the explanatory variables;

ε_t – error term.

Empirical Results

Descriptive Statistics

The corruption variable and revolution variable have lowest standard deviations of 0.45 and 0.52, respectively. The exchange rate variable has the highest mean and highest standard deviation of 185.19 and 545.01, respectively, while the inflation rate variable has also a highest mean and standard deviation of 83.91 and 31.78, respectively (Table 1).

Based on the summary statistics of the variables used in the study, the authors note that the standard deviation of the variables over this period is relatively small, particularly for the political stability related variable (1.50). Occasional observation shows that, in most cases, standard deviations are less than 10%, with the exception of *INF* (29.90) and *BF* (13.53). It is clear that the quality of the institutional framework is a major handicap for FDI inflows into the Arab region. Governance seems to be relatively better in countries as Bahrain, Jordan, Kuwait, Oman, Qatar, Tunisia, and the United Arab Emirates. In sum, the data show that MENA countries mainly suffer from a weak regulatory framework, a high level of corruption, and a low level of political stability. These indicators reflect a risk-prone area that hinders foreign investors despite the investment opportunities in MENA region.

This study adopts the linear model based on panel data with fixed effects (Olley & Pakes, 1996; Levinsohn & Petrin, 2003). This model controls the invariable heterogeneity over time between different countries and is relatively robust through omitted variables (Chamberlain, 1978; Hausman & Taylor, 1981).

Since the presence of individual effects is confirmed, it is necessary to determine how these effects should be modeled and which hypothesis to use: the fixed effects hypothesis or the random effects hypothesis. To find out which model to retain for our sample, the authors perform a Hausman specification test analysis to choose between fixed and random effect model. This test looks at whether the individual impacts are uncorrelated with different regresses in the model. If the null hypothesis is rejected, a fixed effect model is applied. However, after applying Hausman test, it is revealed that fixed effect is appropriate for this model. The hypothesis tested concerns the correlation between individual effects and explanatory variables. The results of the Hausman's test (Hausman & Taylor, 1981) give the statistic $X_2(13) = 122.423$. The P-value is below the 5% confidence level. Thus, the null hypothesis is rejected, and therefore, the authors use the fixed-effects model estimators that are unbiased (Table 2).

Table 1. Descriptive statistics, 2003-2017

	Mean	Std.Dev.	Skew.	Kurt.	J-Bera
ExchR	185.19	545.01	2.98	11.94	1321.32***
InfR	83.91	31.78	-0.86	4.94	53.25***
LGDP	1.78	1.53	-0.32	4.13	32.48***
LGDPC	1.58	1.23	-0.59	4.16	21.65***
UnempR	12.15	6.15	0.15	2.75	3.65
PolSt	-0.32	1.35	8.83	123.17	1564.46***
RevIn	0.59	0.52	-0.25	3.87	36.43***
LFDI	21.01	1.55	-1.19	6.26	132.16***
CorrupL	-0.24	0.45	0.39	3.49	4.53*
BusFr	65.95	12.57	-0.76	5.42	54.53***
MonFr	74.95	8.15	-1.38	5.49	126.18***
TradFr	63.87	16.39	-0.61	3.67	41.49***
InvF	46.93	16.64	-0.59	3.52	6.93*
FincFr	44.91	18.41	-0.58	5.54	5.43*

Note: ExchR – exchange rate; InfR – inflation rate; LGDP – GDP logarithm; LGDPC – per capita GDP logarithm; UnempR – unemployment rate; PolSt – political freedom; RevIn – revolution; LFDI – FDI logarithm; CorrupL – corruption; BusFr – business freedom; MonFr – monetary freedom; TradeFr – trade freedom; InvF – investment freedom; FincFr – financial freedom

Source: Authors' development

Table 2. Hausman test results

Test summary	Chi-Sq. Stat	Chi-Sq. d.f.	Prob.
Cross-section random	122.423	13	0.000

Source: Authors' development

Correlation Analysis

Correlation analysis is conducted before applying panel regression to measure the degree of multicollinearity among all the variables of the study. In this study, the correlation coefficient is used as a method to detect strength of linear association among the dependent and the independent variables. Results in Table 3 reveal that the highest correlation of 0.83 is between *LGPDC* and *LGPD*. But, overall, the correlation of all other independent variables is less than 0.80 which indicate that there is no multicollinearity among the independent variables. The correlation test helps to identify the most significant factors in the list of the independent variables (Gathogo & Ragui, 2014; Soleimani & Dnyanoba, 2017).

Panel Analysis Results

In order to determine the main factors that explain the probability of attracting FDI inflows in MENA countries, the authors perform many panel regressions. As it is well documented in the literature, the level of development is strongly correlated with the level of growth. Thus, this study first estimates all

Table 3. Correlation matrix

	ExchR	InfR	LGDP	LGDPC	UnempR	PolSt	RevIn	LFDI	CorrupL	BusFr	MonFr	TradFr	InvFr	FincFr
ExchR	1.00													
InfR	0.13	1.00												
LGDP	-0.02	-0.09	1.00											
LGDPC	-0.13	-0.17	0.83	1.00										
UnempR	-0.15	-0.06	0.13	0.21	1.00									
PolSt	-0.21	0.08	0.09	0.12	-0.04	1.00								
RevIn	0.22	0.02	-0.04	0.06	-0.03	-0.22	1.00							
LFDI	0.14	0.20	-0.06	-0.14	-0.07	-0.06	0.06	1.00						
CorrupL	-0.29	0.16	-0.23	-0.22	-0.44	0.32	-0.31	0.15	1.00					
BusFr	-0.16	0.09	-0.32	-0.31	-0.36	0.11	-0.13	-0.03	0.45	1.00				
MonFr	0.08	0.06	-0.21	-0.23	-0.27	0.07	-0.25	0.05	0.41	0.27	1.00			
TradFr	0.03	0.42	-0.09	-0.12	-0.32	0.03	-0.08	0.24	0.35	0.15	0.04	1.00		
InvFr	0.05	0.21	-0.32	-0.31	-0.03	0.13	0.04	0.05	0.21	0.36	0.15	0.08	1.00	
FincFr	0.29	0.36	-0.36	-0.45	-0.34	0.06	0.06	0.07	0.43	0.40	0.30	0.33	0.51	1.00

Source: Authors' development

the determinants of FDI's inflows (Model 1). Next, the authors estimate all the determinants of the FDI's inflows except *LGDP* (Model 2) since it represents a strong correlation with *LGDPC* variable. Then, the authors estimate all the determinants of FDI's inflows except *LGDPC* (Model 3) since it represents a strong correlation with *LGDP* variable.

Taken together, the results strongly suggest that the explanatory variables have the power to determine net FDI flows, as the *p*-values associated with *F*-statistics for regressions are indistinguishable from zero (it means that the coefficient is irrelevant) (Asiedu, 2002; Busse & Hefeker, 2007). The value of the Fisher statistic for the three models is 6.75, 6.47, and 6.85, respectively. This value, which gives the information on the overall significance of the model, is high with zero probability and means that the model is globally significant. The Model 1 displays the most significant determination coefficient (*R2*) with 0.58%. Results clearly indicate the presence of significant and positive relationship between economic, political, and institutional factors and FDI inflows in MENA countries during period of study. The analysis focus is to identify the main determinants of FDI and highlight the crucial barriers to foreign investment in MENA region. Panel regression results show that among market seeking factors, *LNGDP* show a significant and positive relationship with foreign direct investment. This result is consistent with the results of Mohamed and Sidiropoulos (2010) who illustrate that GPD contributes to the increase in FDI flows. GPD, as an accurate indication of an economy's size is, by far, the most widely accepted significant determinant of FDI flows. This implies that FDI is attracted to countries with large markets. Therefore, *LNGDPC* is significantly positively associated with foreign direct investment. *LNGDPC* appears also as a source of macroeconomic stability that the foreign investor needs.

Inflation rate is revealed to have a statistically significant positive relationship with FDI inflows at 1% level with *p*-value of 0.0584. This suggests that the inflation rate is a factor that economic managers should control to encourage more FDI inflows. This result is contrary to the findings of Asiedu (2002) and Koukpo (2005) who found that FDI flows are negatively correlated with the level of inflation. Therefore, policy makers must give importance to this variable and ensure monetary policies in order to absorb the negative impact of inflation rates and reduce its effects.

Real exchange rate appears to be negative and significant at 1% level with *p*-value of 0.052482. This implies that exchange rate depreciation has a negative influence on FDI inflows to the host country. It appears that the instability of this rate can hinder FDI inflows because it generates uncertainty in the financial plan of foreign investors. Real exchange rate is also an important element for policy makers. A summary of the results of the panel data estimates is presented in Table 4 through three different regressions.

The unemployment rate variable has negative and significant effect on FDI inflows. The negative effect of this variable would be due to inadequate training programs. Despite a series of reforms, MENA has remained stuck in a low-learning, low-skills level. The current situation in MENA requires a renewed focus on education in order to prepare students for a productive future and therefore to ensure that training programs meet the needs of foreign expectations. A highly skilled and competitive workforce can be a key element in attracting FDI and thus promoting foreign investors' choice of location.

Other variables that influence foreign direct investment in MENA region are the variables related to political risks factors. Results indicate the presence of significant and negative relationship between the political risks factors related variables (i.e. political stability, revolution, and corruption) and FDI inflows in MENA countries during the period of study. These results imply that countries with an unstable political situation will be a major disincentive for foreign investors. Related to political stability is the level of corruption and quality of institutions. In fact, weak institutions promote corruption, which,

Table 4. Panel data analysis: estimation of the fixed-effects model

Variable	Model 1	Model 2	Model 3
C	19.85123***	20.352485***	22.54875***
BusFr	-0.049624***	-0.056231***	0.039524
ExchR	-0.052482*	-0.005482**	-0.005698*
UnempR	-0.284759**	-0.076325*	-0.059632*
CorrupL	-0.284167**	-0.315384*	0.365982
FincFr	-0.054824	-0.025418*	-0.025486
InvFr	0.058475	0.035856	0.025687*
InfR	0.058468*	0.006895**	0.006985
LGDP	0.462584***		0.448652***
LGDPC	0.287513**	0.256248**	
MonFr	-0.056321	-0.056984	-0.0369574
RevIn	-0.185374**	-0.254876*	0.305842
PolSt	-0.156941***	0.058472*	0.039584
TradFr	0.018625***	0.035624***	0.038547***
R-squared	0.581257	0.398547	0.4412587
F-statistic	6.75896***	6.475865***	6.852147***
DW	1.285324	1.269541	1.275145

Note: Model 1 refers to the estimation of all determinants of FDI, model 2 refers to the estimation of all FDI determinants except the LGDP variable since it represents a strong correlation with that of the LGDPC variable and model 3 refers to the estimation of all determinants of FDI

Source: Authors' development

in turn, leads to higher investment costs and consequently lower investor profits. The authors conclude that political stability associated with institutional quality is a key determinant for several reasons. First, political stability, low corruption levels and trust in institutions provide confidence to foreign investors and make business and investment climate more conducive to MNEs. Second, institutional quality and political stability could lead to higher economic growth, which should attract FDI inflows. Third, the high sunk cost of FDI makes investors very sensitive to political risk factors, uncertainty and corruption that can result from poor quality institutions.

Free trade is positive and significant at 10%. This result indicates that free trade and economic openness of countries can be analyzed as an important factor in stimulating foreign investment in the region. Indeed, when a country is open to international trade, and where the volume of trade is significant, foreign investors can be better informed about local conditions. This study reveals the insignificance of monetary freedom, financial freedom and freedom of investment. As a result, MENA countries must strengthen their global position in these fields by improving their position in the external market. To conclude, these results can have several implications for policy makers. Therefore, policy makers should strengthen investment policy frameworks in order to compensate for risks faced by investors in MENA region.

SOLUTIONS AND RECOMMENDATIONS

The aim of the present research was three-fold. The first aim was to identify the main determinants of FDI in MENA countries. The study empirically examines the economic, political and institutional determinants of FDI inflows in MENA countries. The study conducts multiple-regression model for the estimation of a time series data. The sample comprises fourteen Arab countries over the period 2003-2017. The second aim was to deduce the crucial barriers to invest in this region. The empirical results demonstrate that macroeconomic stability and political stability are two important factors in the attractiveness of FDI which implies that political instability combined with macroeconomic instability constitutes the major barriers to investment decisions in MENA region. The barriers can be divided into three factors; economic factors (effect of macroeconomic variables and exchange rate on FDI), political risks related factors (political stability, revolution/Arab Spring and corruption level), and institutional factors. The third aim was to identify some implications for policy makers and the action necessary to attract FDI in the region. The study suggests that economic managers should take some economic policy measures in order to reduce or mitigate risks to investors and promote investment in MENA region.

FUTURE RESEARCH DIRECTIONS

Many studies have provided evidence that FDI can convey great advantages to host countries and can have important positive effects on their development efforts and economic growth. In relation to FDI in MENA region, future research could examine the impact of various explanatory organizational and country-level variables on the volume of direct investment. A hypothesis about the significant role of the quality of institutions to attract FDI in MENA region should be investigated and tested.

CONCLUSION

The study found positive and significant impact from market size variables on FDI inflows which mean that MENA countries can attract more FDI by increasing GDP per capita and GDP growth rate. Results also indicate that inflation control can attract FDI inflows as it reflects macroeconomic stability. Moreover, the results display a negative relationship between FDI and exchange rate and between FDI and unemployment rate. Therefore, results show that business freedom, financial freedom, and monetary freedom have negative and significant effect in attracting FDI inflows to MENA economies. It implies that enhancing trade freedom by relaxing trade barriers and increasing preferential trade agreements would attract more FDI. Therefore, the development level of financial institutions and business freedom is vital because they facilitate the financial services to MNEs. The results confirm that institutional quality performance variables, government stability, and investment freedom are important elements in attracting FDI inflows in host countries. This research will be useful for policy makers as it clearly identifies a set of actions necessary to attract FDI.

REFERENCES

Abu-Bader, S., & Abu-Qarn, A. S. (2003). Causality Evidence from Egypt, Israel, and Syria Government Expenditures, Military Spending and Economic Growth. *Journal of Policy Modeling*, *25*(6-7), 567–583. doi:10.1016/S0161-8938(03)00057-7

Ades, A., & Chua, H. (1997). The Neighbor's Curse: Regional Instability and Economic Growth. *Journal of Economic Growth*, *2*(3), 279–304. doi:10.1023/A:1009782809329

Aizenman, J., & Glick, R. (2006). Military Expenditure, Threats, and Growth. *The Journal of International Trade & Economic Development*, *15*(2), 129–155. doi:10.1080/09638190600689095

Alfaro, L., Chanda, A., Kalemli-Ozcan, S., & Sayek, S. (2004). FDI and Economic Growth: The Role of Local Financial Markets. *Journal of International Economics*, *64*(1), 89–112. doi:10.1016/S0022-1996(03)00081-3

Argimón, I., González, J. M., & Roldán, J. M. (1997). Evidence of Public Spending Crowding-Out from a Panel of OECD Countries. *Applied Economics, 29*(8), 001-1010.

Arunatilake, N., Jayasuriya, S., & Kelegama, S. (2001). The Economic Cost of the War in Sir Lanka. *World Development*, *29*(9), 1483–1500. doi:10.1016/S0305-750X(01)00056-0

Asiedu, E. (2002). On the Determinants of Foreign Direct Investment to Developing Countries: Is Africa Different? *World Development*, *30*(1), 107–119. doi:10.1016/S0305-750X(01)00100-0

Barro, R. J. (1990). Government Spending in a Simple Model of Endogenous Growth. *Journal of Political Economy*, *98*(5, Part 2S5), 103–125. doi:10.1086/261726

Borensztein, E., De Gregorio, J., & Lee, J.-W. (1998). How Does Foreign Direct Investment Affect Economic Growth? *Journal of International Economics*, *45*(1), 115–135. doi:10.1016/S0022-1996(97)00033-0

Botric, V., & Škuflic, L. (2006). Main Determinants of Foreign Direct Investment in the Southeast European Countries. *Transition Studies Review*, *13*(2), 359–377. doi:10.100711300-006-0110-3

Brozen, Y. (1958). Means for Maintaining Economic Stability. *Journal of Farm Economics*, *40*(5), 1069–1078. doi:10.2307/1234973

Busse, M., & Hefeker, C. (2007). Political Risk, Institutions and Foreign Direct Investment. *European Journal of Political Economy*, *23*(2), 397–415. doi:10.1016/j.ejpoleco.2006.02.003

Chamberlain, G. (1978). Omitted Variable Bias in Panel Data: Estimating the Returns to Schooling. *Annales de l'INSEE*, *30/31*(30/31), 49–63. doi:10.2307/20075285

Deger, S. (1986). Economic Development and Defense Expenditure. *Economic Development and Cultural Change*, *34*(4), 677–701.

Devereux, M. B., & Smith, G. W. (2007). Transfer Problem Dynamics: Macroeconomics of the Franco-Prussian War Indemnity. *Journal of Monetary Economics*, *54*(8), 2375–2398. doi:10.1016/j.jmoneco.2007.06.027

Dumas, B. (1978). The Theory of the Trading Firm Revisited. *The Journal of Finance*, *33*(3), 1019–1030. doi:10.1111/j.1540-6261.1978.tb02041.x

Dunning, J. H. (1973). The Determinants of International Production. *Oxford Economic Papers*, *25*(3), 289–336. doi:10.1093/oxfordjournals.oep.a041261

Dutta, N., & Roy, S. (2009). The Impact of Foreign Direct Investment on Press Freedom. *Kyklos*, *62*(2), 239–257. doi:10.1111/j.1467-6435.2009.00434.x

Erokhin, V. (Ed.). (2016a). *Global Perspectives on Trade Integration and Economies in Transition*. Hershey, PA: IGI Global. doi:10.4018/978-1-5225-0451-1

Erokhin, V. (2016b). Rising Economic Powers among Economies in Transition: Is There Enough Space on the Global Market? In V. Erokhin (Ed.), *Global Perspectives on Trade Integration and Economies in Transition* (pp. 1–25). Hershey, PA: IGI Global. doi:10.4018/978-1-5225-0451-1.ch001

Erokhin, V. (2017). How to Shape the Market: China's One Belt One Road Initiative. In M. Malovic, & K. Roy (Eds.), *The State and the Market in Economic Development: In Pursuit of Millennium Development Goals* (pp. 144–156). Brisbane, Australia: The IIDS Australia Inc.

Fosu, A. K. (1992). Political Instability and Economic Growth: Evidence from Sub-Saharan Africa. *Economic Development and Cultural Change*, *40*(4), 829–841. doi:10.1086/451979

Gathogo, G., & Ragui, M. (2014). Capital Structure of Kenyan Firms: What Determines It? Research. *Journal of Finance and Accounting*, *5*(5), 118–125.

Grier, K. G., & Tullock, G. (1989). An Empirical Analysis of Cross-National Economic Growth. *Journal of Monetary Economics*, *24*(2), 259–276. doi:10.1016/0304-3932(89)90006-8

Gupta, S., Kangur, A., Papageorgiou, C., & Wane, A. (2014). Efficiency-Adjusted Public Capital and Growth. *World Development*, *57*(C), 164–178. doi:10.1016/j.worlddev.2013.11.012

Hausman, J., & Taylor, W. (1981). Panel Data and Unobservable Individual Effects. *Econometrica, 49*(6), 1377–1398. doi:10.2307/1911406

Jensen, N. (2003). Democratic Governance and Multinational Corporations: Political Regimes and Inflows of Foreign Direct Investment. *International Organization, 57*(3), 587–616. doi:10.1017/S0020818303573040

Kosteletou, N., & Liargovas, P. (2000). Foreign Direct Investment and Real Exchange Rate. *Open Economies Review, 11*(2), 135–148. doi:10.1023/A:1008383821669

Koukpo, M. (2005). *Analyse des déterminants des investissements directs étrangers dans les pays de l'UEMOA*. Dakar, Senegal: African Institute for Economic Development and Planning.

Landau, D. (1983). Government Expenditure and Economic Growth: A Cross-Country Study. *Southern Economic Journal, 49*(1), 783–792. doi:10.2307/1058716

Laubach, T. (2009). New Evidence on the Interest Rate Effects of Budget Deficits and Debt. *Journal of the European Economic Association, 7*(4), 858–885. doi:10.1162/JEEA.2009.7.4.858

Levinsohn, J., & Petrin, A. (2003). Estimating Production Functions Using Inputs to Control for Unobservables. *The Review of Economic Studies, 70*(2), 317–341. doi:10.1111/1467-937X.00246

Li, X., & Liu, X. (2005). Foreign Direct Investment and Economic Growth: An Increasingly Endogenous Relationship. *World Development, 33*(3), 393–407. doi:10.1016/j.worlddev.2004.11.001

Mohamed, S. E., & Sidiropoulos, M. G. (2010). Another Look at the Determinants of Foreign Direct Investment in MENA Countries: An Empirical Investigation. *Journal of Economic Development, 35*(2), 75–95. doi:10.35866/caujed.2010.35.2.005

Olley, S., & Pakes, A. (1996). The Dynamics of Productivity in the Telecommunications Equipment Industry. *Econometrica, 64*(6), 1263–1297. doi:10.2307/2171831

Prabhakar, A. (2016). Trade and Economic Integration in BRICS: Towards Multi-Polarity. In V. Erokhin (Ed.), *Global Perspectives on Trade Integration and Economies in Transition* (pp. 45–57). Hershey, PA: IGI Global. doi:10.4018/978-1-5225-0451-1.ch003

Prabhakar, A. (2017). *The Current Global Recession: A Theoretical and Empirical Investigation into Developed and BRICS Economies*. London, UK: Emerald Group.

Prabhakar, A. (2018). *Comparative Economic Systems and Welfare Economics*. New Delhi, India: ISARA.

Schneider, F., & Frey, B. S. (1985). Economic and Political Determinants of Foreign Direct Investment. *World Development, 13*(2), 161–175. doi:10.1016/0305-750X(85)90002-6

Sekkat, K., & Veganzones-Varoudakis, M. (2004). *Trade and Foreign Exchange Liberalization, Investment Climate and FDI in the MENA Countries*. Brussels, Belgium: Free University of Brussels.

Sims, C. A. (1994). A Simple Model for Study of the Determination of the Price Level and the Interaction of Monetary and Fiscal Policy. *Economic Theory, 4*(3), 381–399. doi:10.1007/BF01215378

Soleimani, A., & Dnyanoba, J. R. (2017). A Study of Economics Implications of Foreign Direct Investment. *International Journal of Research in Humanities, Arts, and Literature*, *5*(2), 63–72.

Wheeler, D., & Mody, A. (1992). International Investment Location Decisions. The Case of U.S. Firms. *Journal of International Economics*, *33*(1-2), 57–76. doi:10.1016/0022-1996(92)90050-T

ADDITIONAL READING

Ajaga, E., & Nunnenkamp, P. (2008). *Inward FDI, Value Added and Employment in US States: A Panel Cointegration Approach*. Kiel: Kiel Institute for the World Economy.

Alptekin, A., & Levine, P. (2012). Military Expenditure and Economic Growth: A Meta-Analysis. *European Journal of Political Economy*, *28*(4), 636–650. doi:10.1016/j.ejpoleco.2012.07.002

Asiedu, E., & Lien, D. (2011). Democracy Foreign Direct Investment and Natural Resources. *Journal of International Economics*, *84*(1), 99–111. doi:10.1016/j.jinteco.2010.12.001

Bakkalci, A. C., & Argin, N. (2013). Internalization of Foreign Trade in the Context of Labor Market Induced by Foreign Investment. *Journal of Labour Relations*, *4*(1), 71–97.

Balcerzak, A., & Zurek, M. (2011). Foreign Direct Investment and Unemployment: VAR Analysis for Poland in the Years 1995-2009. *European Research Studies*, *14*(1), 3–14.

Balimounoune, L. M. (2004). Does FDI Contribute to Economic Growth? *Business Economics (Cleveland, Ohio)*, *39*(2), 49–56.

Bandera, V. N., & White, T. (1968). U.S. Direct Investments and Domestic Markets in Europe. *Economia Internazionale*, *21*, 739–773.

Billington, N. (1999). The Location of Foreign Direct Investment: An Empirical Analysis. *Applied Economics*, *31*(1), 65–76. doi:10.1080/00036846.2019.12067087

Brunetti, A., & Weder, B. (1998). Investment and Institutional Uncertainty: A Comparative Study of Different Uncertainty Measures. *Review of World Economics*, *134*(3), 513–533.

Caves, R. (1996). *Multinational Enterprises and Economic Analysis*. Cambridge: Cambridge University Press.

Culem, C. G. (1988). The Locational Determinants of Direct Investments among Industrialized Countries. *European Economic Review*, *32*(4), 885–904. doi:10.1016/0014-2921(88)90051-7

Darrat, A., Kherfi, S., & Soliman, M. (2005). FDI and Economic Growth in CEE and MENA Countries: A Tale of Two Regions. In *Proceedings of ERF 12th Annual Conference*. Cairo: Economic Research Forum.

Eltayeb, M., & Sidiropoulos, M. G. (2010). Does Workers' Remittances Affect Growth: Evidence from Seven MENA Labor Exporting Countries. *International Research Journal of Finance and Economics*, *46*, 181–194.

Gouider, M., Nouira, R., & Sboui, F. (2018). La relation croissance-chômage en Tunisie: Validation de la spécification non linéaire de la loi d'Okun. *Région et Développement*, *47*, 27–41.

Habib, S. (2013). Impact of Foreign Direct Investment on Employment Level in Pakistan: A Time Series Analysis. *Journal of Law. Policy and Globalization*, *10*, 2224–3240.

Kohlhagen, S. W. (1987). The Effect of Exchange Rate Uncertainty on the Prices and Volume of International Trade. *Journal of International Economics*, *8*(4), 483–511.

Kostoska, O., & Mitrevski, P. (2008). Estimating the FDI Impact on Economic Growth and Export Performances of the European Economies in Transition. *The Young Economists Journal*, *11*(1), 115–126.

Laabas, B. (2002). *Arab Development Challenges of the Millennium*. Hampshire: Ashgate Publishing Limited.

Lee, J., & Edwin, M. (1996). Intellectual Property Protection and U.S. Foreign Direct Investment. *The Review of Economics and Statistics*, *78*(2), 181–186. doi:10.2307/2109919

Lipsey, R. (2001). *Foreign Direct Investment and the Operations of Multinational Firms: Concepts, History, and Data*. Cambridge, MA: National Bureau of Economic Research. doi:10.3386/w8665

Loree, W., & Guisinger, E. (1995). Policy and Non-Policy Determinants of U.S. Equity Foreign Direct Investment. *Journal of International Business Studies*, *26*(2), 281–299. doi:10.1057/palgrave.jibs.8490174

Lunn, J. (1980). Determinants of U.S. Direct Investment in the E.E.C.: Further Evidence. *European Economic Review*, *13*(1), 93–101. doi:10.1016/0014-2921(80)90048-3

Meschi, E. (2006). FDI and Growth in MENA Countries: An Empirical Analysis. In *Proceedings of the 5th International Conference of the Middle East Economic Association*. Sousse: Middle East Economic Association.

Miyamoto, K. (2003). *Human Capital Formation and Foreign Direct Investment in Developing Countries*. Paris: OECD Development Centre.

Nigh, D., & Schollhammer, H. (1987). Foreign Direct Investment, Political Conflict and Co-operation: The Asymmetric Response Hypotheses. *Managerial and Decision Economics*, *8*(4), 307–312. doi:10.1002/mde.4090080407

Nonnemberg, M. B., & de Mendonca, M. J. C. (2004). *The Determinants of Foreign Direct Investment in Developing Countries*. Retrieved October 9, 2019, from https://ssrn.com/abstract=525462

Noorbakhsh, F., Paloni, A., & Youssef, A. (2001). Human Capital and FDI Inflows to Developing Countries: New Empirical Evidence. *World Development*, *29*(9), 1593–1610. doi:10.1016/S0305-750X(01)00054-7

Nunnenkamp, P., & Spatz, J. (2002). *Determinants of FDI in Developing Countries: Has Globalization Changed the Rules of the Game?* Kiel: Institute for the World Economy.

Rizvi, S. Z. A., & Nishat, M. (2009). The Impact of Foreign Direct Investment on Employment Opportunities: Panel Data Analysis: Empirical Evidence from Pakistan, India and China. *Pakistan Development Review*, *48*(4), 841–851. doi:10.30541/v48i4IIpp.841-851

Sadik, A., & Bolbol, A. (2001). Capital Flows, FDI, and Technology Spillover: Evidence from Arab countries. *World Development*, *29*(12), 2111–2125. doi:10.1016/S0305-750X(01)00083-3

Thomas, D. E., & Grosse, R. (2001). Country-of-Origin Determinants of Foreign Direct Investment in an Emerging Market: The Case of Mexico. *Journal of International Management*, *7*(1), 59–79. doi:10.1016/S1075-4253(00)00040-5

Tsai, P. (2014). Determinants of Foreign Direct Investment and Its Impact on Economic Growth. *Journal of Economic Development*, *19*(1), 137–163.

Vacchiani-Marcuzzo, C. (2007). Mondialisation, investissements étrangers et évolution du système des villes sud-africaines'. *Géographie et cultures, l'Harmattan, 658*, 628-644.

Wei, J. (2000). How Is Taxing Corruption on Internal Investors. *The Review of Economics and Statistics*, *82*(1), 1–11. doi:10.1162/003465300558533

Wisniewski, T. P., & Pathan, S. K. (2014). Political Environment and Foreign Direct Investment: Evidence from OECD Countries. *European Journal of Political Economy*, *36*(C), 13–23. doi:10.1016/j.ejpoleco.2014.07.004

Zhang, K. (2005). *How Does FDI Affect a Host Country's Export Performance: The Case of China.* Retrieved from https://faculty.washington.edu/karyiu/confer/xian05/papers/zhang.pdf

KEY TERMS AND DEFINITIONS

Correlation: A connection or relationship between two or more facts or numbers.

Developing Economy: A country with a less developed industrial base and a low Human Development Index relative to other countries.

Foreign Direct Investment: An investment in the form of a controlling ownership in a business in one country by an entity based in another country.

Macroeconomic Stability: A national economy that has minimized vulnerability to external shocks, which in turn increases its prospects for sustained growth.

MENA Countries: An acronym for the Middle East and North Africa region, an extensive region extending from Morocco in Northwest Africa to Iran in Southwest Asia. It generally includes all the Arab Middle East and North Africa countries, as well as Cyprus, Iran, Israel, and Turkey.

Regression: A technique for determining the statistical relationship between two or more variables where a change in a dependent variable is associated with, and depends on, a change in one or more independent variables.

Risk: A probability or threat of damage, injury, liability, loss, or any other negative occurrence that is caused by external or internal vulnerabilities, and that may be avoided through preemptive action.

Chapter 13
Latin America:
Problems and Opportunities of Integration

Tanima Dutta
Lovely Professional University, India

Anupam Rawat
Bhimrao Ambedkar University of Social Sciences, India

Arti Mishra
Gauri Shankar Mahavidyalaya, India

ABSTRACT

Latin America has been often termed as the lost continent but over the last two decades, both Europe and America have adjusted their policies as per the requirements and opportunities offered by these countries which shows that everything has not been lost. The geopolitical importance of these countries is also immense because of the huge oil reserves that they have apart from other important minerals and materials. These countries have also regrouped since the 1980s and developed the Atlantic Triangle and the Pacific Triangle to take advantage of their strengths. The chapter traces the development of globalization and regionalization in this continent and what it means to the current politico-economic world of today.

INTRODUCTION

In the conditions of globalization, the effectiveness of national economy and sustainability of economic development are increasingly influenced by foreign economic and trade relations. However, the character of such an influence is different for developed and developing countries (Erokhin, 2016a, 2016b). The balance of economic power from the West (which dominated during the last four-five centuries) has been dramatically shifting to the East since 2007 when major capitalist developed countries including the USA faced economic recession (Prabhakar, 2016, 2017, 2018; Erokhin, 2017).

DOI: 10.4018/978-1-7998-1730-7.ch013

In Latin America, most of the countries have gone through this euphoric rise and fall in the past three decades, thereby changing the geopolitics of the region as well as the socio-economic fabric of all the countries. One of the economies, Venezuela, is now going through one of its worst economic phases and has become the poster boy for showcasing what economies should not be doing and how an oil-rich country becomes cash poor with an exorbitant inflation rate of one million percent. As per the latest United Nations report (United Nations High Commissioner for Refugees [UNHCR], 2018), about four million people have fled the country though the numbers are not exact and in future, it may rise further. President Nicolás Maduro is facing stiff opposition not just from the political parties of the country but also from the USA and the UN who have been critical of his moves like blocking the UN and the US aid that was directed to his country as he said that his country is not a beggar, taking away the power of the National Assembly and severing diplomatic ties with the USA and asking all its diplomats to leave the country within 72 hours. The military is ready for coup with support from the Trump government, however, experts believe that a change in the leadership will not help the country as the very same military personnel at the upper echelons of power are hands in glove with the present regime in terms of its policies and corruption.

This case of Venezuela is a classic textbook case of Latin American countries and other developing nations who are rich in resources but have been under the hegemony of America and the West, thereby making them pawn in the game of international power. There are economists, experts, and policymakers who have been advocating the sovereignty of the developed nations especially America for the development of these countries and make them to appear on the world map.

The change that have come about in the Latin American countries since the 1980s have a deep meaning for studying and analyzing the trends of regionalization and its impact on the respective countries which have then led to the disbanding of the regional blocs or their weakening in the post-WTO era with a comeback of western dominance especially of America and European Union. The sea-saw nature of these countries' economies led to political instability or vice-versa, depending on which spectrum is one standing on while analyzing these countries. The re-emergence of protectionism in the light of the US-China economic feud makes it imperative to construct a framework of analysis of the developing nations and the various regional blocs that have emerged in the post-Bretton-Woods era. This chapter focuses on the Latin American nations, their regional blocs, relations amongst the member countries and their relationship vis-à-vis North America, political and economic impact of their integration and why the superpowers are desperate for them to disintegrate.

BACKGROUND

The discussion on regionalization is incomplete without dealing with the various facets of global trade, the various power centers and how they have emerged in the Post II World War scenario because the understanding of the superstructure depends on the premise on which it is built. The pre First World War had a different set of world leaders in terms of economy and polity as the European nations fathomed the capacity of the then underdeveloped, poor countries to supply the raw material for industrial development and also act as consumers, thereby, leading to the increase in the double bounty of these developed nations of Europe. The Second World War saw the shift in this power center from Europe to North America and the emergence of war fed economy. The basic difference between the two hegemony was that Europe concentrated on trade by building colonies and then ruling them by plundering their wealth but at the same time bringing technology too, in the areas which were deemed beneficial for them. On the other hand, America followed the path of military invasion either directly or by placing handpicked governments who would be at their mercy and therefore compliant to all the legitimate, illegitimate demands made by them. The decade of seventies has been a decade of political and economic churning all over the world especially in the newly independent colonized countries with many of them taking the initial steps towards self-reliance, forging new partnerships amongst themselves, with the alternate power center, the USSR which by then had become a competition for America thereby giving rise to new world order. It is important to remember that the decade between seventies and eighties saw huge investment in the Latin American countries as bank lending increased from \$696 million to \$15.7 billion, private investment increased from \$1.07 billion to \$7.49 billion, thus injecting huge capital in these countries. As a corollary to these investments, there was a huge outflow of funds too in the form interest payment but the net balance was in favor of Latin America till 1982. The Latin American countries were no different, with Brazil and Argentina leading the pack started the initial round of regionalization with a new political order at the helm of these countries after facing numerous military coups and armed regimes. In the late 1980s, there was again change in the political leadership in these countries with regimes favoring free trade taking over and the signing of the Buenos Aires Act for having a common market by 1994 replacing the earlier Alfonsin-Sarney FTA. The coming together of these big countries in the continent had a cascading effect on other countries giving birth to regional blocs with countries wanting to increase domestic trade which would just not strengthen their trade but also their currencies thus reducing dependence on the developed nations.

Economic relations among the nations of Latin America have entered a new stage. The last twenty years have seen a dramatic shift in Latin American economic policies away from protectionism and import substitution industrialization policies toward liberalization and the promotion of exports (Aggarwal & Espach, 2003). The level of intraregional trade, however, is still very low, in juxtaposition to interregional trade. It is explained by the expected efficiency gains from trade. These are very low as trade among similar Latin American economies often heightens competition in primary goods, driving down profits. It does little to increase technology or productivity since competition among manufacturing firms remains meager. This situation also makes bilateral trade agreements between neighboring Latin American countries a rarity; exceptions were typically part of a larger program of political and security cooperation (Aggarwal & Espach, 2003; Ruiz-Dana, Goldschagg, Claro, & Blanco, 2007).

MAIN FOCUS OF THE CHAPTER

Latin America's Tryst With Globalization

The continent of Latin America is often termed as the "lost continent" or the one that did not take the full advantage of globalization with both Europe and America having favorable relations with it. However, statistics show that in the first decade of the XXI century, if Latin America lost out in terms of global trade as its share declined from 7.6% in 1963 to 5.6% in 2005, then the share of the captain, America also declined and that too at a much faster rate. This fall in the share of the Americans have been gained by the Asian tigers that is China and India as China has been aggressive in investing in these countries. Russia has also renewed its interest in this area as there has been regimes which are sympathetic to them as they have common interests to pursue as their political ideology is the same. There has been attempts to change the narrative of globalization which has been propagated by the West by the new countries increasing their exports thereby creating a balance of payment crisis in America and other countries.

The age of globalization is perceived to have started in the second last decade of the last century culminating in the formation of the WTO in 1994, thereby taking the entire world in its grip, making way for a new economic order which gave American hegemony a new lease of life to dominate the world in terms of economy and polity. However, globalization is an age-old phenomenon where the western world through its advancement in technology, means of production and colonization practiced in all their colonies by using the route of trade first and then their military prowess to seize control. The nature of globalization before the establishment of the trinity of the IMF, the World Bank, and the WTO was different then what emerged in the post-second world war situation as the newly de-colonized nation-states changed the world dynamics. They provided both an opportunity for the developed western nations in the form of markets where they sold their technologically superior goods as well also became hindrance by the mid-seventies as they became self-reliant in technology and started to consolidate their positions by forming regional blocs. Latin American countries were no different than the other emerging nations of the world and its proximity to America added to its charm.

According to Petras and Morley (1991), the divergent outcomes resulting from the crises in eastern Europe and Latin America are not the result of the demise of economic systems or the superiority of one system over the other but have more to do with the willingness and capacity of the US to reshuffle political regimes while retaining strategic ties to the underlying authoritarian states and economic elite structures. In contrast to the Soviet withdrawal of support for its client regimes, Washington acts quickly to prop up and buttress regional allies: military aid helps repress dissident nationalists; civilian-military pacts provide the electoral facades that perpetuate the continent-wide pillage.

The liberalization of Latin America started in Chile, in 1989-1990, with the transition towards a civilian 'democratic' regime; in Mexico, with the assumption in 1988 of slate power by Salinas de Gortieri; in Peru, with the eclipse of Alan Garcia's populist regime and the election of Fujimori; in Argentina, in 1986 but particularly in 1990, with the pronounced shift to the right by Menem; in Venezuela, in 1989, with the installation of a macroeconomic adjustment program that led to the events of 1992 and the regime's most severe political crisis to date; in Ecuador, with the installation of the government formed in August 1992 by Sixto Duran Ballen and the implementation of austerity measures as draconian as those of neighboring Peru; and elsewhere, including Bolivia, an important test case of the neo-liberal model in its most orthodox form (Veltmeyer, 1993).

It is clear that Washington's policy is operating on four tracks in Latin America. In Central America where there is a mobilized population pressing for democracy and structural change, Washington has opted for the 'terror-with-demonstration elections' formula, attempting to destroy the social movements and then promote (and publicize) elections among local loyalists that will ratify the status quo, The second track, used in South America, involves supporting elections where liberal politicians have gained hegemony over the mass movements and are willing to trade off socio-economic policies acceptable to the banks and armed forces for political democracy. The third track may be seen in operation in Chile. There the mass movements are powerful and mobilized, as in Central America, so that the core policy is one of continued support of authoritarian rule and state terror, with a subsidiary thrust of gently urging (but not insisting upon) gradual accommodation with center-right civilian political forces. The fourth track, and the main thrust in Washington's Central American policy today is to escalate the economic, political, and military assault on Nicaragua. By neutralizing US liberals and their Latin American civilian counterparts with rhetoric on 'resurgent democracy', the Reagan administration hopes to obtain a free hand in securing a military victory against this dangerously vital example of social and economic (as well as political) democracy in Central America (Herman & Petras, 1985).

Regional Blocs in Latin America

Union of South American Nations

The Union of South American Nations (USAN) is an intergovernmental regional organization established to build integration in the cultural, economic, social and political areas while respecting the current situation of each of the member nations. The challenge is to eliminate socioeconomic inequality, achieve social inclusion, increase citizen participation, strengthen democracy and reduce existing asymmetries while taking into account the sovereignty and independence of each of the member states.

USAN is made up of all twelve countries in the South American region: Argentina, Bolivia, Brazil, Colombia, Chile, Ecuador, Guyana, Paraguay, Peru, Suriname, Uruguay, and Venezuela. Initially, The South American Community of Nations was created in 2004. In 2007, the Heads of State changed its name from the South American Community of Nations to the Union of South American Nations. In 2008, the Treaty of the Union of South American Nations was approved, and UNASUR went into force in 2011.

Specific goals of the UNASUR include:

- Strengthen political dialogue between Member States in order to reinforce the South American integration and the participation of UNASUR in the international arena.
- Social and human development with equity and inclusion in order to eradicate poverty and overcome inequalities in the region.
- Illiteracy eradication, equal access to quality education and the regional recognition of courses and degrees.
- Energy integration for the sustainable and fair use of the resources of our Region.
- Infrastructure development to guarantee the interconnection of the region and our peoples according to criteria of sustainable social and economic development.
- Adopt mechanisms compatible with the economic and fiscal policies of Member States which will promote financial integration among them.
- Protection of our biodiversity, water resources and ecosystems as well as cooperation among Member States in matters of disaster prevention and the fight against the causes and effects of climate change.
- Achieving equitable integration in order to overcome asymmetries through the development of concrete and effective mechanisms.
- Progressive recognition of the rights of Member State citizens residing in any of the other Member States with the aim of attaining a citizenship of the other Member State.
- Equal access to Social Security and health services.
- Unrestricted respect for human and labor rights through migratory regularization and harmonization of policies.
- Economic and trade cooperation to achieve progress and consolidation of an innovative, dynamic, transparent, equitable and balanced process.

- Promote growth and economic development in order to overcome asymmetries through the complementation of the economies of all the Member Countries as well as promoting the welfare of all sections of the population and the reduction of poverty.
- Giving attention to small and medium enterprises, cooperative companies, networks and other forms of production organizations with the aim of creating unity in the Industrial and Productive areas.
- Creation and implementation of complementary policies and projects of research, innovation, technology transfer and production in order to increase capacity, sustainability, and proper scientific and technological development.
- Strengthening of the identities of the peoples of the region of our Member States through encouragement of expression of knowledge and memory with the aim of promoting cultural diversity.
- Citizen participation through mechanisms for interaction and dialogue between UNASUR and the various social organizations for the creating of South American integration policies.
- While taking into account international standards and laws, and through coordination between the specialized agencies of the Member States, strengthen the fight against terrorism, corruption, the global drug problem, trafficking of people, trafficking of small guns and light weapons, transnational organized crime and other threats as well as disarmament, non-proliferation of nuclear weapons of mass destruction and demining.
- Promote cooperation between the judicial authorities of the Member States of UNASUR.
- Exchange of information and experience on defense.
- Cooperation to strengthen public safety.
- Sectoral cooperation in order to deepen South American integration through the exchange of information, experience, and training.

The UNASUR was created with the aim of integrating regional processes developed in the region of Latin Americas by the Caribbean Community (CARICOM), the Mercosur, and the Andean Community. Out of twelve member states of the Union of South American Nations, two belong to CARICOM, four belong to the Andean Community of Nations (CAN), and four to Mercosur.

Caribbean Community

Caribbean Community is an organization of Caribbean nations and dependencies, which main purposes are to promote economic integration and cooperation among its members, to ensure that the benefits of integration are equitably shared, and to coordinate foreign policy.

CARICOM is a grouping of twenty countries: fifteen member states (Antigua and Barbuda, Bahamas, Barbados, Belize, Dominica, Grenada, Guyana, Haiti, Jamaica, Montserrat, Saint Kitts and Nevis, Saint Lucia, Saint Vincent and the Grenadines, Suriname, Trinidad and Tobago) and five associate members (Anguilla, Bermuda, British Virgin Islands, Cayman Islands, Turks and Caicos Islands). Also, there are eight observer states (Aruba, Colombia, Curacao, Dominican Republic, Mexico, Puerto Rico, Saint Maarten, Venezuela). CARICOM came into being in 1973.

CARICOM rests on four main pillars: economic integration; foreign policy coordination; human and social development; and security.

The economic integration of CARICOM is largely conceived through a single economic space; the benefits of which include the sustainable economic development of the Community and improved quality of life for its people. The CARICOM Single Market and Economy (CSME) is the heart of CARICOM's economic integration. Better opportunities to produce and sell goods and services competitively and to attract investment; greater economies of scale; increased competitiveness; full employment and improved standards of living for the Community's people are some of the benefits of the CSME, which ultimate goal is to provide the foundation for growth and development.

Safeguarding and promoting the Community's interests within the global environment through the coordination of foreign and external relations and deepening the integration movement and building its resilience to facilitate a socially cohesive Community, underlie the Community's foreign and community relations pillar of integration.

In the sphere of human and social development, an improved and acceptable quality of life for the people of CARICOM and a socially resilient region, capable of taking on the challenges of globalization, underlie the Community's human and social development pillar of integration.

A safe and secure community for its people and an economically and socially resilient region is the aim of CARICOM's Security pillar of integration.

These pillars underpin the following objectives:

- to improve standards of living and work;
- the full employment of labor and other factors of production;
- accelerated, coordinated and sustained economic development and convergence;
- expansion of trade and economic relations with Third States;
- enhanced levels of international competitiveness;
- organization for increased production and productivity;
- achievement of a greater measure of economic leverage;
- effectiveness of Member States in dealing with Third States, groups of States and entities of any description;
- the enhanced coordination of Member States' foreign and foreign economic policies and enhanced functional cooperation.

Andean Community

The Andean Community of nations, previously known as the Andean Pact, is an intergovernmental organization created with the aim to promote the expansion of markets and guarantee an effective economic development to the region. The original Andean Pact was founded in 1969 by Bolivia, Chile, Colombia, Ecuador, and Peru. In 1973 the pact gained its sixth member, Venezuela. In 1976 however, its membership was again reduced to five when Chile withdrew. Venezuela announced its withdrawal in 2006, reducing the Andean Community to four member states. With the cooperation agreement with Mercosur, the Andean Community gained four new associate members: Argentina, Brazil, Paraguay, and Uruguay.

In 1993 a free-trade zone was created for Bolivia, Colombia, Ecuador, and Venezuela. That year the Andean Group also began negotiations to harmonize its customs policy and reached an agreement in 1994 on a common external tariff that covered 90% of imports. ACN later endorsed an accord between Colombia, Venezuela, and Mexico to phase out tariffs and began developing a framework to define a joint foreign policy in 1998. In the same year, negotiations with Mercosur resulted in an agreement to establish a free-trade zone from Mexico to Argentina. Following extensive negotiations, the free-trade zone went into effect on July 1, 2004.

Currently, CAN community deals with the following issues: trade in goods, trade in services, customs union, circulation of persons, common market, common foreign policy, border development, social agenda, sustainable development, and economic policies

Mercosur

Mercosur is a sub-regional bloc established with a purpose to promote free trade and the fluid movement of goods, people, and currency between participating countries. Mercosur's full members are Argentina, Brazil, Paraguay, and Uruguay. Venezuela joined the group in 2012, but the political and economic crisis in the country has revealed fractures within the group. Mercosur members suspended Venezuela in December 2016 for failing to comply with the group's rules on trade and democracy. Mercosur's associate countries are Bolivia, Chile, Peru, Colombia, Ecuador, and Suriname. Observer countries are New Zealand and Mexico.

Mercosur calls for the free movement of goods, services, and factors of production between countries. Its members agreed to eliminate customs duties, implement a common external tariff of 35% on certain imports from outside the bloc, and adopt a common trade policy toward outside countries and blocs.

The Southern Common Market promotes:

- Free transit of produced goods, services, and factors of production among member states. Among other things, this includes eliminating customs rights and lifting of nontariff restrictions on the transit of goods or any other measures with similar effects
- Fixing of a common external tariff and adopting of a common trade policy with regard to non-member states or groups of states, and the coordination of positions in regional and international commercial and economic meetings
- Coordination of macroeconomic and sectorial policies of member states relating to foreign trade, agriculture, industry, taxes, monetary system, exchange and capital, services, customs, transport and communications, and any others they may agree on, to ensure free competition between member states.
- Commitment by member states to necessary adjustments to their laws to strengthen the integration processes. Mercosur residents may live and work anywhere within the bloc.

Mercosur went beyond simply coordinating trade policy, creating political institutions that aim to go deeper than most free trade agreements. The bloc's highest decision-making body is the Common Market Council, which gathers the members' foreign and economy ministers. The group's presidency of the group rotates among its full members in alphabetical order every six months. Other governing bodies include the Common Market Group, which coordinates macroeconomic policies among members; a trade commission; a parliament, known as Parlasur; and the Structural Convergence Fund (FOCEM), which coordinates regional infrastructure projects. Mercosur's founders had hoped to go beyond creating a free trade area to form a common market similar to the European Union, and even considered introducing a common currency.

Mercosur's five full members have a combined GDP of roughly $2.8 trillion, making it one of the world's largest economic blocs. Mercosur was created in large part to cement a rapprochement between longtime rivals Argentina and Brazil, and the two countries loom large over the group: in 2015, the countries had a combined GDP of $2.3 trillion, roughly 83% of the group's economy. Around 250 million of the bloc's roughly 292 million inhabitants live in Argentina or Brazil. Trade among Mercosur members was roughly $108 billion in 2015, nearly three times what it had been in 2000, but it had dropped about 5 percent in that time as a share of members' total trade. Experts say this reflects a lag in integrating Mercosur economies to create value-added supply chains or regional production hubs. Mercosur countries have also failed to coordinate their trade policies toward third countries, such as China, on whom Brazil has unilaterally imposed antidumping restrictions on steel imports. Latin America's traditional reliance on low-value-added commodity exports, particularly to China, continued during the commodities price boom of the 2000s.

Venezuela's suspension from Mercosur came amid political turmoil in its largest economies. Falling commodity prices and what critics describe as economic mismanagement have contributed to negative growth in the region: Brazil's economy shrank by nearly 4% in 2015. Argentina confirmed in 2016 that its economy was in recession; economists projected a 1% contraction in its economy in 2016. Paraguay and Uruguay saw 3% 1% growth, respectively. Mercosur's future largely hinges on decisions made in Brazil and Argentina. These countries are two of each other's most important trading partners. Especially because they are going through a difficult economic time, they would benefit from opening of their markets more generally. The challenge for Mercosur is whether they can do it together. New leadership in Argentina and Brazil and the Venezuela's suspension from the group could either revive Mercosur or make it irrelevant. In September 2016 the group issued a call to continue talks with the EU, with the goal of reaching a free trade agreement by 2018. Some EU members' resistance to agriculture imports, fallout from Brexit, and growing anti-trade sentiment in Europe may hinder efforts on the EU side. Meanwhile, Argentina became an official observer to the Pacific Alliance in June 2016, signaling an opening in the country's trade policies and possibly a willingness to look beyond Mercosur to increase trade.

Pacific Alliance

The Pacific Alliance is an initiative of regional integration between Latin American countries, which border the Pacific Ocean. Chile, Colombia, Mexico, and Peru are the four founding members, which officially established the Pacific Alliance in 2011.

Objectives of the Pacific Alliance are:

- Build in a participatory and consensual way an area of deep integration to move progressively towards the free movement of goods, services, resources, and people.
- Drive further growth, development and competitiveness of the economies of its members, focused on achieving greater well-being, overcoming socioeconomic inequality and promote the social inclusion of its inhabitants.
- Become a platform of political articulation, economic and commercial integration and projection to the world, with emphasis on the Asia-Pacific region.

Members keep a network of trade agreements among them and with other countries worldwide. In the sphere of reducing trade barriers, Pacific Alliance promotes commercial, investment, innovation and technological exchange with the most competitive regions around the world. In addition to reducing trade barriers, the Pacific Alliance has begun several other projects for regional integration, including visa-free travel, a common stock exchange. The Mercado Integrado Latinoamericano (MILA) originally integrated the stock markets of Colombia (Colombia Stock Exchange), Chile (Santiago Stock Exchange), and Peru (Lima Stock Exchange), and is seen as a foundation for the Alliance's economic integration. With the entry of Mexico into MILA, the integrated stock market now counts 780 issuers among the four countries, making it the biggest market by number of listed companies in Latin America, and the biggest in terms of market capitalization

Asia-Pacific Economic Cooperation

In the region of the Pacific Ocean, the Pacific Alliance competes with the Asia-Pacific Economic Cooperation (APEC), which is a regional economic forum established in 1989 to leverage the growing interdependence of the Asia-Pacific and to create greater prosperity for the people of the region by promoting balanced, inclusive, sustainable, innovative and secure growth and by accelerating regional economic integration.

APEC has 21 members, including most countries with a coastline on the Pacific Ocean. However, the criterion for membership is that the member is a separate economy, rather than a state. As a result, APEC uses the term member economies rather than member countries to refer to its members. One result of this criterion is that membership of the forum includes Taiwan (officially the Republic of China, participating under the name "Chinese Taipei") alongside People's Republic of China as well as Hong Kong, which entered APEC as a British colony but it is now a Special Administrative Region of the People's Republic of China.

APEC's primary goal is to support sustainable economic growth and prosperity in the Asia-Pacific region. Other goals include building a dynamic and harmonious Asia-Pacific community by championing free and open trade and investment, promoting and accelerating regional economic integration, encouraging economic and technical cooperation, enhancing human security, and facilitating a favorable and sustainable business environment.

APEC ensures that goods, services, investment, and people move easily across borders. Members facilitate this trade through faster customs procedures at borders; more favorable business climates behind the border; and aligning regulations and standards across the region.

The pursuit of trade and investment liberalization, business facilitation, and economic and technical cooperation will be guided by the goal of democratizing the fruits of economic growth – empowering individuals, businesses and communities to take advantage of the opportunities of regional economic integration, as well as withstand and address economic risks and challenges such as rising income gaps, economic inequity, natural disasters, and food security.

Current APEC's priorities are enhancing the regional economic integration agenda, fostering small and medium enterprises' participation in regional and global markets, investing in human capital development, building sustainable and resilient communities.

Following APEC's multi-year initiative towards the free trade and investment, and the realization of a Free Trade Area of the Asia-Pacific (FTAAP), APEC will expand the regional economic integration agenda to include initial building blocks such as the collective strategic study on the FTAAP, and forward-looking plans based on the review of APEC's Growth Strategy, among others.

Discussions on the possible pathways to the Free Trade Area of the Asia-Pacific (FTAAP) continue. In 2014, APEC Leaders endorsed the Beijing Roadmap for APEC's Contribution to the Realization of the Free Trade Area of Asia-Pacific (FTAAP) to translate the vision of the FTAAP into reality. The roadmap provides for a Collective Strategic Study on Issues related to the Realisation of the FTAAP to be concluded in 2017, as well as enhanced information sharing and capacity building. The study will provide an analysis of potential economic and social benefits and costs, analyze the various pathways towards a Free Trade Area of the Asia-Pacific, and identify challenges economies may face in realizing the FTAAP.

SOLUTIONS AND RECOMMENDATIONS

The initiatives of the countries of Latin America in the sphere of integration should focus on connectivity and trade facilitation, particularly in the areas that promote trade in services and the ease of doing business. Structural reform, financial inclusion measures, and good governance will also place high on the agenda to support efforts to build more inclusive value and production chains in Latin America.

Recognizing the potential of small and medium enterprises to generate employment and serve as engines of economic development, the countries of Latin America should place SMEs front and centers on the trade liberalization and facilitation agenda. SMEs, which comprise more than 90% of businesses in many economies, are key stakeholders in regional economic integration particularly in reaping the benefits of Free Trade Agreements and Regional Trade Agreements. While SMEs are most at risk to economic shocks and challenges of globalization, they continue to adapt as sources of innovative business models and new technologies. To support the entrepreneurial nature of SMEs and their valuable contribution to overall economic growth, the countries of Latin America will align its capacity-building initiatives to the needs of SMEs. They should will continue to support SMEs through trade facilitation measures to link SMEs to global value chains and promote their full participation in markets by removing barriers to entry and promoting greater access to finance, technology, training programs, and tools.

Given the changing global environment and disasters such as typhoons, earthquakes, volcanic eruptions and health pandemics, the countries of Latin America should prioritize the goals of resilience, sustainability, and food security. As trade in the Asia-Pacific continues to be increasingly integrated and interlinked by production and supply chains, disaster-related disruptions in these interwoven chains can hurt both the supply and demand side. The cross-border effects of disasters thus make regional mechanisms and contingencies more necessary. Preparedness such as investing in resilient infrastructure, rather than just relief and recovery, are coming to the fore of international collaboration agenda in Latin America. The countries of the region should look to create and promote risk reduction and management, build SMEs' resilience to disaster, and ensure business continuity. Faced by the need to better manage its food and energy requirements, the collaboration agenda should also include the initiatives to enhance food security across the continent by promoting coastal management, sustainable fishing, and marine conservation.

FUTURE RESEARCH DIRECTIONS

Currently, the countries of Latin America underscore the importance of investing in human capital development in achieving sustained and broad-based growth. Recognizing that economic growth is anchored by the quality of its human resources, the countries of Latin America should continue to pursue the long-term goal of building a skilled and adaptable community of nations through cross-border education, science and technology-based education and skills development, and innovation-driven capacity-building programs. Placed within the context of new technologies that increase the volume, velocity, and variety of knowledge and information flows, research initiatives should be designed to foster economic competitiveness coupled with equal opportunity. The countries of Latin America should enhance cooperation between education providers and businesses as employers – to help realize research, educational, and human resource development goals.

CONCLUSION

The coexistence of various integration formats in one continent, as well as the existing institutional disorder of Latin American regionalism, should not be confused with the absence of regional regimes in the area. In fact, Latin America shares common values and norms regarding peace and security, such as the peaceful settlement of disputes, nonintervention, and the prohibition of arms of mass destruction, which are comparable to other regions of the world. Additionally, it has adopted common norms for the protection of human rights, democracy, and the rule of law (Van Klaveren, 2017). Although the latter have not always been respected in all of the countries, they still stand as the most elaborate regional regime in the developing world. Some of the regional regimes have emerged from existing regional institutions, as was the case of the human rights regime, developed within the Inter-American framework. Others have evolved from strong historical and legal traditions, as was the case of the peaceful settlement of disputes. Others were the result of ad hoc negotiations. In sum, despite all of the confusion and limitations of Latin American regionalism, there is still a considerable degree of regional dimension, which has led to a Latin American international society ruled by common norms and shared practices. The fact that no institution in the region has been capable of regulating and governing this regional dimension adds another complexity to the study of Latin American regionalism.

REFERENCES

Aggarwal, V. K., & Espach, R. H. (2003). *Diverging Trade Strategies in Latin America: An Analytical Framework. Berkeley, CA*: University of California.

Erokhin, V. (Ed.). (2016a). *Global Perspectives on Trade Integration and Economies in Transition*. Hershey, PA: IGI Global. doi:10.4018/978-1-5225-0451-1

Erokhin, V. (2016b). Rising Economic Powers among Economies in Transition: Is There Enough Space on the Global Market? In V. Erokhin (Ed.), *Global Perspectives on Trade Integration and Economies in Transition* (pp. 1–25). Hershey, PA: IGI Global. doi:10.4018/978-1-5225-0451-1.ch001

Erokhin, V. (2017). How to Shape the Market: China's One Belt One Road Initiative. In M. Malovic, & K. Roy (Eds.), *The State and the Market in Economic Development: In Pursuit of Millennium Development Goals* (pp. 144–156). Brisbane, Australia: The IIDS Australia Inc.

Herman, E. S., & Petras, J. (1985). 'Resurgent Democracy' in Latin America: Rhetoric or Reality. *Economic and Political Weekly*, *20*(27), 1147–1152.

Petras, J., & Morley, M. (1991). Latin America: Poverty of Democracy and Democracy of Poverty. *Economic and Political Weekly*, *26*(30), 103–111.

Prabhakar, A. (2016). Trade and Economic Integration in BRICS: Towards Multi-Polarity. In V. Erokhin (Ed.), *Global Perspectives on Trade Integration and Economies in Transition* (pp. 45–57). Hershey, PA: IGI Global. doi:10.4018/978-1-5225-0451-1.ch003

Prabhakar, A. (2017). *The Current Global Recession: A Theoretical and Empirical Investigation into Developed and BRICS Economies*. London, UK: Emerald Group.

Prabhakar, A. (2018). *Comparative Economic Systems and Welfare Economics*. New Delhi, India: ISARA.

Ruiz-Dana, A., Goldschagg, P., Claro, E., & Blanco, H. (2007). *Regional Integration, Trade, and Conflict in Latin America*. Winnipeg, Canada: International Institute for Sustainable Development.

United Nations High Commissioner for Refugees. (n.d.). *Venezuela Situation*. Retrieved October 10, 2019, from https://www.unhcr.org/venezuela-emergency.html?query=venezuela

Van Klaveren, A. (2017). *Regionalism in Latin America. Navigating in the Fog*. Bern, Switzerland: World Trade Institute. doi:10.2139srn.3129996

Veltmeyer, H. (1993). Liberalisation and Structural Adjustment in Latin America: In Search of an Alternative. *Economic and Political Weekly*, *35*(28), 2080–2086.

ADDITIONAL READING

Agarwal, M., & Dipankar, S. (1999). Structural Adjustments in Latin America: Policies and Performances. *Economic and Political Weekly*, *34*(44), 3129–3136.

Beaton, K., Cebotari, A., Ding, X., & Komaromi, A. (2017). *Trade Integration in Latin America: A Network Perspective*. Washington, DC: International Monetary Fund.

Bhojwani, D. (2016). China's Involvement in Latin America, Lessons for India. *Economic and Political Weekly*, *51*(6), 27–29.

Bhupatiraju, S., & Sirohi, R. (2017). Is the 'Pink Tide' Ebbing? Achievements and Limitations of the Latin American Left. *Economic and Political Weekly*, *52*(6), 34–41.

Child, J. (1979). Geopolitical Thinking in Latin America. *Latin American Research Review*, *14*(2), 89–111.

Hakim, P. (2000). Is Latin America Doomed to Failure? *Foreign Policy*, *117*, 104–119.

Hannan, S. A. (2017). *The Impact of Trade Agreements in Latin America using the Synthetic Control Method*. Washington, DC: International Monetary Fund.

Manzetti, L. (1994). The Political Economy of Mercosur. *Journal of Interamerican Studies and World Affairs*, *35*(4), 101–141. doi:10.2307/165956

Nofal, M. (1993). *Economic Integration of Argentina-Brazil, MERCOSUR, and Regionalization in the Southern Cone Market*. Buenos Aires: Nofal & Asociados.

Nolte, D., & Wehner, L. E. (2015). *Geopolitics in Latin America, Old and New*. London, UK: Routledge.

Octavio, M. (1982). Nemesis without Hubris. *Economic and Political Weekly*, *51*(17), 2038–2039.

Petras, J. (1986). Latin America – Dialectics of Growth and Regression. *Economic and Political Weekly*, *41*(21), 1783–1786.

Petras, J. (2001). Unemployed Workers in Argentina. *Economic and Political Weekly*, *45*(36), 4265–4270.

Quigley, J. (1990). The Legality of the United States Invasion of Panama. *The Yale Journal of International Law*, *15*(2), 276–315.

Reisman, W. M. (1983). The Struggle for the Falklands. *The Yale Law Journal*, *93*(2), 287–317. doi:10.2307/796308

Werner, A. (2018). *Latin America and the Caribbean in 2018: An Era in the Making*. Retrieved October 9, 2019, from https://blogs.imf.org/2018/01/25/latin-america-and-the-caribbean-in-2018-an-economic-recovery-in-the-making/

Whiting, V. R. (1993). The Dynamics of Regionalization: Road Map to an Open Future? In P. H. Smith (Ed.), *The Challenge of Integration: Europe and the Americas*. New Brunswick, NJ: Transaction Publishers.

KEY TERMS AND DEFINITIONS

Andean Community: An intergovernmental organization created with the aim to promote the expansion of markets and guarantee an effective economic development to the region. The original Andean Pact was founded in 1969 by Bolivia, Chile, Colombia, Ecuador, and Peru. In 1973 the pact gained its sixth member, Venezuela. In 1976 however, its membership was again reduced to five when Chile withdrew. Venezuela announced its withdrawal in 2006, reducing the Andean Community to four member states. With the cooperation agreement with Mercosur, the Andean Community gained four new associate members: Argentina, Brazil, Paraguay, and Uruguay.

Asia-Pacific Economic Cooperation: A regional economic forum established in 1989 to leverage the growing interdependence of the Asia-Pacific and to create greater prosperity for the people of the region by promoting balanced, inclusive, sustainable, innovative and secure growth and by accelerating regional economic integration.

Caribbean Community: An organization of Caribbean nations and dependencies, which main purposes are to promote economic integration and cooperation among its members, to ensure that the benefits of integration are equitably shared, and to coordinate foreign policy.

Mercosur: A sub-regional bloc established with a purpose to promote free trade and the fluid movement of goods, people, and currency between participating countries. Mercosur's full members are Argentina, Brazil, Paraguay, and Uruguay. Venezuela joined the group in 2012, but the political and economic crisis in the country has revealed fractures within the group. Mercosur members suspended Venezuela in December 2016 for failing to comply with the group's rules on trade and democracy. Mercosur's associate countries are Bolivia, Chile, Peru, Colombia, Ecuador, and Suriname. Observer countries are New Zealand and Mexico.

Pacific Alliance: An initiative of regional integration between Latin American countries, which border the Pacific Ocean. Chile, Colombia, Mexico, and Peru are the four founding members, which officially established the Pacific Alliance in 2011.

Union of South American Nations: An intergovernmental regional organization established to build integration in the cultural, economic, social and political areas while respecting the current situation of each of the member nations. The challenge is to eliminate socioeconomic inequality, achieve social inclusion, increase citizen participation, strengthen democracy and reduce existing asymmetries while taking into account the sovereignty and independence of each of the member states.

Chapter 14
Regional Trade and Green Innovation Development Under the NAFTA:
Territory Democratization and Institutional Design

Jose Vargas-Hernandez
https://orcid.org/0000-0003-0938-4197
University of Guadalajara, Mexico

ABSTRACT

This chapter analyzes the elements of an environmentally sustainable regional trade and development under the NAFTA based on the decentralization of the infrastructure. The author assesses how the democratization of the territory and innovations in the sphere of institutional design address the complexity of the trade and development challenges. The method employed is the critical analysis supported by a review of the literature and consultation with the experts in the field. It is concluded that the environmentally sustainable capacity planning has a critical role in regional innovation development in specific areas of regional trade and development, economic growth, social inclusion and equality, environmental sustainability, health, education, and business. To achieve these aims, environmentally sustainable regional trade and development require the democratization of the territory and the new institutional design.

INTRODUCTION

Cities are very different lively ecosystems brooding places of regional innovation, imagination, and creativity. Cities shape and are shaped by the vision of regional green innovation ecosystem elements that anchor investments into environmental and sustainable development. Larger cities generate more innovations because the interactions between people socially distant to each other and weak ties, aggregating information when they meet (Arbesman, Kleinberg, & Strogatz, 2009; Granovetter, 1973). Large cities have more educated and transient people (Arbesman et al., 2009).

DOI: 10.4018/978-1-7998-1730-7.ch014

Regional green innovation may have the objective to improve the high technology and services business labor market while restructuring old regional industrial and shrinking areas creating new regional development mixing economic, science, media, leisure and living activities. Green innovative technologies processes supporting the green regional environment may become more complex when affecting the pace of changing the city. Regional green innovation challenges sustainable and environmental development of the city at various scales and across sectors. The multi-level conceptual analysis of regional green innovation takes into consideration the micro, meso and macro levels the corresponding niche-innovations, sociotechnical regimes, and socio-technical landscapes.

Defining need of regional green innovation is a first step required to advocating investment in specific local spaces and areas and encouraging external funding support. The intention to introduce regional green innovation requires an enhanced level of corporate governance environmental responsibility and sustained level of implementation of the city's environmental strategies and policies to put regional green projects into practice and overcoming of environmental challenges and risks. Integrating environmental sustainability, economic growth, and social development issues into regional green innovation into an in-depth approach represents a challenge. Other innovative regional green projects are related with alternative and renewable energy-saving buildings, neighborhoods, and spaces.

There are different approaches can be used, each one with different reasons and ends, for example: radical versus incremental, environmental performance, etc. Regional green innovation essentially intends to respond to the environmental changes and new societal expectations, integrate sustainability issues into the achievement of economic growth, social development, environmental sustainability, community welfare and good.

Regional green innovation practices contribute to sustainable regional planning of infrastructure and regional green areas. The cities and regional undertakings are innovation hubs for regional green areas with relevant impacts on economy, technology, social, organizational, etc. Regional green areas are a potential testing ground for innovations in several issues and disciplines. Regional green areas are hot spots for green innovation (Burch & De Luca, 1984; Krott, 1998). Innovation can be social, technical, socio-technical, ecological, socio-ecological and environmental.

BACKGROUND

The regional innovation ecosystem has the levels of interaction shaping, implementing and operating. The regional plan based on an regional green innovation ecosystem is interconnected and supported by a network of organizations, firms, local government, educational centers, communities, etc., aimed to create an inclusive economy based on innovation and encouraged by local business to make local improvements. The regional green innovation ecosystem is interconnected and supported by a network of communities, neighborhoods, social organizations, business firms, local governments and authorities, educational and research centers, etc., are the foundations for the environmental regional planning and design.

Regional innovation and entrepreneurship network systems in the local ecosystem play a crucial role to promote and adapt to new situations (Granovetter, 1973). A green innovation ecosystem is form with regional planning and development programs, living labs and future internet experimental facilities for users and citizens, policy-makers, researchers, scientists, ICT business companies, etc. Regional cyberspace is crucial in technological innovation in city management of digital cities to deliver benefits to people in green public spaces and developing civic networks in areas of economic regeneration and community building.

Regional green innovation may contribute significantly to regional sustainable development providing an opportunity for research to define a new direction for green environments (Cronon, 1991; Goudie, 1994; Forman, 1995).

There are three fundamental elements of regional green innovation: Guarantee the public interest, decentralize the infrastructure to democratize the territory and innovating the institutional design to address the complexity of the challenges in the city.

MAIN FOCUS OF THE CHAPTER

Decentralize the Infrastructure to Democratize the Territory

The debate around the regional public space, the housing and regional justice revolve around the proper object of the struggles for the right to land, city infrastructure and territorial order. Public space emerges as a situation of paradigmatic spatial transition, from a space that is a box or vehicle, to a space that is an entity in itself. It is a collective presence rather than social movements in the city and in public spaces, it is a different type of claim to space.

The green regional resources and infrastructure for innovation, research and innovation networks between governments, business and higher education and research institutions are determinants of the city welfare. The position of the different actors in the innovation network facilitates the access to diverse information and knowledge flows and provides the potential to create and develop innovative opportunities (Burt, 2002, 2005). For example, Green roofing is an innovative practice in design and wastewater technologies. The use of innovative practices in green roof are in both in the promotional policies and in construction as tools in a broader plan to create green infrastructure for ecosystem services, although may not completely mitigate the ecological footprint in regional ecosystems.

The dominant constructions of territory, land and regional space in the contemporaneity are the complementarity of capitalism and the large-scale colonialism brought about by geospatial concentrations and the creation of great inequalities in cities. The spatial regional organization shows dysfunctionalities such as the abandonment of public spaces, organization in a way that hinders the agglomeration of people, the distancing of institutions from city centers in such a way that access is difficult. Democratizing democracy has a very broad meaning.

The territorial unitary vision of regional spaces is problematic in the sense that they are the reflection of the production of hegemonic imaginaries and fictions, from colonial fictions to nationalist fictions. Alongside authoritarian regional spaces, the spaces of the excluded coexist as a response, which gives rise to the struggle for public spaces that show many dimensions to accommodate regional social movements. The public space of the new social movements today is the space itself, the space itself is the value, it is the question of the political arena.

The extractivism of natural resources territorializes economic and political relations, giving rise to a contradiction in the processes of economic globalization under the assumption that it considered the deterritorialization of production, distribution and consumption processes. The processes of deterritorialization is just one of the sides of the condition of globalization as opposed to the processes of reterritorialization because there are certain elements inherent to the processes of production, distribution, and consumption in certain places.

The struggle for land, territory and regional space is a struggle against the colonial and capitalist heritage of territorial space. Cities considered plurinational in geopolitical terms and may have territorial autonomy that is not merely administrative or political, so they are not independent territories. This type of autonomy is the result of the recognition of the existence of other ways of administering the territory, Cosmo visions, cultures, etc. The land and its natural resources today are within a geopolitics of the territory much more complex than the one that had been built before.

The struggles for land, territory and regional space prosecuted by the new social movements form a front that is common to territorial fascism with its forms of colonial domination and exploitation of the territory for the defense of territorial ecological conceptions in the face of capitalist pressures and colonialists. Territorial fascism refers to the logic of the territory that crosses the cities and ends up fracturing them, giving rise to spaces within cities that have an abysmal line between civilized areas, private regionalizations that go against public spaces and wild areas, where the popular classes live. These wild areas proliferate in cities that do not have the capacity to accommodate populations in a reasonable, socially and politically decent way.

The different forms of territorial fascism exist in spite of political and legal homogeneity, but where institutions are able to act in a totally different way according to whether they consider the enemy territory or not in a civilized or savage conception of war. The internal territory can be a very poor neighborhood or groups of terrorists, etc. The internal territories are subject to forms of internal geopolitics that import the relations of international conflicts for the territory itself and that reproduces internal colonial relations.

A great innovation based on a new idea of territory that focuses on the neoliberal capitalist logic that validates the function of the territory as it is exploited is the consideration of the original groups that hold the logic that the territory has no commercial value. A great alteration occurs at the beginning of the 20th century in the conception of the land, because previously there was a conception, if you will, more human of the territory and of the earth.

The social struggle around territorial land in regional centers in Latin America is part of the logic of geopolitical concentration of territory and land through colonial history and colonial cultures. These situations that condition the current struggles over land and territory become relevant to the discourse of hegemonic and dominant practices. There are many international pressures for the exploitation of primary goods, foodstuffs, and speculation about minerals, and consequently, the pressure on land and territory is causing all political conquests to be undermined by the governments that have instituted them.

The counter-hegemonic movements are movements that fight for territory, land and regional spaces. Movements that fight for a more equitable distribution of land are movements of indigenous peoples, populations that today are largely indigenous or aboriginal. The territory is the very root of the cultural identity that is expressed in regional spaces where they try to recover the memory destroyed by capitalism and colonialism. The emergent political protagonism of colonialism consider that for certain social groups there is no dignity without territory. This is the case of indigenous peoples who try to claim respect for their culture and knowledge with respect for their lands and territories, in such a way that they seek to guarantee their dignity with the guarantee of territorial autonomy.

The nature, the territory, the use of the land and space have colonial, capitalist and ecological dimensions. The ecological dimension marks the ecological limits of the other two dimensions. What is at the bottom of the cause is a change of civilization that forces to modify the habits of production, distribution, and consumption. The conceptual foundations of Southern epistemologies, the ecology of knowledge, the sociology of absences and emergencies, and of intercultural translation well established as reference frameworks, can help developed countries with a colonizing past, recognize more experiences and the knowledge to value the origins that come from the colonized territories.

In the traditional conception of regional territorial space, there is a conceptual attempt to create the idea of a regional territorial space that would be outside the hegemonic space of subaltern colonialism that was constructed as such, rather than settler's colonialism, colonialism of intense and direct occupation, within a very unequal colonial relationship. Colonialism created an arrogance that has incapacitated the colonizing countries to learn from experience and to teach the world because they despise all the innovations that may come from the colonized countries that have always been considered inferior.

The pressures of the international institutions of neoliberalism argue that the comparative advantage of less developed territories are mineral resources and that they should be exploited already. For this reason, extraordinary initiatives that had been designed to completely alter the development model based on extractivism, to protect biodiversity requires financing projects with a lot of political will. From a question of struggle for a distribution of land as an agricultural resource for a political construction of a territory with its own cultural identity, it has changed to become the reservoir of biodiversity precisely when the great orgy of natural resources occurs.

The concept of green bio-economy is rationalized based on territorial decision making for smart city investments and capitalize on business models (Belissent, 2010; McGeough & Newman, 2004). Smart city solutions must start with the city solutions, not the smart solutions (Belissent, 2010). The term smart city was coined in the 1990s to suggest that regional planning and development was incorporating innovation, information and communication technologies inserted in globalization processes (Gibson, Kozmetsky, & Smilor, 1992).

Smart city is an initiative that promotes innovation and efficiency of regional planning and design of public services, facilitates access to government information and communication. To create, develop and promote regional green innovation values are needed the relevant contribution of instruments for and innovative communication. Innovation is a novel way of doing useful things embodied and implemented through recursive communication and alignment in regional social networks. Regional social networks underpin green areas innovation.

The Smart City model aims to foster the creation and development of knowledge, innovation, and creativity, increase the efficiency and provides information access and cohesiveness for all the parties involved in sustainable regional development. The policy formulation and implementation of regional green innovation ecosystems must be supported by a sustainable regional planning involving structures and resources.

From another territorial perspective of green regional sustainable planning, smart embedded technology devices are a characteristic of smart cities to distinguish it from intelligent cities and used to create territorial innovation ecosystems by sharing and supporting cooperation between knowledge-intensive activities, institutions for learning and knowledge development, and web-based devices and applications to generate collective intelligence (Komninos, 2008, 2002). Living Labs (European Commission, 2010) is a user-driven open research and innovation ecosystem to facilitate creative roles of users with the goal to involve communities of users in local regional contexts territories.

Open regional innovation and open business models are two concepts elaborated by Chesbrough (2003). The Living Labs concept is user-driven open regional innovation ecosystems which can be applied to smart cities embodying an open business model based on willingness and relationships of collaboration between the citizenry, local governments, social and non-governmental organizations and business enterprises to engage in innovation activities in a kind of deterritorialized space.

Finally, territorial collaboration for regional green innovation systems is based on the concept of competitive advantage (Porter, 1990) and is driven by regional and regional development policies aiming to create the best conditions for sustainable development.

Innovating the Institutional Design

Innovative regional governments tend to be more democratic and accountable supported by institutional and cultural frameworks that allow development of the population in general while providing local funds for initiatives to benefit low-income groups and communities (Satterthwaite, 2002).

Researchers have focused on distinctive theoretical approaches and practices of green area innovation by analyzing radical and incremental innovativeness from different perspectives such as energy-based, material-driven, pollution-prevention, etc. Innovation is incremental and radical changes in ideas, practices, changing rules and institutions, ways of organizing society. Both radical and incremental innovativeness in green areas have a relevant impact on addressing the challenges of the regional environmental and sustainable development. Therefore, regional planning must provide green areas innovation to contribute to sustainable development and economic growth.

The innovation ecosystem is a strategic concentration and interrelations of intensive knowledge-based activities provided by different institutions such as business incubators, technology parks, technology transfer centers, efficient energy centers (Barcelona Field Studies Centre, 2011; Duchesneau, Cohn, & Dutton, 1979), etc. Regional planning and designing are challenged by innovative abilities and an innovative culture to capitalize on the creation of regional green innovation ecosystems to attract individuals and business (McGeough & Newman, 2004; Atkinson & Castro, 2008; Organization for Economic Cooperation and Development [OECD], 2003; The Creative Class, 2011). The model of smart city can promote the public involvement framed under at improving and exploiting the regional cultural heritage.

The regional natural and green resources and infrastructures are basic elements in the innovation ecosystems that can be capitalized and may develop into new business models. Innovation ecosystems start from the formulation and implementation of regional green innovation policies supported by regional planning, resources, and structures. Regional and surrounding areas can evolve towards open, sustainable innovation ecosystems to boost research and experimentation of services driven by users in real-life environments.

Regional green area innovation is characterized as incremental versus radical, radical versus routine, revolutionary versus evolutionary, discontinuous versus incremental innovation, new versus extensions, pioneering versus modifying, original versus adapted and basic versus improvements, etc., by scholars and practitioners (Anderson & Tushman, 1990; Nord & Tucker, 1987; Baker & Sweeney, 1978; Stahl & Steger, 1977; Van de Ven, 1988; Zaltman, Duncan, & Holbeck, 1973). The context of the last 40 years is a context that is not in any way revolutionary, but perhaps counter-revolutionary. In a counter-revolutionary context, expectations are frustrated and democratic institutions do not respond.

Regional green innovation projects can capture an old and shrinking area of the city and turns it into restructured and revitalized creative metropolis. Attractive and cost-effective projects of green innovation should take into account innovative planned building and green spaces outside. Redevelopment of vacant and abandoned regional spaces and buildings in shrinking cities for farming is a green innovation for revitalization. Adopting regional green innovation practices correlates with institutional design and policy changes that empower regional planning and development.

Some examples of regional green innovation projects are community gardens and farms, forestry projects, etc., which support biological diversity and spatial heterogeneity (Tidball & Krasny, 2007). All require investments, active participation and involvement in decision-making process by local residents. Community gardens in the form green innovation exhibiting different types of management offer an opportunity for innovation in green space governance with innovative solutions to individuals, business, communities, etc. These different types of management are formed by local government, private organizations, health centers, schools, an organized group of gardeners, etc. (Lawson, 2005; Hou, Johnson, & Lawson, 2009).

Regional green innovation can be steered toward an opportunity for sustainable knowledge, practices, institutions, and solutions. Citizens and business demands for regional green innovation and green services quality are potential welfare of regional areas. An regional green innovation ecosystem use user-driven innovation methods and requires the support of an open platform for heterogeneous technologies intended to be used for designing and implementing innovative and creative green cases. However, the use of innovative technologies requires also an innovative institutional design.

Operational innovative institutional mechanisms such as differential land taxes and payments for environmental services to support sustainable regional greening activities that contribute to benefits such as carbon sequestration. Stressed regional green innovation systems require an institutional design shifting from the industrial economy and innovative bio-economy towards a more ecological economy to effectively support the generation and use of regional ecosystem services. Regional innovation processes can use industrialization aimed to reach sustainable economy. Regional research, experimentation and innovation technology-oriented ecosystems may be aimed to contributing and developing potentially attractive environments to fulfill the needs of the citizenry.

For example, innovations in regional planning and policies on land use can integrate farming into multi-functional buildings. Regional farming in open rooftop generate several green-roof effects such as reducing the rooftop surface temperatures, reducing summer cooling load and heat losses, insulation against cold, etc. The spread of regional agriculture and gardens development and adaptation requires technological involvement, social organization techniques, diffusion and extension of production techniques. Comprehensive regional planning of cities and food policies can include farming and agriculture as a regional green innovation.

The creation of a collaborative approach to regional green innovation ecosystems is based on sustainable partnerships among the stakeholders from citizens, local government, leaders of the community, business firms, social organizations, etc. aimed to achieve resources and specific goals. The institutional design of the regional space is an object to attract considerable scientific-technological innovations interested in meeting the needs of people and supporting collaboration for the development of innovative solutions to sustainability issues. Smart Cities initiatives are more characterized by public interventions than by new technology deployment in policies of innovation and social inclusion aimed at creating societal and institutional design conditions.

The public space is used to carry out demands in which the public was not in itself a vindication: it was the new work code, the rights of women, and from then on. If the population goes through the non-institutional space it is because the institutions are not democratic or lack vitality and democratic force and therefore the understanding between institutions and institutional spaces is not achieved. Democratic institutional design does not fulfill their mission because they deviate from their functions. The people who have been expelled from the institutions are manifested in the streets depending on the capacity of democracy to respond. That is to say, the transition is manifested in a struggle for real democracy initiated by those who feel expelled and that is historically uncertain. What is claimed is an entry that implies a fundamental reform of the institutions.

Popular knowledge, rescued by the ecologies of knowledge, is knowledge that is often embedded in a practice that is born of struggle, is born in struggle knowledge, and only exists in the practical contexts in which it exists and does not exist. in the institutions of knowledge production. The theory and ecological knowledge as a practice opens spaces to multiplicity and diversity, insofar as it maintains that link to the social and moves away from privileging a certain type of knowledge, the knowledge that triumphed from the seventeenth century, scientific knowledge and the Eurocentric philosophical tradition.

The ecology of knowledge brings some hope in the post-institutional design times because it is carried out in other instances than the traditional ones because the institutions no longer manage to accommodate the echoes of the new generations, which in some way makes new and diverse forms of action are positioning themselves in the regional space, opening new political spaces.

The political struggle takes place in that space because the indignados believe that the institutional spaces were colonized by neoliberalism, neutralizing the right to political manifestation within the institutions, under the conceptualization of post-institutionalist. The post-institutional design moment is also translated into that occupation of spaces, and the logic is the same: it is a political response to a situation of frustration of expectations that were built in the last 40 years, obviously not accrediting institutions, nor in the rights that sustain them, because the right to private property is violated and the right to public property is violated.

Social movements are engaging in cultural innovation challenging conceptual frameworks an identity of the city and regional communities. The new forms of structural articulation between regional social movements and institutions, as well as lines of formalization between a micro and a macro policy, are essential components to improve regional green innovation processes. The acknowledgment of the role of social movements occurs in a neo-liberal pressure boom for natural resources that causes the re-primarization of the economy, that is, a return to that idea, which is the curse from colonialism, that Latin America it exports nature, exports commodities, exports natural resources, exports raw materials, and not industrial goods.

The occupation movement is more a dimension of the post-institutional design movement, which in this case is rape or private property or public property. Private property belongs to the owner, public property is subject to the rules of the State, so those who do not comply with the rules cannot occupy, these are the two dimensions of ownership. An opportunity for innovation for institutional design governance frameworks is a challenge that requires filling the knowledge gaps. Innovation in green regional systems at different scales and across sectors with the involvement of local society provide solutions to improve the quality of life of the regional communities.

A multidimensional measure of radical innovation is required to be applied across different institutional, community and organizational settings with acceptable reliability and validity. Radical innovation of R&D projects is a multidimensional factor which can be measured using a construct of innovation radicalness described by the amount of technological uncertainty, technical expertise, business practices, and costs.

Local policies play an important role in creating the right institutional design setting to foster human capital for research and innovation capabilities to support the creation, establishment, and development of incubators for hi-tech start-ups connected to global-scaled innovation systems. Cities exhibit some weaknesses and strengths on innovation capabilities. Cities located in less developed countries are more active in fostering innovation capabilities than in cities on well-developed countries that are more active in hard domains. Governments are encouraged to increase investments in research and innovation to promote ICTs (Van Winden, Van den Berg, & Pol, 2007).

Environmentally Sustainable Regional Trade and Development

Global, transnational, regional and national regulatory regimes are converging in harmonization of actions in international standards in trade and environmental sustainability, leaving less important roles to the States in the creation and enforcement of rules. The States are the most important institutions of global society who legitimize trade and environmentally sustainable development regulations through international organizations, conference, and meetings, etc. (Klabbers, 2013). Global forces of markets have increased their influence on the interaction between trade and environmental sustainability while local forces have decreased as markets have become more open. Even under conditions of less open market, the economic agents follow the global signals.

The emergence of a global and international administrative space for interactions of trade and environmental commissions involve both domestic and international organizations and institutions, intergovernmental organizations, transnational networks, and coordination arrangements, all of which give rise to concerns about transparency and accountability (Krisch & Kingsbury, 2006). An international regime of a free trade agreement does require that the trade and environmentally sustainable development regime have a formal organization in order to exist. Strategic choice across different national market domains on trade and environmental sustainability issues must take into consideration differences in natural resource endowments, geographic factors, infrastructure, etc.

The free trade agreements have a normative role in environmental sustainability. The approach of NAFTA to trade-environment is more normative than practical and overlaps management interaction with environmentally sustainable development issues internally, informally and quite limited. The Mexican government implemented NAFTA to stimulate sustainable development. The Mexican sustainable development is a guideline of the operation of free trade agreements aimed at the optimal use of natural resources and seeks to protect and preserve the environment. NAFTA is slowly shaping the relationship trade-environment politics, which is becoming increasingly relevant and contributes to organizational legitimacy by setting the regulations, norms, and processes.

Trade regimes are developing trade judicial and administrative capacities in trade adjudication and the creation of centralized bodies to deal with and manage the relationships and interactions in cross-fertilization between trade and environment. However, centralization of a sided agreement to regulate the implications of trade on environmentally sustainable development under the authority of the free trade agreement leads to decision making that is prone to political deadlock and difficulty in adaption and correction.

The administrative and judiciary functions of NAFTA grapple with trade jurisprudence to better accommodate domestic policies to address sustainable development and to develop green economy policies and strategies. Administrative and adjudicatory functions of free trade agreements should grapple with trade jurisprudence that may better accommodate for domestic policies intended to address sustainable development concerns, other international organizations are engaging in developing global strategies for sustainable development.

The concept of sustainable development has been accepted since the mid-1980's when in Rio Declaration on Environment and Development declared that human beings are entitled to a healthy and productive life in harmony with nature. An important advancement in these subjects has been to identify the relationships between trade and environmental measures and to identify the linkages between trade and sustainable development to promote environmentally sustainable development and formulate policies to encourage precatory approaches.

The principle of sustainable development is incorporated in the free trade agreements in order to achieve a balance between economic and non-economic rights and concerns of current and future generations. Furthermore, it has become relevant to analyze social issues and implement policies that may intersect with trade and sustainable development, protection and preservation of natural resources and to address climate change concerns. Also, the linkages between trade principles, economic growth, sustainable consumption, social issues, climate change concerns, and environmentally sustainable development must need to be promoted and raise awareness by policy-makers at domestic and regional levels.

Fertilizations of cross-border trade and environmental sustainability issues enhance the collaboration among the nations involved in the free trade agreement toward more green and clean domestic economies. According to Trujillo (2013), the dialogical approach highlights the adjudicatory and administrative capacities of the trade agreement and the fragmented nature of trade governance.

The dialogic approach provides a nonhierarchical framework for the analysis of interactions between trade and environmental sustainability issues. Trujillo (2013) uses a dialogical approach to frame trade governance and to explain the adjudicatory and administrative functions in cross-fertilization between trade and environmental sustainability issues towards a convergence between domestic and global environmental and trade regulations. International organizations may support convergence with the States through different forms of cooperation in the development and implementation of trade and environmentally sustainable development regulations. The manner in which trade regimes deal with environmental policies influences the link of economic development with sustainable development.

There is an increasing convergence among these variables that may lead to a model of sustainable development. The emerging regime is one of furthering trade principles with green economic growth and environmentally sustainable development goals. The thesis of convergence and inevitability is a polity theory developed by Wittrock (2002), who argues that modernity is a global condition affecting all actions, interpretations, and habits across nations. These dynamics allow cross-fertilization of environmentally sustainable development concerns into cross-border trade negotiations. Fragmentation in trade adjudication is relevant to analyze cross-fertilization between trade and environmental sustainability issues.

The cross-fertilization processes between cross-border trade and environmental sustainability issues incorporate domestic regulations on this subject into the legal free trade agreement framework to recognize its legitimacy. Non-state parties' participation in the trade framework enhances cross-fertilization and dialogue among the different parties. The free trade agreement itself has provided a forum for a jurisdictional regime through adjudicatory processes in a regional arrangement in interaction with the trade agreement and recognizing the cross-border trade and environmental sustainability relationships. It may be argued that the free trade agreement may not be the correct forum to resolve issues on environmental sustainability, despite the impacts that they have on cross-border trade.

NAFTA was the first free trade agreement to incorporate trade concerns into environmental sustainability issues through the formalization of NAAEC. NAAEC has an adjudicatory mechanism to claim environmental sustainability disputes although it is not being used at all. NAFTA involves complex exchange relationships of trade and environmental sustainability issues between the three countries which involve cross-border supply chains and technological changes. This mechanism has been useful in cross-fertilization processes of environmental and trade concerns. This process of cross-fertilization between trade and environmental sustainability issues within the NAFTA trade jurisdiction has an impact on the convergence of national regimes.

Under the assumption that not all countries and regions have developed the same capacities to integrate due to the interactions of local-global forces and economic, political, social, geographical differences, infrastructure, and production regimes. Country members of NAFTA have developed some limited capacities for domestic networks of institutions and organizations across trade and environmental sustainability concerns. Nevertheless, the magnitude of these influences may change over time.

Recent developments in sustainable development elements indicate that it plays a relevant role in investment policies. However, what is the best for investment regimes is not always good for trade and environmental sustainability and development. The free trade agreement is based on the assumption that free trade and investment must guarantee sustainable development for the participating countries. Foreign investments and international cooperation for economic development are relevant and have a positive impact on the sustainable development of the host country. Policymaking on sustainable development has emphasized the role of foreign investment.

Sustainable development is the main objective of foreign investment policymaking of any country to achieve integration and balance of economic, social and environmentally sustainable development aimed at common interests between the home and host countries. Host countries should not consider foreign investment as a barrier considering that they play a relevant role in enacting environmental regulations for sustainable development. Sustainable development has been universally accepted as a common objective for contracting parties to meet the needs of capital-importing states and the needs of economic, social and environmentally sustainable development of host states. In response to various challenges, recent investment agreements promoted by the States places greater emphasis on preserving the regulatory capacities of host states to pursue environmentally sustainable development as public welfare objectives.

The relationships between advocating foreign investment, trade, and sustainable development should be emphasized and balanced with the pursuits of economic growth objectives through environmentally sustainable growth. Free trade agreements may directly impose foreign investment national regulations upon sustainable development. Furthermore, policymaking includes foreign investment and international governance for sustainable development and integration of investment policies. NAFTA's Environmental Side Agreement began to direct attention to the relevance of an agenda for foreign investment and sustainable development. The best endeavor clause does not impose proper substantive obligations upon contracting parties but the right to adopt, maintain and enforce measures considered appropriate to ensure sensitive investments to environmentally sustainable development concerns. Besides, the parties may consult each other.

NAFTA should contribute to the sustainable development of the countries. Foreign investment policy for sustainable development should be aligned with investment for inclusive economic growth, social issues, and environmental concerns. Foreign investment policies in host countries must be aligned and integrated with its sustainable development strategy. Protection of foreign investment should not hinder the power of the host state to regulate public interests for public health, safety, social issues, and environmentally sustainable development concerns. Passive action of host states reduces the operation costs of foreign investments and cannot claim rights.

However, the administrative capacity has allowed some overlaps between public and private rights of action when considered as a dynamic regime. This overlapping between public and private rights of action is illustrated with the conflict between the United Mexican States and the Corn Products International. Other trade disputes resulted in negotiations and dealings with the environmentally sustainable regulations. The economic, social and political capacities of safety nets for trade and environmental sustainability across countries are influenced by dependent and interdependent interactions in international negotiations, public outreach and dispute settlements among the parties.

Complex economic, social and political changes initiated during the 1980s in Mexico had an impact on the economic organization and social structure of rural development and rural livelihoods. Despite the fact that rural communities were strained, corn persists as the main crop of livelihood strategy (De Janvry, Sadoulet, & de Anda, 1995; Eakin, Perales, Appendini, & Sweeney, 2014; Wiggins et al., 2002). Regional cross-border integration in agriculture under the trade framework of NAFTA is provided by the cross-border cattle trade. The disruption of the process of integration of the red meats industry occurred across borders (Veeman, 2017).

This situation has created some concerns for Mexicans regarding food security and food sovereignty. Food security is considered the permanent supply of 'basic and strategic staples' for the population and 'food sovereignty' is the priority accorded to national production for supplying the staples, according to the Mexican Law of Rural Sustainable Development (December 2001) (Cámara de Diputados, 2003). The environmentally sustainable development policy and strategy may be implemented by voluntary schemes through business, non-governmental organizations and local communities to improve performance.

Environmental sustainable development is being considered in the renegotiated NAFTA, now under the acronymic the USA, Mexico, and Canada, as an important and critical issue for the development of commercial exchanges. In fact, the new agreement proves the importance that the institutional capital already created and developed has been essential for the renegotiations of the new agreement.

SOLUTIONS AND RECOMMENDATIONS

Local authorities of the city as the founding ground must have the potential to promote the vision of the regional green innovation ecosystem as assemblies of planning policies. Local authorities must provide support to enhance green innovation capacity and business-intelligence through discussion, debates, and analysis of policies, research programs, and other forms to find solutions to meet the regional green spaces challenges.

Local authorities of the city as the founding ground must have the potential to promote the vision of the regional green innovation ecosystem as assemblies of planning policies. Local authorities must provide support to enhance green innovation capacity and business-intelligence through discussion, debates, and analysis of policies, research programs, and other forms to find solutions to meet the regional green spaces challenges.

The regional planning policies of local government have the potential to promote an regional green innovation ecosystem. Smart local government of a city has the capacity to generate service innovation and communication to deliver to local residents (González & Rossi, 2011). Cities more active in improving their capacity to sense and act through ICT systems are also less likely to differentiate soft domains initiatives related to innovation, human capital, and cultural heritage capabilities.

Fostering the city capacity for regional green innovation requires the implementation of human capital investment and improvement of quality of life initiatives supported by motivated local residents, innovative business, entrepreneurs and investors, talented persons, etc., able to start up new enterprises (Caragliu, Del Bo, & Nijkamp, 2009; Correia & Wünstel, 2011; Giffinger et al., 2007; Hollands, 2008; Rios, 2008; Toppeta, 2010).

Smart cities must instrument local regional green innovation ecosystems and the knowledge of innovation bio-economy overall to face the challenge of securing high living standards. Future Internet technology arrangements in regional green environments involve large business and enterprises, micro, small, medium and enterprises (MSMEs), universities, research centers, etc. Future Internet facilities are used for developing and validating some service concepts and applications supported by the Living Labs approaches for smart cities.

FUTURE RESEARCH DIRECTIONS

Regional green innovation projects have a relationship with other environmentally innovative activities such as green infrastructure, energy efficiency, water quality, drinking water infrastructure, and wastewater, etc. Regional green innovation projects are opportunities for producing goods, food, bioenergy, biomedicine, resource efficiency, farming technologies, new regional spaces, new forms of regional mobility and transportation, etc. Development of innovative regional green planning is required to make use of some prospective studies and methodological tools focused on improving the regional green ecosystem in various elements such as water, waste treatment, energy, etc. Regional green planning and design might integrate risk management in transition periods to incorporate innovative projects such as from fighting against water to living with water (Rijke, De Graaf, Van de Ven, Brown, & Biron, 2008; Newman, Ashley, Molyneux-Hodgson, & Cashman, 2011).

CONCLUSION

This paper has analyzed the interrelationships between the fundamental principles of regional trade and development innovation: decentralize the infrastructure to democratize the territory and innovating the institutional design to address the complexity of the challenges in the city.

The innovation capacity on the use and development of technologies in ecosystems is incorporating parameters of sustainable and environmental regional green innovation planning projects. Regional green innovation planning projects is a strategy to stimulate organizational economic growth. Research and development programs embody regional green innovation planning to anticipate meeting the needs and aspirations of citizens to provide them green public services. Regional innovation planning has a critical role in regional innovation development in specific areas of inclusion, environment, health, education, business, etc.

Future Internet technologies engages users and citizens to enhance participation in the transformation process of individual and collective behaviors and social norms to discover and design sustainable scenarios to implement regional green innovation projects. To this, Learning Alliance can operate in the context of research action referring to the risk management in regional development projects. Learning action alliances are used for regional green innovation in different sectors.

The reference model of regional green innovation ecosystems can evaluate its innovative capacity to identify complementarities and inconsistencies in regional planning and designs. All the opportunities should be explored to build on the innovative regional green capacity of the cities to develop and transform a multifunctional green infrastructure into a more regional green innovation ecosystem. Location of source of experimentation and innovation in green regional areas help to build capacities to face uncertainties and enable changes and transitions in regional governance.

REFERENCES

Anderson, P., & Tushman, M. L. (1990). Technological Discontinuities and Dominant Designs: A Cyclical Model of Technological Change. *Administrative Science Quarterly*, *35*(4), 604–633. doi:10.2307/2393511

Arbesman, S., Kleinberg, J. M., & Strogatz, S. H. (2009). Superlinear Scaling for Innovation in Cities. *Physical Review*, *79*, 1–5. PMID:19257115

Atkinson, R., & Castro, D. (2008). *Digital Quality of Life: Understanding the Personal and Social Benefits of the Information Technology Revolution*. Retrieved October 6, 2019, from https://papers.ssrn.com/sol3/papers.cfm?abstract_id=1278185

Baker, N. R., & Sweeney, D. J. (1978). Toward a Conceptual Framework of the Process of Organized Technological Innovation within the Firm. *Research Policy*, *7*, 150–174. doi:10.1016/0048-7333(78)90003-3

Barcelona Field Studies Centre. (2011). *Barcelona Regional Studies*. Retrieved October 6, 2019, from http://geographyfieldwork.com/barcelona.htm

Belissent, J. (2010). *Getting Clever about Smart Cities: New Opportunities Require New Business Models*. New York, NY: Forrester Research.

Burch, W. R., & De Luca, L. R. (1984). *Measuring the Social Impact of Natural Resource Policies*. Albuquerque, NM: University of Mexico Press.

Burt, R. S. (2002). The Social Capital of Structural Holes. In M. F. Guillen, R. Collins, P. England, & M. Meyer (Eds.), *The New Economic Sociology: Developments in an Emerging Field* (pp. 148–189). New York, NY: Sage.

Burt, R. S. (2005). *Brokerage and Closure: An Introduction to Social Capital*. Oxford, UK: Oxford University Press.

Cámara de Diputados. (2003). *Compilación de leyes para el campo, México, El campo no aguanta más (2002), Seis propuestas para la salvación y revaloriza- ción del campo mexicano*, mimeo (12 organizations signing).

Caragliu, A., Del Bo, C., & Nijkamp, P. (2011). Smart Cities in Europe. *Journal of Urban Technology*, *18*(2), 65–82. doi:10.1080/10630732.2011.601117

Chesbrough, H. W. (2003). *Open Innovation: The New Imperative for Creating and Profiting from Technology*. Boston, MA: Harvard Business School Press.

Correia, L. M., & Wünstel, K. (2011). *Smart Cities Applications and Requirements*. Retrieved October 7, 2019, from http://www.scribd.com/doc/87944173/White-Paper-Smart-Cities-Applications

Cronon, W. (1991). *Nature's Metropolis: Chicago and the Great West*. New York, NY: W.W. Norton & Company.

De Janvry, A., Sadoulet, E., & de Anda, G. G. (1995). NAFTA and Mexico's Maize Producers. *World Development, 23*(8), 1349–1362. doi:10.1016/0305-750X(95)00056-I

Duchesneau, T. D., Cohn, S. E., & Dutton, J. E. (1979). *A Study of Innovation in Manufacturing: Determining Process and Methodological Issues*. Orono, ME: University of Maine.

Eakin, H., Perales, H., Appendini, K., & Sweeney, S. (2014). Selling Maize in Mexico: The Persistence of Peasant Farming in an Era of Global Markets. *Development and Change, 45*(1), 133–155. doi:10.1111/dech.12074

European Commission. (2010). *DG INFSO: Advancing and Applying Living Lab Methodologies*. Brussels, Belgium: European Commission.

Forman, R. (1995). *Land Mosaics: The Ecology of Landscapes and Regions*. Cambridge, MA: Cambridge University Press. doi:10.1017/9781107050327

Gibson, D. V., Kozmetsky, G., & Smilor, R. W. (Eds.). (1992). *The Technopolis Phenomenon: Smart Cities, Fast Systems, Global Networks*. New York, NY: Rowman & Littlefield.

Giffinger, R., Fertner, C., Kramar, H., Kalasek, R., Pichler-Milanović, N., & Meijers, E. (2007). *Smart Cities: Ranking of European Medium-Sized Cities*. Vienna, Austria: Vienna University of Technology.

González, J. A., & Rossi, A. (2011). *New Trends for Smart Cities, Open Innovation Mechanism in Smart Cities*. Retrieved October 7, 2019, from http://opencities.net/sites/opencities.net/files/contentfiles/repository/D2.2.21%20New%20trends%20for%20Smart%20Cities.pdf

Goudie, A. (1994). *The Human Impact on the Natural Environment*. Cambridge, MA: MIT Press.

Granovetter, M. (1973). The Strength of Weak Ties. *American Journal of Sociology, 76*(6), 1360–1380. doi:10.1086/225469

Hollands, R. G. (2008). Will the Real Smart City Please Stand Up? Intelligent, Progressive or Entrepreneurial? *City, 12*(3), 303–319. doi:10.1080/13604810802479126

Hou, J., Johnson, J. M., & Lawson, L. J. (2009). *Greening Cities, Growing Communities: Learning from Seattle's Regional Community Gardens*. Seattle, WA: University of Washington Press.

Klabbers, J. (2013). Unity, Diversity, Accountability: The Ambivalent Concept of International Organisation. *Melbourne Journal of International Law, 14*(1), 149–170.

Komninos, N. (2002). *Intelligent Cities: Innovation, Knowledge Systems and Digital Spaces*. London, UK: Taylor & Francis.

Komninos, N. (2008). *Intelligent Cities and Globalisation of Innovation Networks*. London, UK: Routledge. doi:10.4324/9780203894491

Krisch, N., & Kingsbury, B. (2006). Introduction: Global Governance and Global Administrative Law in the International Legal Order. *European Journal of International Law*, *17*(1), 1–13. doi:10.1093/ejil/chi170

Krott, M. (1998). Regional Forestry: Management within the Focus on People and Trees. In M. Krott, & K. Nilsson (Eds.), *Multiple-Use of Town Forests in International Comparison* (pp. 9–19). Wuppertal, Germany: IUFRO Working Group.

Lawson, L. J. (2005). *City Bountiful: A Century of Community Gardening in America*. Berkeley, CA: University of California Press.

McGeough, U., & Newman, D. (2004). *Model for Sustainable Regional Design with Expanded Sections on Distributed Energy Resources*. Des Plaines, IL: Gas Technology Institute.

Newman, R., Ashley, R. M., Molyneux-Hodgson, S., & Cashman, A. (2011). Managing Water as a Socio-Technical System: The Shift from 'Experts' to 'Alliances'. *Proceedings of the Institution of Civil Engineers. Engineering Sustainability, 164*(ES1), 95-102.

Nord, W. R., & Tucker, S. (1987). *Implementing Routine and Radical Innovations – As Substantive Areas Including Employee Attitudes*. Lexington, MA: Lexington Books.

Organization for Economic Cooperation and Development. (2003). *The E-Government Imperative: Main Findings*. Paris, France: Organization for Economic Cooperation and Development.

Porter, M. (1990). *The Competitive Advantage of Nations*. New York, NY: Free Press. doi:10.1007/978-1-349-11336-1

Rijke, J. S., De Graaf, R. E., Van de Ven, F. H. M., Brown, R. R., & Biron, D. J. (2008). Comparative Case Studies towards Mainstreaming Water Sensitive Regional Design in Australia and the Netherlands. In *Proceedings of the 11th International Conference on Regional Drainage (ICUD)*. Edinburgh, UK.

Rios, P. (2008). *Creating "The Smart City"*. Retrieved October 7, 2019, from http://dspace.udmercy.edu:8080/dspace/bitstream/10429/20/1/2008_rios_smart.pdf

Satterthwaite, D. (2002). Local Funds and Their Potential to Allow Donor Agencies to Support Community Development and Poverty Reduction. *Environment and Regionalization*, *14*(1), 179–188.

Stahl, M. J., & Steger, J. A. (1977). Innovation and Productivity in R&D Tuning Management. *R & D Management*, *7*, 71–76.

The Creative Class. (2011). *The Creative Class*. Retrieved October 7, 2019, from http://www.creativeclass.com/

Tidball, K. G., & Krasny, M. E. (2007). From Risk to Resilience: What Role for Community Greening and Civic Ecology in Cities? In A. Wals (Ed.), *Social Learning Towards a More Sustainable World* (pp. 149–164). Wageningen, The Netherlands: Wageningen Academic Publishers.

Toppeta, D. (2010). *The Smart City Vision: How Innovation and ICT Can Build Smart, "Liveable", Sustainable Cities*. Retrieved October 7, 2019, from http://www.thinkinnovation.org/file/research/23/it/Toppeta_Report_005_2010.pdf

Trujillo, E. (2013). A Dialogical Approach to Trade and Environment. *Journal of International Economic Law*, *16*(3), 535–585. doi:10.1093/jiel/jgt019

Van de Ven, A. (1988). *Progress Report on the Minnesota Innovation Research Project*. Minneapolis, MN: University of Minnesota.

Van Winden, W., Van den Berg, L., & Pol, P. (2007). European Cities in the Knowledge Economy: Towards a Typology. *Regional Studies*, *44*(3), 525–549.

Veeman, M. (2017). Keynote Address. North American Trade Policy for Agriculture and Forestry: Can Economics Trump Politics? *Canadian Journal of Agricultural Economics*, *65*(1), 43–68. doi:10.1111/cjag.12135

Wiggins, S., Keilbach, N., Preibisch, K., Proctor, S., Herrejón, G. R., & Muñoz, G. R. (2002). Discussion – Agricultural Policy Reform and Rural Livelihoods in Central Mexico. *The Journal of Development Studies*, *38*(4), 179–202. doi:10.1080/00220380412331322461

Wittrock, B. (2002). Modernity: One, None, or Many? European Origins and Modernity as a Global Condition. *Daedalus*, *129*, 31–60.

Zaltman, G., Duncan, R., & Holbeck, J. (1973). *Innovations and Organizations*. New York, NY: Wiley.

ADDITIONAL READING

Barrionuevo, J. M., Berrone, P., & Ricart, J. E. (2012). Smart Cities, Sustainable Progress. *IESE Insight*, *14*(14), 50–57. doi:10.15581/002.ART-2152

Chen, T. M. (2010). Smart Grids, Smart Cities Need Better Networks. *IEEE Network*, *24*(2), 2–3. doi:10.1109/MNET.2010.5430136

Guan, L. (2012). Smart Steps to a Battery City. *Government News*, *32*(2), 24–27.

Johnson, D. G. (1975). World Agriculture, Commodity Policy, and Price Variability. *American Journal of Agricultural Economics*, *57*(5), 823–828. doi:10.2307/1239087

Komninos, N., & Sefertzi, E. (2009). Intelligent Cities: R&D Offshoring, Web 2.0 Product Development and Globalization of Innovation Systems. In *Proceedings of the Second Knowledge Cities Summit*. Shenzhen: The Hong Kong Polytechnic University.

Lima de Oliveira, A., & Grangeiro da Silva Castro, G. (2019). Smart Cities: Communication and Consumption of a Prescribed Future in Urban Space. *Interin*, *24*(1), 209–225. doi:10.35168/1980-5276.UTP.interin.2019.Vol24.N1.pp209-225

Nasir, M., Salman, M., Ahmad, F., & Siddiquee, T.A.R. (2019). Critical Assessment of Smart City Mission – A Research of Gwalior Smart City Proposals. *International Journal of Innovative Technology and Exploring Engineering, 8*(6S4), 1181-1187.

So, J., Kim, T., Kim, M., Kang, J., Lee, H., & Choi, J. M. (2019). A Study on the Concept of Smart City and Smart City Transport. *Journal of the Korean Society for Transplantation*, *37*(2), 79–91. doi:10.7470/jkst.2019.37.1.079

KEY TERMS AND DEFINITIONS

Democratization: A process of distributing or dispersing functions, powers, persons from the State or central government to regional and local administrations.

Infrastructure: A set of technical means, services and facilities necessary for the development of an activity or for a place to be used.

Institutional Design: The projects carried out for organizations that play a social interest function.

Regional: Makes reference to that belonging to or relating to the city.

Regional Trade: A freely determined geographical area, which does not necessarily coincide with political boundaries. The meeting and exchange with local producers and artisans in the region, a space to discover quality products and various artisanal productions.

Sustainable Development: A type of development obtained to meet the needs of the present generation without compromising the ability of future generations to meet their own needs.

Territory: An extension of land that belongs to a state, province or other type of political division.

Compilation of References

Abhayaratne, A. S. P. (1996). Foreign Trade and Economic Growth Evidence from Sri Lanka, 1960-1992. *Applied Economics Letters*, *9*(3), 567–570. doi:10.1080/135048596355961

Abu-Bader, S., & Abu-Qarn, A. S. (2003). Causality Evidence from Egypt, Israel, and Syria Government Expenditures, Military Spending and Economic Growth. *Journal of Policy Modeling*, *25*(6-7), 567–583. doi:10.1016/S0161-8938(03)00057-7

Ades, A., & Chua, H. (1997). The Neighbor's Curse: Regional Instability and Economic Growth. *Journal of Economic Growth*, *2*(3), 279–304. doi:10.1023/A:1009782809329

Africa Export-Import Bank, & Export-Import Bank of India. (2018). *Deepening South-South Collaboration: An Analysis of Africa and India's Trade and Investment*. Heliopolis: Africa Export-Import Bank.

African Union. (2012). *The First Sino-African Media Forum on Cooperation – Beijing, China*. Retrieved October 5, 2019, from https://au.int/en/newsevents/20120822-0

African Union. (2014a). *Countries in Africa and China Renew Their Commitment to Jointly Eliminating Poverty – Africa-China Poverty Reduction and Development Conference*. Retrieved October 5, 2019, from https://au.int/en/newsevents/14665/countries-africa-and-china-renew-their-commitment-jointly-eliminating-poverty

African Union. (2014b). *Statement by the Chairperson of the African Union Commission*. Addis Ababa: African Union.

African Union. (2016). *The 3rd Forum on China-Africa Media Cooperation, Beijing, People's Republic of China, 21 June 2016*. Retrieved October 5, 2019, from https://au.int/en/newsevents/30802/3rd-forum-china-africa-media-cooperation-beijing-people-s-republic-china

Aggarwal, V. K., & Espach, R. H. (2003). *Diverging Trade Strategies in Latin America: An Analytical Framework. Berkeley, CA*: University of California.

Aidehou, K. C. L., Yang, S. Y., & Ehikioya, B. (2014). Ecowas Member Countries Trade with China: Analysis of Structural Transformation. *International Journal of Innovation and Applied Studies*, *8*(2), 756–769.

Aizenman, J., & Glick, R. (2006). Military Expenditure, Threats, and Growth. *The Journal of International Trade & Economic Development*, *15*(2), 129–155. doi:10.1080/09638190600689095

Akira, K. (2000). *A Note on Globalization and Regional Integration*. Retrieved August 22, 2019, from https://project.iss.u-tokyo.ac.jp/kikkawa/iss-1.pdf

Alfaro, L., Chanda, A., Kalemli-Ozcan, S., & Sayek, S. (2004). FDI and Economic Growth: The Role of Local Financial Markets. *Journal of International Economics*, *64*(1), 89–112. doi:10.1016/S0022-1996(03)00081-3

Alguacil, M., Cuadros, A., & Orts, V. (2011). Inward FDI and Growth: The Role of Macroeconomic and Institutional Environment. *Journal of Policy Modeling*, *33*(3), 481–496. doi:10.1016/j.jpolmod.2010.12.004

Anderson, J. E. (1979). A Theoretical Foundation for the Gravity Equation. *The American Economic Review*, *69*(1), 106–116.

Anderson, P., & Tushman, M. L. (1990). Technological Discontinuities and Dominant Designs: A Cyclical Model of Technological Change. *Administrative Science Quarterly*, *35*(4), 604–633. doi:10.2307/2393511

Anwar, S., & Sun, S. (2011). Financial Development, Foreign Investment and Economic Growth in Malaysia. *Journal of Asian Economics*, *22*(4), 335–342. doi:10.1016/j.asieco.2011.04.001

Arbesman, S., Kleinberg, J. M., & Strogatz, S. H. (2009). Superlinear Scaling for Innovation in Cities. *Physical Review*, *79*, 1–5. PMID:19257115

Arellano, M., & Bond, S. (1991). Some Tests of Specification for Panel Data: Monte Carlo Evidence and an Application to Employment Equations. *The Review of Economic Studies*, *58*(2), 277–297. doi:10.2307/2297968

Argimón, I., González, J. M., & Roldán, J. M. (1997). Evidence of Public Spending Crowding-Out from a Panel of OECD Countries. *Applied Economics, 29*(8), 001-1010.

Arunatilake, N., Jayasuriya, S., & Kelegama, S. (2001). The Economic Cost of the War in Sir Lanka. *World Development*, *29*(9), 1483–1500. doi:10.1016/S0305-750X(01)00056-0

Asiedu, E. (2002). On the Determinants of Foreign Direct Investment to Developing Countries: Is Africa Different? *World Development*, *30*(1), 107–119. doi:10.1016/S0305-750X(01)00100-0

Asongu, S., & Kodila-Tedika, O. (2015). *Conditional Determinants of FDI in Fast Emerging Economies: An Instrumental Quantile Regression Approach*. Yaounde, Cameroon: African Governance and Development Institute.

Asongu, S., & Odhiambo, N. M. (2018). Drivers of Growth in Fast Emerging Economies: A Dynamic Instrumental Quantile Approach to Real Output and Its Rates of Growth in BRICS and MINT Countries, 2001-2011. *Applied Econometrics and International Development*, *18*(1), 5–22.

Asteriou, D., Masatci, K., & Pılbeam, K. (2016). Exchange Rate Volatility and International Trade: International Evidence from the MINT Countries. *Economic Modelling*, *58*, 133–140. doi:10.1016/j.econmod.2016.05.006

Atkinson, R., & Castro, D. (2008). *Digital Quality of Life: Understanding the Personal and Social Benefits of the Information Technology Revolution*. Retrieved October 6, 2019, from https://papers.ssrn.com/sol3/papers.cfm?abstract_id=1278185

Attri, V. N. (2016). *An Emerging New Development Paradigm of the Blue Economy in IORA; A Policy Framework for the Future*. Retrieved September 27, 2019, from https://www.iora.int/media/23838/the-blue-economy-and-iora-2016.pdf

Awokuse, T. O. (2007). Causality between Exports, Imports, and Economic Growth: Evidence from Transition Economies. *Economics Letters*, *94*(3), 389–395. doi:10.1016/j.econlet.2006.08.025

Awokuse, T. O. (2008). Trade Openness and Economic Growth: Is Growth Export-Led or Import-Led? *Applied Economics*, *40*(2), 161–173. doi:10.1080/00036840600749490

Awokuse, T. O., & Christopoulos, D. K. (2009). Nonlinear Dynamics and the Exports-Output Growth Nexus. *Economic Modelling*, *26*(1), 184–190. doi:10.1016/j.econmod.2008.06.009

Azam, M., & Lukman, L. (2010). Determinants of Foreign Direct Investment in India, Indonesia and Pakistan: A Quantitative Approach. *Journal of Managerial Sciences*, *4*(1), 31–43.

Baert, F., Scaramangli, T., & Soderbaum, F. (Eds.). (2014). *Intersecting Regionalism. Regions, Global Governance and The EU*. London, UK: Springer. doi:10.1007/978-94-007-7566-4

Bajpai, S., & Sharma, A. K. (2018). An Empirical Test of the Select Multifactor Asset Pricing Models with GMM. *International Journal of Business Innovation and Research*, *15*(3), 357–380. doi:10.1504/IJBIR.2018.089753

Baker, N. R., & Sweeney, D. J. (1978). Toward a Conceptual Framework of the Process of Organized Technological Innovation within the Firm. *Research Policy*, *7*, 150–174. doi:10.1016/0048-7333(78)90003-3

Balassa, B. (1965). Trade Liberalization and Revealed Comparative Advantage. Manchester School of Economics and Social Science, 33, 99-123.

Balassa, B. (1965). Trade Liberalization and Revealed Comparative Advantage. *The Manchester School of Economic and Social Studies*, *33*(2), 99–123. doi:10.1111/j.1467-9957.1965.tb00050.x

Balasubramaniam, A., Mansor, S. A., & Puah, C.-H. (2016). The Relationship between Trade Integration and Economic Growth: Case of ASEAN-5 Countries. *Global Economy Journal*, *16*(4), 745–768. doi:10.1515/gej-2016-0024

Banaji, J. (2000). *Foreign Portfolio Investment in Indian Equity Markets: Has the Economy Benefited?* Oxford, UK: Queen Elizabeth House.

Banik, N. (2006). How Promising Is BIMSTEC? *Economic and Political Weekly*, *41*(51), 5264–5268.

Barcelona Field Studies Centre. (2011). *Barcelona Regional Studies*. Retrieved October 6, 2019, from http://geography-fieldwork.com/barcelona.htm

Barro, R. J. (1990). Government Spending in a Simple Model of Endogenous Growth. *Journal of Political Economy*, *98*(5, Part 2S5), 103–125. doi:10.1086/261726

Bartenstein, K. (2015). The "Common Arctic": Legal Analysis of Arctic and non-Arctic Political Discourses. In L. Heininen, H. Exner-Pirot, & J. Plouffe (Eds.), *Arctic Yearbook 2015* (pp. 264–280). Akureyri: Northern Research Forum.

Basu, S., Deepthi, D., & Reddy, J. (2011). *Country Risk Analysis in Emerging Markets: The Indian Example*. Bangalore, India: Indian Institute of Management Bangalore.

Batra, A. (2010). Asian Economic Integration and Sub-Regionalism: A Case Study of the BIMSTEC. *International Studies*, *47*(1), 1–25. doi:10.1177/002088171104700101

Batra, A., & Khan, Z. (2005). *Revealed Comparative Advantage: An Analysis for India and China*. New Delhi, India: Indian Council for Research on International Economic Relations.

Bawa, A., Bohler-Muller, N., Fikeni, S., Zondi, S., & Naidu, S. (Eds.). (2013). *BRICS and Africa: Partnership for Development, Integration and Industrialisation*. Pretoria, South Africa: The Department of International Relations and Cooperation.

Beatty, E. (2000). The Impact of Foreign Trade on the Mexican Economy: Terms of Trade and the Rise of Industry 1880-1923. *Journal of Latin American Studies*, *32*(2), 399–433. doi:10.1017/S0022216X00005794

Begum, S., & Shamsuddin, A. F. M. (1998). Exports and Economic Growth in Bangladesh. *The Journal of Development Studies*, *35*(1), 89–114. doi:10.1080/00220389808422556

Belissent, J. (2010). *Getting Clever about Smart Cities: New Opportunities Require New Business Models*. New York, NY: Forrester Research.

Benesova, I., Maitah, M., Smutka, L., Tomsik, K., & Ishchukova, N. (2017). Perspectives of the Russian Agricultural Exports in Terms of Comparative Advantage. *Agricultural Economics – Czech, 63*, 1-13.

Bergstrand, J. H. (1985). The Gravity Equation in International Trade: Some Microeconomic Foundations and Empirical Evidence. *The Review of Economics and Statistics, 67*(3), 474–481. doi:10.2307/1925976

Bhardwaj, A. (2019). Fourth Industrial Revolution: Decay of Liberalism and Withering Away of the Left. *Economic and Political Weekly, 54*(30), 12–14.

Bhattacharya, S. K., & Bhattacharya, B. N. (2006). *Prospects of Regional Cooperation in Trade, Investment and Finance in Asia: An Empirical Analysis on BIMSTEC Countries and Japan.* Retrieved October 4, 2019, from https://ssrn.com/abstract=905761

Bhattacharya, S. K. (2007). *Does BIMSTEC-Japan Economic Cooperation Promote Intra-Regional Trade? The Case for Free Trade Arrangement.* Delhi, India: Centre for Studies in International Relations and Development.

Billington, N. (1999). The Location of Foreign Direct Investment: An Empirical Analysis. *Applied Economics, 31*(1), 65–76. doi:10.1080/00036846.2019.12067087

Bondaz, A., Cohen, D., Godement, F., Kratz, A., & Pantucci, R. (2015). *One Belt, One Road: China's Great Leap Outward.* London, UK: European Council on Foreign Relations.

Borensztein, E., De Gregorio, J., & Lee, J.-W. (1998). How Does Foreign Direct Investment Affect Economic Growth? *Journal of International Economics, 45*(1), 115–135. doi:10.1016/S0022-1996(97)00033-0

Botric, V., & Škuflic, L. (2006). Main Determinants of Foreign Direct Investment in the Southeast European Countries. *Transition Studies Review, 13*(2), 359–377. doi:10.100711300-006-0110-3

Brautigam, D., Diao, X., McMillan, M., & Silver, J. (2017). *Chinese Investment in Africa: How Much Do We Know?* Washington, DC: International Food Policy Research Institute.

Broadman, H. G., Isik, G., Plaza, S., Ye, X., & Yoshino, Y. (2006). *Africa's Silk Road: China and India's New Economic Frontier.* Washington, DC: World Bank. doi:10.1596/978-0-8213-6835-0

Brozen, Y. (1958). Means for Maintaining Economic Stability. *Journal of Farm Economics, 40*(5), 1069–1078. doi:10.2307/1234973

Bugajski, J. (2008). *Expanding Eurasia: Russia's European Ambitions.* Washington, DC: Center for Strategic and International Studies.

Burch, W. R., & De Luca, L. R. (1984). *Measuring the Social Impact of Natural Resource Policies.* Albuquerque, NM: University of Mexico Press.

Burt, R. S. (2002). The Social Capital of Structural Holes. In M. F. Guillen, R. Collins, P. England, & M. Meyer (Eds.), *The New Economic Sociology: Developments in an Emerging Field* (pp. 148–189). New York, NY: Sage.

Burt, R. S. (2005). *Brokerage and Closure: An Introduction to Social Capital.* Oxford, UK: Oxford University Press.

Busse, M., & Hefeker, C. (2007). Political Risk, Institutions and Foreign Direct Investment. *European Journal of Political Economy, 23*(2), 397–415. doi:10.1016/j.ejpoleco.2006.02.003

Caleb, G., Mazanai, M., & Dhoro, N. L. (2014). Relationship between International Trade and Economic Growth: A Cointegration Analysis for Zimbabwe. *Mediterranean Journal of Social Sciences, 20*(5), 621–627.

Cámara de Diputados. (2003). *Compilación de leyes para el campo, México, El campo no aguanta más (2002), Seis propuestas para la salvación y revaloriza- ción del campo mexicano*, mimeo (12 organizations signing).

Caragliu, A., Del Bo, C., & Nijkamp, P. (2011). Smart Cities in Europe. *Journal of Urban Technology*, *18*(2), 65–82. doi:10.1080/10630732.2011.601117

Chakrabarti, R. (2001). FII Flows to India: Nature and Causes. *Money and Finance, 2*(7). Retrieved October 2, 2019, from https://papers.ssrn.com/sol3/papers.cfm?abstract_id=649852

Chakrabarti, A. (2001). The Determinants of Foreign Direct Investments: Sensitivity Analyses of Cross-Country Regressions. *Kyklos*, *54*(1), 89–114. doi:10.1111/1467-6435.00142

Chakrabarti, S., & Ghosh, I. (2014). FDI in Africa: A Comparison of the Indian and Chinese Experience. *Procedia: Social and Behavioral Sciences*, *157*, 340–352. doi:10.1016/j.sbspro.2014.11.038

Chakrabarty, M. (2018). *Indian Investments in Africa: Scale, Trends, and Policy Recommendations*. New Delhi, India: Observer Research Foundation.

Chakraborty, D. (2007a). India's New Regionalism in Asia: Look East and BIMSTEC Interface. In T. Nirmala Devi (Ed.), *India and Bay of Bengal Community: The BIMSTEC Experiment* (pp. 106–121). New Delhi, India: Gyan Publishing House.

Chakraborty, D. (2007b). *Trade Performance and Integration Experience of BIMSTEC: A Review of Issues*. Kolkata, India: Centre for Studies in International Relations and Development.

Chamber of Commerce and Industry of the Republic of Bashkortostan. (2019). *The Fifth Small Business Forum of the SCO and BRICS Regions Takes Place on September 26-27, 2019*. Retrieved August 24, 2019, from https://sco-brics.ru/en/registration-reliz/

Chamberlain, G. (1978). Omitted Variable Bias in Panel Data: Estimating the Returns to Schooling. *Annales de l'INSEE*, *30/31*(30/31), 49–63. doi:10.2307/20075285

Chandrasekhar, C. P. (2019). *Looming Economic War*. Retrieved August 22, 2019, from https://frontline.thehindu.com/columns/C_P_Chandrasekhar/article27546724.ece

Cheru, F., & Obi, C. (2010). *The Rise of China and India in Africa: Challenges, Opportunities, and Critical Interventions*. London, UK: Zed Books.

Chesbrough, H. W. (2003). *Open Innovation: The New Imperative for Creating and Profiting from Technology*. Boston, MA: Harvard Business School Press.

China-Africa Development Fund. (2013). General Introduction. Beijing: China-Africa Development Fund.

Chittedi, K. R. (2008). Volatility of Indian Stock Market and FIIs. *European Business Review*, *15*(31), 22–34.

Chowdhury, A. B., & Neogi, D. (2014). Trade Complementarity and Similarity between India and BIMSTEC Countries in the Context of the Regional Trade Agreement (RTA). [IJRESS]. *International Journal of Research in Economics & Social Sciences*, *4*(6), 5–14.

Coates, K. S., & Holroyd, C. (2017). Non-Arctic States and Their Stake in Arctic Sustainability. In K. Keil & S. Knecht (Eds.), *Governing Arctic Change* (pp. 207–228). Cham, Switzerland: Springer. doi:10.1057/978-1-137-50884-3_11

Correa, C. (2019). *Financing for Development*. Washington, DC: United Nations.

Correia, L. M., & Wünstel, K. (2011). *Smart Cities Applications and Requirements*. Retrieved October 7, 2019, from http://www.scribd.com/doc/87944173/White-Paper-Smart-Cities-Applications

Cosset, J. C., & Roy, J. (1991). The Determinants of Country Risk Ratings. *Journal of International Business Studies*, *22*(1), 135–142. doi:10.1057/palgrave.jibs.8490296

Cronon, W. (1991). *Nature's Metropolis: Chicago and the Great West*. New York, NY: W.W. Norton & Company.

De Janvry, A., Sadoulet, E., & de Anda, G. G. (1995). NAFTA and Mexico's Maize Producers. *World Development*, *23*(8), 1349–1362. doi:10.1016/0305-750X(95)00056-I

Deger, S. (1986). Economic Development and Defense Expenditure. *Economic Development and Cultural Change*, *34*(4), 677–701.

Deichmann, J. I. (2001). Distribution of Foreign Direct Investment among Transition Economies in Central and Eastern Europe. *Post-Soviet Geography and Economics*, *42*(2), 142–152. doi:10.1080/10889388.2001.10641167

Delgado, D. L. (2015). Discourse, Identity, and International Development Cooperation: China, Africa and FOCAC. *Asia-Pacific Social Science Review*, *15*(2), 1–18.

De, P. (2013). Assessing Barriers to Trade in Services in India: An Empirical Investigation. *Journal of Economic Integration*, *28*(1), 108–143. doi:10.11130/jei.2013.28.1.108

Devereux, M. B., & Smith, G. W. (2007). Transfer Problem Dynamics: Macroeconomics of the Franco-Prussian War Indemnity. *Journal of Monetary Economics*, *54*(8), 2375–2398. doi:10.1016/j.jmoneco.2007.06.027

Devi, T. N. (2007). Economic Cooperation in BIMSTEC: Emerging Trends and Prospects. In T. Nirmala Devi (Ed.), *India and Bay of Bengal Community: The BIMSTEC Experiment* (pp. 128–154). New Delhi, India: Gyan Publishing House.

Diamonte, R. L., Liew, J. M., & Stevens, R. L. (1996). Political Risk in Emerging and Developed Markets. *Financial Analysts Journal*, *52*(3), 71–76. doi:10.2469/faj.v52.n3.1998

Diener, A. C. (2015). Parsing Mobilities in Central Eurasia: Border Management and New Silk Roads. *Eurasian Geography and Economics*, *56*(4), 376–404. doi:10.1080/15387216.2015.1078736

Dodaro, S. (1993). Exports and Growth: A Reconsideration of Causality. *Journal of Developing Areas*, *27*(2), 227–244.

Dollar, D., & Kraay, A. (2004). Trade, Growth, and Poverty. *Economic Journal (London)*, *493*(114), F22–F49. doi:10.1111/j.0013-0133.2004.00186.x

Dornbusch, R., & Park, Y. C. (1995). *Financial Integration in a Second Best World: Are We Still Sure About Our Classical Prejudices*. Seoul, South Korea: Korea Institute of Finance.

Doyle, T. (2018). Blue Economy and the Indian Ocean Rim. *Journal of the Indian Ocean Region*, *14*(1), 1–6. doi:10.1080/19480881.2018.1421450

Dragneva, R., & Wolczuk, K. (2017). *The Eurasian Economic Union: Deals, Rules and the Exercise of Power.* London, UK: Chatham House, the Royal Institute of International Affairs.

Dritsaki, M., Dritsaki, C., & Adamopoulos, A. (2004). A Causal Relationship between Trade, Foreign Direct Investment and Economic Growth for Greece. *American Journal of Applied Sciences*, *3*(1), 230–235.

Duchesneau, T. D., Cohn, S. E., & Dutton, J. E. (1979). *A Study of Innovation in Manufacturing: Determining Process and Methodological Issues*. Orono, ME: University of Maine.

Dumas, B. (1978). The Theory of the Trading Firm Revisited. *The Journal of Finance*, *33*(3), 1019–1030. doi:10.1111/j.1540-6261.1978.tb02041.x

Dunning, J. H. (1973). The Determinants of International Production. *Oxford Economic Papers*, *25*(3), 289–336. doi:10.1093/oxfordjournals.oep.a041261

Durotoye, A. (2014). The MINT Countries as Emerging Economic Power Bloc: Prospects and Challenges. *Developing Country Studies*, *15*(4), 99–106.

Dutta, N., & Roy, S. (2009). The Impact of Foreign Direct Investment on Press Freedom. *Kyklos*, *62*(2), 239–257. doi:10.1111/j.1467-6435.2009.00434.x

Eakin, H., Perales, H., Appendini, K., & Sweeney, S. (2014). Selling Maize in Mexico: The Persistence of Peasant Farming in an Era of Global Markets. *Development and Change*, *45*(1), 133–155. doi:10.1111/dech.12074

East African Community. (2011). *Press Release: EAC and China Sign Framework Agreement to Boost Trade, Investment.* Retrieved October 5, 2019, from https://assets.aspeninstitute.org/content/uploads/files/content/images/ghd/China_EAC_Press_Release_11.17.2011.pdf

East African Community. (2017). *China Accredits Envoy to EAC Bloc.* Retrieved October 5, 2019, from https://www.eac.int/press-releases/151-international-relations/899-china-accredits-envoy-to-eac-bloc

East African Community. (2018). *EAC, China Sign Financing Agreement.* Retrieved October 5, 2019, from https://www.eac.int/press-releases/155-resource-mobilization/1293-eac,-china-sign-financing-agreement

East African Community. (2019). *EAC-China Forum on Air Traffic Management Concludes in Arusha.* Retrieved October 5, 2019, from https://www.eac.int/press-releases/629-1106-662-eac-china-forum-on-air-traffic-management-concludes-in-arusha

Economic and Commercial Section of the Consulate General of the People's Republic of China in Lagos. (2012). *China, ECOWAS Move to Strengthen Ties.* Retrieved October 5, 2019, from http://ng2.mofcom.gov.cn/article/bilateralvisits/201212/20121208488755.shtml

Economic Community of West African States. (2018). *ECOWAS Signs MOU with China for the Construction of the New ECOWAS Commission Headquarters.* Retrieved October 5, 2019, from https://www.ecowas.int/ecowas-signs-mou-with-china-for-the-construction-of-the-new-ecowas-commission-headquarters/

Economic Community of West African States. (2019). *History.* Retrieved October 5, 2019, from https://www.ecowas.int/about-ecowas/history/

Ekanayake, E. M. (1999). Exports and Economic Growth in Asian Developing Countries: Cointegration and Error-Correction Models. *Journal of Economic Development*, *24*(2), 43–56.

Ekanayake, E. M., Mukherjee, A., & Veeramacheneni, B. (2010). Trade Blocks and the Gravity Model: A Study of Economic Integration among Asian Developing Countries. *Journal of Economic Integration*, *25*(4), 627–643. doi:10.11130/jei.2010.25.4.627

Elisabeth, A. (2017). Diversity, Community, Cooperation: Cultural Intersections in the Indian Ocean Region. *Journal of the Indian Ocean Region*, *13*(3), 277–280. doi:10.1080/19480881.2017.1374674

Embassy of the People's Republic of China in the Federal Republic of Nigeria. (2016). *Gu Xiaojie Met with New President of ECOWAS Commission.* Retrieved October 5, 2019, from http://ng.china-embassy.org/eng/zt/ecowas/t1358045.htm

Erokhin, V. (2015). Contemporary Reshaping of Eurasian Integration: Russia's Policies and their Implication for the EU and EurAsEC. *Procedia Economics and Finance*, *22*, 402–411. doi:10.1016/S2212-5671(15)00313-5

Erokhin, V. (2016). Rising Economic Powers among Economies in Transition: Is There Enough Space on the Global Market? In V. Erokhin (Ed.), *Global Perspectives on Trade Integration and Economies in Transition* (pp. 1–25). Hershey, PA: IGI Global. doi:10.4018/978-1-5225-0451-1.ch001

Erokhin, V. (2017). Factors Influencing Food Markets in Developing Countries: An Approach to Assess Sustainability of the Food Supply in Russia. *Sustainability*, *9*(8), 1313. doi:10.3390u9081313

Erokhin, V. (2017). How to Shape the Market: China's One Belt One Road Initiative. In M. Malovic, & K. Roy (Eds.), *The State and the Market in Economic Development: In Pursuit of Millennium Development Goals* (pp. 144–156). Brisbane, Australia: The IIDS Australia Inc.

Erokhin, V. (2018). Contemporary Foreign Trade Policy of China in the Region of Central and Northeast Asia. In A. C. Ozer (Ed.), *Globalization and Trade Integration in Developing Countries* (pp. 27–54). Hershey, PA: IGI Global. doi:10.4018/978-1-5225-4032-8.ch002

Erokhin, V. (2019). Arctic Connectivity for Sustainable Development: Major Actors, Policies, and Approaches. In V. Erokhin, T. Gao, & X. Zhang (Eds.), *Handbook of Research on International Collaboration, Economic Development, and Sustainability in the Arctic* (pp. 24–54). Hershey, PA: IGI Global. doi:10.4018/978-1-5225-6954-1.ch002

Erokhin, V. (Ed.). (2016). *Global Perspectives on Trade Integration and Economies in Transition*. Hershey, PA: IGI Global. doi:10.4018/978-1-5225-0451-1

Erokhin, V., & Gao, T. (2018). Competitive Advantages of China's Agricultural Exports in the Outward-Looking Belt and Road Initiative. In W. Zhang, I. Alon, & C. Lattemann (Eds.), *China's Belt and Road Initiative: Changing the Rules of Globalization* (pp. 265–285). London, UK: Palgrave Macmillan. doi:10.1007/978-3-319-75435-2_14

Erokhin, V., Gao, T., & Zhang, X. (Eds.). (2019). *Handbook of Research on International Collaboration, Economic Development, and Sustainability in the Arctic*. Hershey, PA: IGI Global. doi:10.4018/978-1-5225-6954-1

European Commission. (2010). *DG INFSO: Advancing and Applying Living Lab Methodologies*. Brussels, Belgium: European Commission.

European Commission. (2019). *East African Community (EAC)*. Retrieved October 5, 2019, from https://ec.europa.eu/trade/policy/countries-and-regions/regions/eac/

Fajana, O. (1979). Trade and Growth: The Nigerian Experience. *World Development*, *7*(1), 73–78. doi:10.1016/0305-750X(79)90009-3

Fan, C. C. (1992a). Foreign Trade and Regional Development in China. *Geographical Analysis*, *24*(3), 240–256. doi:10.1111/j.1538-4632.1992.tb00264.x

Fan, C. C. (1992b). Regional Impacts of Foreign Trade in China, 1984-1989. *Growth and Change*, *23*(2), 129–159. doi:10.1111/j.1468-2257.1992.tb00576.x

Fan, S. (1997). Production and Productivity Growth in Chinese Agriculture: New Measurement and Evidence. *Food Policy*, *22*(3), 213–228. doi:10.1016/S0306-9192(97)00010-9

Fanta, A. B. (2017). Bond Markets, Stock Markets, Banks and Growth: A System GMM Analysis. *Global Business and Economics Review*, *19*(1), 1–14. doi:10.1504/GBER.2017.080779

Federal State Statistics Service of the Russian Federation. (2019). *Russia in Figures*. Retrieved June 13, 2019, from http://www.gks.ru/wps/wcm/connect/rosstat_main/rosstat/en/main/

Feder, G. (1983). On Exports and Economic Growth. *Journal of Development Economics*, *12*(1-2), 59–73. doi:10.1016/0304-3878(83)90031-7

Fedorenko, V. (2015). *Eurasian Integration: Effects on Central Asia*. Washington, DC: Rethink Institute.

Fischer, B. (1995). Foreign Portfolio Equity Investment in Emerging Markets: A Panacea for Economic Development. *Savings and Development*, *19*(2), 149–173.

Forman, R. (1995). *Land Mosaics: The Ecology of Landscapes and Regions*. Cambridge, MA: Cambridge University Press. doi:10.1017/9781107050327

Forum on China-Africa Cooperation. (2006). *Forum on China-Africa Cooperation. Beijing Action Plan (2007-2009)*. Retrieved October 5, 2019, from https://www.focac.org/eng/zywx_1/zywj/t280369.htm

Forum on China-Africa Cooperation. (2015). *The Forum on China-Africa Cooperation. Johannesburg Action Plan (2016-2018)*. Retrieved October 5, 2019, from https://www.focac.org/eng/zywx_1/zywj/t1327961.htm

Foster, V., Butterfield, W., Chen, C., & Pushak, N. (2008). *Building Bridges: China's Growing Role as Infrastructure Financier for Sub-Saharan Africa*. Washington, DC: International Bank for Reconstruction and Development.

Fosu, A. K. (1992). Political Instability and Economic Growth: Evidence from Sub-Saharan Africa. *Economic Development and Cultural Change*, *40*(4), 829–841. doi:10.1086/451979

Francesco, S., & Ardita, T. (2015). Markets' Globalization and Emerging Economies. MINTs Economic Growth: Developments and Prospects. *International Journal of Business and Commerce*, *5*(2), 38–55.

Gale, F., Hansen, J., & Jewison, M. (2015). *China's Growing Demand for Agricultural Imports*. Washington, DC: U.S. Department of Agriculture, Economic Research Service.

Gamage, R. N. (2016). Blue Economy in Southeast Asia: Oceans as the New Frontier of Economic Development. *Maritime Affairs: Journal of the National Maritime Foundation of India*, *12*(2), 1–15.

Gao, T. (2017). Food Security and Rural Development on Emerging Markets of Northeast Asia: Cases of Chinese North and Russian Far East. In V. Erokhin (Ed.), *Establishing Food Security and Alternatives to International Trade in Emerging Economies* (pp. 155–176). Hershey, PA: IGI Global.

Gao, T. (2019). Going North: China's Role in the Arctic Blue Economic Corridor. In V. Erokhin, T. Gao, & X. Zhang (Eds.), *Handbook of Research on International Collaboration, Economic Development, and Sustainability in the Arctic* (pp. 133–161). Hershey, PA: IGI Global.

Gao, T., Ivolga, A., & Erokhin, V. (2018). Sustainable Rural Development in Northern China: Caught in a Vice between Poverty, Urban Attractions, and Migration. *Sustainability*, *10*(5), 1467. doi:10.3390u10051467

Garg, R., & Dua, P. (2014). Foreign Portfolio Investment Flows to India: Determinants and Analysis. *World Development*, *59*, 16–28. doi:10.1016/j.worlddev.2014.01.030

Gathogo, G., & Ragui, M. (2014). Capital Structure of Kenyan Firms: What Determines It? Research. *Journal of Finance and Accounting*, *5*(5), 118–125.

Ghatak, S., Silaghi, M., & Daly, V. (2009). Trade and Migration Flows between Some CEE Countries and the UK. *The Journal of International Trade & Economic Development*, *18*(1), 61–78. doi:10.1080/09638190902757426

Ghosh, I., & Ghoshal, I. (2017). Implications of Trade Liberalization for Food Security under the ASEAN-India Strategic Partnership: A Gravity Model Approach. In V. Erokhin (Ed.), *Establishing Food Security and Alternatives to International Trade in Emerging Economies* (pp. 98–118). Hershey, PA: IGI Global.

Gibson, D. V., Kozmetsky, G., & Smilor, R. W. (Eds.). (1992). *The Technopolis Phenomenon: Smart Cities, Fast Systems, Global Networks*. New York, NY: Rowman & Littlefield.

Giffinger, R., Fertner, C., Kramar, H., Kalasek, R., Pichler-Milanović, N., & Meijers, E. (2007). *Smart Cities: Ranking of European Medium-Sized Cities*. Vienna, Austria: Vienna University of Technology.

Golam, M., & Monowar, M. (2018). Eurasian Economic Union: Evolution, Challenges and Possible Future Directions. *Journal of Eurasian Studies*, *9*(2), 163–172. doi:10.1016/j.euras.2018.05.001

González, J. A., & Rossi, A. (2011). *New Trends for Smart Cities, Open Innovation Mechanism in Smart Cities*. Retrieved October 7, 2019, from http://opencities.net/sites/opencities.net/files/contentfiles/repository/D2.2.21%20New%20trends%20for%20Smart%20Cities.pdf

Goudie, A. (1994). *The Human Impact on the Natural Environment*. Cambridge, MA: MIT Press.

Government of India. (n.d.). *Directorate General of Commercial Intelligence and Statistics*. Retrieved October 1, 2019, from http://dgciskol.gov.in/

Government of India. (n.d.). *Latest Trade Figures*. Retrieved August 22, 2019, from https://commerce.gov.in

Granovetter, M. (1973). The Strength of Weak Ties. *American Journal of Sociology*, *76*(6), 1360–1380. doi:10.1086/225469

Grier, K. G., & Tullock, G. (1989). An Empirical Analysis of Cross-National Economic Growth. *Journal of Monetary Economics*, *24*(2), 259–276. doi:10.1016/0304-3932(89)90006-8

Gupta, S., Kangur, A., Papageorgiou, C., & Wane, A. (2014). Efficiency-Adjusted Public Capital and Growth. *World Development*, *57*(C), 164–178. doi:10.1016/j.worlddev.2013.11.012

Hänggi, H. (2000). Interregionalism: Empirical and Theoretical Perspectives. Paper presented at the *Workshop "Dollars, Democracy and Trade: External Influence on Economic Integration in the Americas"*. Los Angeles.

Harrison, A. (1996). Openness and Growth: A Time-Series, Cross-Country Analysis for Developing Countries. *Journal of Development Economics*, *48*(2), 419–447. doi:10.1016/0304-3878(95)00042-9

Hartwell, C. A. (2016). Improving Competitiveness in the Member States of the Eurasian Economic Union: A Blueprint for the Next Decade. *Post-Communist Economies*, *28*(1), 49–71. doi:10.1080/14631377.2015.1124554

Harvey, C. H. (2004). Country Risk Components, the Cost of Capital, and Returns in Emerging Markets. In S. Wilkin (Ed.), *Country and Political Risk: Practical Insights for Global Finance* (pp. 71–102). London, UK: Risk Books. doi:10.2139srn.620710

Hatemi-J, A. (2002). Export Performance and Economic Growth Nexus in Japan: A Bootstrap Approach. *Japan and the World Economy*, *14*(1), 25–33. doi:10.1016/S0922-1425(01)00071-8

Hausman, J., & Taylor, W. (1981). Panel Data and Unobservable Individual Effects. *Econometrica*, *49*(6), 1377–1398. doi:10.2307/1911406

Hayakawa, K., Kimura, F., & Lee, H. H. (2013). How Does Country Risk Matter for Foreign Direct Investment? *The Developing Economies*, *51*(1), 60–78. doi:10.1111/deve.12002

Heidari, H., Katircioglu, S., & Davoudi, N. (2012). Trade and Growth Nexus in Iran: An Application of Bounds Test Approach to Level Relationship. *Economic Computation and Economic Cybernetics Studies and Research, 46*(3), 241–254.

Heininen, L. (2012). Arctic Strategies and Policies. Inventory and Comparative Study. Akureyri: The Northern Research Forum; The University of Lapland.

Helpman, E., Melitz, M., & Rubinstein, Y. (2008). Estimating Trade Flows: Trading Partners and Trading Volumes. *The Quarterly Journal of Economics, 123*(2), 441–487. doi:10.1162/qjec.2008.123.2.441

He, M., Huang, Z., & Zhang, N. (2016). An Empirical Research on Agricultural Trade between China and "The Belt and Road" Countries: Competitiveness and Complementarity. *Modern Economy, 7*(14), 1671–1686. doi:10.4236/me.2016.714147

Henriques, I., & Sadorsky, P. (1996). Export-Led Growth or Growth-Driven Exports? The Canadian Case. *The Canadian Journal of Economics. Revue Canadienne d'Economique, 29*(3), 540–555. doi:10.2307/136249

Herman, E. S., & Petras, J. (1985). 'Resurgent Democracy' in Latin America: Rhetoric or Reality. *Economic and Political Weekly, 20*(27), 1147–1152.

Hill, C. (2008). International Business: Competing in the Global Market Place. *Strategic Direction, 24*(9). doi:10.1108d.2008.05624iae.001

Hollands, R. G. (2008). Will the Real Smart City Please Stand Up? Intelligent, Progressive or Entrepreneurial? *City, 12*(3), 303–319. doi:10.1080/13604810802479126

Hou, J., Johnson, J. M., & Lawson, L. J. (2009). *Greening Cities, Growing Communities: Learning from Seattle's Regional Community Gardens*. Seattle, WA: University of Washington Press.

Huang, J., Wei, W., Cui, Q., & Xie, W. (2017). The Prospects for China's Food Security and Imports: Will China Starve the World via Imports? *Journal of Integrative Agriculture, 16*(12), 2933–2944. doi:10.1016/S2095-3119(17)61756-8

Huang, J., & Yang, G. (2017). Understanding Recent Challenges and New Food Policy in China. *Global Food Security, 12*, 119–126. doi:10.1016/j.gfs.2016.10.002

Information Office of the State Council. (2013). *China-Africa Economic and Trade Cooperation (2013)*. Beijing, China: Information Office of the State Council.

International Monetary Fund. (2019). *GDP, Current Prices*. Retrieved October 5, 2019, from https://www.imf.org/external/datamapper/NGDPD@WEO/CHN/AFQ

International Monetary Fund. (n.d.). *Coordinated Direct Investment Survey*. Retrieved October 1, 2019, from http://data.imf.org/site_moved.html

International Trade Centre. (2019). South-South Trade Helps Firms Build Competitiveness, Met Growth Goals. Retrieved August 23, 2019, from http://www.intracen.org/news/South-South-trade-helps-firms-build-competitiveness-meet-growth-goals/

International Trade Centre. (2019). *Trade Map*. Retrieved September 27, 2019, from https://www.trademap.org/Index.aspx

Ishchukova, N., & Smutka, L. (2013a). Comparative Advantage: Products Mapping of the Russian Agricultural Exports. *AGRIS On-Line Papers in Economics and Informatics, 5*(3), 13–24.

Ishchukova, N., & Smutka, L. (2013b). Revealed Comparative Advantage of Russian Agricultural Exports. *Acta Universitatis Agriculturae et Silviculturae Mendelianae Brunensis, 61*(4), 941–952. doi:10.11118/actaun201361040941

Jacques, M. (2005). *China Is Well on Its Way to Being the Other Superpower*. Retrieved August 23, 2019, from https://www.theguardian.com/world/2005/dec/08/china.comment.

Janicki, H. P., & Wunnava, P. V. (2004). Determinants of Foreign Direct Investment: Empirical Evidence from EU Accession Candidates. *Applied Economics*, *36*(5), 505–509. doi:10.1080/0003684041000168214

Jayachandran, G., & Seilan, A. (2010). A Causal Relationship between Trade, Foreign Direct Investment and Economic Growth for India. *International Research Journal of Finance and Economics*, *42*, 74–88.

Jensen, N. (2003). Democratic Governance and Multinational Corporations: Political Regimes and Inflows of Foreign Direct Investment. *International Organization*, *57*(3), 587–616. doi:10.1017/S0020818303573040

Jipson, J., & Jitheesh, P. M. (2018). *There Is a Structural Crisis of Capitalism*. Retrieved August 22, 2019, from https://frontline.thehindu.com/other/there-is-a-structural-crisis-of-capitalism/article10107168.ece

Johnston, L. A., & Yuan, C. (2014). China's Africa Trade and Investment Policies: Review of a "Noodle Bowl". *African East-Asian Affairs*, *4*, 6–41.

Jung, W. S., & Marshall, P. J. (1985). Exports, Growth and Causality in Developing Countries. *Journal of Development Economics*, *18*(1), 1–12. doi:10.1016/0304-3878(85)90002-1

Jun, K., & Singh, H. (1996). The Determinants of Foreign Direct Investment in Developing Countries. *Transnational Corporations*, *5*(2), 67–105.

Kabir, M., & Salim, R. (2010). Can Gravity Model Explain BIMSTEC's Trade? *Journal of Economic Integration*, *25*(1), 143–165. doi:10.11130/jei.2010.25.1.144

Kalirajan, K. P. (2000). Indian Ocean Rim Association for Regional Cooperation (IOR-ARC): Impact on Australia's Trade. *Journal of Economic Integration*, *15*(4), 533–547. doi:10.11130/jei.2000.15.4.533

Kalirajan, K., & Bhattacharya, S. K. (2011). Export Potentials among BIMSTEC and Japan: An Empirical Measurement. *The Journal of World Economic Review*, *6*(2), 173–188.

Kaur, M., & Dhillon, S. S. (2010). Determinants of Foreign Institutional Investors Investment in India. *Eurasian Journal of Business and Economics*, *3*(6), 57–70.

Kavoussi, R. M. (1984). Export Expansion and Economic Growth. *Journal of Development Economics*, *14*(1), 241–250. doi:10.1016/0304-3878(84)90052-X

Keck, A., & Raubold, A. (2006). *Forecasting Trade*. Geneva, Switzerland: World Trade Organization.

Kelegama, S. (1998). Can Open Regionalism Work in the Indian Ocean Rim Association for Regional Co-operation? *ASEAN Economic Bulletin*, *15*(2), 153–167. doi:10.1355/AE15-2D

Kembayev, Z. (2016). Towards a Silk Road Union? *Chinese Journal of International Law*, *15*(3), 691–699.

Khan, S. M., & Arora, K. (2017). Scope of India's and China's Investment in African Continent. *Procedia Computer Science*, *122*, 691–697. doi:10.1016/j.procs.2017.11.425

Khan, T. (2011). Identifying an Appropriate Forecasting Model for Forecasting Total Import of Bangladesh. *International Journal of Trade, Economics, and Finance*, *2*(3), 242–246.

Kim, S. J., & Wu, E. (2008). Sovereign Credit Ratings, Capital Flows and Financial Sector Development in Emerging Markets. *Emerging Markets Review*, *9*(1), 17–39. doi:10.1016/j.ememar.2007.06.001

Klabbers, J. (2013). Unity, Diversity, Accountability: The Ambivalent Concept of International Organisation. *Melbourne Journal of International Law*, *14*(1), 149–170.

Kokotović, F., & Kurečić, P. (2016). The MINT Countries: A Regression Analysis of the Selected Economic Features. *International Journal of Management Science and Business Administration*, *5*(2), 21–31.

Komninos, N. (2002). *Intelligent Cities: Innovation, Knowledge Systems and Digital Spaces*. London, UK: Taylor & Francis.

Komninos, N. (2008). *Intelligent Cities and Globalisation of Innovation Networks*. London, UK: Routledge. doi:10.4324/9780203894491

Kongcharoen, C., & Kruangpradit, T. (2013). Autoregressive Integrated Moving Average with Explanatory Variable (ARIMAX) Model for Thailand Export. In *Proceedings of the 33rd International Symposium on Forecasting*. Seoul, South Africa: International Institute of Forecasters.

Kosteletou, N., & Liargovas, P. (2000). Foreign Direct Investment and Real Exchange Rate. *Open Economies Review*, *11*(2), 135–148. doi:10.1023/A:1008383821669

Koukpo, M. (2005). *Analyse des déterminants des investissements directs étrangers dans les pays de l'UEMOA*. Dakar, Senegal: African Institute for Economic Development and Planning.

Kravchenko, A., & Sergeeva, O. (2014). China Policy in the Area of Food Security: Modernization of Agriculture. *Pacific Rim: Economics, Politics, Law*, *32*(4), 57–65.

Krisch, N., & Kingsbury, B. (2006). Introduction: Global Governance and Global Administrative Law in the International Legal Order. *European Journal of International Law*, *17*(1), 1–13. doi:10.1093/ejil/chi170

Krott, M. (1998). Regional Forestry: Management within the Focus on People and Trees. In M. Krott, & K. Nilsson (Eds.), *Multiple-Use of Town Forests in International Comparison* (pp. 9–19). Wuppertal, Germany: IUFRO Working Group.

Kudaibergenova, D. (2016). Eurasian Economic Union Integration in Kazakhstan and Kyrgyzstan. *European Political Science*, *17*(1), 97–112.

Kukushkina, J., & Ostrovskaya, E. (2013). Current Issues and Prospects of Eurasian and European Economic Integration. *International Organizations Research Journal*, *8*(4), 214–228.

Kumari, B. R. (2007). Gender Mainstreaming in Trade Policies in BIMSTEC. In T. Nirmala Devi (Ed.), *India and Bay of Bengal Community: The BIMSTEC Experiment* (pp. 348–354). New Delhi, India: Gyan Publishing House.

Lall, S. (2000). *The Technological Structure and Performance of Developing Country Manufactured Exports, 1985-1998*. Oxford, UK: University of Oxford.

Landau, D. (1983). Government Expenditure and Economic Growth: A Cross-Country Study. *Southern Economic Journal*, *49*(1), 783–792. doi:10.2307/1058716

Laubach, T. (2009). New Evidence on the Interest Rate Effects of Budget Deficits and Debt. *Journal of the European Economic Association*, *7*(4), 858–885. doi:10.1162/JEEA.2009.7.4.858

Lawrence, G., & McMichael, P. (2012). The Question of Food Security. *International Journal of Sociology of Agriculture and Food*, *19*(2), 135–142.

Lawson, L. J. (2005). *City Bountiful: A Century of Community Gardening in America*. Berkeley, CA: University of California Press.

Leela, P. (2007). Evolution of BIMSTEC: Towards a Bay of Bengal Economic Community. In T. Nirmala Devi (Ed.), *India and Bay of Bengal Community: The BIMSTEC Experiment* (pp. 172–178). New Delhi, India: Gyan Publishing House.

Lenee, T. L., & Oki, J. (2017). Capital Market Development and Economic Growth: Evidence from the MINT Countries. *Journal of Economic and Sustainable Development*, *8*(2), 68–107.

Levinsohn, J., & Petrin, A. (2003). Estimating Production Functions Using Inputs to Control for Unobservables. *The Review of Economic Studies*, *70*(2), 317–341. doi:10.1111/1467-937X.00246

Lewer, J. J., & van den Berg, H. (2003). How Large Is International Trade's Effect on Economic Growth? *Journal of Economic Surveys*, *17*(3), 363–396. doi:10.1111/1467-6419.00198

Libanio, G. A. (2005). Unit Roots in Macroeconomic Time Series: Theory, Implications and Evidence. *Nova Economia*, *15*(3), 145–176. doi:10.1590/S0103-63512005000300006

Linn, J. F., & Tiomkin, D. (2006). The New Impetus towards Economic Integration between Europe and Asia. *Asia Europe Journal*, *4*(1), 31–41. doi:10.100710308-006-0046-6

Li, S., & Filer, L. (2007). The Effects of the Governance Environment on the Choice of Investment Mode and the Strategic Implications. *Journal of World Business*, *42*(1), 80–98. doi:10.1016/j.jwb.2006.11.006

Liu, X., Burridge, P., & Sinclair, P. J. N. (2002). Relationships between Economic Growth, Foreign Direct Investment, and Trade: Evidence from China. *Applied Economics*, *34*(11), 1433–1440. doi:10.1080/00036840110100835

Li, X., & Liu, X. (2005). Foreign Direct Investment and Economic Growth: An Increasingly Endogenous Relationship. *World Development*, *33*(3), 393–407. doi:10.1016/j.worlddev.2004.11.001

Lunenborg, P. (2019). *"Phase 1B" of the African Continental Free Trade Area (AfCFTA) Negotiations*. Geneva, Switzerland: The South Centre.

Mahendra Dev, S., & Zhong, F. (2015). Trade and Stock Management to Achieve National Food Security in India and China? *China Agricultural Economic Review*, *7*(4), 641–654. doi:10.1108/CAER-01-2015-0009

Mahmood, A. (2005). Export Competitiveness and Comparative Advantage of Pakistan's Non-agricultural Production Sectors: Trends and Analysis. *Pakistan Development Review*, *43*(4), 541–561.

Makarov, I., & Sokolova, A. (2016). The Eurasian Economic Union and the Silk Road Economic Belt: Opportunities for Russia. *International Organisations Research Journal*, *11*(2), 40–57. doi:10.17323/1996-7845-2016-02-40

Makki, S. S., & Somwaru, A. (2004). Impact of Foreign Direct Investment and Trade on Economic Growth: Evidence from Developing Countries. *American Journal of Agricultural Economics*, *86*(3), 795–801. doi:10.1111/j.0002-9092.2004.00627.x

Mariani, B. (2013). *China's Role and Interests in Central Asia*. London, UK: Saferworld.

McGeough, U., & Newman, D. (2004). *Model for Sustainable Regional Design with Expanded Sections on Distributed Energy Resources*. Des Plaines, IL: Gas Technology Institute.

McMillan, M. (2019). *Chinese Investment in Africa*. Retrieved September 2, 2019, from https://www.theigc.org/blog/chinese-investment-africa/

Mehmood, S. (2012). Forecasting Pakistan's Exports to SAARC: An Application of Univiriate Arima Mode. *Journal of Contemporary Issues in Business Research*, *3*(1), 96–110.

Mehta, R. (2002). *Establishment of Free Trade Arrangement among BIMSTEC Countries Some Issues*. New Delhi, India: Research and Information System for Developing Countries.

Ministry of Human Resource Development of India. (n.d.). *All India Survey on Higher Education*. Retrieved October 1, 2019, from https://www.india.gov.in/all-india-survey-higher-education-ministry-human-resource-development

Mishra, A. K., Gadhia, J. N., Kubendran, N., & Sahoo, M. (2015). Trade Flows between India and Other BRICS Countries: An Empirical Analysis Using Gravity Model. *Global Business Review*, *16*(1), 107–122. doi:10.1177/0972150914553523

Mittra, S. (2017). *Blue Economy: Beyond an Economic Proposition*. New Delhi, India: Observer Research Foundation.

Mohamed, S. E., & Sidiropoulos, M. G. (2010). Another Look at the Determinants of Foreign Direct Investment in MENA Countries: An Empirical Investigation. *Journal of Economic Development*, *35*(2), 75–95. doi:10.35866/caujed.2010.35.2.005

Mohan, T. T. R. (2006). Neither Dread nor Encourage Them. *Economic and Political Weekly*, *41*(2), 95–99.

Mohanty, S. K., Franssen, L., & Saha, S. (2019). *The Power of International Value Chains in the Global South*. Geneva, Switzerland: International Trade Centre.

Molchanov, M. (2016). Russia's Leadership of Regional Integration in Eurasia. In S. Kingah, & C. Quiliconi (Eds.), *Global and Regional Leadership of BRICS Countries* (pp. 113–133). Cham, Switzerland: Springer International Publishing. doi:10.1007/978-3-319-22972-0_7

Moyo, S. (2016). Perspectives on South-South Relations: China's Presence in Africa. *Inter-Asia Cultural Studies*, *17*(1), 58–67. doi:10.1080/14649373.2016.1138615

Mukherji, I. N., & Paswan, N. K. (2007). India's Trade and Investment Opportunities in BIMSTEC. In T. Nirmala Devi (Ed.), *India and Bay of Bengal Community: The BIMSTEC Experiment* (pp. 60–105). New Delhi, India: Gyan Publishing House.

Musila, J. W., & Yiheyis, Z. (2015). The Impact of Trade Openness on Growth: The Case of Kenya. *Journal of Policy Modeling*, *37*(2), 342–354. doi:10.1016/j.jpolmod.2014.12.001

Nag, B., & De, D. (2007). *Asian Integration Process and BIMSTEC*. Kolkata, India: Centre for Studies in International Relations and Development. doi:10.2139srn.2819875

Nashier, T. (2015). Financial Integration between BRICS and Developed Stock Markets. *International Journal of Business and Management Invention*, *4*(1), 65–71.

Nath, R., Luan, Y., Yang, W., Yang, C., Chen, W., Li, Q., & Cui, X. (2015). Changes in Arable Land Demand for Food in India and China: A Potential Threat to Food Security. *Sustainability*, *7*(5), 5371–5397. doi:10.3390u7055371

National Bureau of Statistics of China. (2018). *China Statistical Yearbook*. Beijing, China: National Bureau of Statistics of China.

Nayyar, R., & Aggarwal, P. (2014). *Africa-India's New Trade and Investment Partner*. Retrieved October 1, 2019, from https://papers.ssrn.com/sol3/papers.cfm?abstract_id=2757798

Newman, R., Ashley, R. M., Molyneux-Hodgson, S., & Cashman, A. (2011). Managing Water as a Socio-Technical System: The Shift from 'Experts' to 'Alliances'. *Proceedings of the Institution of Civil Engineers. Engineering Sustainability*, *164*(ES1), 95-102.

Nord, W. R., & Tucker, S. (1987). *Implementing Routine and Radical Innovations – As Substantive Areas Including Employee Attitudes*. Lexington, MA: Lexington Books.

Nowak, W. (2016). China-Africa and India-Africa Trade in the Years 2000-2014. *Procedia Economics and Finance, 39*, 140–146. doi:10.1016/S2212-5671(16)30261-1

Ofori-Atta, P. (2016). *Backward Integration Key to Africa's Growth Prospects*. Retrieved September 2, 2019, from https://www.theafricareport.com/1743/backward-integration-key-to-africas-growth-prospects/

Olley, S., & Pakes, A. (1996). The Dynamics of Productivity in the Telecommunications Equipment Industry. *Econometrica, 64*(6), 1263–1297. doi:10.2307/2171831

Organization for Economic Cooperation and Development. (2003). *The E-Government Imperative: Main Findings*. Paris, France: Organization for Economic Cooperation and Development.

Pal, P. (1998). Foreign Portfolio Investment in Indian Equity Markets: Has the Economy Benefited? *Economic and Political Weekly, 33*(11), 589–598.

Parletun, J. (2008). *The Determinants of Foreign Direct Investment: A Regional Analysis with Focus on Belarus*. Retrieved October 2, 2019, from http://lup.lub.lu.se/luur/download?func=downloadFile&recordOId=1336912&fileOId=1646641

Patnaik, P. (2019). *The Global Shift to the Right*. Retrieved August 22, 2019, from https://peoplesdemocracy.in/2019/0602_pd/global-shift-right

Petras, J., & Morley, M. (1991). Latin America: Poverty of Democracy and Democracy of Poverty. *Economic and Political Weekly, 26*(30), 103–111.

Pham, C. S., & Martin, W. (2008). *Estimating the Gravity Equation when Zero Trade Flows Are Frequent*. Washington, DC: World Bank.

Pirolli, M. (2014). *ECOWAS: From Economic Cooperation and Development to Security. A Revision of the Mandate of Progress towards Future Rules?* Retrieved October 5, 2019, from http://mediterraneanaffairs.com/ecowas-from-economic-cooperation-and-development-to-security-a-revision-of-the-mandate-or-progress-towards-future-rules-part-2/

Pistoresi, B. (2000). *Investimenti diretti esteri e fattori di localizzazione: L'America Latina e il Sud Est asiatico*. Retrieved October 2, 2019, from http://www.rivistapoliticaeconomica.it/2000/feb.php

Porter, M. (1990). *The Competitive Advantage of Nations*. New York, NY: Free Press. doi:10.1007/978-1-349-11336-1

Portes, R., & Rey, H. (2005). The Determinants of Cross-Border Equity Flows. *Journal of International Economics, 65*(2), 269–296. doi:10.1016/j.jinteco.2004.05.002

Porwal, A., Kumar, H., & Gupta, R. (2005). The Stock Market Volatility. *The Journal of Accounting and Finance, 20*(1), 31–44.

Poyhonen, P. (1963). A Tentative Model for the Volume of Trade between Countries. *Weltwirtschaftliches Archiv, 90*, 93–100.

Prabhakar, A. (2005). Globalisation, Poverty & Inequality: A Study of India, China, the USA and OECD, *VIKLP*.

Prabhakar, A. (2005). Globalisation, Poverty, & Inequality: A Study of India, China, the USA and OECD, *VIKLP*.

Prabhakar, A. (2003). A Critical Reflection on Globalisation and Inequality: A New Approach to the Development of the South. *African and Asian Studies, 2*(3), 307–345. doi:10.1163/156920903322661735

Prabhakar, A. (2014). *South-South Trade and Technological Cooperation: A Case Study of India and East Africa*. New Delhi, India: Shodh Ganga.

Prabhakar, A. (2016). Trade and Economic Integration in BRICS: Towards Multi-Polarity. In V. Erokhin (Ed.), *Global Perspectives on Trade Integration and Economies in Transition* (pp. 45–57). Hershey, PA: IGI Global. doi:10.4018/978-1-5225-0451-1.ch003

Prabhakar, A. (2017). *The Current Global Recession: A Theoretical and Empirical Investigation into Developed and BRICS Economies*. London, UK: Emerald Group.

Prabhakar, A. (2018). *Comparative Economic Systems and Welfare Economics*. New Delhi, India: ISARA.

PricewaterhouseCoopers. (2017). *The Long View. How Will the Global Economic Order Change by 2050?* London, UK: PricewaterhouseCoopers.

Priyadarshi, S. (2015). *South-South Trade and Its Implications for the World Economy*. Retrieved August 23, 2019, from https://internationalbanker.com/finance/south-south-trade-and-its-implications-for-the-world-economy/

Radulescu, I. G., Panait, M., & Voica, C. (2014). BRICS Countries Challenge to the World Economy New Trends. *Procedia Economics and Finance*, *8*, 605–613. doi:10.1016/S2212-5671(14)00135-X

Rahman, M. M. (2003). *A Panel Data Analysis of Bangladesh's Trade: The Gravity Model Approach*. Sydney, Australia: University of Sydney.

Rahman, M. M., & Kim, C. (2016). Prospects for Economic Integration of BIMSTEC: Trade and Investment Scenario. *International Journal of u- and e- Service. Science and Technology*, *9*(4), 235–248.

Rai, K., & Bhanumurthy, N. R. (2004). Determinants of Foreign Institutional Investment in India: The Role of Return, Risk, and Inflation. *The Developing Economies*, *42*(4), 479–493. doi:10.1111/j.1746-1049.2004.tb00246.x

Rajanayagam, S. (2019). *South-South Trade. Trade between Developing Countries Is Evolving*. Retrieved August 23, 2019, from https://www.gbm.hsbc.com/insights/global-research/south-south-trade

Rampa, F., & Bilal, S. (2011). *Emerging Economies in Africa and the Development Effectiveness Debate*. Maastricht, The Netherlands: European Centre for Development Policy Management.

Rao, B. M., & Rao, S. S. (2007). Re-Envisioning India-Myanmar Relations. In T. Nirmala Devi (Ed.), *India and Bay of Bengal Community: The BIMSTEC Experiment* (pp. 218–234). New Delhi, India: Gyan Publishing House.

Rasoulizhad, E., & Jabalameli, F. (2018). Do BRICS Countries Have Similar Trade Integration Patterns? *Journal of Economic Integration*, *33*(1), 1011–1045. doi:10.11130/jei.2018.33.1.1011

Raza, S. A., Sbia, R., Shahbaz, M., & Rousan, S. (2018). Trade-Growth Nexus and the Rolling Window Analysis in United Arab Emirates. *Journal of Asia Business Studies*, *12*(4), 469–488. doi:10.1108/JABS-07-2016-0098

Renard, M.-F. (2011). *China's Trade and FDI in Africa. Belvedere*. African Development Bank.

Richards, A. (2002). Big fish in small ponds: The momentum investing and price impact of foreign investors in Asian emerging equity markets. *Journal of Financial and Quantitative Analysis*, *40*(1), 1–27. doi:10.1017/S0022109000001721

Rijke, J. S., De Graaf, R. E., Van de Ven, F. H. M., Brown, R. R., & Biron, D. J. (2008). Comparative Case Studies towards Mainstreaming Water Sensitive Regional Design in Australia and the Netherlands. In *Proceedings of the 11th International Conference on Regional Drainage (ICUD)*. Edinburgh, UK.

Rios, P. (2008). *Creating "The Smart City"*. Retrieved October 7, 2019, from http://dspace.udmercy.edu:8080/dspace/bitstream/10429/20/1/2008_rios_smart.pdf

Rowland, D. B. (2009). *U.S.-Chinese Relation with the Southern African Development Community (SADC) Countries: How It Can Make A Difference*. Washington, DC: Georgetown University.

Roy, S. (2013). *India and Africa Ties: Challenges and Opportunities*. Retrieved October 1, 2019, from https://blogs.lse.ac.uk/africaatlse/2013/07/03/india-and-africa-ties-challenges-and-opportunities/

Roy, S. (2014). *China and India, "Rising Powers" and African Development: Challenges and Opportunities*. Uppsala, Sweden: The Nordic Africa Institute.

Ruiz-Dana, A., Goldschagg, P., Claro, E., & Blanco, H. (2007). *Regional Integration, Trade, and Conflict in Latin America*. Winnipeg, Canada: International Institute for Sustainable Development.

Saraogi, R. (2008). *Determinants of FII Inflows: India*. Retrieved October 2, 2019, from https://mpra.ub.uni-muenchen.de/22850/

Satoglu, E. B. (2017). Emerging through Foreign Investment: Investment Development Path Estimation of MINT Economies. *Advances in Economics and Business*, *5*(5), 256–264. doi:10.13189/aeb.2017.050503

Satterthwaite, D. (2002). Local Funds and Their Potential to Allow Donor Agencies to Support Community Development and Poverty Reduction. *Environment and Regionalization*, *14*(1), 179–188.

Saxena, S., & Bhadauriya, S. (2012). India and BIMSTEC: An Analysis of India's Trade Performance & Prospects. *Business Analyst: A Refereed Journal of Shri Ram College of Commerce*, *33*(1), 103-114.

Schneider, F., & Frey, B. S. (1985). Economic and Political Determinants of Foreign Direct Investment. *World Development*, *13*(2), 161–175. doi:10.1016/0305-750X(85)90002-6

Sekkat, K., & Veganzones-Varoudakis, M. (2004). *Trade and Foreign Exchange Liberalization, Investment Climate and FDI in the MENA Countries*. Brussels, Belgium: Free University of Brussels.

Semančíková, J. (2016). Trade, Trade Openness and Macroeconomic Performance. *Procedia: Social and Behavioral Sciences*, *220*, 407–416. doi:10.1016/j.sbspro.2016.05.515

Shamsuddin, A. F. (1994). Economic Determinants of Foreign Direct Investment in Less Developed Countries. *Pakistan Development Review*, *33*(1), 41–51. doi:10.30541/v33i1pp.41-51

Shaygani, B., Abolhasani Hastiani, F., Ghaffari, A., Sadeghi Shahdani, M., & Fadaee, M. (2015). Effects of Exchange Rate Arrangements on Trade Cooperation in BRICS Countries. *Asian Economic and Financial Review*, *5*(3), 563–578. doi:10.18488/journal.aefr/2015.5.3/102.3.563.578

Shohibul, A. (2013). Revealed Comparative Advantage Measure: ASEAN-China Trade Flows. *Journal of Economics and Sustainable Development*, *4*(7), 136–145.

Silva, J. S., & Tenreyro, S. (2006). The Log of Gravity. *The Review of Economics and Statistics*, *88*(4), 641–658. doi:10.1162/rest.88.4.641

Sims, C. A. (1994). A Simple Model for Study of the Determination of the Price Level and the Interaction of Monetary and Fiscal Policy. *Economic Theory*, *4*(3), 381–399. doi:10.1007/BF01215378

Singhania, M., & Gupta, A. (2011). Determinants of Foreign Direct Investment in India. *Journal of International Trade Law and Policy*, *10*(1), 64–82. doi:10.1108/14770021111116142

Soleimani, A., & Dnyanoba, J. R. (2017). A Study of Economics Implications of Foreign Direct Investment. *International Journal of Research in Humanities, Arts, and Literature*, *5*(2), 63–72.

Solomon, S. (2018). *Once Influential in Africa, Taiwan Loses All but One Ally.* Retrieved October 5, 2019, from https://www.globalsecurity.org/wmd/library/news/taiwan/2018/taiwan-180526-voa01.htm

Southern African Development Community. (2012). *About SADC.* Retrieved October 5, 2019, from https://www.sadc.int/about-sadc

Southern African Development Community. (2016). *China and the SADC Secretariat Commit to Enhance Cooperation.* Retrieved October 5, 2019, from https://www.sadc.int/news-events/news/china-and-sadc-secretariat-commit-enhance-cooperation/

Srinivasan, P., & Kalaivani, M. (2013). Determinants of Foreign Institutional Investment in India: An Empirical Analysis. *Journal of Academic Research in Economics*, *5*(3), 361–375.

Srivastava, S. (2019). *India Is Said to Have Cut Trade Deficit with China by $10 Billion.* Retrieved August 22, 2019, from https://economictimes.indiatimes.com/small-biz/trade/exports/insights/india-is-said-to-cut-trade-deficit-with-china-by-10-billion/articleshow/68902529.cms?from=mdr

Stahl, M. J., & Steger, J. A. (1977). Innovation and Productivity in R&D Tuning Management. *R & D Management*, *7*, 71–76.

Steinbock, D. (2017). *The Global Economic Balance of Power Is Shifting.* Retrieved August 22, 2019, from https://www.weforum.org/agenda/2017/09/the-global-economic-balance-of-power-is-shifting

Strutt, A. (2008). Dynamic Analysis of a BIMSTEC-Japan Free Trade Area. In *Proceedings of 11th Annual Conference in Global Trade Analysis*. Helsinki, Finland.

Stuenkel, O. (2015). *BRICS and SCO: Russia's Big Summit.* Retrieved August 24, 2019, from https://www.postwestern-world.com/2015/07/01/brics-russias-summit/

Taffler, R. J., & Abassi, B. (1984). Country Risk: A Model for Predicting Debt Servicing Problems in Developing Countries. *Journal of the Royal Statistical Society. Series A (General)*, *147*(4), 541–568. doi:10.2307/2981843

Tah, K. A., Czerniak, C., Levine, A., Wiggin, K., & Osondu, I. N. (2019). Foreign trade and economic growth in South Africa. *Asia-Pacific Journal of Accounting & Economics*, *17*(1), 1–10. doi:10.1080/16081625.2019.1567352

Temiz Dinç, D., Gökmen, A., Nakip, M., & Azari, N. M. (2017). The Impact of Foreign Trade Issues on Economic Growth in Some Developing Countries Including Iran and Turkey. *Journal of Transnational Management*, *22*(3), 171–202. doi:10.1080/15475778.2017.1346455

Tharakan, P. K. M., Beveren, I. V., & Ourti, T. V. (2005). Determinants of India's Software Exports and Goods Exports. *The Review of Economics and Statistics*, *87*(4), 776–780. doi:10.1162/003465305775098161

The Creative Class. (2011). *The Creative Class.* Retrieved October 7, 2019, from http://www.creativeclass.com/

The World Bank. (2018). *Central Asia. China (and Russia) 2030 – Implications for Agriculture in Central Asia*. Washington, DC: The World Bank.

Tian, D., Hu, N., Wang, X., & Huang, L. (2016). Trade Margins, Quality Upgrading, and China's Agri-Food Export Growth. *China Agricultural Economic Review*, *8*(2), 277–298. doi:10.1108/CAER-12-2013-0156

Tidball, K. G., & Krasny, M. E. (2007). From Risk to Resilience: What Role for Community Greening and Civic Ecology in Cities? In A. Wals (Ed.), *Social Learning Towards a More Sustainable World* (pp. 149–164). Wageningen, The Netherlands: Wageningen Academic Publishers.

Tinbergen, J. (1962). *An Analysis of World Trade Flows in Shaping the World Economy*. New York, NY: Twentieth Century Fund.

Tonami, A. (2014). Future-Proofing Japan's Interests in the Arctic: Scientific Collaboration and a Search for Balance. *Asia Policy*, *18*(1), 52–58. doi:10.1353/asp.2014.0027

Toppeta, D. (2010). *The Smart City Vision: How Innovation and ICT Can Build Smart, "Liveable", Sustainable Cities*. Retrieved October 7, 2019, from http://www.thinkinnovation.org/file/research/23/it/Toppeta_Report_005_2010.pdf

Tripathi, S., & Leitao, N.C. (2013). India's Trade and Gravity Model: A Static and Dynamic Panel Data. *MPRA Paper 45502*.

Trujillo, E. (2013). A Dialogical Approach to Trade and Environment. *Journal of International Economic Law*, *16*(3), 535–585. doi:10.1093/jiel/jgt019

Tsai, P. L. (1994). Determinants of Foreign Direct Investment and Its Impact on Economic Growth. *Journal of Economic Development*, *19*(1), 137–163.

United Nations Commodity Trade Statistics. (n.d.). *UN Comtrade Database*. Retrieved September 29, 2019, from https://comtrade.un.org/

United Nations Conference on Trade and Development. (2018). *Trade and Development Report 2018*. Geneva, Switzerland: United Nations Conference on Trade and Development.

United Nations Conference on Trade and Development. (2019). *Statistics Database* [Data file]. Retrieved August 24, 2019, from http://unctad.org/en/Pages/Statistics.aspx

United Nations Conference on Trade and Development. (2019). *Statistics Database* [Data file]. Retrieved June 14, 2019, from http://unctad.org/en/Pages/Statistics.aspx

United Nations Conference on Trade and Development. (2019). *Statistics Database* [Data file]. Retrieved October 3, 2019, from http://unctad.org/en/Pages/Statistics.aspx

United Nations Conference on Trade and Development. (2019). *Statistics Database* [Data file]. Retrieved October 4, 2019, from http://unctad.org/en/Pages/Statistics.aspx

United Nations Conference on Trade and Development. (2019). *Statistics Database*. Retrieved September 1, 2019, from http://unctad.org/en/Pages/Statistics.aspx

United Nations Conference on Trade and Development. (2019). *World Investment Report 2019: Special Economic Zones*. Geneva: United Nations Conference on Trade and Development.

United Nations Development Programme. (2013). *Human Development Report 2013. The Rise of the South – Human Progress in a Diverse World*. New York, NY: United Nations Development Programme.

United Nations High Commissioner for Refugees. (n.d.). *Venezuela Situation*. Retrieved October 10, 2019, from https://www.unhcr.org/venezuela-emergency.html?query=venezuela

Upadhyay, S. (2006). FIIs in the Stock Market and the Question of Volatility. *Portfolio Organizer*, 22-30.

Uperti, B. C. (2007). Development of BIMSTEC: Nature, Direction, Challenges and Issues. In T. Nirmala Devi (Ed.), *India and Bay of Bengal Community: The BIMSTEC Experiment* (pp. 184–196). New Delhi, India: Gyan Publishing House.

Valle, V. M. (2008). *A Case Study of the European Union and Mercosur*. Mexico: University of Mexico.

Van de Ven, A. (1988). *Progress Report on the Minnesota Innovation Research Project*. Minneapolis, MN: University of Minnesota.

Van den Berg, H., & Schmidt, J. R. (1994). Foreign Trade and Economic Growth: Time Series Evidence from Latin America. *The Journal of International Trade & Economic Development*, *3*(3), 249–268. doi:10.1080/09638199400000016

Van Klaveren, A. (2017). *Regionalism in Latin America. Navigating in the Fog*. Bern, Switzerland: World Trade Institute. doi:10.2139srn.3129996

Van Winden, W., Van den Berg, L., & Pol, P. (2007). European Cities in the Knowledge Economy: Towards a Typology. *Regional Studies*, *44*(3), 525–549.

Veeman, M. (2017). Keynote Address. North American Trade Policy for Agriculture and Forestry: Can Economics Trump Politics? *Canadian Journal of Agricultural Economics*, *65*(1), 43–68. doi:10.1111/cjag.12135

Veltmeyer, H. (1993). Liberalisation and Structural Adjustment in Latin America: In Search of an Alternative. *Economic and Political Weekly*, *35*(28), 2080–2086.

Vinokurov, E. (2017). Eurasian Economic Union: Current State and Preliminary Results. *Russian Journal of Economics*, *3*(1), 54–70. doi:10.1016/j.ruje.2017.02.004

Vollrath, T. (1985). *Dynamics of Comparative Advantage and the Resistance to Free Trade*. Washington, DC: United States Department of Agriculture.

Wagner, C. (2019). *India's Africa Policy*. Berlin, Germany: German Institute for International and Security Affairs.

Warr, P. (2011). *Food Security vs. Food Self-Sufficiency: The Indonesian Case*. Canberra, Australia: The Australian National University.

Wenping, H. (2006). Engaging with NEPAD: A View from China. Johannesburg, South Africa: Royal African Society; South African Institute of International Affairs.

Were, M. (2015). Differential Effects of Trade on Economic Growth and Investment: A Cross-Country Empirical Investigation. *Journal of African Trade*, *2*(1-2), 71–85. doi:10.1016/j.joat.2015.08.002

Wethal, U. (2018). Beyond the China Factor: Challenges to Backward Linkages in the Mozambican Construction Sector. *The Journal of Modern African Studies*, *56*(2), 325–351. doi:10.1017/S0022278X18000150

Wheeler, D., & Mody, A. (1992). International Investment Location Decisions: The Case of US Firms. *Journal of International Economics*, *33*(1-2), 57–76. doi:10.1016/0022-1996(92)90050-T

Wiggins, S., Keilbach, N., Preibisch, K., Proctor, S., Herrejón, G. R., & Muñoz, G. R. (2002). Discussion – Agricultural Policy Reform and Rural Livelihoods in Central Mexico. *The Journal of Development Studies*, *38*(4), 179–202. doi:10.1080/00220380412331322461

Wijayasiri, J., & Mel, D. D. (2008). *BIMSTEC-Japan Cooperation in Trade and Investment: A Sri Lankan Perspective*. Kolkata, India: Centre for Studies in International Relations and Development.

Wiradanti, B., Pettit, S., Potter, A., Abouarghoub, W., & Beresford, A. (2016). Trends in Trade and Port Development of Rising Economies: Mexico and Indonesia. In *Proceedings of Logistics Research Network (LRN) Conference*. Hull: Chartered Institute of Logistics and Transport.

Wittrock, B. (2002). Modernity: One, None, or Many? European Origins and Modernity as a Global Condition. *Daedalus, 129*, 31–60.

World Bank. (2019). *Global Economic Prospects, June 2019: Heightened Tensions, Subdued Investment*. Washington, DC: World Bank.

World Trade Integrated Solution. (2019). *China Product Exports by Country*. Retrieved October 5, 2019, from https://wits.worldbank.org/CountryProfile/en/Country/CHN/Year/LTST/TradeFlow/Export/Partner/by-country/Product/Total

Yu, W., Elleby, C., & Zobbe, H. (2015). Food Security Policies in India and China: Implications for National and Global Food Security. *Food Security, 7*(2), 405–414. doi:10.100712571-015-0432-2

Yu, Y., Feng, K., Hubacek, K., & Sun, L. (2016). Global Implications of China's Future Food Consumption. *Journal of Industrial Ecology, 20*(3), 593–602. doi:10.1111/jiec.12392

Yu, Z., & Bai, X. (2017). From Southeast Asia to the Gulf: Analysis of the Prospect of Indian Ocean Integration. *Asian Journal of Middle Eastern and Islamic Studies, 11*(3), 90–106. doi:10.1080/25765949.2017.12023312

Zaltman, G., Duncan, R., & Holbeck, J. (1973). *Innovations and Organizations*. New York, NY: Wiley.

Zhang, H. (2016). Food in Sino-U.S. Relations. From Blessing to Curse? In F. Wu & H. Zhang (Eds.), *China's Global Quest for Resources. Energy, Food and Water* (pp. 100–118). London, UK: Routledge.

Zhu, Y. (2016). International Trade and Food Security: Conceptual Discussion, WTO and the Case of China. *China Agricultural Economic Review, 8*(3), 399–411. doi:10.1108/CAER-09-2015-0127

About the Contributors

Akhilesh Chandra Prabhakar is a Professor in Economics at Mittal School of Business, Lovely Professional University, India. In his academic journey of over 24 years, he has obtained M.Phil. & Ph.D. degrees from Jawaharlal Nehru University (India). During the Ph.D. study, he visited Kenya, Uganda, and Tanzania in 2000. Thereafter, as a social scientist, he joined the project "Global Democracy Initiatives: The Art of Possible in the Era of Globalization" run by KEPA (Finland) and CSDS (India). With the same organizations, he has also served as Research Associate in the project "South Asian Perspectives on North-South Cooperation and Impact of Foreign Funding on People's Organization". In 2011-2015, Dr. Prabhakar served as Senior Lecturer at Universiti Utara Malaysia. He worked with Hankuk University of Foreign Studies (South Korea) and served as Assistant Professor at AAU, UoG, DBU, and DTU for seven years (invited by the Ministry of Education of Ethiopia) under the UNDP). Dr. Prabhakar was associated as a Research Assistant with the project of "Evaluation of Rural Technology" (funded by CSIR) at the National Institute of Science Technology and Development Studies (India), and he actively participated in the workshop on Multi-Sectoral Production Networks at IIT (India). In total, he has attended 20+ conferences, workshops, training programs, and retreat programs in Malaysia, Ethiopia, and India for continuous teaching-learning. Dr. Prabhakar served as a member of international committee and publishing committee at the UUM (Malaysia) and reviewed conference papers of the 3rd International Conference on Rural Entrepreneurship (ICORE-15) organized by Hebei University (China) as collaborated with the UUM (Malaysia) and the University of Indonesia in 2015. He has presented several research papers in national & international conferences and seminars (including India-Africa Conference at IIC, New Delhi). Dr. Prabhakar has written two modules for Distance Learning Education in Ethiopia and published 60+ research papers (including ten Scopus-indexed and refereed) in international and national level journals. He has published two books, including the one with Emerald (UK), and one book chapter with IGI Global (USA). He has supervised MPhil and Ph.D. students. Dr. Prabhakar has served as Editor-in-Chief of the International Journal of Social Sciences, Guest Editor of IJSS, and currently Associate Editor of IJSS. He has been working as Director of Third World Social Networks (TWSN).

Gurpreet Kaur is an Assistant Professor at Mittal School of Business, Lovely Professional University, India. Dr. Kaur obtained his Ph.D. degree in Economics from Lovely Professional University, India and received a UGC research fellowship. Dr. Kaur's expertise entails the areas of international economics, finance, and econometric models. Dr. Kaur has publications in journals, edited books, and conference proceedings in the areas of international economics and finance and econometric models. Dr. Kaur has presented several papers in international and national level seminars and participated in various workshops and FDP's. Dr. Kaur published thirteen research papers in journals and one research chapter in the refereed edited book and attended thirteen national and international conferences. Dr. Kaur has supervised three M.Sc. dissertation projects.

Vasilii Erokhin is an Associate Professor, School of Economics and Management, Harbin Engineering University, China. Since 2017, Dr. Erokhin is a researcher at the Center for Russian and Ukrainian Studies (CRUS) and Arctic Blue Economy Research Center (ABERC) Harbin Engineering University, China. In 2018, Dr. Erokhin also joined Key West University (Florida, USA) as an Adjunct Professor in Macroeconomics, Microeconomics, and History of Economic Thought. Dr. Erokhin is an author of over 190 scientific works in the areas of international trade, globalization, sustainable development, food security issues with a focus on emerging markets, developing countries, and economies in transition. His major book titles include Global Perspectives on Trade Integration and Economies in Transition (2016), Establishing Food Security and Alternatives to International Trade in Emerging Economies (2017), Handbook of Research on International Collaboration, Economic Development, and Sustainability in the Arctic (2018), and Handbook of Research on Globalized Agricultural Trade and New Challenges for Food Security (2019). Dr. Erokhin is an Editor of MDPI Sustainability special issue "Sustainable Economic Development: Challenges, Policies, and Reforms", Guest Editor at MDPI Sustainability and MDPI Economies; an Associate Editor at Springer's Journal of Knowledge Economy; a member of the Editorial Review Board at IGI International Journal of Sustainable Economies Management (IJSEM); an editorial board member at a number of international journals and publications. Dr. Erokhin is a holder of the honorary awards from the Ministry of Agriculture of the Russian Federation and the Ministry of Education and Science of the Russian Federation. He is a holder of Publons Peer Review Award 2018 "Top 1% of Reviewers in the Spheres of Environment and Ecology" for elite contribution to scholarly peer review and editorial pursuits internationally and outstanding commitment to protecting the integrity and accuracy of published research. In 2019, Dr. Erokhin is named among the Publons top peer reviewers in cross-field studies and environment and ecology.

* * *

Mohamad Aslam is an Assistant Professor at the Mittal School of Business, Lovely Professional University, India. Dr. Aslam obtained his M.A. in Economics from Panjab University, India and M.Phil. from Jawaharlal Nehru University, India. He had received an ICSSR Doctoral Fellowship for M.Phil. In M.Phil., his work was on the employment and education linkages among scheduled tribes of Northeast and Central states and found that education is the best tool for successful transformation and to get the benefit of all government schemes including reservation. Dr. Aslam currently works on marginalized groups like Schedule Tribes (Gujjar and Gaddis of Himachal Pradesh). In teaching, his specialization is in Econometrics and Statistical Analysis. Dr. Aslam pursues Ph.D. from Panjab University, India. As a researcher, he is interested in economic concerns of laborers, tribal communities, agrarian structure and development, and social exclusion and marginalization. Besides teaching and research, he helps more than six research scholars from different universities in spare time in methodology and data analysis, especially in cross-sectional primary studies.

Jasdeep Kaur Dhami is an Associate Professor at CT University, India. Dr. Dhami obtained her Doctorate degree in Business Studies from Punjabi University. She is a Ph.D. in Economics and pursued B.Sc. in Economics, PGDCA, and M.Sc. degree in IT. She has also gained a vast experience of 19 years in academics and research. Dr. Dhami has published over 90 papers in various International conferences and referred journals. She supervises eight doctorate students in Management. Six Ph.D. and seven M.Phil scholars were awarded their degrees under her guidance. She has professional membership in the

East Asian Economic Association, Japan and Indian Economic Association. Her main area of research is international trade and environmental economics. She has been a member of various international editorial boards. Dr. Dhami has served as a member of review board of Independent Journal of Management & Production, Brazil; International Committee member for Scientific and Technical Committee & Editorial Review Board on Economics and Management Engineering, World Academy of Science, Engineering and Technology, USA; International Journal of Economics and Financial Management, Kardan Journal of Economics and Management Sciences, Kardan University, Kabul, Afghanistan. She acted as a convener for various national and international conferences. Dr. Dhami has attended various refresher/short term courses on research methodology, SPSS, curriculum development, environmental sciences, and time series analysis.

Kunal Dutta is an Assistant Professor at Mittal School of Business, Lovely Professional University, India. He has been an academician for the past five years served initially at D.A.V College for Girls, Yamuna Nagar, and Haryana in the period of 2014-2016. Over his tenure, Dr. Dutta has been a resource person for the SPSS workshop for three days held at D.A.V College for girls, Yamuna Nagar, Haryana in 2015. As a responsible citizen, he has been associated with NSS working on street children's education, adolescent girl education, and empowerment during the graduation time period. Dr. Dutta is a member of the Indian Society for Ecological Economics. As a perceptive researcher, he has presented several research papers in national and international conferences and seminars. He has published three research papers in the reviewed journals and one chapter in the IGI Global Publishers book project.

Tanima Dutta is an Associate Professor at the Department of Economics, School of Business, Lovely Professional University, India. She has an eighteen yearlong academic and administrative experience. She completed her Ph.D. at the Department of Regional Planning and Economic Growth, Barkatullah University Bhopal in 2011. Her past experience is from one of the premier institutes of Bhopal where she worked from 2000 to 2018. Dr. Dutta worked in the projects funded by Madhya Pradesh Council of Science and Technology, District Urban Development Authority, Ministry of Women and Child Welfare (Madhya Pradesh), and State Bank of India. Her papers have been published nationally and internationally. One of her papers on Financial Inclusion was listed as the top ten download list of SSRN.

Tonny Dian Effendi is a Lecturer at the Department of International Relations, Universitas Muhammadiyah Malang, Indonesia. His research focuses on international relations in East Asia, diplomacy, diaspora, and China-Indonesia studies.

Marwa Ben Salem Fakhfakh is a Ph.D. in Economics at the University of Sfax, Tunisia.

Akriti Gupta is a Research Scholar of Finance at Mittal School of Business, Lovely Professional University, India. Her research niche lies in stock market analysis, international trade, foreign institutional investments, marketing strategies, and cryptocurrencies. She has also published her research ideas in journals and conference proceedings in the areas of international economics and finance and econometric models.

Krishna Murthy Inumula is an Associate Professor at the Symbiosis International (Deemed University), India. Dr. Inumula is a professional trainer in various fields like market research analytics, statistics, operations management, project management, econometrics, quality control, and business analytics. Dr. Inumula has been constantly enriching the experience through executive education development programs like Faculty Development (FDP), Management Development (MDP), and Executive Development to promote and contribute research and innovation among the knowledge community. Some of the glimpses are, conducted as a resource person Corporate Training Program MDP in Project Management and its contemporary Applications in Evaluating the Port Performance for the Employees of Gujarat Maritime Board (GMB) –Ahmadabad, Gujarat, India. Eight corporate batches were trained span over two years 2009-2011. Executed MDP – Project Management for Petro Bangla to the corporate of Bangladesh Petroleum Company, Bangladesh. Conducted MDP – Materials & Operations Management for Corporate of Oil & Gas Sector, Indian Oil Corporation Ltd. (Pipeline Division), Noida, UP, India. Chairperson for MDP in ISB&M Pune – Small & Medium Enterprises: Agenda for Profitability. Professional data analyst in dealing with complex data models, expertise in various software like SPSS, MINITAB, EVIEWS, and MSPROJECT. Time series data modeling, casual data analysis, and multivariate data analysis are the core expertise. Authored and contributed to management topics 31 papers and articles in various national and international journals and conferences. Some of the journals include Arthshastra: Indian Journal of Economics & Research, NICMAR: Journal of Construction Management, Indian Journal of Finance Prabandhan: Indian Journal of Management and International Journal of Ecological Economics and Statistics. Rich experience in handling hundred plus master's level management dissertation projects and guided so far one M.Phil. and one Ph.D. scholars in the areas of general management-marketing and project management areas respectively.

Souhaila Kammoun is an assistant-Professor at IHEC Sfax and researcher at CODECI, University of Sfax, Tunisia. She got her Phd in Economics at the University of Social Sciences of Toulouse 1, France. She has taught Economics in France and Tunisia. She is the author of a book entitled: Innovation et compétences pour innover des firmes: Modélisation du comportement innovant dans l'industrie française (Editions Universitaires Européennes, 2015). She was member of the PAQ-ES project committee, director of the Master's degree in Entrepreneurship and International Development (Tempus project funded by the European Union) and member of the scientific council at IHEC Sfax. She has held the positions of Head of the Department of Economics, Director of Studies and Vice-Director. She was also Director of IHEC Sfax, Tunisia.

Arti Mishra is a guest lecturer at Gauri Shankar Mahavidyalaya, India. Earlier, Dr. Mishra worked as Assistant Professor at Mittal School of Business, Lovely Professional University, India.

Gaibul Preet is an Assistance Professor of Economics at Mittal School of Business, Lovely Professional University, India. Dr. Preet completed a Post Graduate degree of Masters of Arts in Economics at the Central University of Hyderabad, India with division and first-class and developed acumen on subjects of Applied Microeconomics, Agricultural, Environment, and Labor Economics. Dr. Preet completed graduation from Delhi University in BA Economics (Honours) and worked as a Research Analyst at Indira Gandhi Institute of Research and Development on the "Efficacy of Prohibitionist Laws in the Field of Substance Abuse" and its effects on the Indian society and as a Data Analyst at Institute of Social Sciences on "Forest Rights Act implementation"; analyzing the forest rights claims database of the Ministry of Tribal Affairs, Government of India to find out the linkage between the distribution of titles and the general election at the state level.

Anupam Rawat is an Education Management and Teaching professional with 28+ years of experience as Head of Economics Department, Director, Associate Professor, and more. Currently, Prof. Rawat is the Head of Economics and Dean, School of Agriculture and Rural Development. She has been the Director and Professor of Economics at Symbiosis International University, India. Prof. Rawat has expertise in teaching to UG/PG students, syllabus/curriculum designing and implementation, academic research, administration, budgeting, new strategic innovations, liaising with government/non-government bodies, stakeholder and team management. She is skilled in organizing, coordinating and facilitating seminars/conferences/forums which reflect a passion for economics and environment and social issues. Prof. Rawat is a qualified Ph.D., M.Phil, M.A professional, author/co-author of multiple publications, member of various professional bodies, and contributor in participatory decision making and policy formulation exercises.

Youssra Ben Romdhane is a Ph.D. in Economics at the University of Sfax, Tunisia.

Mahesh Sarva is an Associate Professor at Mittal School of Business, Lovely Professional University, India. He has cross-functional experience in academics as well as in the financial sector industry. Dr. Sarva started his career in the corporate sector with Stock Holding Corporation of India Limited. He also worked as a branch manager in Standard Chartered-STCI Capital Markets Limited in Rajasthan. After shifting his work arena from corporate to academics, Dr. Sarva has worked with Maharishi Arvind Institute of Science and Management Jaipur, Apex Institute of Engineering and Technology Jaipur, Sobhasaria Group of Institutions, Sikar. Expertise entails the areas like security analysis and portfolio management, Indian financial system, management of financial services, derivatives, and risk management. Research interests include a critical perspective on issues of the securities market, efficiency and effectiveness of financial system as well as behavioral finance and investor awareness in the financial market.

Manbir Singh is a Research Scholar at the Department of Management, CT University, India. He is a well-versed graduate from Middlesex University, UK. He believes hard work, mental balance, and promptness is the need of the hour that can lead anybody to success and failure. The success mantra of his life is punctuality and discipline. His areas of interest are international trade and international business.

Rajender Singh is an Associate Professor at Mittal School of Business, Lovely Professional University, India. In the academic career spanning over fifteen years, Dr. Singh has served as Assistant Professor of Economics at JCDM College of Engineering, Sirsa (Hry), Assistant Professor at the Department of Economics, CDLU Sirsa (Hry), Associate Professor of Economics at Mizan Tepi University, Mizan, Ethiopia. He has attended over fifteen relevant training and courses for continuous learning; attended and presented papers in over thirty national and international conferences, and published twenty research papers in national and international journals. He has guided fourteen M.A. projects and completed one major research project on "Impact Assessment of NRHM in Haryana and Punjab: A Comparative Analysis" sponsored by UGC. Dr. Singh is guiding five Ph.D. scholars. Dr. Singh's Ph.D. thesis is titled "Distribution of Foreign Direct Investment in India (A Comparative Analysis of Haryana and Maharashtra)". A comparative analysis was carried out on FDI inflows in Haryana and Maharashtra by taking socio-economic infrastructure (human capital, education, and life expectancy), transport infrastructure (road, rail, air, water), and power availability (per capita) in both states. The study used simple and multiple regression analysis for data analysis. The study found that the availability of physical infrastructure in

Maharashtra is strong than Haryana and Maharashtra has the advantage of coastal region for the attraction of FDI but human capital is almost the same. The study makes the suggestion that Haryana develops the dry port to attract more FDI.

Sundip Solanki is an Associate Professor and Head of International Business, Symbiosis Institute of International Business (SIIB), Symbiosis International (Deemed University), India. He has more than eighteen years of teaching experience in various business schools as a faculty of management. Dr. Solanki is also associated with the Federation of Indian Export Organization (FIEO), Mumbai. He has conducted the Management Development Program for various corporates like TATA, Wipro, Mahindra & Mahindra, Amdocs, Awaya, Welspun, etc. Dr. Solanki has chaired many international and national conferences and invited as a keynote speaker for national and international conferences in India and abroad. More than 35 research papers published in various Scopus, ABDC, UGC indexed journals are also on his credit. He also writes in Times of India and telecasts his radio programs.

Gao Tianming is an Associate Professor, School of Economics and Management, Harbin Engineering University, China. He obtained his Bachelor degree in Industrial External Trade from Harbin Engineering University, Master degree in Management from the Russian Presidential Academy of National Economy and Public Administration under the President of the Russian Federation, and Ph.D. degree in International Economics from Moscow State Institute of International Relations under the Ministry of Foreign Affairs of the Russian Federation. He has over 15 years of professional experience as a general representative of Chinese transnational corporation in Russia and the CIS. He is a Director and Chief Expert of the Center for Russian and Ukrainian Studies (CRUS) and Arctic Blue Economy Research Center (ABERC) at Harbin Engineering University, Deputy Head of the Heilongjiang International Economic and Trade Association, leading consultant of governmental bodies and commercial organizations in the sphere of economic collaboration between China, Russia, and the Republic of Korea. Dr. Gao is an author of many publications related to China's Arctic policy and developments, China-Russia and China-Nordic collaboration in the spheres of economic development, industrial policy, and investment. He is a member of the Scientific Board of the Research Network on Resources Economics and Bioeconomy (RebResNet) and a regular member of the editorial boards in Marketing and Logistics journal, Public Administration Aspects journal, Grani almanac, and Agricultural Bulletin of Stavropol Region.

Jose Vargas-Hernandez is a Research Professor at the University of Guadalajara, Mexico and a member of the National System of Researchers of Mexico. Prof. Vargas-Hernandez has a Ph.D. in Public Administration and a Ph.D. in Organizational Economics. He has undertaken studies in Organizational Behavior and has an MBA degree. He published four books and more than 200 papers in international journals and reviews (some translated to English, French, German, Portuguese, Farsi, Chinese, etc.) and more than 300 essays in national journals and reviews. He has obtained several international awards and recognition.

Index

F

G

I

L

M

N

P

R

S

T

U

W

www.ingramcontent.com/pod-product-compliance
Lightning Source LLC
LaVergne TN
LVHW060423300926
849162LV00006B/1514